April 9–11, 2013
Philadelphia, PA, USA

I0019888

**Association for
Computing Machinery**

Advancing Computing as a Science & Profession

HiCoNS'13

Proceedings of the 2nd ACM International Conference on
High Confidence Networked Systems

Sponsored by:
ACM SIGBED

Supported by:
TRUST

Part of:
CPSWeek 2013

**Association for
Computing Machinery**

Advancing Computing as a Science & Profession

The Association for Computing Machinery
2 Penn Plaza, Suite 701
New York, New York 10121-0701

ISBN: 978-1-4503-1961-4

Additional copies may be ordered prepaid from:

ACM Order Department
PO Box 30777
New York, NY 10087-0777, USA

Phone: 1-800-342-6626 (USA and Canada)
+1-212-626-0500 (Global)
Fax: +1-212-944-1318
E-mail: acmhelp@acm.org
Hours of Operation: 8:30 am – 4:30 pm ET

ACM Order No: 4771301

Printed in the USA

General Chairs' Welcome

It is our great pleasure to welcome you to the *2013 2ⁿᵈ ACM International Conference on High Confidence Networked Systems (HiCoNS'13)* as part of CPSWeek 2013. HiCoNS aims to bring together novel concepts and theories that can help in the development of the science of high confidence networked systems, in particular those considered cyber-physical systems (CPS). The conference will focus on system theoretic approaches to address fundamental challenges to increase the confidence of networked CPS by making them more secure, dependable, and trustworthy. An emphasis will be the control and verification challenges arising as a result of complex interdependencies between networked systems, in particular those at the intersection of cyber and physical areas. In doing so, the conference aims to advance the development of principled approaches to high confidence networked CPS.

This year's conference continues what we hope will be a premier venue for showcasing research focused on improving the confidence of cyber-physical systems, in particular modern control technologies based on embedded computers and networked systems that monitor and control large-scale physical processes.

The conference technical program is exceptionally strong and we were pleased with the interest from so many authors who submitted to the conference. We would like to thank the Program Committee Co-Chairs Linda Bushnell and Larry Rohrbough for their efforts to produce the conference program and the entire Program Committee who worked very hard in reviewing papers and providing feedback to the authors.

We also received significant support and guidance from the CPSWeek 2013 Steering Committee and we would like to especially thank CPSWeek 2013 General Chair Prof. Oleg Sokolsky and his staff for their assistance with the overall organization, coordination, and local arrangements.

Finally, we would like to thank conference sponsor, the ACM Special Interest Group on Embedded Systems (ACM SIGBED), and conference organizer, the Team for Research in Ubiquitous Secure Technology (TRUST), a National Science Foundation Science & Technology Center. Putting together *HiCoNS'13* was truly a team effort!

We hope that you will find this program interesting and thought-provoking and that the conference will provide you with a valuable opportunity to share ideas with other researchers and practitioners from institutions around the world.

S. Shankar Sastry
HiCoNS'13 General Chair
University of California, Berkeley,
USA

Tamer Başar
HiCoNS'13 General Chair
University of Illinois at Urbana-Champaign,
USA

Program Committee Chairs' Welcome

It is our great pleasure to welcome you to the *2013 2ⁿᵈ ACM International Conference on High Confidence Networked Systems (HiCoNS'13)* as part of CPSWeek 2013. HiCoNS aims to foster collaborations between researchers from the fields of control and systems theory, embedded systems, game theory, software verification, formal methods, and computer security who are addressing various aspects of resilience of cyber-physical systems (CPS). HiCoNS continues after growing interest and enthusiasm that was created by the *First Workshop on Secure Control Systems (SCS)* at CPSWeek 2010, the *Workshop on the Foundations of Dependable and Secure Cyber-Physical Systems (FDSCPS)* at CPSWeek 2011, and the *1ˢᵗ ACM International Conference on High Confidence Networked Systems (HiCoNS'12)* as part of CPSWeek 2012.

This year's conference aimed to present novel research, development, and experimentation addressing the security, robustness, and reliability of cyber-physical systems that govern the operation of critical infrastructures such as power transmission, water distribution, transportation, healthcare, building automation, and many more.

The use of Internet-connected devices and commodity IT solutions and the malicious intents of hackers and cybercriminals have made these technologies more vulnerable. Despite attempts to develop guidelines for the design and operation of systems via security policies, much remains to be done to achieve a principled, science-based approach to enhance security, trustworthiness, and dependability of networked cyber-physical systems. The technical program of HiCoNS'13 will present theories and methodologies from such areas as fault-tolerant and networked control systems, game theory for multi-agent dynamics in uncertain environments, and learning and verification theory for secure and trustworthy cyber-physical systems. The technical program includes sessions focused on Resilient Networks, Security Games, Attack Diagnosis, and Security Experimentation. During these sessions, oral presentations will cover both recent research results as well as new directions for future research and development. In addition, the program includes invited talks and panel discussions on emerging topics in resilience of CPS.

We would like to thank our colleagues on the Program Committee who both submitted papers and expended a significant amount of time and energy in reviewing papers and formulating constructive comments and suggestions to the authors.

We hope conference attendees find the program as informative and engaging as we do and that these proceedings will serve as a valuable reference for security researchers and developers.

Linda Bushnell
HiCoNS'13 Program Chair
University of Washington,
USA

Larry Rohrbough
HiCoNS'13 Program Chair
University of California, Berkeley,
USA

Table of Contents

HiCoNS Technical Presentation
(Alphabetical order by lead authors' last names)

HiCoNS 2013 Conference Organization

General Chairs: S. Shankar Sastry *(University of California, Berkeley, USA)*
Tamer Başar *(University of Illinois at Urbana-Champaign, USA)*

Program Chairs: Linda Bushnell *(University of Washington, USA)*
Larry Rohrbough *(University of California, Berkeley, USA)*

Program Committee: Saurabh Amin *(Massachusetts Institute of Technology, USA)*
Hamsa Balakrishnan *(Massachusetts Institute of Technology, USA)*
John Baras *(University of Maryland, USA)*
Alvaro Cárdenas *(University of Texas at Dallas, USA)*
Christian Claudel *(King Abdullah University of Science and Technology (KAUST), Saudi Arabia)*
Emiliano De Cristofaro *(PARC, USA)*
Manimaran Govindarasu *(Iowa State University, USA)*
Tembine Hamidou *(SUPELEC, France)*
Naira Hovakimyan *(University of Illinois at Urbana-Champaign, USA)*
Karl Henrik Johansson *(Royal Institute of Technology (KTH), Sweden)*
Himanshu Khurana *(Honeywell Automation and Control Solutions, USA)*
Xenofon Koutsoukos *(Vanderbilt University, USA)*
Deepa Kundur *(University of Toronto, Canada)*
Cedric Langbort *(University of Illinois at Urbana-Champaign, USA)*
Rahul Mangharam *(University of Pennsylvania, USA)*
Brad Martin *(National Security Agency, USA)*
John Musacchio *(University of California, Santa Cruz, USA)*
Radha Poovendran *(University of Washington, USA)*
Ram Rajagopal *(Stanford University, USA)*
Henrik Sandberg *(Royal Institute of Technology (KTH), Sweden)*
Galina Schwartz *(University of California, Berkeley, USA)*
Uday Shanbhag *(Pennsylvania State University, USA)*
Bruno Sinopoli *(Carnegie Mellon University, USA)*
Pascal Sitbon *(EDF, France)*
Janos Sztipanovits *(Vanderbilt University, USA)*
Paulo Tabuada *(University of California, Los Angeles, USA)*

HiCoNS 2013 Sponsor & Supporter

Sponsor:

Supporter:

Mechanism Design for Robust Resource Management to False Report in Cloud Computing Systems

Yusuke Aoki
Graduate School of
Engineering Science
Osaka University
Toyonaka, Osaka, Japan
aoki@hopf.sys.es.osaka-
u.ac.jp

Takafumi Kanazawa
Graduate School of
Engineering Science
Osaka University
Toyonaka, Osaka, Japan
kanazawa@sys.es.osaka-
u.ac.jp

Toshimitsu Ushio
Graduate School of
Engineering Science
Osaka University
Toyonaka, Osaka, Japan
ushio@sys.es.osaka-
u.ac.jp

ABSTRACT

We consider a resource allocation problem that ensures a fair QoS (Quality of Service) level among selfish clients in a cloud computing system. The clients share multiple resources and process applications concurrently on the cloud computing system. When the available resources are less than the total amount of required resources by all clients, the overload condition occurs. To avoid this, a fair resource allocation is needed. However, when there are selfish clients who want to maximize QoS levels of their applications, they may not report their true QoS functions honestly in order to get more resources than their fairly allocated ones. Then, the performance of the system degrades. Thus, it is important to prevent selfish behaviors of the clients. We propose a resource allocation mechanism that ensures a fair QoS level based on the framework of the mechanism design. In the proposed mechanism, the resource manager cannot know applications which will be processed by the clients but can observe their QoS levels after completing the applications.

Categories and Subject Descriptors

B.8.2 [**PERFORMANCE AND RELIABILITY**]: Performance Analysis and Design Aids; C.4 [**Computer Systems Organization**]: PERFORMANCE OF SYSTEMS— *Fault tolerance*; K.6.2 [**MANAGEMENT OF COMPUTING AND INFORMATION SYSTEMS**]: Installation Management—*Pricing and resource allocation*

Keywords

Cloud Computing, Mechanism Design, Resource Allocation, Fairness

1. INTRODUCTION
1.1 Motivation

The processing of big data is an important issue in the large scale sensor networks, and the necessity of the cloud computing systems is increasing in cyber physical systems [8]. The cloud technology enables us to share the various data in heterogeneous sensor networks. These sensor networks can process various data concurrently by using shared resources in cloud computing systems. The virtualization technology enables us to share the multiple resources more flexibly and cost-effectively [7]. Therefore, it is important how to allocate the computational resources to each sensor network.

A cloud computing system processes multiple applications by using its multiple resources concurrently. When there is an application to which the resource manager cannot allocate a required amount of resources to achieve its best performance, the overload condition occurs. To avoid this, each client needs to process his/her application with fair performances. To measure the degree of fairness, we consider a QoS (Quality of Service) level of each application. The QoS level is a performance index of the provided service such as throughput, delay, jitter, and packet loss rate [14]. When a client processes the application, its QoS level is evaluated and fed back to the resource manager. The resource manager decides a resource allocation to achieve the fairness of observed QoS levels.

To decide a fair QoS resource allocation, the resource manager must know a QoS function of each client, which is the relationship between the QoS level and the allocated resources of each client. However, since the QoS function is private information of each client, he/she may not report the true QoS function to the resource manager. When the clients report false QoS functions selfishly, the fair QoS levels cannot be achieved and the performance of this system may be degraded. Therefore, we need a high-confidence resource management which makes each client decide to report his/her true QoS function.

We formulate the problem using a framework of a mechanism design where we consider each client and his/her QoS level as a player and his/her utility, respectively. In this paper, we propose a fair QoS resource allocation mechanism in the cloud computing system with selfish clients. We assume that the resource manager cannot know which application each client will process beforehand and the clients behaves selfishly such as he/she wants to maximize their own QoS levels. To achieve the fair QoS resource allocation with preventing the reports of the false QoS functions by selfish clients, we propose a mechanism that imposes penalties on clients based on the differences between the true QoS levels of processed applications and the reported QoS levels.

1.2 Related work

There is plenty of work on a distributed system with selfish agents such as clients, servers, and other network users based on the game theory or the mechanism design. A distributed algorithmic mechanism design includes multicast cost sharing or interdomain routing [3]. Zhu and Başar proposed a dynamic game-theoretic approach to model the interactions between a cyber level policy making and a physical level robust control design [15]. Bauso et al. proposed a mechanism design approach to a consensus problem on a network of dynamic agents [2]. Wei et al. proposed a game-theoretic approach to scheduling of cloud-based computing services [13].

The resource allocation is a fundamental issue in cloud computing systems. Efficient resource allocation problems are studied in many settings. Goudarzi and Pedram proposed a SLA-based resource allocation algorithm in a multi-tier cloud computing system [4]. However, it was assumed implicitly that clients do not behave selfishly. Maheswaran and Başar proposed an efficient signal proportional allocation mechanism to yield an allocation which maximizes social welfare at a Nash equilibrium [10]. Ma et al. propose a resource allocation mechanism for cloud computing providers that ensure high service levels [9]. Kong et al. proposed a mechanism that allocates resources among virtual machines in a cloud environment [7]. This mechanism is stochastic and no virtual machine manipulates resource allocations.

A fair QoS resource allocation problem is also an important issue. Tomita and Kuribayashi proposed a fair QoS resource allocation algorithm in cloud computing environments when users do not behave selfishly [12]. Hayashi et al. proposed a control theoretic approach to guarantee a fair QoS level in a multi-tier server system [5]. However, it was assumed implicitly that clients do not behave selfishly.

2. CLOUD COMPUTING SYSTEM AND FAIR QOS

We consider that n clients share a cloud computing system which consists of m divisible resources. Let $N = \{1, \ldots, n\}$ be the set of clients, and $M = \{1, \ldots, m\}$ be a set of resources. The available amount of each resource is normalized to the interval $[0, 1]$ without loss of generality. Then, denoted by $x_{ij} \in [0, 1]$ is an allocation of resource $j \in M$ for client $i \in N$. Let $x_i = (x_{i1}, \ldots, x_{im}) \in [0, 1]^m$ and $x = (x_1, \ldots, x_n) = (x_{11}, \ldots, x_{nm}) \in [0, 1]^{nm}$ be the resource allocation of client i and the resource allocations of all clients, respectively. Thus, the set of possible resource allocations is given by

$$X = \{x \in [0, 1]^{nm} \mid x_{1j} + \cdots + x_{nj} \leq 1, \forall j \in M\}.$$

The resource allocations are decided by a resource manager of the cloud computing system. We consider that each client processes an application on the cloud computing system and evaluates its satisfaction as a QoS level. Suppose that the

QoS level of each application is normalized in the interval $[0, 1]$ without loss of generality. Denoted by $v_i : [0, 1]^m \to [0, 1]$ is a QoS function which represents the relationship between resource allocations and the QoS levels for client i. Suppose that v_i is continuous and $v_i(0, \ldots, 0) = 0$. Denoted by V_i is the set of the QoS functions of applications which can be processed by client i. Let $V = V_1 \times \cdots \times V_n$. Suppose that $F : V \twoheadrightarrow X$ is the correspondence[1] defined by

$$F(v) = \arg\max_{x \in X} \left(\min_{i \in N} v_i(x_i) \right),$$

where $v = (v_1, \ldots, v_n) \in V$.

We define a fair QoS resource allocation as follows:

Definition 1 (fair QoS resource allocation)
Let $v^* = (v_1^*, \ldots, v_n^*) \in V$ be a profile of the true QoS functions of all clients. A resource allocation $x = (x_1, \ldots, x_n) \in X$ is fair if x maximizes $\min_{i \in N} v_i^*(x_i)$, i.e., $x \in F(v^*)$.

We consider that the resource manager decides a fair QoS resource allocation $x \in X$ based on the profile of QoS functions, but the application which will be processed by each client is private information in general. Therefore, the resource manager has to request clients to report the true QoS functions $v^* = (v_1^*, \ldots, v_n^*) \in V$ of the applications. However, since the clients behaves selfishly to get more resources than a fairly allocated one, they may report a false profile of QoS functions $\hat{v} = (\hat{v}_1, \ldots, \hat{v}_n) \in V$ which is different from the true profile v^*.

In order to prevent the false reports, we consider that the resource manager imposes penalties on clients who reported a false QoS function. If clients obtain profits which depend on the QoS levels of processed applications or clients have a consensus on a correspondence between the QoS levels and the monetary value, we can consider a monetary payment as a penalty. However, the penalties need not to restrict to the monetary payment. For example, when we consider the bit rate as QoS, the penalty for each client may be a reduction of the bit rate by reducing the bandwidth directly from that which would be allocated.

Denoted by $p_i \in \mathbb{R}$ is a penalty for client $i \in N$. Let $p = (p_1, \ldots, p_n) \in \mathbb{R}^n$ be penalties of all clients. Each client behaves considering not only his/her true QoS function but also his/her penalty, that is, client i behaves to maximize his/her own utility function defined as follows:

Definition 2 (utility function)
For all $i \in N$, a utility function $u_i : V_i \times [0, 1]^m \times \mathbb{R} \to \mathbb{R}$ is

$$u_i(v_i^*, x_i, p_i) = v_i^*(x_i) - p_i, \tag{1}$$

where $v_i^* \in V_i$ is a true QoS function, $x_i \in [0, 1]^m$ is a resource allocation, and $p_i \in \mathbb{R}$ is a penalty.

The resource manager cannot know the true QoS function v_i^* since it is private information of client i. However, the resource manager can observe the true QoS level $v_i^*(x_i)$ after completing the application of client i.

---

[1] A correspondence F from a set A to a set B, denoted by $F : A \twoheadrightarrow B$, is a function from the set A to the set 2^B, that is, for any $a \in A$, $F(a)$ is a subset of B.

Algorithm 1 Fair QoS mechanism
---

1. Client i decides an application which he/she processes and knows its QoS function $v_i^* \in V_i$.

2. Client i reports a QoS function $\hat{v}_i \in V_i$ of his/her application for the resource managers.

3. The resource manager decides a resource allocation $x = f^x(\hat{v})$ based on the profile $\hat{v} = (\hat{v}_1, \ldots, \hat{v}_n) \in V$ of the reported QoS functions.

4. The resource manager and client i observe the QoS level $v_i^*(x_i) \in [0, 1]$.

5. The resource manager decides penalty $p_i = f_i^p(\hat{v})$ for client i based on the QoS level $v_i^*(x_i) \in [0, 1]$ and the reported QoS function $\hat{v}_i \in V_i$.

6. Client i gains utility $u_i(v_i^*, x_i, p_i)$.

---

3. FAIR QOS MECHANISM

We consider clients as players and reported QoS functions as strategies. Then, we can regard the fair QoS resource allocation problem as a game. In the game, each player selects his/her strategy so as to maximize his/her own utility function defined by (1). Therefore, we can achieve the fair QoS resource allocation using the framework of the mechanism design [6, 11].

We propose a fair QoS mechanism (f^x, f^p), which consists of an allocation function f^x and a penalty function f^p defined as follows:

Definition 3 (allocation function)
An allocation function $f^x : V \to X$ is a function that satisfies the following condition:

$$f^x(\hat{v}) \in F(\hat{v}) = \arg\max_{x \in X} \left(\min_{i \in N} \hat{v}_i(x_i) \right).$$

Definition 4 (penalty function)
For the profile $\hat{v} \in V$ of the QoS functions, a penalty function $f_i^p : V \to \mathbb{R}$ of client i is

$$f_i^p(\hat{v}) = v_i^*(x_i) - \min \left\{ v_i^*(x_i), \min_{j \in N \setminus \{i\}} \hat{v}_j(x_j) \right\},$$

where $v_i^* \in V_i$ is the true QoS function for client i and $x = (x_1, \ldots, x_n) = f^x(\hat{v})$. Then, a penalty function $f^p : V \to \mathbb{R}^n$ is defined by

$$f^p(\hat{v}) = (f_1^p(\hat{v}), \ldots, f_n^p(\hat{v})).$$

The resource manager decides a resource allocation $x = (x_1, \ldots, x_n) = f^x(\hat{v})$ and penalties $p = (p_1, \ldots, p_n) = f^p(\hat{v})$ when a profile of QoS functions $\hat{v} = (\hat{v}_1, \ldots, \hat{v}_n)$ is reported by clients. The utility of client i is $u_i\left(v_i^*, (f^x(\hat{v}))_i, f_i^p(\hat{v})\right) = v_i^*\left((f^x(\hat{v}))_i\right) - f_i^p(\hat{v})$ by Definition 2. Note that the penalty p_i of client i depends on not only the reported QoS functions $\hat{v}$ but also the observed QoS level $v_i^*(x_i)$ of client i. Without penalties, selfish clients may report false QoS functions in order to obtain more resources.

Shown in Algorithm 1 is the detail of the proposed fair QoS mechanism.

The remainder of this section introduces basic notions which will be used in the following sections [1, 6, 11]. The dominant strategy incentive compatibility and the dominant strategy implementability are the basic notations in the mechanism design.

A dominant strategy is defined as follows.

Definition 5 (dominant strategy)
For the true QoS function $v_i^* \in V_i$, a strategy $v_i \in V_i$ of the client i is a dominant strategy under the mechanism (f^x, f^p) if, for any $v' \in V$,

$$u_i\left(v_i^*, \left(f^x\left(v_i, v'_{-i}\right)\right)_i, f_i^p\left(v_i, v'_{-i}\right)\right)$$
$$\geq u_i\left(v_i^*, \left(f^x\left(v'\right)\right)_i, f_i^p\left(v'\right)\right),$$

where $v'_{-i} = (v'_1, \ldots, v'_{i-1}, v'_{i+1}, \ldots, v'_n)$.

A dominant strategy of client i is independent of the QoS functions which are reported by the other clients. Moreover, it is the best report of the QoS function for client i under the mechanism (f^x, f^p).

A dominant strategy equilibrium is defined as follows.

Definition 6 (dominant strategy equilibrium)
For the profile $v^* \in V$ of the true QoS functions, a profile $v = (v_1, \ldots, v_n) \in V$ of clients' strategies is a dominant strategy equilibrium under the mechanism (f^x, f^p) if, for any $i \in N$ and any $v' \in V$,

$$u_i\left(v_i^*, \left(f^x\left(v_i, v'_{-i}\right)\right)_i, f_i^p\left(v_i, v'_{-i}\right)\right)$$
$$\geq u_i\left(v_i^*, \left(f^x\left(v'\right)\right)_i, f_i^p\left(v'\right)\right).$$

A dominant strategy equilibrium corresponds to the situation that each client i reports a dominant strategy.

Dominant strategy incentive compatibility is defined as follows.

Definition 7 (incentive compatibility)
The mechanism (f^x, f^p) is dominant strategy incentive compatible if

$$v^* \in DE(v^*),$$

where $v^* \in V$ is the profile of the true QoS functions and $DE(v^*)$ is the set of dominant strategy equilibria under (f^x, f^p) for $v^* \in V$.

If a mechanism is dominant strategy incentive compatible, then reporting the true QoS function is a dominant strategy. Then, there is no incentive for each client to report any false QoS function.

Dominant strategy implementation is defined as follows.

Definition 8 (dominant strategy implementation)
The mechanism (f^x, f^p) implements the correspondence $F : V \twoheadrightarrow X$ in dominant strategies if

$$DE(v^*) \neq \emptyset \wedge f^x(DE(v^*)) \subseteq F(v^*),$$

where $v^* \in V$ is the profile of the true QoS functions.

If a mechanism implements the correspondence F in dominant strategies, then a fair QoS resource allocation is achieved when each client behaves rationally and the mechanism realizes a fair QoS as a dominant strategy equilibrium.

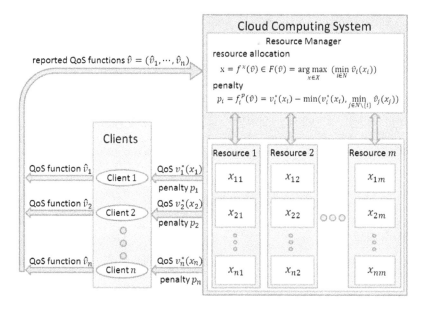

Figure 1: Proposed fair QoS mechanism.

4. PROPERTIES

4.1 General QoS functions

Whatever QoS functions clients report, the resource manager should be able to decide a resource allocation by the allocation function f^x. Therefore, the existence of at least one resource allocation is required for the correspondence F. We show that a resource allocation given by the correspondence F always exists.

Lemma 1
For all profile $\hat{v} \in V$ of QoS functions, there exists at least one resource allocation, i.e., for any $\hat{v} \in V$,

$$F(\hat{v}) \neq \emptyset.$$

PROOF. Let $f : X \to \mathbb{R}$ be $f(x) = \min_{i \in N} \hat{v}_i(x_i)$. X is compact. f is continuous since $\hat{v}_i \in V_i$ is continuous for all $i \in N$. Therefore, from the extreme value theorem, f attains the maximum value. Thus, for all $\hat{v} \in V$, the following condition holds:

$$\begin{aligned} F(\hat{v}) &= \underset{x \in X}{\arg\max} \left(\min_{i \in N} \hat{v}_i(x_i) \right) \\ &= \underset{x \in X}{\arg\max} f(x) \\ &\neq \emptyset. \end{aligned}$$

□

From Lemma 1, since there exists at least one resource allocation, the allocation function f^x is always defined. Then, we show that the proposed mechanism is dominant strategy incentive compatible.

Theorem 1
The mechanism (f^x, f^p) is dominant strategy incentive compatible.

PROOF. Let $v^* = (v_1^*, \ldots, v_n^*)$ be a profile of the true QoS functions for all clients. By Definition 6, it is sufficient to prove that the following condition holds:

$$\forall i \in N, \, \forall v' \in V, \, u_i(v_i^*, x_i, p_i) \geq u_i(v_i^*, x_i', p_i'),$$

where

$$\begin{aligned} x &= f^x(v_i^*, v_{-i}'), \\ x' &= f^x(v'), \\ p_i &= f_i^p(v_i^*, v_{-i}'), \\ p_i &= f_i^p(v'). \end{aligned}$$

We will show the above condition by contradiction. Suppose that there exist $i \in N$ and $v' \in V$ such that,

$$u_i(v_i^*, x_i, p_i) < u_i(v_i^*, x_i', p_i').$$

Then,

$$\begin{aligned} \min &\left\{ v_i^*(x_i), \min_{j \in N \setminus \{i\}} v_j'(x_j) \right\} \\ &< \min \left\{ v_i^*(x_i'), \min_{j \in N \setminus \{i\}} v_j^*(x_j') \right\}. \end{aligned}$$

This contradicts

$$\begin{aligned} x &= f^x(v_i^*, v_{-i}') \\ &\in \underset{\tilde{x} \in X}{\arg\max} \left(\min \left\{ v_i^*(\tilde{x}_i), \min_{j \in N \setminus \{i\}} v_j'(\tilde{x}_j) \right\} \right). \end{aligned}$$

Hence, for any $i \in N$ and any $v' \in V$,

$$u(v_i^*, x_i, p_i) \geq u_i(v_i^*, x_i', p_i').$$

This means that reporting the true QoS function $v_i^* \in V_i$ is a dominant strategy for each client $i \in N$. Thus, the mechanism (f^x, f^p) is dominant strategy incentive compatible. □

We show that the proposed mechanism implements the correspondence $F : V \twoheadrightarrow X$.

Theorem 2
The mechanism (f^x, f^p) implements the correspondence $F : V \twoheadrightarrow X$ in dominant strategies.

PROOF. Since $DE(v^*) \neq \emptyset$ holds from Theorem 1, it is sufficient to prove that the following condition holds: for any $v \in DE(v^*)$,

$$f^x(v) \in F(v^*).$$

Suppose that both $v^* \in V$ and $v \in V$ are dominant strategies. Then, they satisfy the following condition: for any $i \in N$,

$$u\left(v_i^*, (f^x(v^*))_i, f_i^p(v^*)\right) = u_i\left(v_i^*, (f^x(v))_i, f_i^p(v)\right).$$

From the definitions of u_i and f_i^p,

$$u_i\left(v_i^*, (f^x(v^*))_i, f_i^p(v^*)\right) = \min_{i \in N} v_i^*\left((f^x(v^*))_i\right),$$

$$u_i\left(v_i^*, (f^x(v))_i, f_i^p(v)\right)$$
$$= \min\left\{v_i^*\left((f^x(v))_i\right), \min_{j \in N \setminus \{i\}} v_j\left((f^x(v))_j\right)\right\}.$$

Hence, for any $i \in N$,

$$\min_{i \in N} v_i^*\left((f^x(v^*))_i\right)$$
$$= \min\left\{v_i^*\left((f^x(v))_i\right), \min_{j \in N \setminus \{i\}} v_j\left((f^x(v))_j\right)\right\}$$
$$\leq v_i^*\left((f^x(v))_i\right).$$

Then,

$$\min_{i \in N} v_i^*\left((f^x(v^*))_i\right) \leq \min_{i \in N} v_i^*\left((f^x(v))_i\right).$$

From Theorem 1 and the definition of f^x,

$$\max_{x \in X}\left(\min_{i \in N} v_i^*(x_i)\right) = \min_{i \in N} v_i^*\left((f^x(v^*))_i\right)$$
$$= \min_{i \in N} v_i^*\left((f^x(v))_i\right).$$

Therefore,

$$f^x(v) \in \arg\max_{x \in X}\left(\min_{i \in N} v_i^*(x_i)\right) = F(v^*).$$

Hence, for any $v \in V$, $f^x(v) \in F(v^*)$, i.e., $f^x(DE(v^*)) \subseteq F(v^*)$. Thus, the mechanism (f^x, f^p) implements the correspondence $F : V \twoheadrightarrow X$ in dominant strategies. $\square$

We prove that there always exists a fair QoS resource allocation.

Lemma 2
For all $v \in V$, there exists an allocation function $f^x : V \to X$ such that, for all $v \in V$, $v_1\left((f^x(v))_1\right) = \ldots = v_n\left((f^x(v))_n\right)$.

PROOF. Let $x' \in \arg\max_{x \in X}\left(\min_{i \in N} v_i(x_i)\right)$ and $a = \min_{i \in N} v_i(x_i')$, respectively. For all $i \in N$, let $g_i : [0, 1] \to [0, 1]$ be

$$g_i(y_i) = v_i\left(y_i x_i'\right).$$

v_i is continuous. Then, g_i is also continuous. Since $0 \leq a \leq g_i(1) = v_i(x_i')$, there exists $k_i \in [0, 1]$ such that $g_i(k_i) = a$ by the intermediate value theorem. Let $\tilde{x}_i$ be $\tilde{x}_i = k_i x_i'$. Then, $\tilde{x} = (\tilde{x}_1, \ldots, \tilde{x}_n)$ satisfies $v_1(\tilde{x}_1) = \ldots = v_n(\tilde{x}_n)$. Moreover, $\tilde{x} \in F(v)$ since $a = \min_{i \in N} v_i(x_i')$. Let f^x be

$$f^x(v) = \tilde{x}.$$

Then, for any $v \in V$, $f^x : V \to X$ satisfies

$$v_1\left((f^x(v))_1\right) = \ldots = v_n\left((f^x(v))_n\right).$$

$\square$

We prove that there exists a penalty function such that no penalty is imposed on all clients if they report their true QoS functions.

Theorem 3
Let $v^* \in V$ be a profile of the true QoS functions. Then, there exists an allocation function f^x such that the penalty for client i satisfies $f_i^p(v^*) = 0$ for all $i \in N$.

PROOF. From Lemma 2, there is an allocation function $f^x : V \to X$ such that

$$\forall v \in V, v_1\left((f^x(v))_1\right) = \ldots = v_n\left((f^x(v))_n\right)$$

then for all $i \in N$,

$$f_i^p(v^*)$$
$$= v_i^*\left((f^x(v^*))_i\right)$$
$$\quad - \min\left\{v_i^*\left((f^x(v^*))_i\right), \min_{j \in N \setminus \{i\}} v_j^*\left((f^x(v^*))_j\right)\right\}$$
$$= v_i\left((f^x(v^*))_i\right) - \min\left\{v_i\left((f^x(v^*))_i\right), v_i^*\left((f^x(v^*))_i\right)\right\}$$
$$= 0.$$

Thus, $f_i^p(v^*) = 0$ for any $i \in N$. $\square$

Theorem 3 means that the proposed mechanism imposes no penalty on each client if a dominant strategy equilibrium is achieved.

4.2 Strictly increasing QoS functions

For resource allocations $x_i = (x_{i1}, \ldots, x_{im})$ and $x_i' = (x_{i1}', \ldots, x_{im}')$, we denote $x_i < x_i'$ if

$$\left(\forall j \in M, x_{ij} \leq x_{ij}'\right) \wedge \left(\exists j \in M, x_{ij} < x_{ij}'\right).$$

A QoS function $v_i : [0, 1]^m \to [0, 1]$ is said to be strictly increasing if

$$x_i < x_i' \Rightarrow v_i(x_i) < v_i(x_i').$$

In this section, we assume that the QoS function is strictly increasing and show that each f^x decides an allocation which makes the QoS levels of all clients the same value.

Lemma 3
For any $v \in V$, any $x = f^x(v) \in F(v)$ satisfies $v_i(x_1) = \ldots = v_n(x_n)$.

PROOF. We will show Lemma 3 by contradiction. Suppose that $v_i(x_1) = \ldots = v_n(x_n)$ does not hold. Let A, a, B, and b be as follows:

$$A = \arg\max_{i \in N} \hat{v}_i(x_i),$$
$$a = \max_{i \in N} \hat{v}_i(x_i),$$
$$B = \arg\min_{i \in N} \hat{v}_i(x_i),$$
$$b = \min_{i \in N} \hat{v}_i(x_i).$$

If $i \in A$ holds, then there exists $j \in M$ such that $x_{ij} > 0$. Then,

$$\exists \varepsilon > 0, v_i\left(x_{i1}, \ldots, x_{i(j-1)}, x_{ij} - \varepsilon, x_{i(j+1)}, \ldots, x_{im}\right) > b$$

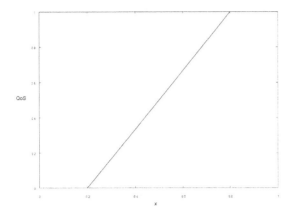

Figure 2: An example of the QoS functions of clients.

since v_i is continuous. Let $|B|$ be the cardinality of B. Then, for all $i' \in B$,

$$v_{i'}\left(x_{i'1}, \ldots, x_{i'(j-1)}, x_{i'j} + \frac{\varepsilon}{|B|}, x_{i'(j+1)}, \ldots, x_{i'm}\right) > b$$

since v_i is strictly increasing. Therefore,

$$\min\left\{\hat{v}_1\left(x_1'\right), \ldots, \hat{v}_n\left(x_n'\right)\right\} > b,$$

where

$$x_k' = \begin{cases} \left(x_{k1}, \ldots, x_{k(j-1)}, x_{kj} - \varepsilon, x_{k(j+1)}, \ldots, x_{km}\right) \\ \qquad\qquad\qquad\qquad \text{if } k = i \in A, \\ \left(x_{k1}, \ldots, x_{k(j-1)}, x_{kj} + \frac{\varepsilon}{|B|}, x_{k(j+1)}, \ldots, x_{km}\right) \\ \qquad\qquad\qquad\qquad \text{if } k \in B, \\ \left(x_{k1}, \ldots, x_{k(j-1)}, x_{kj} - \varepsilon, x_{k(j+1)}, \ldots, x_{km}\right) \\ \qquad\qquad\qquad\qquad \text{if } k \in N \setminus (B \cup \{i\}), \end{cases}$$

which contradicts $x \in F(v) = \arg\max_{x \in X}\left(\min_{i \in N} v_i(x_i)\right)$. $\square$

Finally, the following theorem is shown by Theorem 3 and Lemma 3.

Theorem 4
Let $v^* \in V$ be a profile of the true QoS functions. For any $f^x(v^*) \in F(v^*)$, the penalty of each client $i \in N$ satisfies $f_i^p(v^*) = 0$.

5. EXAMPLE

We consider an allocation of two resources with 3 clients, i.e., $N = \{1, 2, 3\}$ and $M = \{1, 2\}$, respectively. We assume that the QoS level of client $i \in N$ is given by

$$v_i(x_i) = \min\left(g(a_{i1}, b_{i1}, x_{i1}), g(a_{i2}, b_{i2}, x_{12})\right),$$

where

$$g(a_{ij}, b_{ij}, x_{ij}) = \begin{cases} 0 & \text{if } 0 \le x_{ij} \le a_{ij}, \\ \frac{1}{b_{ij} - a_{ij}} x_{ij} - \frac{a_{ij}}{b_{ij} - a_{ij}} & \text{if } a_{ij} < x_{ij} < b_{ij}, \\ 1 & \text{if } b_{ij} \le x_{ij} \le 1, \end{cases}$$

and a_{ij} and b_{ij} are the minimum and the maximum amount of resource j for processing the application of client i, respectively. The QoS level of client i is characterized by a_{i1}, a_{i2}, b_{i1}, and b_{i2}. Shown in Figure 2 is the QoS function of client i for $a_{ij} = 0.2$ and $b_{ij} = 0.8$.

We assume that the true QoS function of client i is

$$\begin{cases} v_1^*(x_1) &= \min\left\{g(0.25, 0.75, x_{11}), g(0.25, 0.75, x_{12})\right\}, \\ v_2^*(x_2) &= \min\left\{g(0.25, 0.75, x_{21}), g(0.25, 0.75, x_{22})\right\}, \\ v_3^*(x_3) &= \min\left\{g(0, 1, x_{31}), g(0, 1, x_{32})\right\}, \end{cases}$$

and the reported QoS function of client i is

$$\begin{cases} \hat{v}_1(x_1) &= \min\left\{g(s, 1-s, x_{11}), g(s, 1-s, x_{12})\right\}, \\ \hat{v}_2(x_2) &= \min\left\{g(t, 1-t, x_{21}), g(t, 1-t, x_{22})\right\}, \\ \hat{v}_3(x_3) &= \min\left\{g(0, 1, x_{31}), g(0, 1, x_{32})\right\}, \end{cases}$$

where $s \in [0, 1]$ and $t \in [0, 1]$. Note that $s = 0.25$ and $t = 0.25$ correspond to the cases that clients 1 and 2 report the true QoS functions, respectively.

As shown in Figure 3, the penalty of client 1 is 0 if $s = 0.25$. If $s > 0.25$ holds, then the penalty is imposed on client 1. The more resource client 1 requests, the more penalty he/she is imposed on. If client 1 requests resources less than the true requirement, i.e., $s < 0.25$, the penalty of client i is 0.

As shown in Figure 4, the penalty of client 3 is always 0, and independent of the report of clients 1 and 2. Figure 5 shows that the utility of client 1 is maximized when he/she reports the true QoS function, i.e., $s = 0.25$. Therefore, reporting the true QoS function is a dominant strategy.

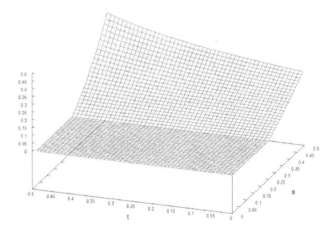

Figure 3: The penalty of client 1.

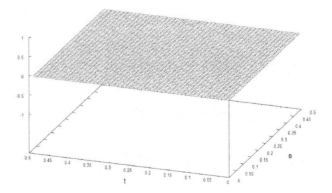

Figure 4: The penalty of client 3.

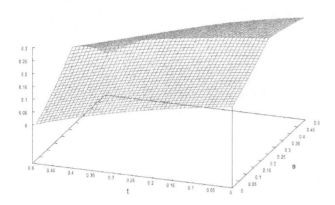

Figure 5: The utility of client 1.

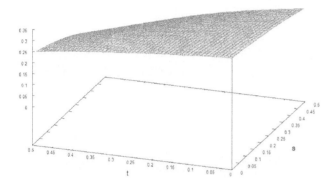

Figure 6: The utility of client 3.

6. CONCLUSION

In this paper, we apply a mechanism design to a fair QoS resource allocation problem in a cloud computing system. We proposed a fair QoS resource allocation mechanism when clients behave selfishly. We proved that clients have no incentive to report a false QoS function if he/she wants to maximize his/her QoS level. A fair QoS resource allocation is realized as a dominant strategy equilibrium by the proposed mechanism. Using an example, we showed efficiency of the proposed mechanism.

7. ACKNOWLEDGMENT

This work was supported by JSPS KAKENHI 24360164.

8. REFERENCES

[1] K. R. Apt and E. Grädel, editors. *Lectures in Game Theory for Computer Scientists*. Cambridge University Press, 2011.

[2] D. Bauso, L. Giarre, and R. Pesenti. Mechanism design for optimal consensus problems. In *Decision and Control, 2006 45th IEEE Conference on*, pages 3381–3386, 2006.

[3] J. Feigenbaum and S. Shenker. Distributed algorithmic mechanism design: Recent results and future directions. In *Proceedings of the 6th International Workshop on Discrete Algorithms and Methods for Mobile Computing and Communications*, pages 1–13, 2002.

[4] H. Goudarzi and M. Pedram. Multi-dimensional SLA-based resource allocation for multi-tier cloud computing systems. In *Proceedings of the 2011 IEEE 4th International Conference on Cloud Computing*, pages 324–331, Washington, DC, USA, 2011.

[5] N. Hayashi, T. Ushio, and T. Kanazawa. Adaptive fair resource management with an arbiter for multi-tier computing systems. In *Proceedings of the 14th IEEE International Conference on Emerging Technologies & Factory Automation*, pages 162–169, Washington, DC, USA, 2009.

[6] M. O. Jackson. Mechanism theory. In *The Encyclopedia of Life Support Systems*. EOLSS Publishers, 2000.

[7] Z. Kong, C.-Z. Xu, and M. Guo. Mechanism design for stochastic virtual resource allocation in non-cooperative cloud systems. In *Proceedings of the 2011 IEEE 4th International Conference on Cloud Computing*, pages 614–621, 2011.

[8] C. Luo, F. Wu, J. Sun, and C. W. Chen. Compressive data gathering for large-scale wireless sensor networks. In *Proceedings of the 15th Annual International Conference on Mobile Computing and Networking*, pages 145–156, New York, NY, USA, 2009.

[9] R. T. Ma, D. M. Chiu, J. C. Lui, V. Misra, and D. Rubenstein. On resource management for cloud users: A generalized kelly mechanism approach. Technical report, Electrical Engineering, May 2010.

[10] R. T. Maheswaran and T. Başar. Efficient signal proportional allocation (ESPA) mechanisms: decentralized social welfare maximization for divisible resources. *IEEE Journal on Selected Areas in Communications*, 24(5):1000–1009, 2006.

[11] Y. Shoham and K. Leyton-Brown. *Multiagent Systems: Algorithmic, Game-Theoretic, and Logical Foundations*. Cambridge University Press, 2009.

[12] T. Tomita and S. Kuribayashi. Congestion control method with fair resource allocation for cloud computing environments. In *Proceedings of the 2011 IEEE Pacific Rim Conference on Communications, Computers and Signal Processing*, 2011.

[13] G. Wei, A. V. Vasilakos, Y. Zheng, and N. Xiong. A game-theoretic method of fair resource allocation for cloud computing services. *The Journal of Supercomputing*, 54(2):252–269, 2010.

[14] F. Xia, L. Ma, J. Dong, and Y. Sun. Network QoS management in cyber-physical systems. In *Proceedings of the 2008 International Conference on Embedded Software and Systems Symposia*, pages 302–307, Washington, DC, USA, 2008. IEEE Computer Society.

[15] Q. Zhu and T. Başar. A dynamic game-theoretic approach to resilient control system design for cascading failures. In *Proceedings of the 1st International Conference on High Confidence Networked Systems*, pages 41–46, New York, NY, USA, 2012.

An Inverse Correlated Equilibrium Framework for Utility Learning in Multiplayer, Noncooperative Settings

Aaron Bestick, Lillian J. Ratliff, Posu Yan, Ruzena Bajcsy, S. Shankar Sastry

Department of Electrical Engineering and Computer Sciences
University of California, Berkeley
Berkeley, CA 94720-1776
{abestick, ratliffl, pyan, bajcsy, sastry}@eecs.berkeley.edu

ABSTRACT

In a game-theoretic framework, given parametric agent utility functions, we solve the inverse problem of computing the feasible set of utility function parameters for each individual agent, given that they play a correlated equilibrium strategy. We model agents as utility maximizers, then cast the problem of computing the parameters of players' utility functions as a linear program using the fact that their play results in a correlated equilibrium. We focus on situations where agents must make tradeoffs between multiple competing components within their utility function. We test our method first on a simulated game of Chicken-Dare, and then on data collected in a real-world trial of a mobile fitness game in which five players must balance between protecting their privacy and receiving a reward for burning calories and improving their physical fitness. Through the learned utility functions from the fitness game, we hope to gain insight into the relative importance each user places on safeguarding their privacy vs. achieving the other desirable objectives in the game.

Categories and Subject Descriptors

J.2 [**Physical Sciences and Engineering**]: Engineering

Keywords

game theory; privacy; mobile health; utility learning

1. INTRODUCTION

Game theory is a powerful tool for modeling engineering problems due to the fact that it considers the strategic nature of agents, and hence, the agents' intent. In particular, game theory aids in modeling humans which inherently have varied preferences and are strategic by nature. As the human element appears more frequently in engineering problems, it becomes imperative to find ways of accurately modeling their behavior.

In the context of healthcare, human factors engineering has grown in importance as technology is increasingly used to both collect data on patient behavior and deliver care more effectively [8, 14]. A major issue in bringing technology into the doctor-patient relationship is one of privacy. It is important to develop an understanding of how people value their privacy, particularly when it concerns data about their physical person. In addition to user preference aspects of privacy that influence the way patients interact with data collection devices, there is a regulatory or policy aspect to privacy in healthcare [6, 9]. As a result, developing an understanding of the role privacy plays in healthcare is becoming a priority.

In this paper, our goal is to learn the utility function of each player in a multiplayer competitive environment based on observed player behavior. We are particularly concerned with environments where players must make tradeoffs between competing goals (e.g: protecting their privacy vs. achieving some other desirable outcome).

There are several existing methods that could be employed to solve the utility learning problem. These include descriptive statistics, Q-learning, and other reinforcement learning algorithms [7, 10, 15]. However, descriptive statistics do not explicitly capture the strategic nature of players, much less the decision making aspect of multi-agent interactions. While Q-learning and other reinforcement learning formulations are possible frameworks in which to model the utility learning process, we chose to use a game-theoretic framework, as we believe this approach most directly captures the strategic interaction of the players.

We model the agents as decision makers who are interested in maximizing their expected gain (minimizing their expected regret). We characterize gain by comparing the expected utility an agent receives under one strategy versus another. A well known property of correlated equilibria is that if all agents in a game independently play a regret-minimization strategy, and if the game is repeated infinitely many times, then the empirical frequency of play for all joint strategies converges to the set of correlated equilibria [3, 17].

The method we propose uses the correlated equilibrium concept and inverse optimization techniques to determine the utility functions of agents in a game. There has been considerable literature on computing correlated equilibria given the utility functions of the players in a game (see [11, 13] and references therein). In addition, there have been attempts at the inverse correlated equilibrium problem of computing player utility functions given a correlated equilibrium distribution. For instance, the authors in [18] develop an algorithm to learn a universal reward function for all agents and an estimated distribution over the joint strategy space for predicting behavior. However, learning a single reward function for all agents does not allow for differentiation of agents based on preferences.

In this paper, we present a method for computing the feasible set of parameter values for individual player utility functions based on observed player behavior. We assume a static game with a discrete, finite action space, finite number of players, and agent utility functions which live in a class of linear, parameterized functions described in Section 4.2. Our approach poses the problem as a linear program which can be solved efficiently using existing methods, given the low dimensionality of the problem in applications we consider. In contrast to existing work, the method we propose allows us to learn each agent's individual utility function.

We apply the proposed method of computing the utility functions of agents to two scenarios. The first is a simulated game of Chicken-Dare, in which we validate our method for recovering user utility functions given observations of a known correlated equilibria. The second is a mobile fitness game in which players are given a choice of privacy setting, and must make a tradeoff between protecting their privacy and maximizing their score to win a reward. In this case, the score is a function of each player's calorie expenditure and represents the benefit to their health from increased physical activity. We attempt to learn user utility functions based on the empirical joint action distribution observed over many iterations of the game. Because players play a large number of repetitions of the game and can observe the actions of other players and optimize their own strategies, we assume each player is playing a regret-minimization strategy, and that the empirical joint action distribution over the series of repeated games therefore approximates a correlated equilibrium.

The paper is organized in the following fashion. In Section 2, we define the game of interest. In Section 3, we recall the definition of a correlated equilibria and provide justification for its use in the model. In Section 4, we describe the inverse problem of utility learning and present the main result for learning agents' preferences. In Section 5, we validate the proposed method for computation of agent preferences via application to the well known game of Chicken-Dare. In Section 6, we describe the experimental set up for the fitness game and apply the proposed method for computing agents preferences. We discuss the trade-off between privacy and desire to win in the context of the fitness game. In Section 7, we make concluding remarks and discuss directions for future work.

2. GAME DEFINITION

In this section, we review definitions and notation from the theory of finite games.

2.1 Standard normal form game

Recall the definition of a normal form game.

Definition 1. Define $\mathcal{G} = \{\mathcal{N}, \mathcal{A}, \mathcal{U}\}$ where

- $\mathcal{N} = \{1, \ldots, n\}$ is the player index set and n is the total number of players,

- $\mathcal{A} = A_1 \times \ldots \times A_n$ is the *joint action* space where A_i is the finite set of actions for player i, and

- $\mathcal{U} = \{U_1, \ldots, U_n\}$ is the set of all players' utility functions where player i's *utility function* is $U_i : \mathcal{A} \to \mathbb{R}$.

In the execution of the game, each player i chooses an action $a_i \in A_i$. The tuple $a = (a_1, \ldots, a_n)$ of every player's individual choice of action then forms the joint action $a \in \mathcal{A}$. Each player i then collects a payoff, or *utility*, of $U_i(a)$. Note that in this standard formulation, each player's utility is completely determined by the joint action a, and may depend not only on player i's action, but on the actions of other players.

2.2 Normal form game with uncertain parameters

We may more accurately capture the non-deterministic nature of real world scenarios by modeling players utilities as functions parameterized by random variables that are independent of the choice variables of the players. We now specify that the utility function of each player is not only a function of the choice variable of each player but is also parameterized by some random variables that represent the variability in nature and its impact on the game. Specifically, define a parameter vector $k = (k_1, \ldots, k_m) \in \mathbb{R}^m$, which is sampled from the probability distribution κ. As before, $\mathcal{U}$ is the set of utility functions U_i for each player i. However, since the utility of each player is now dependent on the vector of uncertain parameters k, each utility function now takes the form $U_i : (\mathcal{A}, \mathbb{R}^m) \to \mathbb{R}$. The game itself is stateless, and the value of the parameter vectors k in a given realization of the game is independent of past games (i.e. each vector k is drawn from the distribution κ, and is independent of the value of k in all past and future games).

We assume that each player knows the distribution κ (e.g. they have observed the distribution of the random variables over many previous games), but does not know the value of k in the current game. As before, each player i makes a strategy choice $a_i \in A_i$. Players still choose a strategy which will maximize their utility, but now each player's choice is made based on the expected payoff she will receive where the expectation is with respect to the random vector k which is distributed as κ. Note that each player's utility is no longer a deterministic function of a. Consequently, in multiple realizations of the game, an identical joint strategy may produce different payoffs.

3. CORRELATED EQUILIBRIA

Given a noncooperative game as defined above, one might wonder whether there exist strategies for each player which are optimal in the sense that if each player adopts the strategy, then the player's expected utility is maximized and no player has an incentive to deviate from that strategy. Recall that, informally, a joint strategy is said to be a Nash equilibrium if no individual player can increase their expected utility by unilaterally deviating from the strategy.

The correlated equilibrium concept generalizes the Nash equilibrium and was proposed in a seminal work by Aumann [2]. It is known that the correlated equilibrium concept is consistent with Bayesian rationality [1]. This makes it a more ideal equilibrium concept in that it is consistent with the Bayesian view of the world. In addition, each player still plays a best response (as in the case of the Nash equilibrium concept) yet some cooperation is allowed to take place giving the opportunity for players to reach a solution which provides them more utility.

Probably the most crucial argument for using the correlated equilibrium is that in contrast to a Nash equilibrium, there exist learning dynamics which, when used independently by each player in a game, cause their joint action distribution to converge to a correlated equilibrium [4, 5]. In general, when players in a game use a strategy which minimizes their expected regret based on the joint actions and utilities observed in past games, the joint action distribution for the game will approach a correlated equilibrium as the number of repetitions grows large. Thus, it is plausible that the joint action distribution observed in an arbitrary game with rational players would represent a correlated equilibrium.

3.1 Correlated equilibrium conditions

Let us now describe the correlated equilibrium concept. Suppose we have some probability distribution σ over a game's joint action space $\mathcal{A}$. In each game, a joint strategy a is sampled from σ, and each player i is informed only of his or her portion, a_i, of this joint action. Then, informally, we define the distribution σ to be a correlated equilibrium for the game if no player, with knowledge only of σ, a_i, and κ, can increase their expected utility by choosing an action different from a_i. Note that the correlated equilibrium concept is a superset of the Nash equilibrium, and as such, any Nash equilibrium is also a correlated equilibrium.

For notational convenience, we will often write the joint action a as the tuple (a_i, a_{-i}), where a_i is the action of player i, and $a_{-i} \in \mathcal{A}_{-i}$ is the joint action of all players *except* player i. Additionally, we use $\sigma(a) = \sigma(a_i, a_{-i})$ to denote the probability of a given joint action a, and $\sigma(a_{-i}|a_i)$, to denote the probability of the joint action (a_i, a_{-i}) given that player i has chosen the action a_i.

First, we define the *gain* function $G_i(a'_i, a_i, a_{-i})$. The gain function gives the amount by which player i can increase his or her utility by switching from strategy a_i to strategy a'_i, given that the other players have played the strategy a_{-i}. The function is defined as

$$G_i(a'_i, a_i, a_{-i}) := U_i(a'_i, a_{-i}) - U_i(a_i, a_{-i}) \quad (1)$$

Given this definition, we can then define the *expected gain* for player i when switching from action a_i to action a'_i, given a probability distribution σ over $\mathcal{A}$, as

$$E_{a_{-i} \sim \sigma_{a_{-i}|a_i}}[G_i(a'_i, a_i, a_{-i})] =$$
$$\sum_{a_{-i} \in \mathcal{A}_{-i}} \sigma(a_{-i}|a_i) G_i(a'_i, a_i, a_{-i}) \quad (2)$$

where $\sigma_{a_{-i}|a_i}$ is the distribution of a_{-i} given that a_i is equal to some chosen value.

Definition 2. The distribution σ is a *correlated equilibrium* if $E_{a_{-i} \sim \sigma_{a_{-i}|a_i}}[G_i(a'_i, a_i, a_{-i})] \leq 0$ for all $i \in \mathcal{N}$, and for all possible $(a'_i, a_i) \in A_i^2$, where $a'_i \neq a_i$. Equivalently, the linear constraint

$$\sum_{a_{-i} \in \mathcal{A}_{-i}} \sigma(a_i, a_{-i}) G_i(a'_i, a_i, a_{-i}) \leq 0 \quad (3)$$

must be satisfied for all $i \in \mathcal{N}$, and for all possible $(a'_i, a_i) \in A_i^2$, $a'_i \neq a_i$.

We may relax the definition of a correlated equilibrium with the following definition.

Definition 3. The distribution σ is an *ε-correlated equilibrium* if $E_{a_{-i} \sim \sigma_{a_{-i}|a_i}}[G_i(a'_i, a_i, a_{-i})] \leq \varepsilon$ for all $i \in \mathcal{N}$, and for all possible $(a'_i, a_i) \in A_i^2$, where $a'_i \neq a_i$. Equivalently, the constraint

$$\sum_{a_{-i} \in \mathcal{A}_{-i}} \sigma(a_{-i}|a_i) G_i(a'_i, a_i, a_{-i}) \leq \varepsilon \quad (4)$$

must be satisfied for all $i \in \mathcal{N}$, and for all possible $(a'_i, a_i) \in A_i^2$, $a'_i \neq a_i$.

Given the above definition, for a game with n players, each with a finite strategy space A_i with cardinality q, a correlated equilibrium σ must satisfy a system of $n \times q \times (q-1)$ linear constraints (one constraint for every possible combination (a_i, a'_i) with $a_i \neq a'_i$, multiplied by the number of players).

3.2 Correlated equilibrium conditions with uncertain parameters

We can extend these conditions to a game with uncertain parameters with a simple modification. Because each player's utility function U_i is now dependent on the parameter vector k as well as the joint action a, the gain function G_i becomes

$$G_i(a'_i, a_i, a_{-i}, k) = U_i(a'_i, a_{-i}, k) - U_i(a_i, a_{-i}, k) \quad (5)$$

To compute the expected gain, we must then take the expectation over all values of both k and a_{-i}. The expression for expected gain is now

$$E_{a_{-i} \sim \sigma_{a_{-i}|a_i}}[E_{k \sim \kappa}[G_i(a'_i, a_i, a_{-i}, k)|a_{-i}]] =$$
$$\sum_{a_{-i} \in \mathcal{A}_{-i}} \sigma(a_{-i}|a_i) E_{k \sim \kappa}[G_i(a'_i, a_i, a_{-i}, k)]. \quad (6)$$

The method used to compute the inner expectation depends on whether k is a discrete or continuous random variable. The definitions for correlated and ε-correlated equilibria extend in the obvious way to the case where the gain function $G(\cdot, \cdot, \cdot, \cdot)$ is a function of a random variable, i.e. replace each G_i in Definitions (2) and (3) with the expected gain function.

For the remainder of this paper, we will concern ourselves with games which include uncertain parameters.

4. UTILITY LEARNING

In the previous section we described how, given a game $\mathcal{G}$, we can write constraints that a joint action distribution σ must satisfy to be a correlated equilibrium. However, the central focus of this paper is the inverse of this problem: Given an empirically observed joint action distribution σ and parameterized utility functions U_i for each player, what is the feasible set of parameter values for each player such that σ is a correlated equilibrium for the game?

4.1 Conceptual outline

Suppose we observe a group of players playing a game which can be modeled in the normal form with uncertain parameters as described in Section 2.2. We know the set of players in the game ($\mathcal{N}$), which action choices are available to each player ($\mathcal{A}$), and any environmental variables which might affect players' strategy decisions

If we observe a sequence of games and record each player's action in each game, we can compute an empirical distribution σ over the joint action space $\mathcal{A}$ via existing statistical methods.

From this point on, our analysis rests on three assumptions about the game's players:

ASSUMPTION 1. *When making their strategy choices, the players each seek to maximize some utility function. The players are* utility maximizing.

ASSUMPTION 2. *The players are* rational. *When presented with incomplete information or a situation with an uncertain outcome, they maximize their expected utility, which we assume they can compute.*

ASSUMPTION 3. *The empirical distribution σ is a correlated equilibrium.*

Based on these assumptions, we will use the correlated equilibrium constraints defined previously to estimate the unknown player utility function parameters based on the observed joint strategy distribution σ.

4.2 Utility functions

In order to estimate the player utility functions from observed data, we must first hypothesize what form the functions take. Our goal is to create a general, parameterized utility function, for which we can then estimate the parameter values based on observed player behavior.

Intuitively, each player's utility function should associate some reward or penalty with various features of each game's outcome. Therefore, we write the utility function as the product of two factors.

First, we define a *feature vector* $\theta_i(a, k) \in \mathbb{R}^d$ for each player i. The feature vector for each player contains d values, each of which represents an element in the game's outcome that player i's utility function may either reward or penalize. The feature vector for each player is a function only of the joint strategy a and the uncertain parameter values k in a particular round of the game. In our analysis, we take the feature vector for each player to be given *a priori*.

Second, we define a *feature weighting vector* $w_i \in \mathbb{R}^d$ for each player i. The values in this vector represent the non-negative weight which player i's utility function places on each of the elements of the feature vector. Our analysis will estimate the feature weighting vector w_i for each player.

We can now define the parameterized utility function for player i as

$$U_i(a_i, a_{-i}, k; w_i) = \langle \theta_i(a_i, a_{-i}, k), w_i \rangle \quad (7)$$

where the vector w_i is the parameter which we wish to estimate and $\langle \cdot, \cdot \rangle$ is the usual inner product. Thus, each player's utility function is a weighted sum of the elements of that player's feature vector. The entries in w_i represent the coefficients by which each feature is multiplied in the utility function.

4.3 Utility function constraints

We now formally describe the inverse correlated equilibrium problem for a general, partially specified normal form game. Assume we have observed a sequence of games and computed an empirical joint strategy distribution σ.

We substitute the parameterized utility function for U_i into the gain function defined in Equation (5) to get

$$G_i(a_i', a_i, a_{-i}, k; w_i) = \langle \theta_i(a_i', a_{-i}, k), w_i \rangle$$
$$- \langle \theta_i(a_i, a_{-i}, k), w_i \rangle \quad (8)$$

Factoring out the feature weighting vector w_i gives

$$G_i(a_i', a_i, a_{-i}, k; w_i) = w_i^T [\theta_i(a_i', a_{-i}, k)$$
$$- \theta_i(a_i, a_{-i}, k)] \quad (9)$$

For notational clarity, define the function Φ_i as

$$\Phi_i(a_i', a_i, a_{-i}, k) = \theta_i(a_i', a_{-i}, k) - \theta_i(a_i, a_{-i}, k) \quad (10)$$

The expected gain is then given by

$$E_{a_{-i} \sim \sigma_{a_{-i}|a_i}}[E_{k \sim \kappa}[G_i(a_i', a_i, a_{-i}, k; w_i)|a_{-i}]] =$$

$$w_i^T \left(\sum_{a_{-i} \in \mathcal{A}_{-i}} \sigma(a_{-i}|a_i) E_{k \sim \kappa}[\Phi_i(a_i', a_i, a_{-i}, k)|a_{-i}] \right)$$
$$(11)$$

Finally, define the constraint function C as

$$C_i(a_i', a_i, \sigma, \kappa) :=$$
$$\sum_{a_{-i} \in \mathcal{A}_{-i}} \sigma(a_{-i}|a_i) E_{k \sim \kappa}[\Phi_i(a_i', a_i, a_{-i}, k)|a_{-i}]. \quad (12)$$

Using the constraint function, we can define a polytope for each player i which must contain that player's feature weighting vector w_i, in order for the observed distribution σ to be a correlated equilibrium. The polytope in which player i's weighting vector must lie is defined as follows.

$$S_i := \{w_i \in \mathbb{R}^d | w_i^T C_i(a_i', a_i, \sigma, \kappa) \le 0$$
$$\forall (a_i', a_i) \in A_i^2, \ a_i' \ne a_i, \ ||w_i||_1 = 1, w_i \ge 0\} \quad (13)$$

where w_{ij} denotes the j-th entry of the vector w_i. Similarly, we may define the polytope containing the weights that make σ a ε-correlated equilibria:

$$S_i^\varepsilon := \{w_i \in \mathbb{R}^d | w_i^T C_i(a_i', a_i, \sigma, \kappa) \le \varepsilon$$
$$\forall (a_i', a_i) \in A_i^2, \ a_i' \ne a_i, \ ||w_i||_1 = 1, w_i \ge 0\}. \quad (14)$$

We can then state the following theorem, specifying when a set of utility functions $\mathcal{U}$ exists that makes the observed joint action distribution σ a correlated equilibrium.

THEOREM 1. *Suppose the feature vectors $\theta_i(a_i, a_{-i}, k)$, $\forall i \in \mathcal{N}$, and an observed probability distribution σ over a joint action space $\mathcal{A}$ are given. Then, there exist utility functions of the form $\langle \theta_i(a_i, a_{-i}, k), w_i \rangle$ for each $i \in \mathcal{N}$ such that*

(i) σ is a correlated equilibrium if and only if $S_i \ne \emptyset$,

(ii) σ is an ε-correlated equilibrium if and only if $S_i^\varepsilon \ne \emptyset$ for some $\varepsilon > 0$.

is satisfied for all $i \in \mathcal{N}$.

PROOF. The proof follows from the definition of correlated equilibrium (resp. ε-correlated equilibrium) and the linearity of the utility functions in the weights. $\square$

For an arbitrary joint strategy distribution σ observed from a series of games, there is, in general, no guarantee that the conditions of Theorem 1(i) are satisfied, and therefore no guarantee that there exist weighting vectors which satisfy the constraints for σ to be a correlated equilibrium. We do know, however, that there exists some $\varepsilon > 0$ such that weighting vectors exist which make the observed distribution σ an ε-correlated equilibrium (see Theorem 1(ii)). Therefore, we pose an optimization problem to find the smallest value of ε such that there exist w_i for all $i \in \mathcal{N}$ which satisfy the correlated equilibrium constraints.

First, define the matrix of all player utility weighting vectors

$$W := \begin{bmatrix} w_1^T \\ \vdots \\ w_n^T \end{bmatrix} \qquad (15)$$

The optimization problem is then

$$\begin{aligned} \underset{\varepsilon,\, W}{\text{minimize}} \quad & \varepsilon \\ \text{s.t.} \quad & w_i^T C_i(a_i', a_i, \sigma, \kappa) \leq \varepsilon \\ & \|w_i\|_1 = 1, w_i \geq 0, \\ & \forall i \in \mathcal{N}, \forall (a_i', a_i) \in A_i^2, a_i' \neq a_i \end{aligned} \qquad (\text{P-1})$$

where the constraint that $\|w_i\| = 1$ for each $i \in \mathcal{N}$ excludes the trivial solution where $w_i = 0$.

By finding the set of utility weighting vectors which satisfy the correlated equilibrium conditions with the smallest possible ε, we are identifying the utility functions for which the observed distribution σ represents the *strongest* possible correlated equilibrium, in the sense that players incur the largest possible penalty for deviating from the suggested action. A similar optimization problem is used in [16] for the forward problem of .

5. APPLICATION TO CHICKEN-DARE

After defining the algorithm in Section 4 above, we would like to test its ability to recover user utility functions from observed behavior that is known to be a correlated equilibrium. For this we use the well known Chicken-Dare game [12].

The game simulates two players arriving simultaneously at an intersection. In each game, each player chooses to either go or wait. Each player's utility function includes a small reward for making it though the intersection successfully, a small penalty for waiting while the other player crosses the intersection, and a large penalty for crashing, when both players choose to go.

For our test, we will first define the game in normal form as described previously, then compute a correlated equilibrium distribution for the game. Next, we will sample from this distribution to simulate observations of individual games, and attempt to recover the feature weighting vectors used in the initial game definition.

5.1 Game Definition

The game has two players ($\mathcal{N} = \{1, 2\}$). In every game, each player can choose to either stop or go, so $A_i = \{stop, go\}$, and $\mathcal{A} = A_1 \times A_2$.

Define the utility functions for each player in the form

described in Section 4.2. Define two features:

$$\theta_{i,1}(a) = c_i(a) = \begin{cases} -10, & \text{if } a_i = go, a_{-i} = go \\ 0, & \text{otherwise} \end{cases}$$

$$\theta_{i,2}(a) = m_i(a) = \begin{cases} -1, & \text{if } a_i = stop, a_{-i} = go \\ 1, & \text{if } a_i = go, a_{-i} = stop \\ 0, & \text{otherwise} \end{cases}$$

The *crash* function, $c_i(a)$, penalizes a player's utility if he or she crashes. The *move* function, $m_i(a)$, rewards a player for making it through the intersection safely, and penalizes the player for allowing the other player to pass safely.

We can then define each player's feature vector as $\theta_i(a) = [c_i(a) \; m_i(a)]^T$, and each player's utility function as $U_i(a) = \langle \theta_i(a), w_i \rangle$, where w_i is the feature weighting vector specific to player i. For this test, we choose the feature weighting vectors arbitrarily as $w_1 = [.3\; .7]^T$, $w_2 = [.6\; .4]^T$. This fully specifies the normal form game $\mathcal{G}$.

Next, we compute the unique maximum entropy correlated equilibrium σ^* for this game using the algorithm in [11]. Note that the game has other correlated equilibria which may give different results in our analysis.

5.2 Utility Learning

We now apply our algorithm to learn the feature weighting vectors for both players. We sample from σ^* to simulate observations of real player behavior. We generate three different observed distributions $\tilde{\sigma}$ using 500, 1000, and 5000 samples.

Next, we use our algorithm to compute the polytopes of feasible weighting vectors given the distributions $\tilde{\sigma}$. The results are presented in Figure 1.

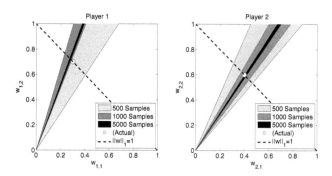

Figure 1: Learned weighting vector polytopes. Note that as the number of observations of the game increases, the feasible weighting vectors contained in the polytopes more closely approximate the true feature weights.

The figure clearly shows that as the number of observed games increases, the polytopes which must contain each w_i grow smaller, approaching the original w_i values from the game definition. This is consistent with the property of correlated equilibria that when players play a regret-minimization strategy, the empirical frequency of play approaches the set of correlated equilibria as the game is repeated a large number of times.

6. APPLICATION TO FITNESS GAME

In order to collect a real world dataset on which to test the utility learning algorithm, a multiplayer mobile fitness game was designed. Each player in the game carried a smartphone that tracked their GPS location and calorie expenditure continuously. Data on each player's physical activity and GPS location was continuously uploaded to and displayed on a web interface accessible to the other players of the game, as well as the researchers running the experiment.

The trial was run for a period of five days, and included five players. The trial was divided into a total of 1440 individual five-minute games. At the beginning of each game, each player chooses a privacy setting of either *high* or *low*. This privacy setting determines how much of their location and activity data is visible to the game's other players. Each player's score for that game is then equal to their total calorie expenditure over the five minute period times a privacy multiplier of 1 if they select *high* privacy, or 2 if they select *low* privacy. At the end of each game, the player with the highest score received a small monetary reward. In this way, the game creates a tradeoff between players' desire to protect their privacy, and their desire to maximize their score to win a reward.

6.1 Game Definition

Our first step is to write a partially specified normal form definition of the fitness game. Our game has five players, thus we specify the player index set $\mathcal{N} = \{1, 2, 3, 4, 5\}$.

Next, we define the joint strategy space $\mathcal{A}$. At the beginning of each game, each of the five players is given a choice of either *high* or *low* privacy. Thus, each player's action space is $A_i = \{high, low\}$, and the joint action space for each game is $\mathcal{A} = \times_{i \in \mathcal{N}} A_i$.

In an effort to isolate players' preferences on privacy, for each player $i \in \mathcal{N}$ we model calorie expenditure in the game as a random variable k_i with distribution κ_i. Each κ_i describes the calorie expenditure for player i. We define κ to the joint distribution over the players' calorie expenditure and $k \in \mathbb{R}^5$ as the vector of random variables k_i. We will assume that each κ_i is a univariate normal distribution and that the random variables k_i are independent.

Modeling calorie expenditure as a random variable assumes that players do not alter their normal level of physical activity for the purposes of winning the game. We assume that any deviations are captured in the variance of the distributions κ_i. This simplification allows us to focus our analysis strictly on the tradeoff between player privacy and competition, and allows us to model each player's action space as a discrete set of choices. We leave the extension to infinite games for future work.

Finally, we must define the parameterized utility function for each player, $U_i(a, k)$. Specifically, we must choose what features to include in each player's feature vector $\theta_i(a, k)$. This choice is perhaps the most important to the outcome of our analysis, as the weights we learn are associated with the selected features, and hence, define the predictive power of the solution.

First, we must hypothesize what features of the game are most important to each player's decision making process. As described previously, the fitness game was designed to study how each player negotiates a tradeoff between protecting their personal privacy and winning a reward. Therefore, the feature vector should include two features which represent, in some way, each of these competing factors.

The first feature we define will represent each player's desire to win the game. Define the score multiplier function $\mathrm{m} : A_i \to \mathbb{R}$ as

$$\mathrm{m}(a_i) = \begin{cases} 1, & \text{if } a_i = high \\ 2, & \text{if } a_i = low \end{cases}$$

Then each player's score in a given realization of the game is given by the score function $\mathrm{s} : (A_i, \mathbb{R}) \to \mathbb{R}$, which is equal to

$$\mathrm{s}(a_i, k_i) = \mathrm{m}(a_i) \cdot k_i$$

We can then define the first feature, $\theta_{i,1}(a, k)$, as

$$\theta_{i,1}(a, k) = \mathrm{s}(a_i, k_i) - \max_{j \in \mathcal{N}}(\mathrm{s}(a_j, k_j))$$

This feature gives the difference between the score of player i and the score of the winning player in a given game realization. Thus, if player i is the winner of the game, $\theta_{i,1}(a, k) = 0$, and if player i did not win, then $\theta_{i,1}(a, k)$ is a negative quantity which represents how far player i's score lagged behind the lead score. This feature will impose a penalty on player i's utility whenever she does not win a given game.

Next, we define a feature to represent each player's desire to protect his or her privacy. This feature should be some function of player i's privacy setting, which we defined above as the action $a_i \in A_i$. We define the privacy function $\sigma : A_i \to \mathbb{R}$, as

$$\mathrm{p}(a_i) = \begin{cases} 500, & \text{if } a_i = high \\ -500, & \text{if } a_i = low \end{cases}$$

We then define the second feature, $\theta_{i,2}(a, k)$ as

$$\theta_{i,2}(a, k) = \mathrm{p}(a_i)$$

If player i selects *high* privacy, this feature adds a constant reward to player i's utility function, and, alternately, if player i selects *low* privacy, the feature adds a penalty. Note that the specific reward and penalty values of 500 and -500 are, in general, arbitrary, but are chosen to be on the same order of magnitude as typical values of the first feature, $\theta_{i,1}(a, k)$.

We can now write the complete feature vector for player i as

$$\theta_i(a, k) = \begin{bmatrix} \mathrm{s}(a_i, k_i) - \max_{j \in \mathcal{N}}(\mathrm{s}(a_j, k_j)) \\ \mathrm{p}(a_i) \end{bmatrix}$$

This completes the partial specification of the normal form representation of the fitness game.

6.2 Game observations

We now analyze the data from several real world trials of the fitness game. Observations are collected from a sequence of 1440 games. Let the index t indicate the game under consideration, i.e. $t \in \{1, \dots, 1440\}$.

In each game, we observe two pieces of data for each user: privacy setting (action choice) and calorie expenditure (uncertain parameter). Therefore, in the t-th game, we observe a joint action $a^{(t)} = [a_1^{(t)} \cdots a_n^{(t)}]^T$ with $a_i^{(t)} \in \{\text{high, low}\}$, $\forall i \in \mathcal{N}$ as well as a calorie expenditure $k^{(t)} = [k_1^{(t)} \cdots k_n^{(t)}]^T$ with $k_i^{(t)} \in \mathbb{R}$, $\forall i \in \mathcal{N}$.

Using a frequentist methodology, we compute an empirical joint mixed action distribution σ from our observations of the joint action $a^{(t)}$. We also compute statistics for the distribution of each player's calorie expenditures which is assumed to be normally distributed. Denote the sample means of each distribution with the vector $\mu \in \mathbb{R}^n$, and the sample standard deviations with the vector $\nu \in \mathbb{R}^n$.

6.3 Utility computation

We now apply the utility learning methods described in Section 4. Using the distribution for κ calculated from user behavior, we precompute the expected value of each player's feature vector $\theta_i(a_i', a_{-i}, k)$ for all possible combinations of a_i and a_{-i}. Next, we calculate the constraint vectors $C_i(a_i', a_i, \sigma, \kappa)$ for each player i and each combination of a_i' and a_i, using Equation 12.

We can then solve the optimization problem (P-1) for the weights of each player.

6.4 Results

The results of the game are displayed below. Figure 2 shows the privacy settings selected by each of the five users over the five day trial.

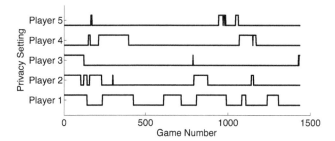

Figure 2: User privacy settings vs. game number. A raised line indicates that the given user selected high privacy for a particular game, while a lowered line indicates low privacy.

Users displayed a wide range of strategies, ranging from that of Player 1, who selected high privacy in 49.6% of games, to Player 5, who selected high privacy in only 4.2% of games.

Figure 3 plots the cumulative number of games won by each player over the course of the game.

The proportion of games won by each player appears to be strongly correlated with both a player's average calorie expenditure and his or her average privacy setting. We can see this connection in Table 1, where the player who won the largest number of games (Player 3), also expended the largest average number of calories. Conversely, Player 1, who won the fewest number of games, expended the lowest number of calories per game, on average.

Parameter	Player				
	1	2	3	4	5
μ (mean)	10.6	13.6	15.2	11.2	12.1
σ^2 (variance)	84.9	136.1	139.9	79.7	64.6

Table 1: Empirical mean and variance of each player's calorie expenditure over the five day trial.

Finally, we applied our utility learning algorithm to the observed data as described in Section 6 to obtain the feature

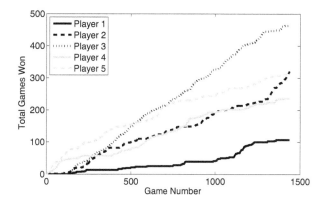

Figure 3: Total games won vs. game number. The total reward received by each player was proportional to the number of games he or she won. Of the five players, Player 3 won the most games, followed by players 2, 5, 4, and 1.

weighting vectors in Table 2. The weighting vector for each player was the computed from the optimization problem P-1. These weights should, in theory, represent the relative importance each user places on protecting their privacy and winning the game.

Parameter	Player				
	1	2	3	4	5
w_1 (Winning)	.693	.695	.700	.680	.663
w_2 (Privacy)	.307	.305	.300	.320	.337

Table 2: The learned feature weighting vectors for each player based on the observed joint strategy distribution over 1440 games.

We can make a number of observations when we compare the learned weights to each player's observed behavior. First, note that players 2 and 3, the players for whom the learned weight for winning was the largest, also won the largest total number of games, at 321 and 464, respectively. This result is logical, as we would expect the players who value winning the most, and thus privacy the least, will choose low privacy more often, increasing their scores and their chances of winning. Indeed, players 2 and 3 selected low privacy in 79% and 91% of games, respectively - a higher percentage than all other players except for player 5, who selected low privacy in 96% of games.

Second, examine players 2 and 5, who won almost identical numbers of games (321 and 311, respectively). However, the utility learning algorithm assigned player 2 a winning feature weight of 0.695, while player 5 was assigned a winning weight of 0.663. This result seems more sensible, however, when we examine each player's average calorie expenditure and privacy setting. Player 2 selected high privacy in 21% of games and expended, on average, 13.6 calories per game. Conversely, player 5 expended an average of 12.1 calories, but chose high privacy in only 4% of games. These weights suggest that although player 5 may value her privacy slightly more than player 2, the fact that she consistently expended fewer calories than player 2 forced her to choose low privacy more often to keep her score competitive with that of the other players.

Of course, any interpretation of people's behavior in a real world scenario such is as this is subjective. These initial observations, however, suggest that our inverse correlated method may be a promising approach to multiagent player preference learning problems.

7. CONCLUSION

Using a game theoretic framework, we model agents in a multiplayer, noncooperative game as utility maximizers that maximize the expected gain of employing one strategy over another. In this framework, when the game is played a large number of times, the joint strategy distribution converges to a correlated equilibrium. Using this fact, we utilize tools of inverse optimization to develop a method by which we can learn individual parametrized utility functions of the agents and hence their preferences. The result is a linear program. We apply the theory to the game of Chicken-Dare to validate the method of determining the utility functions. Finally, we apply the proposed method to data collected in a fitness game where agents are allowed to select their privacy setting. We find that the learned weights are reasonable in the context of the observed user behavior.

In future work, we will examine the robustness of the learning algorithm with different correlated equilibrium distributions and varied choices of feature vector. Maximum entropy correlated equilibria are of particular interest in the context of this inverse problem. We also hope to compare our results to those obtained various reinforcement learning formulations, and to extend the theory presented here to games with infinite strategy spaces.

Acknowledgments

This work is supported in part by HHS grant number 90TR0003/01 and by the NSF TRUST center under award CCF-0424422.

The authors would like to thank Daniel Aranki for his helpful suggestions on the formulation of the game theoretic model, and Maurice Grant and Girum Ibssa for their help in the development of the fitness game.

8. REFERENCES

[1] R. Aumann. Correlated equilibrium as an expression of Bayesian rationality. *Econometrica: Journal of the Econometric Society*, pages 1–18, 1987.

[2] R. Aumann. Subjectivity and correlation in randomized strategies. *Journal of Mathematical Economics*, 1(1):67–96, 2012.

[3] A. Blum and Y. Monsour. *Algorithmic Game Theory*, Learning, regret minimization, and equilibria. Cambridge University Press, 2007.

[4] D. Foster and R. Vohra. Regret in the on-line decision problem. *Games and Economic Behavior*, 29(1):7–35, 1999.

[5] S. Hart and A. Mas-Colell. Uncoupled dynamics do not lead to Nash equilibrium. *The American Economic Review*, 93(5):1830–1836, 2003.

[6] M. Li, R. Poovendran, and S. Narayanan. Protecting patient privacy against unauthorized release of medical images in a group communication environment. *Computerized Medical Imaging and Graphics*, 29(5):367–383, 2005.

[7] L. Mac Dermed, C. Isbell, and L. Weiss. Markov games of incomplete information for multi-agent reinforcement learning. In *Workshops at the 25th AAAI Conference on Artificial Intelligence*, 2011.

[8] J. Mathe, A. Ledeczi, A. Nadas, J. Sztipanovits, J. Martin, L. Weavind, A. Miller, P. Miller, and D. Maron. A model-integrated, guideline-driven, clinical decision-support system. *IEEE Software*, 26(4):54 –61, july-aug. 2009.

[9] J. L. Mathe, S. Duncavage, J. Werner, B. A. Malin, A. Ledeczi, and J. Sztipanovits. Towards the security and privacy analysis of patient portals. *ACM SIGBED Review*, 4(2):5–9, Apr. 2007.

[10] A. Ng and S. Russell. Algorithms for inverse reinforcement learning. In *Proceedings of the 17th International Conference on Machine Learning*, pages 663–670, 2000.

[11] L. Ortiz, R. Schapire, and S. Kakade. Maximum entropy correlated equilibria. Technical report, Massachusetts Institute of Technology Computer Science and Artificial Intelligence Laboratory, 2006.

[12] C. H. Papadimitriou. *Algorithmic Game Theory*, The complexity of finding Nash equilibria. Cambridge University Press, 2007.

[13] C. H. Papadimitriou and T. Roughgarden. Computing correlated equilibria in multi-player games. *Journal of the ACM*, 55(3):14:1–14:29, Aug. 2008.

[14] E. A. R. Breu, J. Sztipanovits. Model-based design of trustworthy health information systems. *Methods of Information in Medicine*, 47(5):389–91, 2008.

[15] C. Rothkopf and C. Dimitrakakis. Preference elicitation and inverse reinforcement learning. *Machine Learning and Knowledge Discovery in Databases*, pages 34–48, 2011.

[16] N. D. Stein, P. A. Parrilo, and A. Ozdaglar. Correlated equilibria in continuous games: Characterization and computation. *Games and Economic Behavior*, 71(2):436–455, 2011.

[17] G. Stoltz and G. Lugosi. Learning correlated equilibria in games with compact sets of strategies. *Games and Economic Behavior*, 59(1):187–208, 2007.

[18] K. Waugh, B. Ziebart, and J. Bagnell. Computational rationalization: The inverse equilibrium problem. *Proceedings of the 28th International Conference on Machine Learning (ICML)*, 2011.

Future Cars: Necessity for an Adaptive and Distributed Multiple Independent Levels of Security Architecture

Alexander Camek
fortiss GmbH
Guerickestr. 25
Munich, Germany
camek@fortiss.org

Christian Buckl
fortiss GmbH
Guerickestr. 25
Munich, Germany
buckl@fortiss.org

Alois Knoll
Technical University Munich
Boltzmannstr.3
Garching, Germany
knoll@in.tum.de

ABSTRACT

Current automotive systems contain security solutions provided as singular solutions. Security mechanisms are implemented for each automotive function individually. This individual security design leads to several problems: combining several functions that are for its own secure may not result in a secure system. Furthermore, the combination of functions might also lead to situations, where mechanisms erroneously detect a security threat. This paper argues that new features, such as Car-2-Car communication or autonomous driving, will result in new information and communication technology (ICT) architectures of cars. The paper will outline basic properties of this architecture and summarize resulting security threads. We will argue that security needs to be treated in a holistic way and that the design must be suitable for adaptive, multiple independent levels of security (MILS) architecture.

Categories and Subject Descriptors

C.2.0 [**General**]: Security and protection (e.g., firewalls); C.2.4 [**C.2.4 Distributed Systems**]: Distributed Applications; D.4.6 [**Security and Protection**]: Security Kernels

General Terms

Security

Keywords

Security; Plug&Play; adaptivity; distributed MILS; secure product lifecycle; automotive

1. INTRODUCTION

Over the past 30 years, information and communication technology (ICT) has made significant innovations in automotive construction possible: from the anti-lock braking system in 1978 to electronic stability control in 1995 and emergency brake assist in 2010. Accordingly, ICT, and especially its software, has expanded significantly, from about 100 lines of code (LOC) in the 1970s to as much as ten million LOC.

This massive usage of software has however also downsides. Different research groups have reported security vulnerabilities of cars. A major reason is that security is not treated as a first-class design issue across the whole ICT architecture. In contrast, the decision if and which security functions are applied is made for each automotive function individually. This individual security design leads to several problems: combining several functions that are for its own secure may not result in a secure system. Furthermore, the combination of functions might also lead to situations, where mechanisms erroneously detect a security threat.

For a recent study [5], we interviewed 240 experts world wide, how the automotive ICT architecture will evolve in the next 20 years. The study was focused on electric cars, but its results can be mapped to cars with internal combustion engines. The study identified several architectural changes. Additionally, it identified functions of future cars that will increase the vulnerability of cars if no adequate measures are applied. All these lead to more severe consequences of successful attacks. This paper will analyze these changes and motivate the necessity of an adaptive, multiple independent layers of security (MILS) architecture.

The paper starts with an overview on the security architecture in today's cars in section 2. Section 3 will then summarize the societal and technological drivers for the upcoming change of the ICT architecture, as identified in the study. The cornerstones of the resulting architecture will be explained in section 4. The main contribution is the analysis described in section 5, which security threats will be the result of this architectural change and the motivation of requirements on the security architecture in section 6. The paper is summarized in section 7.

2. CURRENT AUTOMOTIVE SECURITY SYSTEMS

Currently produced cars contain a lot of electronic control units (ECU). For each functionality, from electronic stability control to high end driver assistance systems, suppliers provide an own ECU. These ECUs are targets to influence the system, to access the whole car, or to conduct a financial damage of the car owner. To avoid such attacks ECU suppliers stock their products with embedded suitable security mechanisms. For example, the immobilizer is such a mechanism, which is directly integrated in the motor control unit and hinders a non-authorized person to start the engine.

As a first version, the security mechanisms were coded directly in the control software of a given ECU. After attacks, these mechanisms were improved and moved to specific hardware components [20], which can be added to standard automotive microcontroller. One of the solutions is the secure hardware extension (SHE). It was developed to provide protection of cryptographic keys and secure boot, among others. In the motor control unit SHE is implemented to secure the immobilizer.

Hardening ECUs at the hardware level was one step. Next, ECUs were hardened at the software level by secure programming. Therefore, three major topics have been identified. At first, ECUs must be programmed only by authorized subjects, e.g., certified ECU manufacturers. This is mostly solved by setting up processes, which guarantees the compliance of regulations. Besides that, the ECUs must be loaded with authorized objects. Here, a lot of effort, standards in specific groups, and research [11] was done. And as third, standard cryptographic algorithms were defined, which shall be used by ECU manufacturers.

But, in modern cars ECUs cannot provide their functionality without data exchange. For example, the immobilizer needs a command, which authorize the ignition of the engine. This command is a combination of unlocking the door and pushing the ignition button or turning a key. It will be sent to the immobilizer through an in-vehicle communication network, such as LIN, CAN, FLEXRAY, or MOST, for data exchange.

These networks become more and more a target for attackers [9]. In the past, it was simple to wiretap and to manipulate the exchanged data, because the communication was not secured at all, as shown in [12]. Later, the communication for specific applications, such as the immobilizer or diagnostics, and their data exchange became encrypted. For example EVITA HSM [1] is a solution, which is used only for vehicle communication. Furthermore, in-vehicle communication systems are topics of ongoing researches, e.g., OVERSEE [2].

Diagnosis is another application, which uses the network to collect information from log files. To get access, an On-Board Diagnostics (OBD) port exists. But, this port is not only used to read reports. It can also be used to update the firmware of an ECU. This capability was a target of attacks [7], which tried to manipulate the messages and install manipulated firmware. After these attacks were published, new standards were introduced to drive secure diagnosis with access control.

All these security mechanisms are single solutions and independent from each other. This can also be seen by analyzing the AUTOSAR standard [1]. Here, the standard only specifies the Crypto Service Manager, a component that offers generic access to standardized cryptographic routines. Higher-level services are not part of the standard and the whole security management has to be implemented application level. As a results, the mechanisms are implemented for each automotive function individually. This individual security design leads to several problems as can be seen from reported attacks: combining several functions that are for its

---

[1]http://evita-project.org/
[2]https://www.oversee-project.com

own secure may not result in a secure system. Furthermore, the combination of functions might also lead to situations, where mechanisms erroneously detect a security threat.

3. TRENDS IN AUTOMOTIVE DOMAIN

This section summarizes the trends identified in the before-mentioned study [5]. Customers will ask essentially for three capabilities: zero accidents, Plug&Play and always-on.

To decrease the number of car accidents and simultaneously enable mobility for the growing number of elderly people, cars will be equipped with more intelligent advances driver assistance systems and even be capable for autonomous driving [19]. These functions impose a twofold challenge to the ICT architecture: first of all they are absolutely safety-critical. A failure of these functions might lead to car damage and even threaten live of the passengers. The second challenge is about the close interconnection of these functions with already existing functions and sensors. Today, the functions can mainly be implemented and integrated into the car in isolated fashion and via additional electronic control units (ECU). For the new interconnected functions, this approach will not be feasible. Therefore, new functions will be rather integrated on a central platform computer.

The second capability of future cars is Plug&Play. In today's cars it is nearly impossible to add new functions after production of the car, except from the infotainment domain. Due to the fast technological progress and the long life cycle of a car, this fact will be no longer tenable. Customers will for example require an update of their five year's old car to the latest ADAS technology.

The third trend is interconnectivity of the car leading to an always-on car. The passengers of the car will require access to their data and to the Internet similar to the smart phone domain. Furthermore the ADAS functions of the car will more and more rely on data from outside the car leading to car-to-car and car-to-infrastructure communication.

Car manufacturers have already picked up these trends and started technological changes to the ICT architecture. The most important trend is to introduce a standardized run-time system called AUTOSAR [1], that enables the integration of new functions at the software component level rather than at the hardware or ECU level. The main goal is to allow several functions to execute on one computer with the final vision of a central platform computer. The required computational power of such computers is anticipated by introducing multi-core technologies.

The challenge derived from increasing connectivity demands is met by introducing high-bandwidth communication technologies such as Ethernet. Using Ethernet as communication backbone has also the advantage of easier integration with the Internet and car-to-X functionality.

4. CORNERSTONES OF FUTURE ICT ARCHITECTURES

Figure 1 depicts a future scenario for future ICT architectures in cars. Advanced functions will be executed on a central platform computer, which may itself consist of several controllers. Smart sensors or actuators will on the other hand read sensor values, preprocess the data and execute local control functions. The preprocessing step will allow a reduction of the required bandwidth. The local control functions will implement control loops with real-time

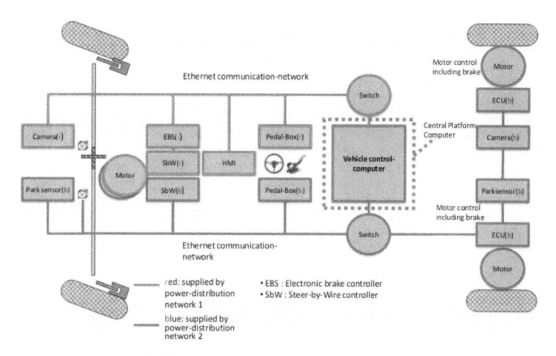

Figure 1: Possible Future ICT Architecture ©RACE, www.race-projekt.de

requirements that cannot be achieved in distributed fashion.

A communication backbone, most probably a real-time Ethernet variant, will connect the smart sensors and actuators. For safety reasons, the communication backbone will be based on physical redundancy. Sensors and actuators that are required for functions with fail-operational execution semantics will be connected to both channels.

All controllers will execute a standardized run-time system. This run-time system will enable the execution of functions with different levels of criticality on one computer. The run-time system will offer services for fault-tolerant execution and other extra-functional requirements including security.

Furthermore, it will provide functionality for Plug&Play. On the one hand, this includes the support to add software functions to the system. On the other hand, it must be possible to detect and integrate new hardware components, such as additional sensors, actuators, or computational units for the central control computer.

5. SECURITY THREATS FOR NEW ARCHITECTURE

Let our new architecture, given in Section 4, serve as a basis for a security analysis.

5.1 Attacker Model

Before we take a closer look of potential security holes, we will setup an attacker model at the beginning. The attackers are inspired by briefly described attacks in Section 2. Therefore, we classify possible attackers into different categories. Such categorizations have been studied in related work.

Howard and Longstaff [10] provide a common model to describe computer security incidents. Here, an incident is a relation of an attacker to an objective. Their seven attacker categories are primarily defined from the perspective of computer and network security. In contrast to our categorization attackers are not divided into internal and external physical access to the system.

In [4] attackers are categorized according to their physical access to the target and their skills. There, the attackers are not specific for automotive systems, and therefore they do not match for us. Bless et al. [6] classified their attackers based on several motivations. But, they do not classify their attackers according to their objectives and their access to the system.

Given that, the available attacker classifications do inadequately suit our kind of architecture. Thus, we propose a suitable attacker classification for automotive systems, which is a combination of the above with additional objectives. We classify our attackers into four skill classes, as given in Table 1:

- **Class A** includes technically unskilled persons searching for a low-risk opportunity to steal and sell some devices, or to attack and change systems. This attacker possesses low technical equipment and uses by experts pre-crafted tools. The members of this category have only minor financial resources. The car owner is part of that category. They want to improve the car's performance without extra payment for the additional functionality or install additional components. We also add the petty criminal to this category. He normally steals devices and wants to sell these. Script kiddies [14] who attack systems only for fun without special knowledge fit in this category. They want only to improve their reputation, but their attacks will harm the system and after those attacks the system is left in an unusable mess.

- **Class B** contains technically low skilled persons who have already attacked systems with weak security, and may have been caught for one of their attacks. This

Table 1: Attacker Classification

Skill Class	Class A	Class B	Class C	Class D
Automotive knowledge	medium	high	high	medium
IT knowledge	low	medium	high	high
Technical equipment	low	medium	medium	high
Financial resources	low	low	medium	high
Possible roles	car owner, petty criminal, or script kiddie	manufacturer, motorcar mechanic, or tuner	device developer, motorcar mechanic, or hacker	terrorist or organized crime

kind of attacker is cunning and experienced. The person only attacks smaller systems or systems with weak security. They possess some technical equipment, where special tools are part of. The members of this category have only minor financial resources. Device or original end manufacturers are part of that category. We also add motorcar mechanics to this category, because they know about the system and possess the needed special tools. In this category we also put tuners who improve the performance or appearance of a car.

- **Class C** covers technically high skilled persons who are specialized in attacking systems. Sometimes they use members of our other classes as a help. We put normal developers of components in this category. Sometimes these people want to increase their reputation or learn something new, known as hackers. But mostly these people attack for money or harming the company. Additionally, motorcar mechanics who are paid by car owners to tune or tweak the system are also part of this category. They know the system and can use insider knowledge. They have the tools and special equipment to perform the attack. The goal of this attacker class is to use their knowledge to improve their personal benefit.

- **Class D** includes technically high skilled or trained persons who have substantial resources. Additionally, the attacker uses members of our other classes as help. One can interpret this category as terrorists or mafia members. We define this category for criminal organizations. The goal of this attacker class is to maximize the impact by harming passengers, and getting the highest possible outcome, such as money or terror.

Furthermore, we distinguish between *restricted* and *unrestricted* physical access of the attacker (Table 2). An attacker with unrestricted access to a car can manipulate, replace, or remove components directly. Attackers with restricted access can manipulate the system only through the ICT infrastructure.

The main paradigm of security is based on the the protection of most valuable assets from the most capable attackers by a single component under the most difficult circumstances. This paradigm matches our Class D attacker. But, defending a system against a Class D attacker is costly and consumes high efforts of mechanisms. Therefore, in the upcoming analysis we will mainly focus on attackers of Class A-C.

Table 2: Physical Access

Physical Access	unrestricted	restricted
Possible roles	car owner, tuner, petty criminal, manufacturer, device developer, or motorcar mechanics	script kiddie, hacker, organized crime, or terrorist

5.2 Analysis of Classical Architectures

As shown in Section 2, a lot of attacks have been assaulted against classical architectures. These attacks were done against single functions or network components, especially at the infotainment domain. This section summaries already known threats that must be also considered in the new architecture. Here, attackers are Class B and Class C ones, who can access the system restricted and unrestricted.

Bypassing of security mechanism is a fundamental problem. For example, this allows tampering of memory content or changes in an execution path.

In [17] communication networks of embedded systems are described to support only rudimentary capabilities or are isolated. To get the best out of these limitations, most data is broadcast as plain text. Such an information leakage allows an attacker to read and manipulate messages.

Covert channels [13] are another problem in embedded systems. Here, information is transferred between two components, which is normally prohibited by the security policy.

For a better administration embedded systems getting more connected to the Internet and isolation is broken up. Thus, they are faced with threats known from IT systems. Malwares, like Stuxnet, can subvert or compromise the system.

With the change from the internal combustion engine to the electric motor new components were added to the old architecture. Thus, attacks against the new components are done with techniques [16], which work mostly in the old architectures.

Other requirements given by attacks based on social engineering and physical access, such as unauthorized changes, malicious use, or insider threats, are out of scope here.

5.3 Analysis of New Architecture

The upcoming changes increase the attractiveness and potential of new attacks for several reasons. Attractiveness is increased due to the fact that more safety-critical functions are introduced to the car and that access to data due to the centralized architecture becomes easier. The potential of new attacks increases as Plug&Play capability and the use of standardized networks offer a basis for new attacks.

We therefore analyzed the potential attacks and grouped them into categories with respect to attacks against the central computer, the smart sensors and actuators, the network, the data handling and the Plug&Play mechanism. In the following, we summarize the results.

Our architecture of a centralized system executes all important functions and applications. Thus, the centralized system will be the main target for an attacker to get access to a specific function. It is also possible to stall an execution or an execution order to get rid of a specific function. At a worst case, an attacker can shut down the entire system by exploiting a flaw. Additionally, functionality can be activated without extra payment by circumvent security mechanism of the centralized system.

Smart sensors and actuators are the smallest components of the new architecture. They are responsible to collect data and execute commands. Therefore, attackers will try to influence them by analyzing, tampering, and circumventing their software. This can be done whether in changing the firmware or providing special crafted data, former recorded data, or malformed data. For example, tuners fake sensor information of an oxygen sensor to manually override the air and fuel settings for an internal combustion engine [3]. Additionally, a sensor could be blinded by sending a jam signal [21]. Malformed data can lead to a denial of service (DoS), when the component is busy with checking the data and cannot execute other functions.

Components are interconnected by a communication network, above described attacks can be also done remote. Additional attacks are removing a component from the system, shutting down components, or collecting information about the system, such as topology or component interconnection. Besides that, an attacker can block a component by a denial of service (DoS) or can influence the temporal behavior by shifting the time basis. These attacks can base upon security holes of communication protocols or connection components, such as switches.

A new feature of our architecture provides the possibility to integrate components by Plug&Play. This adds a potential to attack the system. Software and hardware Plug&Play allows to integrate a component, which is owned by an attacker. Thus, a component can masquerade as another component, emulate to provide better services (aka Sybil attack [8]), denial of sleep of another component, or block another component (DoS). Plug&Play allows also an attacker to collect informations or listen to data exchange, known as man-in-the-middle attack. Additionally, removing a component can tricker a reconfiguration combined with a recalculation of resources, which may block the whole system, known as Chaos attack. It is also possible to integrate software or malware, which allows an attacker to open backdoors for further attacks [15].

To support Plug&Play we need a standardized interface, which are common to developers. These interfaces are a possible target for a first attack. Therefore, an attacker could use weaknesses of the interfaces [3] to get access to the system. This access enables an attacker to start a selective

---

[3]http://www.ehow.com/how_5409757_fake-out-oxygen-sensor.html

attack against system internals. Otherwise, interfaces are a problem of information leakage. Most interfaces provide more knowledge of itself or the underlying system as needed. By a simple interface probing an attacker could gather information and feed the interface with every possible alternative to analyze the reaction. Then the attacker will use the gathered information to get access to the system.

6. REQUIREMENTS OF FUTURE SECURITY ARCHITECTURE

Security is a system property. Current security in vehicle systems is designed to protect either a function or a communication channel. As shown in Section 2 and 5, a lot of attacks exists. Hence, today's attacks and our centralized platform computer motivate holistic security architecture. This implies that a system must be designed with security in mind from the beginning. A decomposition of system functions is needed to generate successively simpler modules. This allows to support the paradigm, simpler is securer. There, it is possible to trust these simple modules to work under all conditions.

One cornerstone of our architecture is the central computer and its interconnection with smart sensors and actuators. These components must be secured by a holistic approach to support the execution of applications with different levels of security. Therefore, high-assurance security architecture is need.

Avionics, robotics, aeronautics, and military domains have already faced similar problems, and as a consequence have abandoned classical architecture approaches. The result was a new paradigm, which is known as multiple independent levels of security (MILS). Here, the concept is based on separation and information control flow. MILS uses three different levels, a separation kernel, middleware, and applications [18]. The security must ensure to be non-bypassable, evaluable, always invoked, and tamperproof. Based on the previous analysis, we believe that future cars must be based on a **MILS architecture**.

The separation kernel provides temporal and spatial partitions to separate parts of the system to avoid interferences. Between partitions the separation kernel establishes a secure transfer of control. Such kernels are very small with 4,000 lines of code. This allows to verify the correctness with mathematical or formal methods.

Upon the separation kernel a variety of middleware can reside in different partitions. These levels are responsible for creating application components. They run in user or non-privileged mode. This avoids to harm the whole system when a problem occurs, and will only affect their own partition. Additionally, it provides a secure end-to-end inter-object message flow.

The application level implements specific security functionality, such as firewalls or cryptographic modules. These components and non-security ones are mostly developed by other vendors. Consequently, MILS architectures are based on composition.

To ensure tamperproofness MILS runs self-tests during initialization. This shall ensure that the integrity of the platform is valid. When the tests fail a recovery mechanism must be provided. Additionally, the systems must isolate faults and must avoid a cascade of faults. Therefore, only the important part of the system, e.g., the separation kernel, must run in privileged mode. All other functionality, such as partitioning communication system (PCS) or the middleware, will only run in user space.

However, implementing just a standard MILS architecture is not enough. As a lot of computational power is required, the central computer will be based on several computers. Therefore, a secure communication between these different computers and also with smart sensors and actuators is required. Hence, future cars will require a **distributed MILS architecture**. Distributed MILS architectures require that the communication between processors be managed by the MILS system [2]. The way how this can be achieved is the focus of several ongoing research projects, e.g., the projects EURO-MILS[4] and D-MILS[5] funded under the Seventh Framework Program.

But even a distributed MILS architecture will not be enough for future cars. As shown Section 4, Plug&Play is one main feature of future vehicle architecture. In contrast to classical MILS systems Plug&Play capable systems need to be more adaptable during runtime. Hence, the configuration of the system should be modifiable to support additional functionality. This allows also to keep an aging security system up-to-date or to equip a system with future security components. In short, Plug&Play motivates **adaptive and distributed MILS**.

With a later installation of components new dependencies are inserted. It must be checked whether these new dependencies break some old ones or whether connections are established, which are not allowed by the security policy. Furthermore, also resource constraints must be taken into account. During installation of a new component, the system must check whether enough resources are available for the new and the already installed applications. At run-time, the resource assumptions must be continuously checked to detect and omit violations.

If components of different criticality levels are installed, the system must ensure that the different levels are separated and no security constraints are violated.

Finally, Plug&Play also enables update of security mechanisms itself. Systems are increasingly attacked, exploits are created for profit, and numbers of malwares are rising. But, simultaneously new technologies evolve and countermeasures are developed, which will lead to changes of security mechanisms. This is especially important for automotive systems, which last more than ten years in usage. However, MILS systems see security as part of the design and as a built into the system from the beginning. Thus, there will be no changes of the system's security mechanism during the lifecycle of MILS. Based on the lifecycle of a car and new arising attacks the architecture needs to be upgradeable. This motivates a secure product life cycle (SPLC), where system internals and important components can be patched or updated. This is another important aspect, which needs to be covered by an adaptive and distributes MILS architecture.

In summary, at least the following research questions need to be answered for a secure automotive future:

- Security Architecture: which mechanism can be implemented at which security layer and what are the appropriate interfaces? It must be clarified at which

level (application, node, system) security mechanisms are implemented.

- Security Goals: which guarantees regarding security can be offered at the level of distributed systems and how can these guarantees be implemented? Furthermore, how can applications state their requirements independent of the concrete implementation? How are these requirements enforced? This includes securing the data flow between the different components according to confidentiality, integrity, and authenticity.

- Automatic Configuration: how can the system derive a valid configuration satisfying the security constraints of the applications? In traditional systems, a system developer takes over the role of the configurator. In the future, the Plug&Play capability including configuration must be offered as a service by the platform.

- Policy Management: how to implement policy management taking into account Plug&Play? In traditional systems, the communicating components are defined at design time. In a Plug&Play-capable system, the communication partners are determined at runtime. Therefore, policies must be formulated in a different fashion. Furthermore, new policies might be introduced and mechanisms must be defined to guarantee their correct and secure behavior within the system.

- Authentication: how to establish a secure communication and interaction in a dynamic distributed system? Mechanisms must be defined to detect and integrate new components. Additionally, hidden malicious components need to be detected and isolated.

- Intrusion Detection: how can the system detect malicious behavior of components and what are appropriate countermeasures? These mechanisms have to be implemented in a way that the platform can still provide a basic set of services to the remaining applications.

- Audit: how to save all data related to security during run-time to enable a retrospective analysis in case of incidents?

- Secure Product Lifecycle: what are the mechanisms to ensure an up-to-date security architecture? New arising attacks and evolving technologies imply the necessity to keep the architecture up-to-date. A concept for upgrading the architecture must be developed.

- Business Models: who is the owner of the data within the car and who is allowed to earn money with the data? In current cars, the access to the data is restricted: the car manufacturer controls access and usage of data ensuring national data privacy laws. In Plug&Play-capable cars, data access rules will be defined most probably by all stakeholders.

7. CONCLUSION

This paper summarized the results of a study on upcoming changes of the ICT architecture in the automotive area. In particular, we focused on the effects on how security is

---

[4]http://www.euromils.eu/
[5]http://www.fortiss.org/en/research/projects/distributed_mils/

achieved in cars. Based on the current state of the art to design security mechanisms for each automotive function individually, we discussed the cornerstones of future ICT architectures and analyzed the new security threats of such an architecture. As a result, we argue that future cars will need an adaptive and distributed MILS system. While MILS architectures are already state of the art in several domains such as avionics and distributed MILS is already an identified research topic, the design to support adaptivity will be an interesting research topic for the future.

Acknowledgments

This work is partially funded by the German Federal Ministry of Economics and Technology under grant no. 01ME12009 through the project RACE[6].

8. REFERENCES

[1] AUTomotive Open System ARchitecture (AUTOSAR) Release 4.0.

[2] J. Alves-Foss, W. S. Harrison, P. Oman, and C. Taylor. The mils architecture for high-assurance embedded systems. *International Journal of Embedded Systems*, 2:239–247, 2006.

[3] R. J. Anderson. What we can learn from api security. In B. Christianson, B. Crispo, J. A. Malcolm, and M. Roe, editors, *Security Protocols Workshop*, volume 3364 of *Lecture Notes in Computer Science*, pages 288–300. Springer, 2003.

[4] R. J. Anderson. *Security Engineering: A Guide to Building Dependable Distributed Systems*. Wiley computer publishing. Wiley, 2nd edition edition, 2008.

[5] M. Bernhard, C. Buckl, V. Döricht, M. Fehling, L. Fiege, H. von Grolman, N. Ivandic, C. Janelle, C. Klein, K.-J. Kuhn, C. Patzlaff, B. Riedl, B. Schätz, and C. Stanek. *The Software Car: Information and Communication Technology (ICT) as an Engine for the Electromobility of the Future, Summary of results of the "eCar ICT System Architecture for Electromobility" research project sponsored by the Federal Ministry of Economics and Technology*. ForTISS GmbH, March 2011.

[6] R. Bless, G. Grotewold, C. Haas, B. Hackstein, S. Hofmann, A. Jentzsch, A. Kiening, C. Krauß, J. Lamberty, M. Müter, P. Schoo, L. Völker, and C. Werle. A security model for future vehicular electronic infrastructures. In *8th Embedded Security in Cars (escar)*, 2010.

[7] S. Checkoway, D. McCoy, B. Kantor, D. Anderson, H. Shacham, S. Savage, K. Koscher, A. Czeskis, F. Roesner, and T. Kohno. Comprehensive experimental analyses of automotive attack surfaces. In *Proceedings of the 20th USENIX conference on Security*, SEC'11, pages 6–6, Berkeley, CA, USA, 2011. USENIX Association.

[8] J. R. Douceur. The sybil attack. In *Revised Papers from the First International Workshop on Peer-to-Peer Systems*, IPTPS '01, pages 251–260, London, UK, UK, 2002. Springer-Verlag.

[9] T. Hoppe, S. Kiltz, and J. Dittmann. Security threats to automotive can networks — practical examples and selected short-term countermeasures. In *Proceedings of the 27th international conference on Computer Safety, Reliability, and Security*, SAFECOMP '08, pages 235–248, Berlin, Heidelberg, 2008. Springer-Verlag.

[10] J. D. Howard and T. A. Longstaff. A Common Language for Computer Security Incidents. Samdia Report SAND98-8667, Sandia National Laboratories, Albuquerque, New Mexico 87185 and Livermore, California 94550, October 1998.

[11] M. S. Idrees, H. Schweppe, Y. Roudier, M. Wolf, D. Scheuermann, and O. Henniger. Secure automotive on-board protocols: a case of over-the-air firmware updates. In *Proceedings of the Third international conference on Communication technologies for vehicles*, Nets4Cars/Nets4Trains'11, pages 224–238, Berlin, Heidelberg, 2011. Springer-Verlag.

[12] K. Koscher, A. Czeskis, F. Roesner, S. Patel, T. Kohno, S. Checkoway, D. McCoy, B. Kantor, D. Anderson, H. Shacham, and S. Savage. Experimental security analysis of a modern automobile. In *Proceedings of the 2010 IEEE Symposium on Security and Privacy*, SP '10, pages 447–462, Washington, DC, USA, 2010. IEEE Computer Society.

[13] B. W. Lampson. A note on the confinement problem. *Commun. ACM*, 16(10):613–615, Oct. 1973.

[14] N. Mead, E. Hough, and T. S. II. Security Quality Requirements Engineering. Technical Report CMU/SEI-2005-TR-009, Software Engineering Institute, Carnegie Mellon University, Pittsburgh, Pennsylvania,, 2005.

[15] T. Nash. An undirected attack against critical infrastructure a case study for improving your control system security. *US-Cert Control Systems Security Center*, 1.2, 2005.

[16] C. Paar, K. Schramm, A. Weimerskirch, and W. Burleson. Securing green cars: It security in next-generation electric vehicle systems.

[17] G. J. Pottie and W. J. Kaiser. *Principles of Embedded Networked Systems Design*. Cambridge University Press, New York, NY, USA, 1st edition, 2009.

[18] J. M. Rushby. Design and verification of secure systems. In *Proceedings of the eighth ACM symposium on Operating systems principles*, SOSP '81, pages 12–21, New York, NY, USA, 1981. ACM.

[19] G. Silberg and R. Wallace. Self-driving cars: The next revolution. Technical report, KPMG, 2012.

[20] M. Wolf and T. Gendrullis. Design, implementation, and evaluation of a vehicular hardware security module. In *Proceedings of the 14th international conference on Information Security and Cryptology*, ICISC'11, pages 302–318, Berlin, Heidelberg, 2012. Springer-Verlag.

[21] W. Xu, K. Ma, W. Trappe, and Y. Zhang. Jamming sensor networks: attack and defense strategies. *Network, IEEE*, 20(3):41 – 47, may-june 2006.

---

[6]http://www.projekt-race.de/

A Framework for Privacy and Security Analysis of Probe-based Traffic Information Systems

Edward S. Canepa[*]

King Abdullah University of Science and
Technology
4700 KAUST, Thuwal
Jeddah, Saudi Arabia
edward.canepa@kaust.edu.sa

Christian G. Claudel[†]

King Abdullah University of Science and
Technology
4700 KAUST, Thuwal
Jeddah, Saudi Arabia
christian.claudel@kaust.edu.sa

ABSTRACT

Most large scale traffic information systems rely on fixed sensors (e.g. loop detectors, cameras) and user generated data, this latter in the form of GPS traces sent by smartphones or GPS devices onboard vehicles. While this type of data is relatively inexpensive to gather, it can pose multiple security and privacy risks, even if the location tracks are anonymous. In particular, creating bogus location tracks and sending them to the system is relatively easy. This bogus data could perturb traffic flow estimates, and disrupt the transportation system whenever these estimates are used for actuation. In this article, we propose a new framework for solving a variety of privacy and cybersecurity problems arising in transportation systems. The state of traffic is modeled by the Lighthill-Whitham-Richards traffic flow model, which is a first order scalar conservation law with concave flux function. Given a set of traffic flow data, we show that the constraints resulting from this partial differential equation are mixed integer linear inequalities for some decision variable. The resulting framework is very flexible, and can in particular be used to detect spoofing attacks in real time, or carry out attacks on location tracks. Numerical implementations are performed on experimental data from the *Mobile Century* experiment to validate this framework.

Categories and Subject Descriptors

C.2.4 [**Computer-Communication Networks**]: Distributed Systems; G.1.6 [**Numerical Analysis**]: Optimization—*Integer programming*

---

[*]E. Canepa is a PhD student, Department of Electrical Engineering
[†]C. Claudel is an assistant professor, Department of Electrical Engineering

Keywords

Cyber-Physical Systems; Privacy analysis

1. INTRODUCTION

The convergence of mobile sensing, communication and computing has led to the rise of a new class of systems known as *cyberphysical systems*, which are physical systems sensed and actuated by "cyber" agents, an example of which is the transportation network. In transportation systems, a new form of sensing has emerged since a few years in the form of *probe vehicles*. In this paradigm, the vehicles themselves transmit their speed and location anonymously [30] to a central server, which uses this data in conjunction with fixed sensor data [31] to generate real-time traffic maps. While systems such as the *Mobile Millennium* system [30] have successfully demonstrated the concept, multiple issues remain in terms of privacy [19] and security. Unlike fixed sensors which are difficult to tamper with, it is relatively easy for an attacker to generate fake data and inject it in the system to modify the estimates with dire consequences, in particular if the traffic estimates are used for optimal traffic control (traffic lights, ramp metering). In addition, since the user data is sent to a central server, privacy breaches are a real possibility, even if the tracks are anonymous [20].

The security and privacy issues of probe-based traffic information systems have been explored in numerous articles such as [25, 20, 15, 19]. However, these articles do not rely on traffic flow models for the analysis of probe data, which can lead to incorrect results. For instance, naive vehicle matching algorithms based on a constant velocity assumption such as the scheme used in [19] are only valid when the vehicle density is uniform on the highway. They lead to overly optimistic results otherwise, since the probe and fixed sensor data constrains the possible density profile of the highway, which brings additional information that an attacker can exploit.

One of the biggest difficulties arising when dealing with probe-based traffic flow information systems is the integration of the effects of the model. Indeed, such systems are traditionally modeled by *partial differential equations* (PDEs), for which very few mathematical tools are available for control and estimation. An additional difficulty is the integration of the probe data into the PDE, which is computationally cumbersome in general [17, 10].

We showed earlier [9, 7] that the constraints of a PDE model can be written in an explicit (and tractable) form whenever the underlying model is a first order scalar conservation law with convex flux function, encoded here by the classical *Lighthill-Whitham-Richards* (LWR) PDE. For general convex or concave flux functions, the model constraints are mixed integer convex, and boil down to mixed integer linear inequalities for specific flux functions such as the triangular flux function [13, 14]. Since the constraints of the model are encoded in a tractable form, the resulting framework is very useful for solving a variety of transportation engineering problems: estimation [7], boundary control, model parameter estimation, which all result in optimization problems with mixed integer convex constraints. The same framework can be extended to study security and user privacy problems, which is the contribution of this article. We show that many security or privacy problems (cyberattack detection, inference attack on location track) can be posed as mixed integer linear programs, which provide a computationally tractable solution to previously open problems. We then illustrate these results by numerical implementations of the corresponding MILPs using real data from the *Mobile Century* experiment [18] and from the *Mobile Millennium* system [30].

2. MODEL DEFINITION

2.1 Hamilton-Jacobi formulation of the LWR traffic flow model

Let us assume that the road section is a spatial domain defined by $X := [\xi, \chi]$, where ξ and χ are the upstream and downstream boundaries respectively. We assume that the state of the system is described by a scalar function $\mathbf{M}(\cdot, \cdot)$ of both time and space, known as *Moskowitz function* [23, 24]. The Moskowitz function is a macroscopic description of traffic flow which can be thought as follows: let consecutive integer labels be assigned to vehicles entering the highway at location $x = \xi$.

One of the most common models used to described traffic flow is know as the *Lighthill-Whitham-Richards* (LWR) model [21, 26]. With this assumption, the Moskowitz function satisfies a *Hamilton-Jacobi* (HJ) PDE evolution equation:

$$\frac{\partial \mathbf{M}(t,x)}{\partial t} - \psi \left(-\frac{\partial \mathbf{M}(t,x)}{\partial x} \right) = 0 \qquad (1)$$

The function $\psi(\cdot)$ defined in equation (1) is the *Hamiltonian*. Several classes of weak solutions to equation (1) exist, such as viscosity solutions [12, 4] or Barron-Jensen/Frankowska (B-J/F) solutions [5, 16] used in the present article. The B-J/F solutions to equation (1) are fully characterized by a *Lax-Hopf* formula [3, 10], which was initially derived using the control framework of viability theory [2].

In the remainder of this article, we assume that the Hamiltonian is given by the following formula:

$$\psi(\rho) = \begin{cases} v_f \rho & : \rho \in [0, k_c] \\ w(\rho - \kappa) & : \rho \in [k_c, \kappa] \end{cases} \qquad (2)$$

where

$$k_c = \frac{-w\kappa}{v_f - w}$$

Such Hamiltonian is often referred to in the transportation literature as *triangular fundamental diagram* [13, 14],

and is commonly used to model traffic flow because of its robustness.

2.2 Lax-Hopf formula

Solving the HJ PDE (1) requires the definition of *value conditions*, which encompass the concept of initial, upstream, downstream and internal boundary conditions.

DEFINITION 2.1. *[Value condition] A value condition* $\mathbf{c}(\cdot, \cdot)$ *is a lower semicontinuous function ranging in* $\mathbb{R} \cup +\infty$. *The* effective domain*[27] of* $\mathbf{c}(\cdot, \cdot)$ *is*
$$\text{Dom}(\mathbf{c}) = \{(t, x) \in \mathbb{R}_+ \times X | \mathbf{c}(t, x) < +\infty\}.$$

In all applications of this work, the value conditions are assumed to be affine functions of space and time, defined on a line segment of $\mathbb{R}_+ \times X$.

Physically, the *effective domain* of definition $\text{Dom}(\mathbf{c})$ of a value condition $\mathbf{c}$ represents the subset of the space time domain $\mathbb{R}_+ \times X$ in which we want the value condition to apply. For instance, imposing an upstream boundary condition $\mathbf{c}_{\text{upstream}}(\cdot, \cdot)$ amounts to constrain the value of the state on the set $\text{Dom}(\mathbf{c}_{\text{upstream}}) = \mathbb{R}_+ \times \{\xi\}$, *i.e.* constraining the value of the state at the upstream boundary, and for all times.

Given an arbitrary value condition $\mathbf{c}(\cdot, \cdot)$, we define its associated solution $\mathbf{M_c}(\cdot, \cdot)$ to (1) by the following Lax-Hopf formula [3, 10].

PROPOSITION 2.2. *[Lax-Hopf formula] Let* $\mathbf{c}(\cdot, \cdot)$ *be a value condition, as in Definition 2.1. The B-J/F solution* $\mathbf{M_c}(\cdot, \cdot)$ *to (1) with hamiltonian (2) associated with* $\mathbf{c}(\cdot, \cdot)$ *is defined [3, 10] by:*

$$\mathbf{M_c}(t, x) = \inf_{(u,T) \in [-v,w] \times \mathbb{R}_+} \left(\mathbf{c}(t - T, x + Tu) + Tk_c(u + v) \right) \qquad (3)$$

The structure of the Lax-Hopf formula (3), implies the following important property, known as *inf-morphism* property.

PROPOSITION 2.3. *[Inf-morphism property] Let the value condition* $\mathbf{c}(\cdot, \cdot)$ *be minimum of a finite number of lower semicontinuous functions:*

$$\forall (t, x) \in [0, t_{\max}] \times X, \quad \mathbf{c}(t, x) := \min_{j \in J} \mathbf{c}_j(t, x) \qquad (4)$$

The solution $\mathbf{M_c}(\cdot, \cdot)$ *associated with the above value condition can be decomposed [3, 10, 11] as:*

$$\forall (t, x) \in [0, t_{\max}] \times X, \quad \mathbf{M_c}(t, x) = \min_{j \in J} \mathbf{M}_{\mathbf{c}_j}(t, x) \qquad (5)$$

The above proposition has considerable importance in experimental problems, in which the value condition function is typically a set of piecewise affine functions [9]. In this case, the value condition $\mathbf{c}(\cdot, \cdot)$ can be decomposed as (4), where the functions $\mathbf{c}_j(\cdot, \cdot)$ are all affine functions. By the Lax-Hopf formula (3), one can easily compute the function $\mathbf{M}_{\mathbf{c}_j}$ associated with $\mathbf{c}_j(\cdot, \cdot)$ analytically, since it amounts to solving a one dimensional linear program with few constraints [11].

2.3 Model constraints for piecewise affine value conditions

In the remainder of this article, we decompose the value condition $\mathbf{c}(\cdot,\cdot)$ into affine block value conditions $\mathbf{c}_j$, $j \in J$ each representing some measurement data. The relation between block value conditions and measurement data is presented in section 3.

One of the specificities of our problem is that the functions $\mathbf{c}_j(\cdot,\cdot)$ are not exactly known from the measurement data: measurement data only constrains the values of some of its coefficients. Thus, from a given experimental dataset, one cannot define all the block value conditions uniquely.

In the remainder of this article, we assume that the model constraints hold for a given value condition candidate $\mathbf{c}(\cdot,\cdot)$ if and only if the following condition is satisfied:

$$\forall (t,x) \in \mathrm{Dom}(\mathbf{c}), \quad \mathbf{M}_{\mathbf{c}}(t,x) = \mathbf{c}(t,x) \qquad (6)$$

Using the inf-morphism property (5), one can rewrite (6) as follows:

PROPOSITION 2.4. *[Model compatibility of block value conditions]* Let $\mathbf{c}(\cdot,\cdot) = \min_{j \in J} \mathbf{c}_j(\cdot,\cdot)$ be given, and let $\mathbf{M}_{\mathbf{c}}(\cdot,\cdot)$ be defined as in (3). The value condition $\mathbf{c}(\cdot,\cdot)$ satisfies (6) if and only if the following inequality constraints are satisfied:

$$\mathbf{M}_{\mathbf{c}_j}(t,x) \geq \mathbf{c}_i(t,x) \ \forall (t,x) \in \mathrm{Dom}(\mathbf{c}_i), \ \forall (i,j) \in J^2 \quad (7)$$

The proof of this proposition is available in [6].

When the above compatibility property is satisfied, all value conditions can be imposed in the strong sense [28], *i.e.* the solution to the HJ PDE (1) will be identical to the value conditions on their respective domains of definition.

In addition to the above proposition, the Moskowitz function $\mathbf{M}_{\mathbf{c}}(\cdot,\cdot)$ has to be continuous by construction [24, 7], which yields additional compatibility conditions. We outline these compatibility conditions in Section 4.

We now define the affine initial, boundary and internal condition functions that will play the role of building blocks to construct the value condition $\mathbf{c}(\cdot,\cdot)$ of the problem, as described in (4).

3. AFFINE INITIAL, BOUNDARY AND INTERNAL CONDITIONS

Multiple types of value conditions can be incorporated into the estimation problem. In the present article, we include initial, boundary and internal conditions. The initial and boundary conditions are typically measured (with some error) using fixed sensors, such as inductive loop detectors, magnetometers or traffic cameras. Similarly, the internal conditions are partially measured using probe vehicle trajectories[29].

3.1 Definition of affine initial, boundary and internal conditions

The formal definition of initial, upstream, downstream and boundary conditions associated with the HJ PDE (1) is the subject of the following definition.

DEFINITION 3.1. *[Affine initial, boundary and internal conditions]* Let us define $\mathbb{K} = \{0, \ldots, k_{\max}\}$, $\mathbb{N} = \{0, \ldots, n_{\max}\}$ and $\mathbb{M} = \{0, \ldots, m_{\max}\}$. For all $k \in \mathbb{K}$, $n \in \mathbb{N}$ and $m \in \mathbb{M}$, we define the following functions, respectively called *initial, upstream, downstream (boundary) and internal conditions:*

$$M_k(t,x) = \begin{cases} -\sum_{i=0}^{k-1} \rho(i)X \\ -\rho(k)(x-kX) & \text{if } t = 0 \\ & \text{and } x \in [kX, (k+1)X] \\ +\infty & \text{otherwise} \end{cases} \quad (8)$$

$$\gamma_n(t,x) = \begin{cases} \sum_{i=0}^{n-1} q_{\mathrm{in}}(i)T \\ +q_{\mathrm{in}}(n)(t-nT) & \text{if } x = \xi \\ & \text{and } t \in [nT, (n+1)T] \\ +\infty & \text{otherwise} \end{cases} \quad (9)$$

$$\beta_n(t,x) = \begin{cases} \sum_{i=0}^{n-1} q_{\mathrm{out}}(i)T \\ +q_{\mathrm{out}}(n)(t-nT) \\ -\sum_{k=0}^{k_{max}} \rho(k)X & \text{if } x = \chi \\ & \text{and } t \in [nT, (n+1)T] \\ +\infty & \text{otherwise} \end{cases} \quad (10)$$

$$\mu_m(t,x) = \begin{cases} L_m + r_m(t - t_{\min}(m)) \\ (\text{if } x = x_{\min}(m) \\ +\frac{x_{\max}(m)-x_{\min}(m)}{t_{\max}(m)-t_{\min}(m)}(t - t_{\min}(m)) \\ \text{and } t \in [t_{\min}(m), t_{\max}(m)]) \\ +\infty \qquad \text{otherwise} \end{cases} \quad (11)$$

.

As stated in the previous section, the initial, boundary and internal conditions defined above are usually not known exactly. In particular, we do not know the exact values of the initial densities $\rho(\cdot)$, the boundary flows $q_{\mathrm{in}}(\cdot)$ and $q_{\mathrm{out}}(\cdot)$, as well as the coefficients L_m and r_m of the internal conditions. Some coefficients such as $\rho(\cdot)$, $q_{\mathrm{in}}(\cdot)$ and $q_{\mathrm{out}}(\cdot)$ can be known with some uncertainty using flow or traffic density sensors, but some coefficients such as L_m and r_m simply cannot be measured experimentally by any traffic sensor. All of these unknown variables will act as part of our decision variable for the Mixed Integer Linear Program (MILP) derived in Section 4. Note that the coefficients $x_{\min}(\cdot)$, $x_{\max}(\cdot)$, $t_{\min}(\cdot)$ and $t_{\max}(\cdot)$ are known with high accuracy since they are typically measured with a GPS, and will thus not be part of the problem's decision variable.

3.2 Analytical solutions to affine initial, boundary and internal conditions

Given the affine initial, upstream, downstream and internal conditions defined above, the corresponding solutions $\mathbf{M}_{M_k}(\cdot,\cdot)$, $\mathbf{M}_{\gamma_n}(\cdot,\cdot)$, $\mathbf{M}_{\beta_n}(\cdot,\cdot)$ and $\mathbf{M}_{\mu_m}(\cdot,\cdot)$ defined by the Lax-Hopf formula (3) can be computed explicitly [6, 22] as closed-form expressions. These expressions can be found in [6, 22] in the case of the fundamental triangular diagram.

The closed-form expressions of $\mathbf{M}_{M_k}(\cdot,\cdot)$, $\mathbf{M}_{\gamma_n}(\cdot,\cdot)$, $\mathbf{M}_{\beta_n}(\cdot,\cdot)$ and $\mathbf{M}_{\mu_m}(\cdot,\cdot)$ are very important: they enable one to compute the solution to the HJ PDE (1) semi-analytically for a very low computational cost using the inf-morphism property [10, 22]. They also enable one to write the model compatibility constraint condition (7) as a set of linear inequalities in a specific decision variable.

4. CONSTRAINTS ARISING FROM MODEL AND MEASUREMENT DATA

We consider a set of block boundary conditions $\mathbf{c}_j$ defined as in Section 3.1, with unknown coefficients. Let us call V the vector space of unknown coefficients. Our measurement data (from the data set) constrains the possible values of these coefficients. Such constraints are called *data constraints*, and are outlined in Section 4.2 below. Similarly, the model compatibility conditions (7) also constrain the possible values of the unknown coefficients. Such constraints are called *model constraints*, and are outlined in Section 4.1. An important and nontrivial result of [6] is that all these constraints are explicit, and also tractable. A list of all constraints can be found in [7, 8].

4.1 Model constraints

While the derivation of the model and continuity constraints is out of the scope of this article, these constraints have the following important property.

FACT 4.1. *[Mixed integer linear inequality property] The model constraints (7) and the continuity constraints [8] are mixed integer linear in the variables $\rho(1), \rho(2), \ldots, \rho(k_{\max})$, $q_{\mathrm{in}}(1), \ldots, q_{\mathrm{in}}(n_{\max}), q_{\mathrm{out}}(1), \ldots, q_{\mathrm{out}}(n_{\max}), L_1, \ldots, L_{m_{\max}}$ and $r_1, \ldots, r_{m_{\max}}.$*

The proof of this proposition is available in [6, 8].

In the remainder of this article, we define y as the decision variable of the problem, containing the continuous variables $\rho(1), \rho(2), \ldots, \rho(k_{\max}), q_{\mathrm{in}}(1), \ldots, q_{\mathrm{in}}(n_{\max}), q_{\mathrm{out}}(1), \ldots,$ $q_{\mathrm{out}}(n_{\max}), L_1, \ldots, L_{m_{\max}}$ and $r_1, \ldots, r_{m_{\max}}$, with additional integer variables. We symbolically write the mixed integer linear constraints resulting from the model and the continuity constraints as

$$Ay \leq b \qquad (12)$$

4.2 Data constraints

Similarly, the unknown coefficients of the initial, boundary and internal conditions have to satisfy data constraints to be compatible with the observations. The data constraints express the fact that the true values of the conditions coefficients should be close to the corresponding measurements, within the corresponding sensor specifications.

HYPOTHESIS 4.2. *[Data constraints] In the remainder of our article, we assume that the data constraints are linear in the unknown coefficients of the initial, boundary and internal conditions, and can thus be written symbolically as*

$$Cy \leq d \qquad (13)$$

where y is the decision variable defined earlier.

Different choices of error models that yield linear data constraints are available in [7].

5. EXAMPLES OF APPLICATIONS TO CYBERSECURITY AND PRIVACY ANALYSIS

We now present some applications of this framework to security and privacy problems occurring in probe-based traffic information systems. Though we present only two examples for compactness, more problems could be posed as mixed integer linear programs in the same framework. Examples of such problems include:

- Real time assessment of vulnerability to attacks
- Offline assessment of worst case effects of attacks
- Real time analysis of probe data to reject identifiable tracks

5.1 Spoofing cyber attack detection as a mixed integer linear feasibility problem

Given the model, continuity and data constraints presented above, we consider the following feasibility problem:

$$\text{Find } y \atop \text{s. t. } \left\{ \begin{array}{l} Ay \leq b \\ Cy \leq d \end{array} \right. \qquad (14)$$

Let us denote by $\bar{y}$ the actual value of the decision variable corresponding to the actual traffic flow scenario. Note that in experimental situations $\bar{y}$ cannot be measured, unless one has complete knowledge of the state of the system.

If (14) is infeasible, there is no set of initial, boundary and internal conditions satisfying at the same time the model and data constraints. Thus, $\bar{y}$ is either violating the model constraints (*i.e.* $A\bar{y} > b$) or the data constraints (*i.e.* $C\bar{y} > d$), or both. The interpretation is as follows:

- If $\bar{y}$ violates the model constraints, then the actual traffic state function does not follow the HJ PDE (1), which can be caused by modeling errors of the flux function (most probable), or by phenomena that are not modeled by the HJ PDE (1) (less likely).

- If $\bar{y}$ violates the data constraints, our error model is incorrect. There can be three main reasons for this to happen:

  1. Incorrect error modeling, for instance caused by wrong sensor specifications
  2. Sensor faults (the error model assumes that all sensors are working according to their specifications, *i.e.* non faulty)
  3. Spoofing attacks

If (14) is feasible, there exists a set of initial, boundary and internal conditions compatible both with the traffic flow model and with the observed data. Note that this does not guarantee that no spoofing attack occurs. Indeed, a spoofing attack could occur, but the complete dataset (actual data and spoofed data) would somehow be compatible with the model and the sensor error model. In the remainder of this article, we assume that a spoofing attack is detected whenever (14) is infeasible, though in practice one has to exclude sensor faults or incorrect error modeling before reaching such a conclusion.

An example of cyberattack detection is shown in Section 6.

5.2 Applications to user privacy analysis

An internal condition of the form (11) can be interpreted as follows. The coefficients L_m and r_m respectively represent the initial value of the Moskowitz function corresponding to the internal condition (at position $x_{\min}(x)$ and at time $t_{\min}(m)$), and the passing rate (number of vehicles passing the probe vehicle per unit time.

By construction, vehicles trajectories correspond to the isolines of the Moskowitz function [24], assuming that no passing occurs. In this situation, two internal conditions μ_m and μ_n are generated by the same vehicle if and only if $L_m = L_n$.

Evidently, the general assumption that vehicles are not allowed to pass each other does not hold in practice, but it is in most situations a very good approximation. Under this approximation, the problem of reidentification [19] (*i.e.* do the internal conditions μ_m and μ_n originate from the same vehicle?) can be posed as:

$$\text{Minimize } |L_m - L_n|$$
$$\text{s. t. } \begin{cases} Ay \le b \\ Cy \le d \end{cases} \tag{15}$$

If the solution to (15) is zero, μ_m and μ_n can originate (though not necessarily) from the same vehicle. In the converse case, μ_m and μ_n are guaranteed to originate from two different vehicles.

An example of vehicle reidentification is shown in Section 6.

6. IMPLEMENTATION

We now present an implementation of the spoofing attack detection framework presented earlier on an experimental dataset. The dataset includes fixed sensor data (obtained from inductive loop detectors in the present case) and mobile sensor data.

6.1 Experimental setup

In these implementations, we use the *Mobile Century* [30, 29] dataset. The *Mobile Century* field experiment demonstrated the use of Nokia N-95 cellphones as mobile traffic sensors in February 2008, and was a joint UC-Berkeley/Nokia project.

For the numerical applications, a spatial domain of 3.858 km is considered, located between the PeMS [31] VDSs (*vehicle detection stations*) 400536 and 400284 on the Highway I - 880 N around Hayward, California. The data used in this implementation was generated on February 8th, 2008, between times $18 : 30$ and $18 : 55$ (local time). In our scenario, we consider inflow and outflow data $q_{in}^{\text{measured}}(\cdot)$ and $q_{out}^{\text{measured}}(\cdot)$ generated by the above PeMS stations, *i.e.* we do not assume to know any initial density data. We also consider internal condition data (*i.e.* probe vehicle data), either real (*i.e.* extracted from the *Mobile Century* dataset) or spoofed.

For all subsequent applications, the data constraints are chosen as $(1-e)q_{\text{in/out}}^{\text{measured}}(n) \le q_{\text{in/out}}(n) \le (1+e)q_{\text{in/out}}^{\text{measured}}(n)$ $\forall n \in [0, n_{\max}]$, where $e = 0.01 = 1\%$ is chosen the worst-case relative error of the flow sensors.

We divided the spatial domain into six segments of equal distance X=643 m. We also set T=30 s as the aggregation time for the flow data (T is determined by the granularity of PeMS data). All MILPs have been implemented using IBM Ilog Cplex working on a Macbook operating MacOS X. The problems described in this article are tractable: they typically involve hundreds of variables and thousands of constraints, and are solved in a few tens seconds.

6.2 Cyber-attack detection example

Our objective is to detect a spoofing attack using the framework defined earlier. For visualizing this specific appli-

cation, the objective function is to maximize the total number of vehicles at initial time, defined by $\sum_{i=0}^{k_{max}} \rho(i)$, though the cyberattack detection algorithm itself is only a feasibility test of the model and data constraints and does not require the definition of an objective function. We consider 20 blocks of upstream (9) and downstream (10) boundary conditions as well as 6 blocks of (real) internal (11) conditions, extracted from the mobile century dataset.

As no spoofed data is injected, (14) is feasible, resulting in Figure 1, top. Note that given our objective function, this computed scenario corresponds to the most "worst case" scenario in terms of traffic, in which the traffic velocity will be minimal. Let us assume that an attacker purposefully sends a "slow" internal condition corresponding to a local traffic speed of 5 *mph*, to perturb the density estimates. In this case, since the speed corresponding to the internal condition mismatches the worst case speed expected by the model, problem (14) becomes infeasible with this new internal condition, leading to the cyberattack detection. This example is illustrated in Figure 1, bottom.

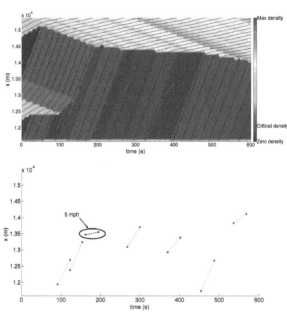

Figure 1: Example of cyber attack detection. This scenario shows how a single internal condition associated with an unreasonable velocity (compared with the model prediction) can result in an infeasibility of problem (14). Top: maximized number of vehicles with no faked internal condition (corresponding to lowest possible average velocity). Bottom: configuration of the internal conditions resulting in an infeasibility of (14). The faked internal condition is highlighted in black, and is corresponding to a speed that is much slower than the worst-case speed forecasted by the model in this area (deep blue corresponds to a free flow velocity).

Of course, the feasibility of (14) does not guarantee that no cyberattack occurs, as a cyberattack could be *stealthy*, in the sense that an attacker could on purpose send data that is compatible with the flow model to be undetected [1]. Also, as stated in Section 5.1, the infeasibility of (14) does not necessarily mean that a cyberattack occurred, since sensor faults or model violations could lead to the same result.

6.3 Vehicle reidentification example

Our objective is now to illustrate the performance of the framework described above on a non trivial case of vehicle reidentification. We consider the same physical setup as previously, with 20 blocks of upstream (9) and downstream (10) boundary conditions. We also consider 3 blocks of (real) internal conditions (11), extracted from the mobile century dataset. Among these 3 blocks, two originate from the same Mobile Century test vehicle, and one originates from another mobile century vehicle. The layout is illustrated in Figure 2.

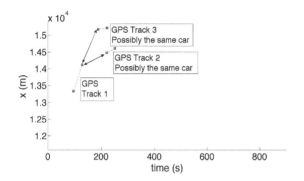

Figure 2: Vehicle reidentification problem layout. In this problem, we consider one block of internal condition (left) generated by a given probe vehicle. We also have two additional blocks of internal condition, generated after the first one. Among these two blocks, one comes from the same vehicle that generated block #1.

Vehicle reidentification problems are at the core of user privacy analysis for probe-based traffic information systems. Indeed, the average *distance to confusion* [19] is an important metric to evaluate user privacy. However typical algorithms such as the one used in [19] do not take into account the effects of the flow model. For instance, the reidentification model used in [19] assumes that the velocity of vehicles is more or less constant, and looks for the best candidate within a region of the space-time domain satisfying this constraint. If we apply this procedure to the problem described in Figure 2, it is easy to visually check that GPS track #3 is the most probable successor of GPS track #1, since it is in the alignment of track #1. However, in this specific case GPS track #2 is actually the successor to GPS track #1, and GPS track #3 has been generated by another probe vehicle. The model-based reidentification scheme (15) is not fooled by the situation: minimizing $|L_1 - L_2|$ gives 0, while minimizing $|L_1 - L_3|$ gives 41. Thus, the nonzero optimal value of (15) rules out GPS track #3 as a possible successor to GPS track #1, a result that does not seem obvious at all by looking at the configuration in Figure 2. The density maps corresponding to the computations of (15) are illustrated in Figure 3.

This result suggests that the framework can help in the vehicle reidentification problem, which is importance for privacy analysis.Indeed, it is very likely that if an attacker gains access to some private probe vehicle data, he or she can also gain access to additional traffic flow measurements from

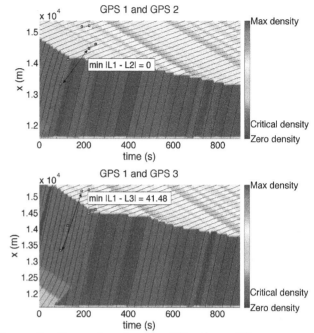

Figure 3: Example of reidentification. The corresponding scenario is decribed in Figure 2. Top: Solution to the reidentification problem (15), with an objective $|L_1 - L_2|$. Bottom: Solution to the same problem with an objective $|L_1 - L_3|$. A nonzero optimum means that both tracks cannot be generated by the same vehicle, according to both the model and the available data.

sensors, which are sometimes even public (for instance the PeMS system operating in California, see [31]). Hence, the example described above suggests that attacks on anonymous location tracks can be much more damaging than initially thought.

Note also that our framework rules out the physical impossibilities, but does not help in choosing a successor whenever problem (15) has an optimal value of 0 for two or more options. However, this model can be used in conjunction with other probabilistic vehicle path inference models to identify the successor.

7. CONCLUSION

In this article, we introduce a new framework for solving some privacy and security problems on systems modeled by Hamilton-Jacobi equations, such as the highway transportation network. Using a semi-analytical expression of the solutions to the Hamilton-Jacobi equation, we formulate the problem of checking the consistency of the data with respect to the model as a Mixed Integer Linear Program (MILP). The method does not require any approximation or Monte-Carlo simulations to operate, and is tractable. We illustrate the performance of the method on an experimental dataset containing fixed sensor as well as probe data.

Future work will be dedicated to the generalization of the method to allow model uncertainty. Another direction is the study of spoofing cyber-attacks on transportation networks, taking into account the coupling effect of junctions and possibly detecting such attacks earlier.

8. REFERENCES

[1] S. AMIN, X. LITRICO, S. SASTRY, and A. BAYEN. Stealthy deception attacks on water scada systems. In *Proceedings of the 13th ACM international conference on Hybrid systems: computation and control*, pages 161–170. ACM, 2010.

[2] J.-P. AUBIN. *Viability Theory*. Systems and Control: Foundations and Applications. Birkhäuser, Boston, MA, 1991.

[3] J.-P. AUBIN, A. M. BAYEN, and P. SAINT-PIERRE. Dirichlet problems for some Hamilton-Jacobi equations with inequality constraints. *SIAM Journal on Control and Optimization*, 47(5):2348–2380, 2008.

[4] M. BARDI and I. CAPUZZO-DOLCETTA. *Optimal Control and Viscosity Solutions of Hamilton-Jacobi-Bellman equations*. Birkhäuser, Boston, MA, 1997.

[5] E. N. BARRON and R. JENSEN. Semicontinuous viscosity solutions for Hamilton-Jacobi equations with convex Hamiltonians. *Communications in Partial Differential Equations*, 15:1713–1742, 1990.

[6] C. G. CLAUDEL and A. M BAYEN. Convex formulations of data assimilation problems for a class of Hamilton-Jacobi equations. *SIAM Journal on Control and Optimization*, 49:383–402, 2011.

[7] E. S. CANEPA and C. G. CLAUDEL. Exact solutions to traffic density estimation problems involving the Lighthill-Whitman-Richards traffic flow model using Mixed Integer Linear Programing. In *Proceedings of the 15th International IEEE Conference on Intelligent Transportation Systems*, Anchorage, AK, September 2012.

[8] E. S. CANEPA and C. G. CLAUDEL. Spoofing Cyber Attack Detection in Probe-based Traffic Monitoring Systems using Mixed Integer Linear Programming. In *Proceedings of the IEEE International Conference on Computing, Networking and Communications*, San Diego, CA, January 2013.

[9] C. G. CLAUDEL and A. M. BAYEN. Convex formulations of data assimilation problems for a class of Hamilton-Jacobi equations. *In preparation for SIAM Journal on Control and Optimization, available from the authors upon request.*, 2009.

[10] C. G. CLAUDEL and A. M. BAYEN. Lax-Hopf based incorporation of internal boundary conditions into Hamilton-Jacobi equation. Part I: theory. *IEEE Transactions on Automatic Control*, 55(5):1142–1157, 2010. doi:10.1109/TAC.2010.2041976.

[11] C. G. CLAUDEL and A. M. BAYEN. Lax-Hopf based incorporation of internal boundary conditions into Hamilton-Jacobi equation. Part II: Computational methods. *IEEE Transactions on Automatic Control*, 55(5):1158–1174, 2010. doi:10.1109/TAC.2010.2045439.

[12] M. G. CRANDALL and P.-L. LIONS. Viscosity solutions of Hamilton-Jacobi equations. *Transactions of the American Mathematical Society*, 277(1):1–42, 1983.

[13] C. DAGANZO. The cell transmission model: a dynamic representation of highway traffic consistent with the hydrodynamic theory. *Transportation Research*, 28B(4):269–287, 1994.

[14] C. F. DAGANZO. On the variational theory of traffic flow: well-posedness, duality and applications. *Networks and heterogeneous media*, 1:601–619, 2006.

[15] S. EICHLER. Anonymous and authenticated data provisioning for floating car data systems. In *Communication systems, 2006. ICCS 2006. 10th IEEE Singapore International Conference on*, pages 1–5. IEEE, 2006.

[16] H. FRANKOWSKA. Lower semicontinuous solutions of Hamilton-Jacobi-Bellman equations. *SIAM Journal of Control and Optimization*, 31(1):257–272, 1993.

[17] N. G.F. A moving bottleneck. *Transportation Research part B: Methodological*, 32:531–537 (7), November 1998.

[18] J. C. HERRERA, D. B. WORK, R. HERRING, X. J. BAN, Q. JACOBSON, and A. M. BAYEN. Evaluation of traffic data obtained via GPS-enabled mobile phones: The Mobile Century field experiment. *Transportation Research Part C: Emerging Technologies*, 2009.

[19] B. HOH, M. GRUTESER, R. HERRING, J. BAN, D. WORK, J. HERRERA, A. M. BAYEN, M. ANNAVARAM, and Q. JACOBSON. Virtual trip lines for distributed privacy-preserving traffic monitoring. to appear, *MobiSys 2008*, Breckenridge, CO.

[20] J. KRUMM. Inference attacks on location tracks. *Pervasive Computing*, pages 127–143, 2007.

[21] M. J. LIGHTHILL and G. B. WHITHAM. On kinematic waves. II. A theory of traffic flow on long crowded roads. *Proceedings of the Royal Society of London*, 229(1178):317–345, 1956.

[22] P. E. MAZARE, A. DEHWAH, C. G. CLAUDEL, and A. M. BAYEN. Analytical and grid-free solutions to the lighthill-whitham-richards traffic flow model. *Transportation Research Part B: Methodological.*, 45(10):1727–1748, 2011.

[23] K. MOSKOWITZ. Discussion of 'freeway level of service as influenced by volume and capacity characteristics' by D.R. Drew and C. J. Keese. *Highway Research Record*, 99:43–44, 1965.

[24] G. F. NEWELL. A simplified theory of kinematic waves in highway traffic, Part (I), (II) and (III). *Transporation Research B*, 27B(4):281–313, 1993.

[25] S. RASS, S. FUCHS, M. SCHAFFER, and K. KYAMAKYA. How to protect privacy in floating car data systems. In *Proceedings of the fifth ACM international workshop on VehiculAr Inter-NETworking*, pages 17–22. ACM, 2008.

[26] P. I. RICHARDS. Shock waves on the highway. *Operations Research*, 4(1):42–51, 1956.

[27] R. ROCKAFELLAR. *Convex Analysis*. Princeton University Press, Princeton, NJ, 1970.

[28] I. S. STRUB and A. M. BAYEN. Weak formulation of boundary conditions for scalar conservation laws. *International Journal of Robust and Nonlinear Control*, 16(16):733–748, 2006.

[29] D. WORK, S. BLANDIN, O. TOSSAVAINEN, B. PICCOLI, and A. BAYEN. A distributed highway velocity model for traffic state reconstruction. *Applied Research Mathematics eXpress (ARMX)*, 1:1–35, April 2010.

[30] http://traffic.berkeley.edu/.

[31] http://pems.eecs.berkeley.edu.

Bio-inspired Strategy for Control of Viral Spreading in Networks *

Chinwendu Enyioha
Department of Electrical and
Systems Engineering
University of Pennsylvania
Philadelphia, PA 19104
cenyioha@seas.upenn.edu

Victor Preciado
Department of Electrical and
Systems Engineering
University of Pennsylvania
Philadelphia, PA 19104
preciado@seas.upenn.edu

George Pappas
Department of Electrical and
Systems Engineering
University of Pennsylvania
Philadelphia, PA 19104
pappasg@seas.upenn.edu

ABSTRACT

We consider a variant of the well-known Susceptible-Infected-Susceptible (SIS) network spreading model, and present a virus control strategy in which nodes in a network are in sleep state or awake state with certain probabilities. Nodes in sleep state are assumed to have a lower infection rate relative to nodes in awake state, hence lower exposure levels to a viral attack on the network. The strategy presented is inspired by the notion of bacteria colony *persistence* to antibiotics in which certain bacteria in the colony hibernate or switch to dormant states as a way of reducing their exposure to antibiotics and helping the colony withstand the effects of the antibiotic attack. Based on a simplified model of persistence, we present a threshold above which a small infection may become an epidemic. Further, we consider the problem of designing the probability of each node being in sleep (less infectious) state with the least effort, allowing the network to control the spread of an infection. Our design strategy for the probabilities of being in sleep state exploits the diagonal dominance property of a non-convex constraint, which enables relaxation of the problem to a Linear Program, for which we compute an exact solution using only local information. Finally, via simulations, we show that the probability of being in sleep state, resulting from our relaxation does, indeed, exploit the network structure in controlling the virus spread.

Categories and Subject Descriptors

D.4.6 [**Security and Protection**]: Optimization, Networks and Graphs

Keywords

Virus propagation; Convex optimization; Network assortativity.

*This work was supported by ONR-MURI HUNT award N00014-08-1-0696.

1. INTRODUCTION

As networks become ubiquitous they also become prone to strategic attacks aimed at causing widespread damage in minimal time. A malicious intruder can, for instance, manipulate or infect one node in the network and have the infection spread to other nodes over time. Occurrence of such attacks are pervasive; examples of this infection spread can be found in computer networks [1], wireless devices, or human populations. Modelling spreading processes in networks is an important topic in epidemiology and has recently attracted substantial research attention. Several deterministic and stochastic models have been proposed to model the spread of biological diseases. A literature review on modelling of epidemics in human populations can be found in [2]. An important concept in mathematical analyses of epidemiological models is the existence of a threshold beyond which a small infection can result in an epidemic. Most recent models represent individuals as nodes or agents that interact in a contact network represented by a graph. In these graph-based models, the epidemic threshold is equal to the inverse of the spectral radius of the contact graph [3, 4, 5].

We investigate how epidemic models can be used to design switching strategies to boost the resilience of the agent population against a contagion. The usual recourse to tackle this problem is to consider immunizing or isolating infected infected nodes. In computer networks, for instance, a solution to the spread of viruses is to install an anti-virus software to clean out the infected computers before the attack spreads to other computer systems on the network. While this approach may work, resources available for anti-viruses or other forms of immunization are usually limited. Determining minimal-cost ways to control and minimize the spread of such network attacks becomes imperative. Though some work has been done on the problem of controlling infection spread in networks, [6, 7]; the approaches presented tend to address the problem from the angle of expending some limited immunization resource.

As an alternative to existing works, we propose a *bio-inspired* strategy to address the problem of controlling a viral spread in a network. The method we present is inspired by bacteria reaction to antibiotics. In particular, our work is inspired by a contagion mitigation strategy well studied in bacteria colonies termed *persistence* (we refer readers to [8, 9, 10] for more information on this behavior). In bacteria colonies, a small portion of the population go into sleep or dormant states, thereby significantly reducing their exposure to attack (by the antibiotic); thus, strengthening the ability of the colony to survive the antibiotic attack and avoid extinction. A more recent work in the control theory research community studying this bacterial phenomenon appears in [11]; where the authors develop a population dynamic model and design methods to minimize the fraction of the network that transition into long-term dormancy using tools from optimal control. Attempts have also been made to link this trait, observed in bacteria, to strategies in human adaptation and survival [12].

In this work, we mathematically formalize a notion of persistence in a networked setting, and study the problem of determining the optimal probabilities of nodes to be in sleep state to prevent a small infection from resulting in an epidemic in the network. We present this strategy as a tool that can be used to defend networks against a viral attack. We employ well-studied, epidemiology-based models to describe a virus spread in a network [13, 14, 15], with a goal of studying the interplay between the probabilities of being in either sleep or awake state and our adapted model of a virus propagation rate from [3]. For our model, we derive a tipping point, by presenting conditions under which the likelihood of infection at each node converges to zero. Furthermore, we consider the problem of optimally designing the probabilities of being in sleep state for the nodes and formulate the problem via a principled convex programming.

The organization of the paper is as follows: In section 2, we briefly review the SIS spreading model, our adapted SIS model and state our problems. Section 3 comprises results on stability of the model presented in 2. We discuss the design of sleep probabilities in section 4, following up with simulations to validate our results in Section 5. In section 6, we introduce assortativity and an important notion of centrality measure in communication networks – betweenness centrality [16, 17]. We numerically show that network structural properties does affect the distribution of protection resources - probabilities of being in sleep mode to prevent an epidemic. In particular, we find that networks with highly assortative mixing patterns have low correlation between distribution of sleep probabilities and the betweenness centrality measure. Concluding remarks follow in Section 7.

2. PROBLEM FORMULATION

In this section, we briefly review the SIS model developed in [3]. We then introduce the SIS model with sleep and awake states as the basis for our developments. First, we introduce some graph-theoretical nomenclature.

Graph theory is the primary mathematical tool to represent the contact topology in an epidemic network. Let $G = (V, E)$ represent a directed graph, with $V = \{1, ..., n\}$ being the set of nodes, and $E \subseteq V \times V$ being the set of edges. In our model, every agent is represented by a node. We assume that G is a simple graph with unweighted, undirected edges and no self-loops. We denote by $N_i = \{j \in V : \{i, j\} \in E\}$ the neighborhood set of node i. We can represent the graph structure using the adjacency matrix $A = [a_{ij}] \in \mathbb{R}^{n \times n}$, where $a_{ij} = 1$ if and only if $\{i, j\} \in E$, otherwise $a_{ij} = 0$. The largest magnitude of the eigenvalues of the adjacency matrix A is called the spectral radius of A and is denoted by $\rho(A)$.

2.1 Standard SIS Model

A set of difference equations was derived in [3], representing the time evolution of the probability of infection for each individual in a network of agents following the SIS epidemic model. In this model, a network of n individuals is considered where each individual is represented by a node and the contact topology is represented by a graph G. A disease in this model is characterized by infection rate $\beta \in \mathbb{R}_+$ and curing rate $\delta \in \mathbb{R}_+$. The SIS model describes the time evolution of the infection probability of the i-th individual, denoted by $p_i \in [0, 1]$, as

$$p_i(t+1) = 1 - \prod_{j \in N_i} (1 - \beta p_j(t)) - \delta p_i(t).$$

After linearizing the above nonlinear, discrete-time model, [3] obtained the following result:

THEOREM 1. *If an epidemic dies out, then it is necessarily true that $\rho(A) < \delta/\beta$, where β is the birth rate, δ is the curing rate and $\rho(A)$ is the largest eigenvalue of the adjacency matrix A.*

This result provides a simple epidemic threshold for arbitrary graphs, such that if the threshold condition is satisfied the epidemic dies out. In the following, we obtain a similar result for the case in which we allow nodes to randomly switch between two states: sleep and awake.

2.2 Hybrid SIS Model

In our model, we assume that each node (regardless of their infection level) or likelihood of infection, can be in one of three states – awake, sleep or infected. Our model is an extension of the traditional SIS model. In particular, we split the susceptible state into two different classes of susceptibility – sleep and awake. These two states are qualitatively similar to the susceptible state in the SIS model and their only difference is in the probabilities of infection. All nodes in the sleep state have an infection rate β_s and a node in the awake state have a higher infection rate $\beta_a > \beta_s$. We also assume that all nodes in the network, independent of which state they are in, have a common virus curing rate δ. The curing rate, δ, can be interpreted as a degree of 'natural immunity' that each node in the network has, irrespective of its state.

Our model assumes that the probability of being in sleep state for node i is l_i (and the probability of being in awake state is $1 - l_i$). At each time step, each node randomly chooses to be awake or asleep, independent of its previous state and the state of its neighbors.

This implies that the infection rate of node i at time t, denoted by $b_i(t)$, is a random variable which is equal to β_s with probability l_i, and is equal to β_a with probability $1 - l_i$. Assuming a discrete-time set-up, at each time-step t, each node i has a probability $p_i(t)$ of being infected at time t. The evolution of the marginal probability of infection can be exactly described via a Markov chain with 3^n states, which in general is extremely large to be of practical interest. Following the mean-field approach proposed in [3], we can approximate the dynamics of the Markov Chain that describes the evolution of the probability of infection at each node. Furthermore, we can linearize the mean-field dynamics around the infection-free state. Following these steps, the evolution of the probability of infection for node i is given by

$$p_i(t+1) = l_i \, \beta_s \sum_{j \in N(i)} a_{ij} p_j(t) \qquad (1)$$

$$+ (1 - l_i)\beta_a \sum_{j \in N(i)} a_{ij} p_j(t) + (1-\delta)p_i(t),$$

which, defining $p(t) = (p_1(t), \ldots, p_N(t))^T$, can be written in matrix-vector form as

$$p(t+1) = BAp(t) + (1-\delta)Ip(t), \qquad (2)$$

where the matrix A is the adjacency matrix of the network and B is the diagonal matrix $B = \mathrm{diag}(\beta_s l_i + \beta_a (1 - l_i))$. We denote by L the diagonal matrix $L = \mathrm{diag}(l_i)$.

The first part of our work considers a case where all nodes in the network have a homogeneous probability of being in sleep state; that is, $l_i = l$. The later part of our analyses considers a heterogeneous model where each node i has a certain probability of being in sleep rate l_i, which results in a particular profile for the infection rate $b_i = \beta_s l_i + \beta_a(1 - l_i)$. Based on (2), next, we state the specific problems addressed in this paper.

2.3 Problem Statements

Given the above model and evolution of probability of infection in (2), we present the problems considered in this work.

PROBLEM 1. *(Epidemic Threshold) Given a network in which nodes have a probability of infection evolving according to (2), what is the point beyond which an infection on one node can propagate and infect other nodes resulting in an epidemic in the network?*

PROBLEM 2. *(Homogeneous Design) Under the assumption that all nodes have a common probability of being in sleep state; that is, $l_i = l$ $\forall i$, what should the optimal probability of being in sleep state be to prevent a virus infection on one node from resulting in an epidemic?*

PROBLEM 3. *(Heterogeneous Design) Let each node i have a distinct probability, l_i, of being in sleep state. What is the optimal l_i to prevent an epidemic?*

To approach the last problem, we derive near-optimal probabilities of being in sleep state via a convex relaxation. These problems are discussed in Sections 3 and 4.

3. STABILITY ANALYSIS

In this section, we consider the stability of (2) when the nodes in the network have a common probability of being in sleep mode. Following an approach similar to the one proposed in [3], we obtain the following result:

THEOREM 2. *Given the discrete-time linear system (2), and any initial condition $p(0)$, the probability of infection $p(t)$ converges to 0, as $t \to \infty$ if and only if*

$$\rho(A) < \frac{\delta}{l\beta_s + (1-l)\beta_a}. \qquad (3)$$

PROOF. (Theorem 2) To study the stability of the linearized model in (2), we only need to locate the eigenvalues of the transition matrix $BA + (1-\delta)I$. It is easy to prove that the eigenvalues of this transition matrix are

$$\lambda_i(BA + (1-\delta)I) = b_i \lambda_i(A) + 1 - \delta,$$

where $B = \mathrm{diag}(b_i)$ with $b_i = b_j$, for all pairs i, j. Hence, for all the eigenvalues of the transition matrix to be in the unit circle, we need the condition in the statement of the theorem to hold. $\square$

For a network under a virus attack, assuming the infection rates for nodes in sleep state in any network varies from those in awake states, a conclusion we can draw from Theorem 2 is that with control over the probabilities of being in sleep or awake state, the network can protect itself from an attack by having some nodes switch to sleep states to prevent a small infection from resulting in an epidemic and destabilizing the network. Two notable things about this resilience strategy are that no assumptions on the network structure are made; second, it is a network protection method that requires no resources for protection - *a passive protection strategy*, since some nodes only need to be in sleep state to reduce exposure to a virus attack.

4. DESIGN PROBLEM

Having established the epidemic threshold, we now consider a design problem of determining optimal probability of being in sleep state to minimize the spectral radius of the system matrix in (2). We consider this problem in two cases:

1. Homogeneous probabilities – In this instance, all nodes have the same probability of being in sleep state, in which case the matrix B can be expressed as $B = bI$.

2. Heterogeneous probabilities – Each node has a distinct probability of being in sleep state, in which case, $B = \mathrm{diag}(b_i)$, for $i = 1, \ldots, N$.

4.1 Homogeneous Sleep Probability

The goal here is to put only few nodes to sleep, by finding the minimum possible common probability of being in sleep state for all nodes, such that the probability of infection, $p(t)$ converges to 0. In other words, we interpret the probability of being in sleep state as a cost, which we want to minimize. We formulate this as the following optimization problem –

$$\begin{aligned}
\underset{l}{\text{minimize}} \quad & l \\
\text{subject to} \quad & (l(\beta_s - \beta_a) + \beta_a)\rho(A) + 1 - \delta \le 1, \quad (4) \\
& 0 \le l \le 1,
\end{aligned}$$

which is equivalent to

$$\begin{aligned}
\underset{l}{\text{minimize}} \quad & l \\
\text{subject to} \quad & (l(\beta_s - \beta_a) + \beta_a)\rho(A) \le \delta, \quad (5) \\
& 0 \le l \le 1.
\end{aligned}$$

As seen in (5), the problem of optimally designing a common sleep probability l, subject to stability constraint is a linear program.

PROPOSITION 1. *The linear optimization problem (5) has a unique optimal solution.*

PROOF. To prove this, note that though the feasible set is constrained, it is non-empty, and imposes a bound on the objective function. Recall that the epidemic threshold is $\rho(A) < \frac{\delta}{l(\beta_s - \beta_a) + \beta_a}$. To get the optimal l, which we denote as l^*, we solve (5) for the l that makes the inequality binding.

Doing so yields

$$l \leq \frac{\left(\frac{\delta}{\rho(A)} - \beta_a\right)}{\beta_s - \beta_a}.$$

In other words,

$$l^* = \inf\left\{l \mid \rho(A) \leq \frac{\delta}{l(\beta_s - \beta_a) + \beta_a}\right\},$$

which implies that if the common probability of being in sleep state is $l \geq l^*$, an epidemic is prevented; and if $l < l^*$, an epidemic results. We note that a trivial solution $l = 0$ will be infeasible, since (4) needs to be satisfied. $\square$

4.2 Heterogeneous Sleep Probabilities

In this case, the nodes have distinct probabilities of being in sleep mode, l_i, which we want to minimize, subject to stability of (2). A related problem was addressed in [18], where the proposed virus taming strategy was to allocate resources in a way that equalizes the propagation impact of each network component. Here, we adopt a disciplined convex formulation of the problem and present a convex relaxation that efficiently, and using only local information, designs the probability of being in sleep state. Our solution in this heterogeneous case has a closed-form expression, and requires only local information. Recall that $B = \beta_a(I - L) + \beta_s L$, where $L = \text{diag}(l_1, \ldots, l_N)$ is a diagonal matrix of the probabilities of being in sleep state. We formally state the optimization problem below:

$$\begin{aligned}
\underset{l_i}{\text{minimize}} \quad & \sum_i^N l_i \\
\text{subject to} \quad & \rho(BA) \leq \delta, \\
& B = \beta_a(I - L) + \beta_s L \\
& 0 \preceq L \preceq I.
\end{aligned} \tag{6}$$

Since B is a function of L and $\beta_s < \beta_a$, we reformulate (6) in terms of B, and make B the optimization variable. If we apply Perron-Frobenius Theorem to the spectral radius constraint in (6), the problem is equivalent to

$$\begin{aligned}
\underset{B}{\text{maximize}} \quad & \text{Trace } B \\
\text{subject to} \quad & \delta B^{-1} - A \succeq 0 \\
& \beta_s I \leq B \leq \beta_a I.
\end{aligned} \tag{7}$$

First, we note that though problem (7) has a linear cost function, it is not a convex program because of the negative exponent in the first summand of the Semidefinite constraint. To address the challenge of nonconvexity from the Semidefinite constraint, we shall use a sufficient condition on diagonally dominant matrices, and eventually arrive at an elegant linear program.

DEFINITION 1. *A matrix is said to be diagonally dominant if for every row of the matrix, the magnitude of the diagonal entry in each row is larger than or equal to the sum of the magnitudes of the off-diagonal entries of that row. More formally, the matrix Z is diagonally dominant if*

$$|z_{ii}| \geq \sum_{j \neq i} z_{ij} \quad \forall i.$$

LEMMA 1. *A diagonally dominant symmetric matrix with non-negative diagonal entries is positive semidefinite.*

See [19] for a proof of Lemma 1. Because we do not allow for self-loops in the network, the diagonal entries of the network adjacency matrix A are 0, and the sum of the off-diagonal entries of row i is the degree of node i in the network, which we denote as $\deg(i)$. In scalar form, we can express the Semidefinite constraint $\delta B^{-1} - A \succeq 0$ as $\frac{\delta}{b_i} - \deg(i) \geq 0$, for each node i, where b_i is the ith element of the diagonal matrix B in (7), and $\deg(i)$ denotes the degree of node i. We can express the constraint $\frac{\delta}{b_i} - \deg(i) \geq 0$ as

$$b_i \leq \frac{\delta}{\deg(i)}. \tag{8}$$

In light of this relaxation, we reformulate problem (7) as an linear program as follows

$$\begin{aligned}
\underset{b_i}{\text{maximize}} \quad & \sum_{i=1}^N b_i \\
\text{subject to} \quad & b_i \leq \frac{\delta}{\deg(i)} \\
& \beta_s \leq b_i \leq \beta_a,
\end{aligned} \tag{9}$$

from which we derive the closed-form solution

$$b_i = \min\left\{\beta_a, \frac{\delta}{\deg(i)}\right\}. \tag{10}$$

After deriving b_i for node i in (10), it is trivial to solve for the probability of being in sleep state l_i.

REMARK 1. *It is remarkable that the solution obtained for the sleep probabilities in the heterogeneous case depend only on local information – individual node degrees. This means that the probability of being in sleep state for each node, can be computed independent of other nodes and complete knowledge of the network. We note that this solution is particularly applicable to large networks where significant costs can be incurred by centrally determining a policy for the probability of being in sleep state and communicating it to the nodes.*

5. SIMULATIONS AND DISCUSSIONS

5.1 Simulations Parameters

In this section, we present results of experiments, indicating how the probabilities of being in sleep states l_i is distributed across the nodes in the network. We solve the problem for a small world network model, and Erdos-Renyi network model as well as networks with homogeneous degrees. For the experiments, we consider a network of size $n = 300$, using a fixed curing rate of $\delta = 0.04$, sleep state infection rate of $\beta_s = 0.5\frac{\delta}{\rho(A)}$ and awake state infection rate of $\beta_a = 1.5\frac{\delta}{\rho(A)}$. In the simulations, we compare how the probabilities of being in sleep state vary with common network centrality measures including eigenvector, betweenness and degree centralities.

5.2 Homogeneous Degree Network

For a network with homogeneous node degrees, we can see in Figure 1 that the optimal probability of being in sleep state to prevent an epidemic is uniform across all nodes in the network, as expected.

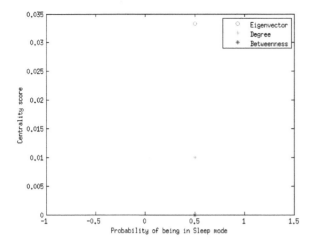

Figure 1: Figure showing sleep probabilities for a complete network

5.3 Erdos-Renyi Network

For an Erdos-Renyi graph with a link probability of 0.13, having a degree distribution that is approximately Poisson, we see that the optimal solution is to allocate higher sleep probabilities to high degree nodes, establishing a largely positive correlation between the sleep probabilities and different network centrality measures, as can be seen in Figure 2.

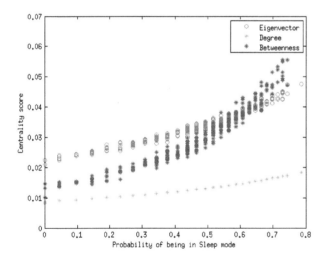

Figure 2: Figure showing sleep probabilities for nodes in an Erdos-Renyi network

5.4 Small-World Network

Finally, we implement our result on a small world network comprising $N = 300$ nodes with probability 0.1 of rewiring each edge. In the small world network, a positive correlation between the probabilities of being in sleep mode and different network centrality measures is also observed. This is captured in Figure 3.

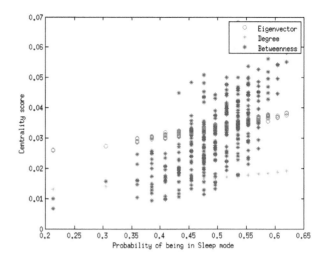

Figure 3: Figure showing sleep probabilities for nodes in a small world network

6. EFFECTS OF NETWORK STRUCTURE

In this section, we briefly introduce assortative mixing patterns in networks, eigenvector and betweenness centrality measures to demonstrate the effect of the network structure on the distribution of the sleep probabilities. The aim of this section is to numerically highlight how the network structure affects the distribution of the sleep probabilities.

6.1 Assortativity in Networks

Assortativity is a property of networks that explains its *mixing pattern* – the tendency for a node to donnect primarily with other nodes of similar degree. Examples of networks exhibiting this property include social networks [20, 21] where people who have similar tastes or interests are more likely to connect and establish relationships with one another. *Disassortativity* explains the converse concept where nodes with high degrees connect to low degree nodes. Assortativity and disassortativity are typically used to explain structural properties in networks and quantify the likelihood for preferential association within the network [22]. More formally,

DEFINITION 2. *The (un-normalized) assortativity of a network, can be defined as*

$$R = \sum_{1 \leq \{i,j\} \leq N} d_i d_j, \qquad (11)$$

where d_i and d_j are the respective degrees of nodes i and j.

6.2 Centrality

Centrality measures in networks are metrics used to capture the level of importance of a given node relative to other nodes in the networks.[1] Here, we focus on betweenness centrality, partly because of its importance as an index in epidemiology and communication networks [16, 17].

---

[1]For more on centrality measures, we refer readers to [23].

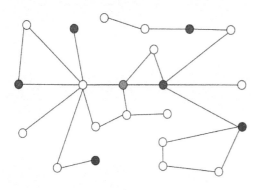

Figure 4: Network centrality depiction

6.2.1 Betweenness Centrality

It is a measure that indicates how relevant a node is in a network using shortest path routing. More formally, the betweenness centrality of a given node i is

$$BC(i) = \sum_{k \neq j : i \notin \{k,j\}} \frac{P_i(k,j)/P(k,j)}{(N-1)(N-2)/2},$$

where $P_i(k,j)$ denotes the number of geodesics (shortest paths) between nodes k and j, that includes i, $P(k,j)$ is the total number of geodesics between k and j. As an example, the red-colored node in Figure 4 has the highest betweenness centrality measure.[2]

6.2.2 Eigenvector centrality

Uses the principal eigenvector of the network adjacency matrix as a measure of importance in the network. More formally, suppose $A = [a_{ij}]$ is the adjacency matrix of the graph, and $a_{ij} = 1$ if node i is connected to node j, and $a_{ij} = 0$, otherwise. The eigenvector centrality score x_i of node i is

$$x_i = \frac{1}{\lambda} \sum_{j \in G} a_{ij} x_j,$$

where λ is a proportionality factor, typically the principal eigenvalue.

6.3 Graph Rewiring

6.4 Rewiring

To modify the degree assortativity of the network, we carry out a degree-preserving rewiring, which has been studied in different contexts [24, 25]. This rewiring can be described as follows: We pick two edges at random. Let's assume that those edges are $\{i, j\}$ and $\{r, s\}$. Notice that a rewiring comprising the removal of edges $\{i, j\}$, $\{r, s\}$, while adding the edges $\{i, s\}$, $\{r, j\}$ does preserve the degrees of nodes i, j, r, s. We can compute the effect of this rewiring on the assortativity as follows

$$\triangle R_{i,j}^{r,s} = d_i d_j + d_r d_s - (d_i d_s + d_r d_j). \quad (12)$$

If $\triangle R_{i,j}^{r,s}$ is greater than 0, the rewiring increases the assortativity of the network. On the other hand, if $\triangle R_{i,j}^{r,s}$ is lower

than 0, the network assortativity is reduced. We can sample through as many edges as we desire, using (12) to determine whether to rewire or not, to tune the assortativity of a network.

6.4.1 Small World Network

We generated a small world network via the following parameters $N = 500$ nodes, with probability 0.15 of rewiring each edge. The assortativity coefficient was first -0.0083. After allowing up to 10^5 rewirings, the assortativity coefficient was increased to 0.8403. Figure 5 shows the relation between the probabilities of being in sleep state and the centrality measures for the original and rewired network. As can be seen, the positive linear correlation between the sleep probabilities and the betweenness centrality measure drops from 0.8014 in the original network to 0.0709 in the rewired network with increased assortativity. And the correlation coefficient between the distribution of sleep probabilities and the eigenvector centrality measure changes from 0.8917 to 0.9428.

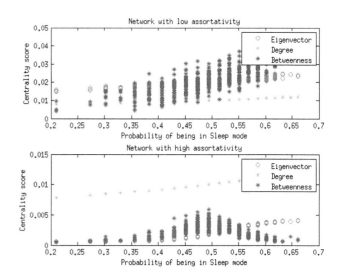

Figure 5: Comparing probabilities of being in sleep state with network Assortativity for a Small World network.

6.4.2 Erdos-Renyi Network

Here, we use $N = 500$ nodes, with an edge probability of 0.13. The assortativity coefficient was first -0.0050. After allowing up to 10^5 rewirings, it was upped to 0.7535. Via the same relaxation of the previous section, we were able to solve the problem for both the original and rewired networks. In Figure 6, the correlation coefficient between the distribution of sleep probabilities and the betweenness centrality measure changes significantly. In particular, it falls from 0.9619 for the original network to 0.0941 for the graph with increased assortativity. And the correlation coefficient between the distribution of sleep probabilities and the eigenvector centrality measure drops from 0.9818 to 0.9451. Figures 5 and 6 indicate that the network structural property affects how the virus spread is controlled.

---

[2]Depending on a network attack objective, the red node is a target.

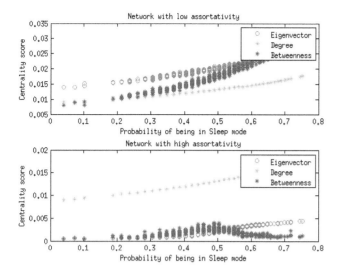

Figure 6: Comparing probabilities of being in sleep state with network Assortativity for an Erdos-Renyi network.

7. CONCLUSIONS

We presented a model of the concept of persistence (observed in bacteria colonies), in a networked setting and presented it as a tool that can be used to prevent a network attack from resulting in an epidemic. Based on our model of persistence, we derived a tipping point under which the probability of infection at each node of the network converges to zero. We also formulated the problem of designing optimal sleep probabilities for nodes in network to ensure an epidemic does not result when the network is under attack. Simulations based on the results from our relaxation showed a positive correlation between the probability of being in sleep state and different network centrality measures. Our simulations, in addition, show that the positive correlation holds for networks with neutral mixing patterns.

Some ongoing work include characterizing other convex approximations and heuristics for our heterogeneous optimization problem, in addition to computing bounds for our relaxation. In a related work, we are studying the problem of simultaneously controlling a contagion, while maximizing information flow in a communication network. We also plan to carry out analyses on the findings highlighted in the preceding section, as understanding the effects of network structural properties on distribution of protection resources can help in the design of resilient cyber-physical networks.

8. ACKNOWLEDGEMENTS

The authors gratefully acknowledge Michael Zargham and Ali Jadbabaie for their comments and suggestions on this work.

9. REFERENCES

[1] M.E.J. Newman, S. Forrest, and J. Balthrop. Email networks and the spread of computer viruses. *Physical Review E*, 66(3):035101, 2002.

[2] Norman TJ Bailey et al. *The mathematical theory of infectious diseases and its applications*. Charles Griffin & Company Ltd, 5a Crendon Street, High Wycombe, Bucks HP13 6LE., 1975.

[3] Y. Wang, D. Chakrabarti, C. Wang, and C. Faloutsos. Epidemic spreading in real networks: An eigenvalue viewpoint. In *Reliable Distributed Systems, 2003. Proceedings. 22nd International Symposium on*, pages 25–34. IEEE, 2003.

[4] Ayalvadi Ganesh, Laurent Massoulié, and Don Towsley. The effect of network topology on the spread of epidemics. In *INFOCOM 2005. 24th Annual Joint Conference of the IEEE Computer and Communications Societies. Proceedings IEEE*, volume 2, pages 1455–1466. IEEE, 2005.

[5] Piet Van Mieghem, Jasmina Omic, and Robert Kooij. Virus spread in networks. *Networking, IEEE/ACM Transactions on*, 17(1):1–14, 2009.

[6] R. Pastor-Satorras and A. Vespignani. Immunization of complex networks. *Arxiv preprint cond-mat/0107066*, 2001.

[7] Y. Chen, G. Paul, S. Havlin, F. Liljeros, and H.E. Stanley. Finding a better immunization strategy. *Physical Review Letters*, 101(5):58701, 2008.

[8] E. Rotem, A. Loinger, I. Ronin, I. Levin-Reisman, C. Gabay, N. Shoresh, O. Biham, and N.Q. Balaban. Regulation of phenotypic variability by a threshold-based mechanism underlies bacterial persistence. *Proceedings of the National Academy of Sciences*, 107(28):12541, 2010.

[9] N.Q. Balaban, J. Merrin, R. Chait, L. Kowalik, and S. Leibler. Bacterial persistence as a phenotypic switch. *Science's STKE*, 305(5690):1622, 2004.

[10] R.W. Kendall, C.P. Duncan, J.A. Smith, and J.H. Ngui-Yen. Persistence of bacteria on antibiotic loaded acrylic depots: a reason for caution. *Clinical orthopaedics and related research*, 329:273, 1996.

[11] N.G. Cooper and A.A. Julius. Bacterial persistence: Mathematical modeling and optimal treatment strategy. In *American Control Conference (ACC), 2011*, pages 3502–3507. IEEE, 2011.

[12] A. Gardner, S.A. West, and A.S. Griffin. Is bacterial persistence a social trait? *PLoS One*, 2(8):e752, 2007.

[13] J.C. Frauenthal and JC Frauenthal. *Mathematical modeling in epidemiology*. Springer-Verlag Berlin, 1980.

[14] J.O. Kephart and S.R. White. Directed-graph epidemiological models of computer viruses. In *Research in Security and Privacy, 1991. Proceedings., 1991 IEEE Computer Society Symposium on*, pages 343–359. IEEE, 1991.

[15] J.O. Kephart and S.R. White. Measuring and modeling computer virus prevalence. In *Research in Security and Privacy, 1993. Proceedings., 1993 IEEE Computer Society Symposium on*, pages 2–15. IEEE, 1993.

[16] K.A. Lehmann and M. Kaufmann. *Decentralized algorithms for evaluating centrality in complex networks*. WSI, 2003.

[17] A. Tizghadam and A. Leon-Garcia. Betweenness centrality and resistance distance in communication networks. *Network, IEEE*, 24(6):10–16, 2010.

[18] Y. Wan, S. Roy, and A. Saberi. Designing spatially

heterogeneous strategies for control of virus spread. *Systems Biology, IET*, 2(4):184–201, 2008.

[19] Abraham Berman and Naomi Shaked-Monderer. *Completely positive matrices*. World Scientific Publishing Company Incorporated, 2003.

[20] M.E.J. Newman. Assortative mixing in networks. *Physical Review Letters*, 89(20):208701, 2002.

[21] M. Catanzaro, G. Caldarelli, and L. Pietronero. Assortative model for social networks. *Physical Review E*, 70(3):037101, 2004.

[22] M.E.J. Newman. Mixing patterns in networks. *Physical Review E*, 67(2):026126, 2003.

[23] M.O. Jackson. *Social and economic networks*. Princeton University Press, 2010.

[24] P. Van Mieghem, H. Wang, X. Ge, S. Tang, and FA Kuipers. Influence of assortativity and degree-preserving rewiring on the spectra of networks. *The European Physical Journal B-Condensed Matter and Complex Systems*, 76(4):643–652, 2010.

[25] C.K. Enyioha, D.C. Tarraf, L. Li, and J.C. Doyle. On the graph of trees. In *Control Applications,(CCA) & Intelligent Control,(ISIC), 2009 IEEE*, pages 246–248. IEEE, 2009.

Using Channel State Feedback to Achieve Resilience to Deep Fades in Wireless Networked Control Systems

Bin Hu
Department of Electrical Engineering
University of Notre Dame
South Bend, Indiana
bhu2@nd.edu

Michael D. Lemmon
Department of Electrical Engineering
University of Notre Dame
South Bend, Indiana
lemmon@nd.edu

ABSTRACT

Wireless networked control systems (WNCS) consist of several dynamical systems that exchange information over a wireless radio (RF) communication network. These RF networks are subject to *deep fades* where the effective link throughput drops precipitously. Deep fading negatively impacts WNCS performance and stability, but in many applications the probability of a deep fade is a function of the system state. This suggests that one can use channel state information (CSI) as a feedback signal to recover some of the performance lost. This paper derives necessary and sufficient conditions for the almost sure stability of WNCS in the presence of deep fading. These conditions relate the channel's state to the WNCS's convergence rate. This paper uses this fact to reconfigure WNCS controllers to recover system performance in the presence of such fades. The results are illustrated using a leader-follower scenario found in vehicle-to-vehicle (V2V) applications.

Categories and Subject Descriptors

B.1.0 [**Control Structures and Microprogramming**]: General; H.1.1 [**Models and Principles**]: Systems and Information Theory—*General Systems Theory*

Keywords

Wireless networked control systems, Deep fading, Resilience, Channel state information, Almost sure stability

1. INTRODUCTION

Wireless networked control systems (WNCS) consist of several dynamical systems that coordinate their behavior by exchanging information over a wireless radio (RF) communication network. Examples of such systems are found in smart transportation [17] applications that anticipate automobiles exchanging information to coordinate their maneuvers. These RF communication channels, however, are subject to *deep fades* where the channel's throughput drops precipitously and remains low for an extended interval of time. Such fades clearly limit the ability of WNCS subsystems to successfully coordinate their actions. This lack of coordination

has obvious negative impacts on the safety of smart transportation applications which could be addressed by developing WNCS that are resilient [13] to deep fading in the sense that the system detects the fade and then adapts its controller to maintain some minimum performance level.

Channel fading is characterized in terms of the channel gain; the ratio of the received signal strength over the transmitted signal strength. This gain is often modeled as an independent and identically distributed (i.i.d.) random process having either a Rayleigh or Rician distribution [16]. This channel model is inadequate for two reasons. In the first place, fading possesses a memory effect which suggests it is better modeled as a Markov process [18] with two states for a high gain condition and a low gain condition. The transition to the low gain state represents a deep fade. In the second place, this model ignores the potential dependence of the channel state on the states of the WNCS subsystems. Vehicle-to-vehicle (V2V) applications provide an example in which the channel state is a function of the velocity and position of both vehicles [1, 12, 3, 4].

The loss of information resulting from a deep fade will negatively impact the performance achievable by WNCS subsystems. Prior work [19, 2, 6, 15, 11] characterized the minimum stabilizing bit rate for linear time-invariant (LTI) systems assuming constant channel gain. But as noted above, the assumption of a constant channel gain is overly simplistic since it ignores channel fading. Initial attempts to study the impact of time-varying channels on a control system's mean square stability have recently appeared [9, 10], but this work has assumed the channel gain is decoupled from the dynamics of the control system. This paper examines a more realistic fading model in which the channel is exponentially bursty [20, 14] and is dependent on the physical plant's state. In particular, this paper characterizes conditions that the physical state of the plant and the exponential bursty channel have to satisfy to assure the stronger stability notion of *almost sure stability*. The paper uses this characterization to propose adaptive schemes that switch feedback controllers in response to changes in the communication channel's state. The results are illustrated on a leader-follower system motivated by smart transportation applications.

2. MATHEMATICAL PRELIMINARIES

Let $\mathbb{R}$ and $\mathbb{Z}$ denote the set of real numbers and integers, respectively. The sets of positive reals and integers are denoted as $\mathbb{R}^+$ and $\mathbb{Z}^+$, respectively. Euclidean n-space is denoted as $\mathbb{R}^n$. The ∞-norm on the vector $x \in \mathbb{R}^n$ is $|x| = \max |x_i| : 1 \leq i \leq n$, and the corresponding induced matrix norm is $\|A\| = \max_{1 \leq i \leq n} \sum_{j=1}^n |A_i^j|$. Given a vector $x \in \mathbb{R}^n$, we let $x_i \in \mathbb{R}$ for $i = 1, 2, \ldots, n$ denote the ith element of vector x. We let $f(\cdot) : \mathbb{R} \to \mathbb{R}^n$ denote a function mapping the real line onto vectors in $\mathbb{R}^n$. We let $f(t) \in \mathbb{R}^n$ denote the value that function f takes at time $t \in \mathbb{R}$. The left-hand limit at $t \in \mathbb{R}$ of a function $f(\cdot) : \mathbb{R} \to \mathbb{R}^n$ is denoted as $f(t^-)$.

Consider a dynamical system whose state trajectory $x(\cdot) : \mathbb{R} \to \mathbb{R}^n$ satisfies the following differential equation

$$\dot{x}(t) = Ax(t) + Bu(t), \quad x(0) = x_0 \quad (1)$$

for all $t \in \mathbb{R}^+$ where $u(\cdot) : \mathbb{R} \to \mathbb{R}^m$ is an input signal, $x_0 \in \mathbb{R}^n$ is the initial state, and the matrices A and B are appropriately dimensioned. Let the *output* of this system be the signal $y(\cdot) : \mathbb{R} \to \mathbb{R}^q$ that satisfies

$$y(t) = Cx(t) + w(t) \quad (2)$$

where C is an appropriately dimensioned matrix, $w(\cdot) : \mathbb{R} \to \mathbb{R}^q$ is the stochastic disturbance process. For any $T > 0$, let $\Phi(T)$ denote the state transition matrix, and its ∞-induced norm is denoted as $\|\Phi(T)\|$.

The probability of a random variable is denoted by $\Pr(\cdot)$ and its expectation by $\mathbb{E}(\cdot)$. Consider a random process $\{x_t\}$, we say this process is almost sure convergent to 0 if for all $\varepsilon > 0$ there exists $\delta > 0$ and $T > 0$ such that

$$\Pr\left\{ \limsup_{t > T} |x_t| > \varepsilon \right\} < \delta$$

One often writes this as $\Pr\{|x_t| \to 0\} = 1$. If the random process $\{x_t\}$ is generated by the system equations (1-2) then we say this system is *almost sure stable*.

The system in equations (1-2) is *almost sure asymptotically observable* if for any $T > 0$ one can use the system inputs and outputs to generate a sequence $\{\hat{x}_k, L_k\}_{k=1}^{\infty}$ such that $e_k = |x(kT) - \hat{x}_k| < L_k$ for all $k = 1, 2, \ldots, \infty$ and $L_k \to 0$ as $k \to \infty$.

The concept of almost sure asymptotic observability may be viewed as a probabilistic extension of the asymptotic observability concept found in [15]. Similar to what is found in [15], a system's almost sure asymptotic observability can be shown to be sufficient for the system to be almost sure stable. This paper establishes that result and then uses it to determine conditions for the almost sure stability of the system under study.

3. SYSTEM MODEL

The proposed system under study is shown in Figure 1. This figure shows a *plant* whose state trajectory $x(\cdot) : \mathbb{R} \to \mathbb{R}^n$ satisfies the system equation (1). The input signal u is generated by a *controller* and its output is the state vector. The plant's state is sampled by an *encoder* at a sequence of time instants $\{\tau_k\}_{k=1}^{\infty}$. The encoder maps the system state $x(\tau_k)$ onto a *codeword*, $c(k) = \{b_i(k)\}_{i=1}^{\overline{R}}$ which is a collection of $\overline{R} \in \mathbb{Z}^+$ blocks of *bits* with block length n. In other words $b_i(k) \in \{0,1\}^n$ is the ith block in the codeword generated by the encoder at sampling time τ_k. The codeword is transmitted over the *channel*. The output of the channel is a codeword, $\hat{c}(k) = \{\hat{b}_i(k)\}_{i=1}^{R_k}$, which is received by the *decoder* at time $a_k = \tau_k + \Delta$. The interval $\Delta > 0$ represents a finite time delay that is constant and known to both the encoder and decoder. The received codeword consists of $R_k \leq \overline{R}$ blocks and we assume that the ith received block, $\hat{b}_i(k)$, is equal to the ith transmitted block $b_i(k)$ for $i = 1, 2, \ldots, R_k$. In other words, the first R_k blocks of bits in the transmitted codeword are reliably received by the decoder. The decoder then uses the received bits in $\hat{c}(k)$ to construct an estimate for the plant's state. We denote this estimate as $\hat{x}_k$ ($k = 1, 2, \ldots, \infty$) and the *controller* uses this state to generate the control signal $u(\cdot) : \mathbb{R} \to \mathbb{R}^m$ used by the plant. More detailed descriptions of the *channel, encoder/decoder*, and *controller* blocks are given below.

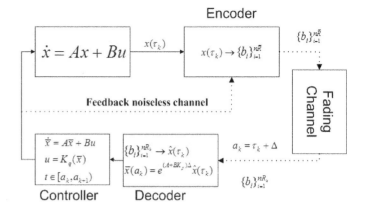

Figure 1: System Structure

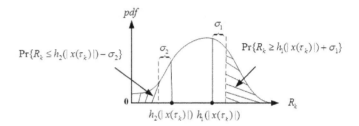

Figure 2: Probability bounds for the channel model

Channel Model: The stochastic nature of the channel is captured by the number of received bits, nR_k, at time instant a_k. In particular, we assume that R_k is a random process and we let $r_k = \frac{nR_k}{\Delta}$ where $\Delta = a_k - \tau_k$ denote the *instantaneous bit rate* for the kth transmission. Let $h_i(\cdot) : \mathbb{R}^+ \to \mathbb{R}^+$ ($i = 1, 2$) and $\zeta_2(\cdot) : \mathbb{R}^+ \to \mathbb{R}^+$ be continuous, non-negative and monotone decreasing functions. Let $\zeta_1(\cdot) : \mathbb{R}^+ \to \mathbb{R}^+$ be continuous, non-negative and monotone increasing function. We assume that the tail of R_k's probability distribution satisfies the following exponential bounds

$$\Pr\{R_k \geq h_1(|x(\tau_k)|) + \sigma_1\} \leq e^{-\zeta_1(|x(\tau_k)|)\sigma_1} \quad (3)$$

$$\Pr\{R_k \leq h_2(|x(\tau_k)|) - \sigma_2\} \leq e^{-\zeta_2(|x(\tau_k)|)\sigma_2} \quad (4)$$

for all real $\sigma_1 \geq 0$ and $\sigma_2 \in [0, h_2(|x(\tau_k)|)]$.

The tail of R_k's probability distribution is shown in figure 2. The left tail of the distribution characterizes the instantaneous low bit rate region while the right tail represents the instantaneous high bit rate region. The low bit rate region at kth transmission interval is the set of all R_k less than $h_2(|x(\tau_k)|)$. One may view $h_2(|x(\tau_k)|)$ as a threshold for the low bit rate region, and varies as a function of the system state. The high bit rate region is constructed in a similar manner.

The probability bounds in (3-4) may be viewed as slight modifications of the *exponentially bounded burstiness*(EBB) model [20]. The only difference lies in our characterization of system state's impact on the model. It is well established that the two state Markov chain commonly used to characterize the fading channel, can be approximated by the *exponentially bounded burstiness* (EBB) model [20]. Although the EBB model may turn out be conservative because it bounds the occurrence of rare events, it is convenient to use for establishing the system's almost sure stability.

The monotone decreasing functions $h_i(\cdot), i = 1, 2$ are introduced to model the basic relationship between channel state and control system's state. Such relationship exists, for example, in typical

V2V applications. In those applications, large separation distance and velocities between vehicles will result in a lower bit rate by reducing the Signal to Noise Ratio (SNR) and coherence time [3, 4]. Such underlying physical relationship reveals the fact that increasing the system state's norm will decrease the channel state and vice versa.

Functions $\zeta_i(\cdot), i = (1,2)$ are used to characterize the exponent in the probability bounds. The selection of $\zeta_i(\cdot), i = (1,2)$ models the fact that the further the state is from the equilibrium, the less likely that the high data rate region will expand, but more likely the low data rate will move toward the origin. It models the fact that channel is more prone to exhibit deep fading when the system states are further from the equilibrium.

Controller: At time instant a_k, the controller receives an estimate of the sampled system state at time instant τ_k. This estimate is denoted as $\hat{x}_k$. To generate the control over the time interval $[a_k, a_{k+1}]$, the controller first selects a control gain, $K \in \mathcal{K}$ where $\mathcal{K} = \{K_1, K_2, \cdots, K_N\}$ is a collection of state feedback gains. We let $K(k)$ denote the controller that was selected over the kth action interval. The controller then generates an estimated state trajectory, $\bar{x}(\cdot) : [a_k, a_{k+1}] \to \mathbb{R}^n$ that satisfies the ODE,

$$\dot{\bar{x}}(t) = (A + BK(k))\bar{x}(t), \quad \bar{x}(a_k) = e^{(A+BK(k-1))\Delta}\hat{x}_k$$

and the control is then

$$u(t) = K(k)\bar{x}(t)$$

for $t \in [a_k, a_{k+1}]$. These equations apply for all $k = 1, 2, \ldots, \infty$.

Encoder/Decoder: The encoder/decoder is characterized by a sequence of $\{(\hat{x}_k, L_k)\}_{k=1}^{\infty}$ which represent the estimated state, $\hat{x}_k$, and the size of the uncertainty set L_k associated with the kth consecutive transmission. It is assumed that at $k = 0$, both encoder and decoder have the same initial state name $\hat{x}_0 = 0$ and $L_0 = \bar{L}$. The encoder then maps the current sampled state, $x(\tau_k)$, onto the bits $b_i(k)$ $(i = 1, 2, \ldots, n\bar{R})$ according to the following series expansion of the sampled state

$$x(\tau_k) = \bar{x}(\tau_k) + \|\Phi(T)\| L_{k-1} \sum_{j=1}^{\infty} \frac{1}{2^j} \bar{b}_j \quad (5)$$

$$\bar{x}(\tau_k) = e^{(A+BK(k-1))(T-\Delta)} \cdot e^{(A+BK(k-2))\Delta} \hat{x}_{k-1}$$

where $\|\Phi(T)\| = \|e^{AT}\|$ and $\bar{b}$ is an n vector whose components are ± 1. This vector is encoded with n bits with bit 0 representing value -1 and bit 1 representing value 1, and the transmitted code word consists of the first $n\bar{R}$ bits.

We assume that the the decoder receives the first nR_k bits (or rather the first R_k blocks) in the transmitted codeword and the reconstructed state is then

$$\hat{x}_k = \bar{x}(\tau_k) + \|\Phi(T)\| L_{k-1} \sum_{j=1}^{R_k} \frac{1}{2^j} \bar{b}_j \quad (6)$$

Figure 3 shows a two-dimensional system with $\bar{R} = 2$ blocks (4 bits) transmitted through the channel, and only one block $R_k = 1$ (2 bits) is received. By using the encoder scheme in equation (5), a codeword $c(k) = \{[1,1],[1,1]\}$ is constructed and used to label the small square on the rightmost corner with true state inside. The decoder only receives the first block of the original codeword, i.e. $\hat{c}(k) = \{[1,1]\}$. The reconstruction equation in (6) gives the estimated state $\hat{x}_k$ marked as red dot in the larger square. It is clear from Figure 3 that the reception of partial information can still guarantee the recovery of the sensor measurement but with a reduced precision. Such reduced precision can be quantitatively bounded if the

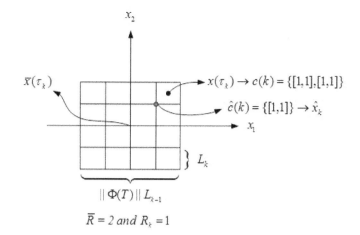

$\bar{R} = 2$ and $R_k = 1$

Figure 3: Encoder and Decoder mapping

synchronization of the information is assured on both encoder and decoder.

From the encoding scheme in equation (5), the information needed to be synchronized includes the prior control gains $K(k-1)$ and $K(k-2)$ as well as the estimated state $\hat{x}_{k-1}$. As shown in Figure 1, this information is obtained from decoder and controller through a feedback noiseless channel at each time interval $[\tau_k, a_k]$. In particular, encoder will construct the estimated state $\hat{x}_{k-1}$ by assessing the actual number of bits nR_{k-1} received at $k-1$th interval. The synchronization on R_{k-1} can be achieved by using acknowledgement signal that indicates the receipt of each block at the decoder side. As for $K(k-1)$ and $K(k-2)$, their corresponding indices will be sent to encoder provided that encoder and decoder share the selection set for the controller.

Such synchronization ensures the encoder and decoder share the estimation error bound at each time instant τ_k as follows,

$$|x(\tau_k) - \hat{x}_k| \leq 2^{-R_k} \|\Phi(T)\| L_{k-1}$$

4. MAIN RESULTS

This section derives necessary and sufficient characterization for the almost sure convergence of sequence $\{L_k\}_{k=0}^{\infty}$, and then proves that the convergence of this sequence guarantees the almost sure asymptotic observability for the system defined in equation (1). Under a *dwell time* assumption (which represents the minimum time between controller switches), we further show that the almost sure asymptotic observability implies almost sure asymptotic stability for the control system in equation (1).

The following proposition bounds the quantization error generated by the proposed encoder/decoder scheme. The proof follows that found in [15].

PROPOSITION 4.1. *Given the sequences $\{\tau_k\}_{k=0}^{\infty}$ and $\{a_k\}_{k=0}^{\infty}$, encoder and decoder scheme in equations (5-6), suppose the initial state $x(0) \in [-\bar{L}, \bar{L}]^n, L_0 > 0$, if the sequence $\{L_k\}_{k=0}^{\infty}$ is constructed by the following equation*

$$L_{k+1} = 2^{-R_{k+1}} \|\Phi(T)\| L_k \quad (7)$$

then the quantization error can be bounded as,

$$\|x(\tau_k) - \hat{x}(\tau_k)\| \leq L_k, \forall k \geq 0 \quad (8)$$

with initial value $L_0 = 2^{-R_0}\bar{L}$, where R_k is the number of blocks received during time interval $[\tau_k, a_k)$.

4.1 Almost sure asymptotic observability

Lemma 4.2 establishes a necessary condition for the almost sure asymptotic convergence of sequence $\{L_k\}_{k=0}^{\infty}$ with convergence rate $\delta \in (0,1]$. The necessary condition is derived based on the probability bound on the high data rate region. The necessity comes from the fact that if the system performance cannot be assured under the high data rate scenario, there will be no way for the system performance to be better under other scenarios.

LEMMA 4.2. *Consider the system in equation (1), suppose the right tail of R_k probability distribution satisfies the probability bound in (3), then a necessary condition to ensure*

$$\mathbb{E}(L_k|L_{k-1}) \leq \delta L_{k-1}, \forall k \in \mathbb{Z}^+$$

is

$$|x(\tau_k)| \leq G_1^{-1}\left(\frac{\delta}{\|\Phi(T)\|}\right), \forall k \in \mathbb{Z} \qquad (9)$$

where $\|\Phi(T)\| = \|e^{AT}\|$, $\delta \in (0,1]$ *and function* $G_1(y) = 2^{-h_1(y)} \cdot \frac{\zeta_1(y)}{\zeta_1(y)+\ln 2}$.

PROOF. In order to prove the necessary condition that ensures $\mathbb{E}(L_k|L_{k-1}) \leq \delta L_{k-1}$, we prove the case that the $\mathbb{E}(L_k|L_{k-1}) > \delta L_{k-1}$ holds when condition (9) is violated, i.e.

$$|x(\tau_k)| > G_1^{-1}(\frac{\delta}{\|\Phi(T)\|}), \forall k \in \mathbb{Z}$$

First, Let us consider the condition that makes $\mathbb{E}(L_k|L_{k-1}) > \delta L_{k-1}$ hold, i.e.

$$\|\Phi(T)\|E[2^{-R_k}] > \delta$$

Let $\tilde{R} := 2^{-R_k}$, $h_{1k} := h_1(|x(\tau_k)|)$ and $\zeta_{1k} := \zeta_1(|x(\tau_k)|)$. The probability bound in (3) implies

$$\Pr\{2^{-R_k} \leq 2^{-(h_{1k}+\sigma_1)}\} = \Pr\{R_k \geq h_{1k}+\sigma_1\} \leq e^{-\zeta_{1k}\sigma_1}$$

Now, the expectation of 2^{-R_k} can be written as

$$\mathbb{E}(\tilde{R}) = \int_0^1 \Pr\{\tilde{R} > x\}dx$$
$$= 1 - \int_0^1 \Pr\{\tilde{R} \leq x\}dx \qquad (10)$$

Since

$$\int_0^1 \Pr\{\tilde{R} \leq x\}dx = \int_0^{2^{-h_{1k}}} \Pr\{\tilde{R} \leq x\}dx + \int_{2^{-h_{1k}}}^1 \Pr\{\tilde{R} \leq x\}dx$$
$$= \int_0^{\infty} \Pr\{\tilde{R} \leq 2^{-h_{1k}-\sigma_1}\}(2^{-h_{1k}} \cdot 2^{-\sigma_1}\ln 2 \cdot d\sigma_1$$
$$+ 1 - 2^{-h_{1k}}$$
$$\leq \int_0^{\infty} e^{-\zeta_{1k}\sigma_1} 2^{-h_{1k}} 2^{-\sigma_1}\ln 2 \cdot d\sigma_1$$
$$+ 1 - 2^{-h_{1k}}$$

we have the following lower bound of $\mathbb{E}(\tilde{R})$

$$\mathbb{E}(\tilde{R}) \geq 2^{-h_{1k}} - 2^{-h_{1k}}\ln 2 \int_0^{\infty} e^{-\zeta_{1k}\sigma_1} 2^{-\sigma_1} d\sigma_1$$
$$= 2^{-h_{1k}} \cdot \frac{\zeta_{1k}}{\zeta_{1k}+\ln 2}$$
$$\triangleq G_1(|x(\tau_k)|) \qquad (11)$$

Taking the derivative of $G_1(y) = 2^{-h_1(y)} \cdot \frac{\zeta_1(y)}{\zeta_1(y)+\ln 2}$ with respect to y, we obtain

$$\dot{G}_1 = -\ln 2 \cdot \dot{h}_1 2^{-h_1}[1 - \frac{\ln 2}{\zeta_1+\ln 2}] + 2^{-h_1} \frac{\ln 2 \cdot \dot{\zeta}_1}{(\zeta_1+\ln 2)^2}$$
$$= \frac{\ln 2 \cdot 2^{-h_1}}{\zeta_1+\ln 2}[-\zeta_1 \cdot \dot{h}_1 + \frac{\dot{\zeta}_1}{\zeta_1+\ln 2}] \qquad (12)$$

Note that the function h_1 is positive and monotone decreasing while function ζ_1 is positive monotone increasing. It is clear that $\dot{G}_1 > 0$ holds. This implies the violation of the condition in (9) will lead to $\mathbb{E}(\tilde{R}) > \frac{\delta}{\|\Phi(T)\|}$, which implies $\mathbb{E}(L_k|L_{k-1}) > \delta L_{k-1}$. Therefore, condition (9) is a necessary condition for $\mathbb{E}(L_k|L_{k-1}) \leq \delta L_{k-1}$ to hold. The proof is complete. $\square$

The following lemma derives a sufficient condition for the controller so that the necessary condition derived in Lemma 4.2 can be achieved.

LEMMA 4.3. *Consider the system in equation (1) with a family of control gain matrices $\{K_i\}_{i=1}^N$, suppose the right tail of R_k probability distribution satisfies the probability bound in (3), if the selected controller $K \in \{K_i\}_{i=1}^N$ satisfies the condition*

$$\|A_K\| \leq \frac{1}{T-\Delta}\ln\frac{G_1^{-1}(\frac{\delta}{\|\Phi(T)\|}) - \|\Phi(T)\|L_{k-1}}{|\hat{x}(a_{k-1})|} \qquad (13)$$
$$A_K = A + BK$$

the necessary condition derived in Lemma 4.2, i.e. $|x(\tau_k)| \leq G_1^{-1}\left(\frac{\delta}{\|\Phi(T)\|}\right), \forall k \in \mathbb{Z}$ is achieved.

PROOF. Consider the upper bound of $|x(\tau_k)|$ that is derived from the dynamics of the quantization error. Using encoding and decoding scheme in (5-6), the quantization error at time τ_k^- can be bounded as

$$|x(\tau_k^-) - \hat{x}(\tau_k^-)| \leq \|\Phi(T)\|L_{k-1} \qquad (14)$$

Because of the continuity of original state at time τ_k^-, $x(\tau_k) = x(\tau_k^-)$, then

$$|x(\tau_k)| = |x(\tau_k^-)| \leq |\hat{x}(\tau_k^-)| + \|\Phi(T)\|L_{k-1} \qquad (15)$$

Since controller reconfiguration will only be conducted at time sequence $\{a_k\}_{k=0}^{\infty}$, $\hat{x}(\tau_k^-)$ can be calculated as follows if a controller K is selected,

$$\hat{x}(\tau_k^-) = e^{(A+BK)(T-\Delta)} \cdot \hat{x}(a_{k-1}) \qquad (16)$$

Now, let the controller K satisfies the condition (13), consider the inequalities (16-15), we have $|x(\tau_k)| \leq G_1^{-1}(\frac{\delta}{\|\Phi(T)\|}), \forall k \in \mathbb{Z}$ holds. The proof is complete. $\square$

It is worth noting that the necessary condition may turn out to be optimistic since it only captures the high data rate region. Lemma 4.4 establishes a sufficient condition for the same performance specification. In contrast, the sufficient conditions are derived based on the probability bound on the low bit rate region, which is the worst case scenario.

LEMMA 4.4. *Consider the system in equation (1), and suppose the left tail of R_k's distribution satisfies the probability bound (4), then a sufficient condition to ensure*

$$\mathbb{E}(L_k|L_{k-1}) \leq \delta L_{k-1}, \forall k \in \mathbb{Z}^+ \qquad (17)$$

is

$$|x(\tau_k)| \le G_2^{-1}\left(\frac{\delta}{\|\Phi(T)\|}\right), \forall k \in \mathbb{Z} \tag{18}$$

where $\|\Phi(T)\| = \|e^{AT}\|$, $\delta \in (0,1]$ *and function* $G_2(y) = e^{-h_2(y)\zeta_2(y)}(1 + h_2(y)\zeta_2(y))$.

PROOF. Unlike the logic used to prove necessary condition, here, we derive a condition that ensures $\mathbb{E}(L_k|L_{k-1}) \le \delta L_{k-1}, \forall k \in \mathbb{Z}^+$. Establishing this is equivalent to proving

$$\|\Phi(T)\|\mathbb{E}[2^{-R_k}] \le \delta, \delta \in (0,1] \tag{19}$$

Since we assume the probability bound (4) holds, we have

$$\Pr\{2^{-R_k} \ge 2^{-h_2(|x(\tau_k)|)+\sigma_2}\} \le e^{-\zeta_2(|x(\tau_k)|)\sigma_2}$$
$$\sigma_2 \in [0, h_2(|x(\tau_k)|)]$$

let $\tilde{R}_k := 2^{-R_k}$, $h_{2k} := h_2(|x(\tau_k)|)$ and $\zeta_{2k} := \zeta_2(|x(\tau_k)|)$, then

$$\mathbb{E}(\tilde{R}_k) = \int_0^1 \Pr\{\tilde{R}_k > x\}dx$$
$$= \int_0^{2^{-h_{2k}}} \Pr\{\tilde{R}_k > x\}dx$$
$$+ \int_{2^{-h_{2k}}}^1 \Pr\{\tilde{R}_k > x\}dx$$

Following the same technique in Lemma 4.2, we obtain

$$\mathbb{E}(\tilde{R}_k) \le 2^{-h_{2k}} + 2^{-h_{2k}}\ln 2 \cdot \int_0^{h_{2k}} e^{-\zeta_{2k}\sigma_2} 2^{\sigma_2} \cdot d\sigma_2 \tag{20}$$

Let $C := \int_0^{h_{2k}} e^{-\zeta_{2k}\sigma_2} 2^{\sigma_2} \cdot d\sigma_2$, integration by parts gives rise to

$$C = \frac{1}{\ln 2}[e^{-\zeta_{2k}\sigma_2} 2^{\sigma_2}|_0^{h_{2k}} + \zeta_{2k}C] \tag{21}$$

Hence, we have

$$C = \frac{e^{h_{2k}(\ln 2 - \zeta_{2k})} - 1}{\ln 2 - \zeta_{2k}} > 0 \tag{22}$$

Substituting equation (22) into inequality (20), $\mathbb{E}(\tilde{R}_k)$ is bounded by

$$\mathbb{E}(\tilde{R}_k) \le \frac{e^{-h_{2k}\zeta_{2k}}\ln 2 - 2^{-h_{2k}}\zeta_{2k}}{\ln 2 - \zeta_{2k}} \tag{23}$$

Note that $2^{-h_{2k}} = e^{-h_{2k}\cdot\ln 2}$, the above upper bound can be further rewritten as

$$\mathbb{E}(\tilde{R}_k) \le \frac{e^{-h_{2k}\zeta_{2k}}[\ln 2 - e^{-h_{2k}\cdot(\ln 2 - \zeta_{2k})}\zeta_{2k}]}{\ln 2 - \zeta_{2k}}$$
$$= e^{-h_{2k}\zeta_{2k}}\left[1 + \zeta_{2k}\cdot\frac{1 - e^{-h_{2k}(\ln 2 - n\zeta_{2k})}}{\ln 2 - \zeta_{2k}}\right] \tag{24}$$

It is easy to check that the right hand side of above inequality is bounded away from zero. Let $\varphi := \ln 2 - \zeta_{2k}$, consider function $f(\varphi) = 1 - e^{-h_{2k}\varphi} - h_{2k}\varphi$, since

$$\frac{df(\varphi)}{dt} = h_{2k}(e^{-h_{2k}\varphi} - 1) \le 0, \varphi \ge 0$$
$$\frac{df(\varphi)}{dt} = h_{2k}(e^{-h_{2k}\varphi} - 1) > 0, \varphi < 0 \tag{25}$$

$f(\varphi)$ obtains maximum value at $\varphi = 0$, i.e. $f(\varphi) \le f(0) = 0$. It implies

$$1 - e^{-h_{2k}\varphi} \le h_{2k}\varphi$$
$$\Rightarrow \frac{1 - e^{-h_{2k}\varphi}}{\varphi} \le h_{2k} \tag{26}$$

By applying the above inequality, $\mathbb{E}(\tilde{R}_k)$ is further bounded as

$$\mathbb{E}(\tilde{R}_k) \le e^{-h_{2k}\zeta_{2k}}[1 + h_{2k}\zeta_{2k}] \tag{27}$$

Recall that $h_{2k} = h_2(|x(\tau_k)|)$ and $\zeta_2(|x(\tau_k)|)$ are both nonnegative and monotone decreasing functions. Hence, function $g(y) = h_2 \cdot \zeta_2$ is also nonnegative and monotone decreasing. Let $G_2(y) = e^{-h_2(y)\zeta_2(y)}(1 + h_2(y)\zeta_2(y))$,

$$\frac{dG_2(y)}{dy} = -\frac{dg(y)}{dy}\cdot g(y)e^{-g(y)} \ge 0 \tag{28}$$

Hence, $G_2(y)$ is nonnegative and monotone increasing function. And we have

$$\mathbb{E}(\tilde{R}_k) \le G_2(\|x(\tau_k)\|) \tag{29}$$

Now, it is clear that if condition (18) holds, with inequality (29), we will have $\mathbb{E}(\tilde{R}_k) \le \frac{\delta}{\|\Phi(T)\|}$, which completes the proof. □

The following corollary proves that the bound given by the necessary condition will always be greater than that obtained from the sufficient condition.

COROLLARY 4.5. *For any* $y \ge 0$, $G_1(y) < G_2(y)$, *i.e.* $G_1^{-1}(y) > G_2^{-1}(y)$.

PROOF. Consider the equations (11) and (20-22), we have

$$G_1(y) = 2^{-h_1(y)} - 2^{-h_1(y)}\frac{\ln 2}{\ln 2 + \zeta_1(y)}$$
$$G_2(y) \ge 2^{-h_2(y)} + 2^{-h_2(y)}\ln 2 \cdot C$$

Since $h_1(y) > h_2(y), \forall y \ge 0, C > 0$ and $\zeta_1(y) \ge 0$, then $G_1(y) < G_2(y)$. Because $G_1(y)$ and $G_2(y)$ are both monotone increasing functions, then $G_1^{-1}(y) > G_2^{-1}(y)$ follows immediately. □

The following lemma derives a sufficient condition for the selection of the controller in the low bit rate region.

LEMMA 4.6. *Consider the system in equation (1) with a family of control gain matrices* $\{K_i\}_{i=1}^N$, *suppose the left tail of* R_k *probability distribution satisfies the probability bound in (4) and let* $A_K = A + BK$. *If the selected controller* $K \in \{K_i\}_{i=1}^N$ *satisfies the condition*

$$\|A_K\| \le \frac{1}{T - \Delta}\ln\frac{G_2^{-1}(\frac{\delta}{\|\Phi(T)\|}) - \|\Phi(T)\|L_{k-1}}{|\hat{x}(a_{k-1})|} \tag{30}$$

then the necessary condition derived in Lemma 4.4, i.e. $|x(\tau_k)| \le G_2^{-1}(\frac{\delta}{\|\Phi(T)\|}), \forall k \in \mathbb{Z}$ *is satisfied.*

PROOF. The proof is omitted since it is similar to what was used in Lemma 4.3. □

With the sufficient conditions in Lemma 4.4 and Lemma 4.6, we proceed to state one of the paper's main theorems, which establishes the almost sure asymptotic observability for the system in equation (1).

THEOREM 4.7. *Given a sequence of $\{L_k\}_{k=0}^{\infty}$ constructed by equation (7), the encoding/decoding scheme in (5-6), and a collection of controller gain matrices $\{K_i\}_{i=1}^{N}$, suppose the communication channel satisfies the probability bounds (3-4). If there exists a sequence of switching signals $\{s_k\}_{k=0}^{\infty}$, in which $s_k \in [1,\ldots,N]$ is constant over $[a_k, a_{k+1}]$, such that the sufficient condition in Lemma 4.6 is satisfied under the selected controller $\{K_{s_k}\}_{k=0}^{\infty}$, then the system in equation (1) is almost sure asymptotically observable.*

PROOF. Suppose there always exists a controller $K \in \{K_i\}_{i=1}^{N}$ such that Lemma 4.6 holds, then we have $\mathbb{E}(L_{k+1}|L_k) \leq \delta L_k, \forall k \in \mathbb{Z}^+$. This also implies [5]

$$\mathbb{E}[L_k] \leq \delta \mathbb{E}[L_{k-1}] \leq \ldots \leq \delta^k L_0$$
$$\Rightarrow \mathbb{E}[L_k] \leq \delta^k L_0 \tag{31}$$

Since $\delta \in [0,1)$, taking the limit $k \to \infty$ leads to

$$\limsup_{k \uparrow \infty} \mathbb{E}[L_k] \leq \lim_{k \uparrow \infty} \delta^k L_0 = 0 \tag{32}$$

which implies almost sure convergence $\Pr(\lim_{k \uparrow \infty} L_k = 0) = 1$. Since L_k is the upper bound for the quantization error, the almost sure asymptotic observability immediately follows. $\square$

Note that the observability result in Theorem 4.7 is stronger than conventional asymptotic notion since it requires δ-convergence property. Such property is useful in real applications because it provides a predictable performance bound at each time instance.

4.2 Almost sure asymptotic stability

The result in Theorem 4.7 indicates that the quantization error will converge to zero with probability 1, however, it does not say anything about the stability of the original system in equation (1). Theorem 4.9 shows that under the dwell-time condition, almost sure asymptotic observability indeed implies the almost sure asymptotic stability for the system in equation (1).

ASSUMPTION 4.8. *(Dwell Time)[7, 8] Given a family of switched closed-loop system $\{A + BK_i\}_{i=1}^{C}$, there exists a constant fixed dwell time τ_D and integer $\pi \in \mathbb{Z}^+$, such that two consecutive switching time interval $\pi * T \geq \tau_D$.*

Since the switching decision is always made at time instant a_k, we know the time interval between two consecutive switches must be a multiple of the sampling period T. One may either select large π or large T to satisfy the dwell-time assumption.

THEOREM 4.9. *Consider the system in (1) and suppose that there exists positive c and λ such that*

$$\left\| e^{A_i t} \right\| \leq c e^{-\lambda t}$$

where $A_i = A + BK_i$ and K_i is the ith controller. If the dwell time assumption holds with $\tau_D > \frac{\ln c}{\lambda}$, then the system in (1) is almost sure asymptotically stable.

PROOF. Without loss of generality we assume $\pi = 1$ in the dwell-time assumption. Consider $t \in [\tau_k, \tau_{k+1})$, we have

$$\hat{x}(\tau_{k+1}^-) = e^{A_q(T-\Delta)} e^{A_p \Delta} \hat{x}(\tau_k) \tag{33}$$

Let $E(\tau_{k+1}) := \hat{x}(\tau_{k+1}) - \hat{x}(\tau_{k+1}^-)$, then

$$\hat{x}(\tau_{k+1}) = e^{A_q(T-\Delta)} e^{A_p \Delta} \hat{x}(\tau_k) + E(\tau_{k+1}) \tag{34}$$

Taking the infinity norm on both sides leads to

$$|\hat{x}(\tau_{k+1})| \leq \|e^{A_q(T-\Delta)}\| \|e^{A_p \Delta}\| |\hat{x}(\tau_k)| + |E(\tau_{k+1})| \tag{35}$$

By inserting inequality (33), we obtain

$$|\hat{x}(\tau_{k+1})| \leq \bar{c} e^{-\lambda T} |\hat{x}(\tau_k)| + |E(\tau_{k+1})| \tag{36}$$

where $\bar{c} := c^2$. The term $|E(\tau_{k+1})|$ can be further bounded by

$$|E(\tau_{k+1})| \leq \|\Phi(T)\| L_k (1 - 2^{-R_{k+1}}) \leq \|\Phi(T)\| L_k \tag{37}$$

Combining inequality (36) and (37) and taking the expectation on both sides gives

$$\mathbb{E}(|\hat{x}(\tau_{k+1})|) \leq \bar{c} e^{-\lambda T} \mathbb{E}(|\hat{x}(\tau_k)|) + \|\Phi(T)\| \mathbb{E}(L_k) \tag{38}$$

Since the almost sure asymptotic observability holds, i.e. $\mathbb{E}(L_k) \leq \delta^k L_0$, we have

$$\mathbb{E}(|\hat{x}(\tau_{k+1})|) \leq \bar{c}^{k+1} e^{-\lambda T(k+1)} \mathbb{E}(|\hat{x}(\tau_0)|)$$
$$+ L_0 \|\Phi(T)\| \delta^k \sum_{i=0}^{k} \left(\frac{\bar{c} e^{-\lambda T}}{\delta} \right)^i$$
$$\leq e^{(k+1)(\ln \bar{c} - \lambda T)} \mathbb{E}(|\hat{x}(\tau_0)|)$$
$$+ \frac{\delta^{k+1} - e^{(k+1)(\ln \bar{c} - \lambda T)}}{\delta - e^{(\ln \bar{c} - \lambda T)}} L_0 \|\Phi(T)\| \tag{39}$$

Here, if the switching time interval $T > \frac{\ln \bar{c}}{\lambda}$, then

$$\lim_{k \to \infty} \mathbb{E}(|\hat{x}(\tau_k)|) \to 0$$

With $\lim_{k \to \infty} \mathbb{E}(L_k) \to 0$, the almost sure asymptotic stability for the original system is achieved, which completes the proof. $\square$

5. SIMULATION

In this section, a vehicle to vehicle tracking example is used to demonstrate Lemma 4.4 and Lemma 4.6 which provide the sufficient conditions for almost sure asymptotic stability. The simulation compares two control strategies, one uses Lemma 4.6 to switch the controller in response to the changes in communication channel state, while the other one applies a non-switching control strategy without using the channel information.

5.1 Vehicle tracking model

Consider the following double integrator vehicle model,

$$\dot{y}_i = v_i$$
$$\dot{v}_i = u_i, i = 1, 2$$

where y_i and v_i represent the position and velocity for each vehicle. u_i is the control policy used by each vehicle to manage their accelerations. The control objective is to maintain a specified separation distance between the leader and follower, and achieve velocity tracking for the follower. To make the tracking problem nontrivial, we consider the case that the leader changes its control profile over time. The control input u_1 to the leader is a piecewise constant signal, which models a vehicle traveling on the road with different speed limits. We assume the leader's control profile changes slowly enough to be perfectly known by the follower. We can therefore develop the following model for the tracking error,

$$\dot{\eta}_1 = \eta_2$$
$$\dot{\eta}_2 = \bar{u} \tag{40}$$

with $\eta_1 = y_1 - y_2 - L_s$, $\eta_2 = v_1 - v_2$ and $\bar{u} = u_1 - u_2$. L_s denotes the safe distance margin for the two vehicles. Since u_1 is known to the follower, it can be treated as a known disturbance. As we can see in the tracking model, in order to achieve the control objective, The leader must transmit its position (y_1) and velocity (v_1)

to the follower in order to meet the control objectives. This transmission is done over a wireless fading channel. which satisfies the probabilistic bounds (3-4).

5.2 Simulation setup

A two-state Markov chain model is used to simulate the communication channel between the two vehicles. One state represents the bad channel condition, the other one represents the good channel condition. The bad channel condition is characterized in terms of those channel states satisfying $R_k \leq 1.8e^{-10^{-4}|\eta|^2}$, while the good channel condition is $R_k \geq 2.4e^{-10^{-4}|\eta|^2}$. The probability associated with the bad state is $p_{11}(|\eta|) = e^{-1.8e^{-0.0251|\eta|^2}}$, while the probability for the good state is $p_{22}(|\eta|) = e^{-2.4e^{0.009|\eta|^2}}$. The corresponding transition probabilities are $1 - p_{11}(|\eta|)$ and $1 - p_{22}(|\eta|)$. Under these assumptions on the Markov chain, one can then evaluate the bounds in equations (3-4) as

$$h_1(|\eta|) = 2.4e^{-10^{-4}|\eta|^2}, h_2(|\eta|) = 1.8e^{-10^{-4}|\eta|^2};$$

$$\zeta_1(|\eta|) = e^{0.001|\eta|^2}, \zeta_2(|\eta|) = e^{-0.025|\eta|^2}.$$

The other simulation parameters are set as follows

$$T = 0.1, \Delta = 0.02, \bar{R} = 2, \delta = 0.8;$$

$$K_1 = [-1 \ -1]; K_2 = [-36 \ -12]$$

By Lemma 4.4, the state set assuring specific performance is determined as $|\eta| \leq G_2^{-1}(\frac{\delta}{\|\Phi(T)\|}) = 20.86$. The initial state $(20, 10)$ is selected to satisfy the sufficient condition. Two controllers $K_1 = [-1 \ -1]; K_2 = [-36 \ -12]$ are selected to ensure different performance levels. K_1 is the controller with small gain, which leads to slow response time but is less sensitive to uncertainty. K_2 is the controller with high gain, which leads to fast response time but is more sensitive to uncertainty.

A Monte Carlo method is used to verify the almost sure asymptotic stability of the system. The simulation is run 1000 times over the time interval from 0 to 10 seconds. Figure 4 shows the maximum and minimum values of each state $\eta_i, i = 1, 2$ as a function of time over all the 1000 runs. The top plot in the figure is the trajectory for state η_1, with maximum value marked as blue solid line, and minimum value marked as red dash line. The black line represents the sufficient bound on the state derived from Lemma 4.4. The bottom plot is for the state η_2. We can see from the plots that the maximum and minimum values of the system state converge to zero almost surely after about 3.5 seconds. These results are consistent with our statement in lemma 4.4 that establishes the almost sure asymptotic stability of the switched system.

We also studied the benefits of switching controllers in response to the changes of channel state. Two control strategies were compared in this simulation. One is the non-switching policy, which applies the conservative controller K_1 all the time without considering the changes of channel state. The other one is the switching control policy that switches the controller in response to the changes of channel state to compensate the deep fading and achieve a fast convergent rate.

In Figure 5, the top plot shows the channel state (R_k) profile along the time line. The bottom plot shows the switching policy that reacts to the changes of channel state. We can see from the top plot that there is a string of zero bits over the time interval $[0, 2]$ which represents a deep fading scenario. At this time interval, the switching policy selects the conservative controller (index 1) to make a safe control decision. Shortly after 2 seconds, the channel state switches to the high bit rate, which makes the system switch to the high gain controller (index 2) to achieve better per-

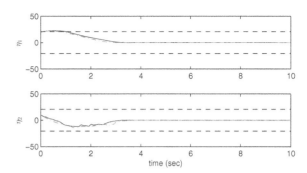

Figure 4: Almost sure asymptotic stability with switching strategy

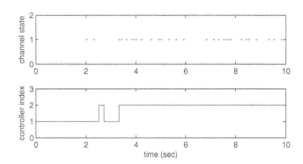

Figure 5: The switching policy in response to the changes of channel state

mance. The channel exhibits another long string of zero bits which is shown between time interval $[2, 4]$. The system detects this deep fade and switches back to small gain controller. After about 3.5 seconds, the high gain controller is always switched on because the channel condition remains good.

Figure 6 shows one path of the system trajectories for both switching policy and non-switching policy. The top plot in the figure shows the comparison for state η_1, while the bottom one is for η_2. The blue solid line represents the trajectory generated by switching policy while the red dashed one is by non-switching policy. As shown in the figure, the system performance is similar for both control policies before 3.5 seconds, since both of them are using low control gain. After 3.5 seconds, the switching policy selects the high gain controller in response to the occurrence of good channel condition. The state converges to the equilibrium at around 4 seconds for the switching strategy, while it takes more than 8 seconds for the non-switching one to converge.

One may argue that this improvement might not be very significant in some applications. However, it is important in vehicle control system because the fast moving vehicles may encounter unexpected emergency that happens within a few seconds. Our preliminary simulations show that switching controllers in response to the changes of channel state may facilitate system's reaction to those unexpected situations.

6. CONCLUSION

This paper studies the almost sure asymptotic stability of the control system in the presence of wireless fading channel whose outages are a function of the system state. Necessary and sufficient conditions are established for a switching controller that assures

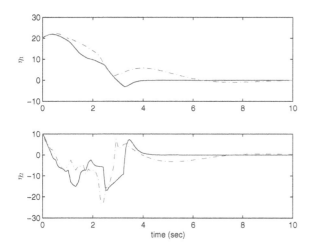

Figure 6: The state trajectory with switching strategy and non-switching strategy

almost sure asymptotic stability. Preliminary simulations results support the analysis.

Acknowledgment

The authors acknowledge the partial financial support of the National Science Foundation (NSF-CNS-1239222).

7. REFERENCES

[1] A. S. Akki and F. Haber. A statistical model of mobile-to-mobile land communication channel. *IEEE Transactions on Vehicular Technology*, 35(1):2–7, 1986.

[2] R. W. Brockett and D. Liberzon. Quantized feedback stabilization of linear systems. *IEEE Transactions on Automatic Control*, 45(7):1279–1289, 2000.

[3] L. Cheng, B. Henty, F. Bai, and D. D. Stancil. Doppler spread and coherence time of rural and highway vehicle-to-vehicle channels at 5.9 ghz. In *Proc. IEEE Global Telecommunications Conf. IEEE GLOBECOM 2008*, pages 1–6, 2008.

[4] L. Cheng, B. E. Henty, D. D. Stancil, F. Bai, and P. Mudalige. Mobile vehicle-to-vehicle narrow-band channel measurement and characterization of the 5.9 ghz dedicated short range communication (dsrc) frequency band. *IEEE Journal on Selected Areas in Communications*, 25(8):1501–1516, 2007.

[5] J. Doob. *Stochastic Processes*. John Wiley & Sons, 1953.

[6] N. Elia and S. K. Mitter. Stabilization of linear systems with limited information. *IEEE Transactions on Automatic Control*, 46(9):1384–1400, 2001.

[7] J. P. Hespanha and A. S. Morse. Stability of switched systems with average dwell-time. In *Proc. 38th IEEE Conf. Decision and Control*, volume 3, pages 2655–2660, 1999.

[8] D. Liberzon. Stabilizing a switched linear system by sampled-data quantized feedback. In *Proc. 50th IEEE Conf. Decision and Control and European Control Conf. (CDC-ECC)*, pages 8321–8326, 2011.

[9] N. C. Martins, M. A. Dahleh, and N. Elia. Feedback stabilization of uncertain systems in the presence of a direct link. *IEEE Transactions on Automatic Control*, 51(3):438–447, 2006.

[10] P. Minero, M. Franceschetti, S. Dey, and G. N. Nair. Data rate theorem for stabilization over time-varying feedback channels. *IEEE Transactions on Automatic Control*, 54(2):243–255, 2009.

[11] G. N. Nair, R. J. Evans, I. M. Y. Mareels, and W. Moran. Topological feedback entropy and nonlinear stabilization. *IEEE Transactions on Automatic Control*, 49(9):1585–1597, 2004.

[12] C. S. Patel, G. L. Stuber, and T. G. Pratt. Simulation of rayleigh-faded mobile-to-mobile communication channels. *IEEE Transactions on Communications*, 53(11):1876–1884, 2005.

[13] C. Rieger, D. Gertman, and M. McQueen. Resilient control systems: next generation design research. In *Human System Interactions, 2009. HSI'09. 2nd Conference on*, pages 632–636. IEEE, 2009.

[14] D. Starobinski and M. Sidi. Stochastically bounded burstiness for communication networks. *Information Theory, IEEE Transactions on*, 46(1):206–212, 2000.

[15] S. Tatikonda and S. Mitter. Control under communication constraints. *IEEE Transactions on Automatic Control*, 49(7):1056–1068, 2004.

[16] D. Tse and P. Viswanath. *Fundamentals of wireless communication*. Cambridge university press, 2005.

[17] P. Varaiya. Smart cars on smart roads: problems of control. *Automatic Control, IEEE Transactions on*, 38(2):195–207, 1993.

[18] H. Wang and N. Moayeri. Finite-state markov channel - a useful model for radio communication channels. *IEEE Transactions on Vehicular Technology*, 44(1):163–171, 1995.

[19] W. S. Wong and R. W. Brockett. Systems with finite communication bandwidth constraints. ii. stabilization with limited information feedback. *IEEE Transactions on Automatic Control*, 44(5):1049–1053, 1999.

[20] O. Yaron and M. Sidi. Performance and stability of communication networks via robust exponential bounds. *IEEE/ACM Transactions on Networking*, 1(3):372–385, 1993.

Privacy-Preserving Release of Aggregate Dynamic Models

Jerome Le Ny
Department of Electrical Engineering
Ecole Polytechnique de Montréal
C.P. 6079, succ. Centre-ville
Montréal, QC H3C 3A7, Canada
jerome.le-ny@polymtl.ca

George J. Pappas
Department of Electrical & Systems Engineering
University of Pennsylvania
200 South 33rd Street
Philadelphia, PA 19104, USA
pappasg@seas.upenn.edu

ABSTRACT

New solutions proposed for the monitoring and control of large-scale systems increasingly rely on sensitive data provided by end-users. As a result, there is a need to provide guarantees that these systems do not unintentionally leak private and confidential information during their operation. Motivated by this context, this paper discusses the problem of releasing a dynamic model describing the aggregate input-output dynamics of an ensemble of subsystems coupled via a common input and output, while controlling the amount of information that an adversary can infer about the dynamics of the individual subsystems. Such a model can then be used as an approximation of the true system, e.g., for controller design purposes. The proposed schemes rely on the notion of differential privacy, which provides strong and quantitative privacy guarantees that can be used by individuals to evaluate the risk/reward trade-offs involved in releasing detailed information about their behavior.

Categories and Subject Descriptors

K.4.1 [**Computers and Society**]: Public Policy Issues—*Privacy*; I.2.8 [**Artificial Intelligence**]: Problem Solving, Control Methods, and Search—*Control theory*; C.3 [**Special-Purpose and Application-Based Systems**]: Signal processing systems

General Terms

Security, Algorithms

Keywords

Differential Privacy; Dynamical Systems; System Identification

1. INTRODUCTION

Many emerging large-scale monitoring and control systems are expected to leverage vast amount of data provided by individual users to provide real-time services more efficiently. Examples include smart grids with advanced metering capabilities [15], intelligent transportation systems exploiting users location traces [11], or real-time population health monitoring systems [16]. The privacy concerns associated with the deployment of such pervasive monitoring networks have often been overlooked, in view of the many promised benefits. However, with certain recent setbacks in the rollout of smart meter projects for example, it is becoming increasingly clear that not addressing these concerns rigorously at design time puts at real risk the adoption of these technologies.

In contrast to these real-time systems, there is extensive work in the statistics and database literature on disclosure limitation and privacy-preserving publication of data [5,6]. In particular, the recently proposed notion of differential privacy [2,6,8] has been adopted in many works as a definition of privacy offering quantitative guarantees. This notion characterizes certain randomized algorithms that produce answers to statistical queries according to a distribution that is not very sensitive to the presence or absence of the data of any single individual. As a result, people contributing their data to a database are guaranteed that they are not dramatically increasing the ability of an adversary to infer private information about them, even by linking the released answers to the queries to other available sources of information.

Previous work on privacy for dynamic systems addressed the problem of releasing time-series, with or without real-time constraints, under various definitions of privacy [3,9, 13,14,18]. In this paper however, we consider the problem of releasing a *model*, rather than actual signals, capturing the aggregate dynamic behavior of a large number of participants, while restricting the accuracy with which the dynamics of any single participant can be inferred. Such models are useful for system simulation, forecasts, or control design. For example, consider an Independent System Operator (ISO) in an electricity market requesting from industrial producers and consumers a model of how fast and by how much they would ramp down and up their production and consumption when exposed to fluctuating spot prices, in order to implement a stable demand response scheme [17]. By observing the actual operation of such a scheme, .e.g., through the temporal behavior of electricity prices, it might be possible to infer some information about these confidential models, such as the equipment owned by specific companies or the value they extract from consuming a certain amount of electricity.

After some preliminaries on differential privacy in Section 2, we formulate in Section 3 a simple aggregate model release scenario of the type described in the previous paragraph, involving linear scalar dynamics to describe the individual subsystems. Three schemes preserving differential privacy for the subsystems are then proposed, based respectively on perturbation of the parameters of the transfer function, on perturbation of the Markov parameters or impulse response of a sampled version of the model, and on sampling and perturbing the frequency response. The ability of these schemes to capture accurately the global input-output behavior of the aggregate system is then discussed using simulated examples in Section 4.

2. TOOLS FOR DIFFERENTIAL PRIVACY

2.1 Definitions

We first introduce the notion of differential privacy [7, 8], which is a property of certain mechanisms accessing datasets containing private information to answer queries. Let us fix some probability space $(\Omega, \mathcal{F}, \mathbb{P})$. Let D be a space of datasets of interest. A *mechanism* is just a map $M : \mathsf{D} \times \Omega \to \mathsf{R}$, for some measurable output space $(\mathsf{R}, \mathcal{M})$, where $\mathcal{M}$ denotes a σ-algebra, such that for any element $d \in \mathsf{D}$, $M(d)$ is a random variable. A mechanism can be viewed as a probabilistic algorithm to answer a specific query q, which is a map $q : \mathsf{D} \to \mathsf{R}$.

Differential privacy is defined with respect to a choice of symmetric binary relation Adj on D, called adjacency, defined so that $\mathrm{Adj}(d, d')$ if and only if d and d' differ by the data of a single participant. A differentially private mechanism produces randomized outputs, with a distribution that does not change much for two adjacent datasets. As a result, an individual choosing to contribute its data is guaranteed that this choice won't dramatically increase the ability of an adversary to infer additional private information about him.

Definition 1. Let D be a space equipped with a symmetric binary relation denoted Adj, and let $(\mathsf{R}, \mathcal{M})$ be a measurable space. Let $\epsilon, \delta \geq 0$. A mechanism $M : \mathsf{D} \times \Omega \to \mathsf{R}$ is (ϵ, δ)-differentially private if for all $d, d' \in \mathsf{D}$ such that $\mathrm{Adj}(d, d')$, we have

$$\mathbb{P}(M(d) \in S) \leq e^{\epsilon} \mathbb{P}(M(d') \in S) + \delta, \quad \forall S \in \mathcal{M}. \quad (1)$$

If $\delta = 0$, the mechanism is said to be ϵ-differentially private.

In this paper, the input data of the participants belongs to a vector space. We now introduce two adjacency relations that are useful for this situation. They bound the variations allowed in the individual input data for which the condition (1) can be guaranteed. Let the space of datasets of interest for n participants be a product vector space $\mathsf{D} = \mathsf{D}_1 \times \ldots \times \mathsf{D}_n$, where D_i is equipped with a norm $\| \cdot \|_i$. Let $x, x' \in \mathsf{D}$ and $\rho \in \mathbb{R}_{>0}^n$. The first binary relation controls the absolute variation

$$\mathrm{Adj}_a^{\rho}(x, x') \text{ iff for some } i, \|x_i - x_i'\|_i \leq \rho_i, \quad (2)$$
$$\text{and } x_j = x_j', \forall j \neq i.$$

Many algorithms, notably in numerical analysis, have a sensitivity that is typically measured by relative variations rather than absolute variations, see, e.g., [19]. To capture these situations, we also introduce the following binary relation, for

$\eta \in \mathbb{R}_{>0}^n$,

$$\mathrm{Adj}_r^{\eta}(x, x') \text{ iff for some } i, \frac{\|x_i - x_i'\|_i}{\min\{\|x_i\|_i, \|x_i'\|_i\}} \leq \eta_i, \quad (3)$$
$$\text{and } x_j = x_j', \forall j \neq i.$$

The relation is undefined is $\min\{\|x_i\|_i, \|x_i'\|_i\} = 0$ in (3). Note that a differentially private mechanism for this adjacency relation produces similar outputs if a single participants changes its data from x_i to any $x_i' = x_i(1 + \tilde{\eta}_i)$, with $|\tilde{\eta}_i| \leq \eta_i$.

A fundamental property of the notion of differential privacy is that no additional privacy loss can occur by simply manipulating an output that is differentially private without looking back at the original data. This result is similar in spirit to the data processing inequality from information theory [4]. To state it, recall that a probability kernel between two measurable spaces $(\mathsf{R}_1, \mathcal{M}_1)$ and $(\mathsf{R}_2, \mathcal{M}_2)$ is a function $k : \mathsf{R}_1 \times \mathcal{M}_2 \to [0, 1]$ such that $k(\cdot, S)$ is measurable for each $S \in \mathcal{M}_2$ and $k(r, \cdot)$ is a probability measure for each $r \in \mathsf{R}_1$.

THEOREM 1 (RESILIENCE TO POST-PROCESSING). *Let* $M_1 : \mathsf{D} \times \Omega \to (\mathsf{R}_1, \mathcal{M}_1)$ *be an* (ϵ, δ)-*differentially private mechanism. Let* $M_2 : \mathsf{D} \times \Omega \to (\mathsf{R}_2, \mathcal{M}_2)$ *be another mechanism, such that there exists a probability kernel* $k : \mathsf{R}_1 \times \mathcal{M}_2 \to [0, 1]$ *verifying*

$$\mathbb{P}(M_2(d) \in S | M_1(d)) = k(M_1(d), S), \ a.s., \quad (4)$$

for all $S \in \mathcal{M}_2$ *and all* $d \in \mathsf{D}$. *Then* M_2 *is* (ϵ, δ)-*differentially private.*

A proof of this theorem can be found in [13]. Note that in (4), the kernel k is not allowed to depend on the dataset d. In other words, this condition says that once $M_1(d)$ is known, the distribution of $M_2(d)$ does not further depend on d. The theorem shows that a mechanism M_2 accessing a dataset only indirectly via the output of a differentially private mechanism M_1 cannot weaken the privacy guarantee. Hence post-processing can be used freely to improve the *accuracy* of an output, without having to worry about a possible loss of privacy.

2.2 Basic Mechanisms for Numerical Queries

Two basic mechanisms [7, 8], introduced in the next theorem, achieve differential privacy by additively perturbing the answers to numerical queries. They involve the following notion of sensitivity of a query.

Definition 2. Let D be a space equipped with an adjacency relation Adj, and R be a normed vector space with norm $\| \cdot \|_{\mathsf{R}}$. The *sensitivity* of a query $q : \mathsf{D} \to \mathsf{R}$ is defined as $\Delta q := \max_{d, d' : \mathrm{Adj}(d, d')} \|q(d) - q(d')\|_{\mathsf{R}}$. In particular, for $\mathsf{R} = \mathbb{R}^k$ equipped with the p-norm $\|x\|_p = \left(\sum_{i=1}^k |x_i|^p \right)^{1/p}$ for $p \in [1, \infty]$, we denote the ℓ_p sensitivity by $\Delta_p q$.

Next, recall that the Laplace distribution with mean zero and scale parameter b, denoted $\mathrm{Lap}(b)$, has density $p(x; b) = \frac{1}{2b} \exp\left(-\frac{|x|}{b}\right)$ and variance $2b^2$. Moreover, for $w \in \mathbb{R}^k$ with w_i iid and $w_i \sim \mathrm{Lap}(b)$, denoted $w \sim \mathrm{Lap}(b)^k$, we have $p(w; b) = (\frac{1}{2b})^k \exp\left(-\frac{\|w\|_1}{b}\right)$, $\mathbb{E}[\|w\|_1] = b$, and $\mathbb{P}(\|w\|_1 \geq tb) = e^{-t}$. The multidimensional normal distribution with mean μ and covariance matrix Σ is denoted $\mathcal{N}(\mu, \Sigma)$. Finally, the $\mathcal{Q}$-function is defined as

$$\mathcal{Q}(x) := \frac{1}{\sqrt{2\pi}} \int_x^\infty e^{-\frac{u^2}{2}} du.$$

THEOREM 2. *Let $q : \mathsf{D} \to \mathbb{R}^k$ be a query. Then the Laplace mechanism $M_q : \mathsf{D} \times \Omega \to \mathbb{R}^k$ defined by $M_q(d) = q(d) + w$, with $w \sim Lap(b)^k$ and $b \geq \frac{\Delta_1 q}{\epsilon}$ is ϵ-differentially private. the Gaussian mechanism $M_q : \mathsf{D} \times \Omega \to \mathbb{R}^k$ defined by $M_q(d) = q(d) + w$, with $w \sim \mathcal{N}(0, \sigma^2 I_k)$, where $\sigma \geq \frac{\Delta_2 q}{2\epsilon}(K + \sqrt{K^2 + 2\epsilon})$ and $K = \mathcal{Q}^{-1}(\delta)$, is (ϵ, δ)-differentially private.*

For the rest of the paper, we define $\kappa(\delta, \epsilon) = \frac{1}{2\epsilon}(K + \sqrt{K^2 + 2\epsilon})$. Note that it can be shown that $\kappa(\delta, \epsilon)$ can be bounded by $2\sqrt{2\ln(2/\delta)}/\epsilon$.

2.2.1 *A Sign-Preserving Mechanism Adapted to Relative Variations*

To conclude this section, we introduce a multiplicative perturbation mechanism, which can be useful to handle relative variations as in (3), and also to maintain sign consistency between an original real-valued query and the result provided by the mechanism. This last feature in particular is used in Section 3.1 to maintain the stability of a dynamic model while perturbing its poles.

Consider a query $q : \mathsf{D} \to \mathbb{R}_{>0}$. We would like to design a differentially private mechanism that preserves the positivity of the output. We have, for two datasets d, d'

$$\begin{aligned} |\ln q(d') - \ln q(d)| &= \left| \ln\left(\frac{q(d')}{q(d)}\right) \right| \\ &\leq \frac{|q(d') - q(d)|}{|q(d)|} \\ &\leq \frac{|q(d') - q(d)|}{\min\{|q(d)|, |q(d')|\}}, \end{aligned}$$

using the fact that $\ln x \leq x - 1$ for all $x > 0$. Suppose now that there exists γ such that for all $d, d' \in \mathsf{D}$,

$$\frac{|q(d') - q(d)|}{\min\{|q(d)|, |q(d')|\}} \leq \gamma \frac{\|d' - d\|}{\min\{\|d\|, \|d'\|\}}. \tag{5}$$

In particular, for d, d' such that $\mathrm{Adj}_r^\eta(d, d')$, we have $\|d' - d\| = \|d_i - d_i'\|_i$ for some i, and moreover $\|d\| \geq \|d_i\|_i$. Hence finally

$$|\ln q(d') - \ln q(d)| \leq \gamma \max_{1 \leq i \leq n} \eta_i =: \Gamma.$$

From Theorem 2, the mechanism $M_1(q) = \ln q(d) + Y$, with $Y \sim \mathrm{Lap}\left(\frac{\Gamma}{\epsilon}\right)$, is ϵ-differentially private, and is (ϵ, δ)-differentially private if $Y \sim \mathcal{N}(0, \kappa(\delta, \epsilon)^2 \Gamma^2)$. Taking exponentials and using Theorem 1, we obtain the following result, where $\lambda = \exp(Y)$.

THEOREM 3. *Let $q : \mathsf{D} \to \mathbb{R}_{>0}$ be a query satisfying (5). Then the mechanism $M(d) = \lambda q(d)$ is ϵ-differentially private for (3) if $\lambda \sim ln\text{-}Lap(\Gamma/\epsilon)$ is a log-Laplace random variable, and is (ϵ, δ)-differentially private if $\lambda \sim ln\text{-}\mathcal{N}(0, \kappa(\delta, \epsilon)^2 \Gamma^2)$ is a log-normal random variable.*

Bounds of the form (5) are frequent in numerical analysis [19]. In the following however, we use this mechanism in its most simple form, with $D = \mathbb{R}_{>0}$ and $q = \mathrm{id}$. Theorem 3

shows in particular that if the data of user i consists of a single positive number x_i, letting each user release $\lambda_i x_i$ with $\lambda_i \sim \mathrm{ln\text{-}Lap}(\eta_i/\epsilon)$ or $\lambda_i \sim \mathrm{ln\text{-}\mathcal{N}}(0, \kappa(\delta, \epsilon)^2 \eta_i^2)$ guarantees ϵ- or (ϵ, δ)-differential privacy for (3) respectively.

3. DYNAMIC MODEL PUBLICATION

In the rest of this paper, we consider the following scenario. A group of n users responds to a common scalar input signal $u : \mathbb{R}_+ \to \mathbb{R}$, according to their own dynamics described by a stable scalar first order differential equation

$$\dot{x}_i = -a_i x_i + b_i u, \quad x_i(0) = x_{0,i} \in \mathbb{R}, \quad a_i > 0, \forall i \in [n],$$

where $[n] := \{1, \ldots, n\}$. The group produces a measured aggregate scalar output signal $y : \mathbb{R}_+ \to \mathbb{R}$, which is a linear combination of the n individual states

$$y = c^T x,$$

where $c \in \mathbb{R}^n$ is a known vector. For example, u could correspond to a price signal, the individual states to deviations with respect to a nominal consumption level (with $b_i \leq 0$), which react to price changes with some inertia, and we could measure the total consumption, i.e., $c = \mathbf{1}_n$.

Each individual user is willing to provide his parameters a_i, b_i to a data aggregator, which then publishes a version $\hat{G}$ of the single input single output (SISO) system $G(s) = c^T(sI - A)^{-1}b$, describing the relationship between the common input and the aggregate output. Once released, this model can then be used by anyone to predict how the global system responds to a given input u. In particular, an adversary with access to the published model $\hat{G}$ is allowed to use any test input u and read the corresponding output y to try to estimate the parameters a_i, b_i of any specific participant. This adversary could have access to arbitrary side information for this purpose, e.g., he could know the parameters a_j, b_j of all the participants except i.

In order to encourage participants to provide their parameters to the data aggregator, we wish to make the mechanism releasing the global system model (ϵ, δ)-differentially private, for the following adjacency relation on $\mathsf{D} = \mathbb{R}_{>0}^n \times \mathbb{R}^n$

$$\mathrm{Adj}^{\eta, \rho}((a, b), (\hat{a}, \hat{b})) \text{ iff } \mathrm{Adj}_r^\eta(a, \hat{a}) \text{ and } \mathrm{Adj}_a^\rho(b, \hat{b}), \tag{6}$$

where $\eta, \rho \in \mathbb{R}_{>0}^n$ and Adj_r^η and Adj_a^ρ are defined in (3) and (2) respectively. Note that we protect relative variations for the location of the individual poles, which is more meaningful than absolute variations, e.g., due to the strong influence of the distance of the poles to the imaginary axis on the dynamics of the system.

The transfer function of the overall system is

$$G(s) = \sum_{i=1}^n \frac{c_i b_i}{s + a_i}. \tag{7}$$

Its order is bounded by n, the number of participants, which is assumed to be large. The data for the participants such that $c_i = 0$ can immediately be discarded, so without loss of generality, we can assume $c_i \neq 0, \forall i$. Up to a linear state transformation by $\frac{1}{n}\mathrm{diag}(c_1^{-1}, \ldots, c_n^{-1})$, we can moreover assume from now on that $c_i = 1/n, \forall i$, which will simplify the notation. Here the normalization factor $1/n$ is chosen to study the performance of the mechanisms more conveniently as n grows.

3.1 Parameter Perturbation

The first mechanism (generally called an input perturbation mechanism in the literature on differential privacy), consists in letting each participant perturb its own data to satisfy the differential privacy property directly, without relying on a central server. A mechanism releasing the scalars

$$\hat{a}_i = \lambda_i a_i, \quad \hat{b}_i = b_i + \mu_i, \ 1 \le i \le n,$$

with μ_i, λ_i chosen as in Theorems 2 and 3, is 2ϵ- or $(2\epsilon, 2\delta)$-differentially private respectively, depending if Laplace or Gaussian random variables are used. According to Theorem 1, we can then publish the model

$$\hat{G}(s) = \frac{1}{n} \sum_{i=1}^{n} \frac{\hat{b}_i}{s + \hat{a}_i} \tag{8}$$

to achieve 2ϵ- or $(2\epsilon, 2\delta)$-differentially privacy.

This approach however can add an excessive amount of noise in some common situations. As an illustration, suppose that all users have the same transfer function $1/(s+1)$. Then $G(s) = 1/(s+1)$. Now, even if only the parameters b_i were to be protected, thus allowing us to leave $\hat{a}_i = 1$ for all i in (8), we would get

$$G(s) - \hat{G}(s) = \frac{1}{s+1} \frac{\sum_{i=1}^{n} \mu_i}{n},$$

i.e., the mean squared error (MSE) of this mechanism scales as $1/n$ at low frequencies, whereas one can reasonably hope to have schemes with an MSE approaching an $1/n^2$ scaling in this case. Another issue in this case is that despite the fact that the original system G is really of order 1, the model with perturbed parameters $\hat{a}_i$ remains of large order $n = 100$ with probability 1.

3.2 Impulse Response Perturbation

The next two schemes try to reduce of amount of privacy-preserving noise by taking advantage of the fact that a single term in (7) changes between two vectors of parameters adjacent according to (6). In this subsection, we produce a differentially private version of the impulse response of the system, and use it to rebuild a differentially private version of G, using again Theorem 1. First, we sample the systems with period h (using a zero-order hold), to obtain the difference equation

$$x_{i,k+1} = \alpha_i x_{i,k} + \beta_i u_k,$$

with $\alpha_i = e^{-a_i h}$, $\beta_i = \int_0^h e^{-a_i \tau} d\tau \, b_i = \frac{1 - e^{-a_i h}}{a_i} b_i$.

We then aim at releasing the impulse response or Markov parameters for the discrete-time system

$$v_0 = 0, \quad v_k = \frac{1}{n} \sum_{i=1}^{n} \beta_i \alpha_i^{k-1}, k \ge 1.$$

Suppose that we wish to publish the first N non-trivial parameters $v = [v_1, \ldots, v_N]^T$. The Laplace mechanism asks that we add to each component v_k a random variable Y_k distributed according to $\mathrm{Lap}(\Delta_1/\epsilon)$, where Δ_1 is the ℓ_1 sensitivity

$$\Delta_1 = \max_{\mathrm{Adj}^{\eta,\rho}((a,b),(\hat{a},\hat{b}))} \|v - \hat{v}\|_1.$$

To compute this sensitivity, consider two adjacent parameter vectors (a, b) and $(\hat{a}, \hat{b})$, differing say by the data of the ith

participant. Then

$$\|v - \hat{v}\|_1 = \frac{1}{n} \sum_{k=0}^{N-1} |\beta_i \alpha_i^k - \hat{\beta}_i \hat{\alpha}_i^k|. \tag{9}$$

Since this quantity scales as $1/n$ (for N fixed), the MSE between the original impulse response and the perturbed one scales as $1/n^2$, which is an improvement over the scaling in Section 3.1. However, we still need to reconstruct a system approximation from the perturbed Markov parameters, which can be very sensitive to the presence of noise and therefore can cancel the benefits of the scaling. To pursue the computation of the sensitivity, we now make the following additional assumption on the location of the parameters of the system.

Assumption 1. There are publicly known scalars $\kappa_a, \kappa_b > 0$ such that $a_i \ge \kappa_a$ and $|b_i| \le \kappa_b$, for all $i \in [n]$.

The following proposition, whose proof can be found in the Appendix, bounds the ℓ_1 sensitivity. For the parameters η, ρ appearing in the (3), we define $\eta_m = \max_{i \in [n]} \eta_i, \rho_m = \max_{i \in [n]} \rho_i$.

PROPOSITION 1. *Under Assumption 1, we have*

$$\Delta_1 \le \frac{h}{n} \left(\frac{(0.3\,\eta_m \kappa_b + \rho_m)(1 - e^{-N\kappa_a h})}{1 - e^{-\kappa_a h}} \right. \tag{10}$$

$$\left. + \frac{(0.37\,\eta_m\,\kappa_b)(1 + (N-1)e^{-N\kappa_a h} - Ne^{-(N-1)\kappa_a h})}{(1 - e^{-\kappa_a h})^2} \right).$$

Let $\bar{\Delta}_1$ denote the right-hand side of (10). Algorithm 1 summarizes our mechanism for publishing a differentially private version of the global dynamical system. From a perturbed sequence of N Markov parameters, we reconstruct an approximate version of G, using the MATLAB function `imp2ss`, which implements a model realization algorithm using an impulse response, proposed initially by Kung [12]. A discrete-time model is constructed first, and the sampling period h is then used to reconstruct a continuous-time system using the inverse Tustin transform [1]. Note finally that the mechanism is ϵ-differentially private, but the computations in the Appendix can be used to obtain the ℓ_2 sensitivity and design an (ϵ, δ)-differentially private mechanism.

Algorithm 1 Dynamic Model Publication via Approximate Realization

---

Require: h, sampling period; N, number of Markov parameters

    Generate $\nu_i \sim \mathrm{Lap}(\bar{\Delta}_1/\epsilon)$, $i \in [n]$

    $y_i \leftarrow v_i + \nu_i$, $i \in [n]$

    $\hat{G} \leftarrow \texttt{imp2ss}(y, h)$

3.3 Frequency Response Perturbation

Instead of releasing the impulse response, it is perhaps more intuitive to release a set of N samples of the transfer function G, measured at a set of a priori fixed frequencies $\omega_1, \ldots, \omega_N$, which can moreover be chosen in the frequency range over which we wish to better approximate G. Let

$$f = [G(j\omega_1), \ldots G(j\omega_N)]$$

be the vector in $\mathbb{C}^N$ to be released. Equivalently, we want to release the real and imaginary parts of $f = [f_R, f_I]$, where

$$f_R = [\Re(G(j\omega_1)), \ldots \Re(G(j\omega_N))],$$
$$f_I = [\Im(G(j\omega_1)), \ldots \Im(G(j\omega_N))].$$

To compute the ℓ_2 sensitivity, consider the variation of the parameters of say participant i. We then compute the change in 2-norm

$$\Delta_{2,i}^2 = \sum_{k=1}^{N} [\Re(G(j\omega_k) - \hat{G}(j\omega_k))]^2 + [\Im(G(j\omega_k) - \hat{G}(j\omega_k))]^2$$

$$= \sum_{k=1}^{N} |G(j\omega_k) - \hat{G}(j\omega_k)|^2$$

$$= \frac{1}{n^2} \sum_{k=1}^{N} \left| \frac{b_i}{j\omega_k + a_i} - \frac{\hat{b}_i}{j\omega_k + \hat{a}_i} \right|^2. \quad (11)$$

We now analyze the terms of the sum (11).

$$\left| \frac{b_i}{j\omega_k + a_i} - \frac{\hat{b}_i}{j\omega_k + \hat{a}_i} \right|^2 = \frac{(b_i\hat{a}_i - \hat{b}_ia_i)^2 + \omega_k^2(b_i - \hat{b}_i)^2}{(a_i^2 + \omega_k^2)(\hat{a}_i^2 + \omega_k^2)}$$

$$= \frac{(b_i(\hat{a}_i - a_i) + (b_i - \hat{b}_i)a_i)^2 + \omega_k^2(b_i - \hat{b}_i)^2}{(a_i^2 + \omega_k^2)(\hat{a}_i^2 + \omega_k^2)}$$

$$\leq \frac{2\kappa_b^2(\hat{a}_i - a_i)^2 + 2\rho_i^2 a_i^2 + \omega_k^2 \rho_i^2}{(a_i^2 + \omega_k^2)(\hat{a}_i^2 + \omega_k^2)}$$

$$\leq \frac{2a_i^2(\kappa_b^2\eta_i^2 + \rho_i^2) + \omega_k^2 \rho_i^2}{(a_i^2 + \omega_k^2)(\hat{a}_i^2 + \omega_k^2)}.$$

Now, using $\frac{a_i^2}{a_i^2 + \omega_k^2} \leq 1$, we get the bound

$$\Delta_2^2 \leq \frac{1}{n^2} \sum_{k=1}^{N} \frac{2(\kappa_b^2\eta_m^2 + \rho_m^2)}{\kappa_a^2 + \omega_k^2} + \frac{\omega_k^2 \rho_m^2}{(\kappa_a^2 + \omega_k^2)(\kappa_a^2 + \omega_k^2)}, \quad (12)$$

under Assumption 1. Note in particular that sampling at high frequencies contributes less to the sensitivity bound, or equivalently, it is harder to publish information about low frequencies than about high frequencies while achieving differential privacy.

Algorithm 2 summarizes our mechanism based on frequency response perturbation. Let $\bar{\Delta}_2^2$ denote the right-hand side of (12). We first perturb the coordinates of the vector (f_R, f_I) using additive Gaussian noise with variance proportional to $\bar{\Delta}_2^2$ to achieve (ϵ, δ)-differential privacy. We then estimate a transfer function $\hat{G}$ based on this frequency response data, using the MATLAB function `tfest` [10]. This function requires the user to specify the order `np` of the model to produce, which should not be chosen too large to avoid overfitting the perturbed values of the frequency response. Note that this order should be chosen a priori without taking the form of G into account, otherwise Theorem 1 would not apply.

4. SIMULATIONS

In this section, we discuss in more details the performance of two of the mechanisms previously presented, namely, the parameter perturbation scheme of Subsection 3.1 and the frequency response perturbation scheme of Subsection 3.3. We fix a priori `np` = 5 in Algorithm 2, and a vector ω of 20 sampled frequencies logarithmically spaced between 0.1

Algorithm 2 Dynamic Model Publication via Frequency Response Estimation

Require: ω, vector of frequencies to sample; `np`, number of poles desired in the released model
  Generate $\nu_{R,i} \sim \mathcal{N}(0, \kappa(\delta, \epsilon)^2 \bar{\Delta}_2^2)$, $i \in [n]$
  Generate $\nu_{I,i} \sim \mathcal{N}(0, \kappa(\delta, \epsilon)^2 \bar{\Delta}_2^2)$, $i \in [n]$
  $\hat{f}_{R,i} \leftarrow f_{R,i} + \nu_{R,i}$, $i \in [n]$
  $\hat{f}_{I,i} \leftarrow f_{I,i} + \nu_{I,i}$, $i \in [n]$
  $\hat{G} \leftarrow$ `tfest`$(\hat{f}_R + i\hat{f}_I, \omega, $`np`$)$

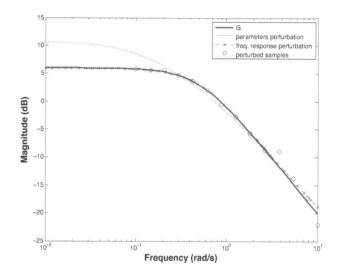

Figure 1: Examples of results produced by the mechanisms based on parameter perturbation and on reconstruction from noisy samples of the frequency response. The samples produced and used by `tfest` in Algorithm 2 are denoted with circles.

rad/s and 100 rad/s. We let $n = 100, \epsilon = \ln 3, \delta = 0.05, \eta_i = 0.2, \rho_i = 0.5, \forall i \in [n]$.

The first example is similar to the case described in Subsection 3.1, with each user associated to the same transfer function $1/(s+0.5)$, which is also equal to G. Sample models produced by the parameter perturbation and frequency response perturbation are shown on Fig. 2. For these particular outputs, the errors measured by the H_∞-norm of the difference between the produced and original models are 1.397 for the parameter perturbation scheme and 0.043 for Algorithm 2. In this case the parameter perturbation method produced a model with a large error at low frequencies.

The second example consists of a randomly generated model, where the parameters a_i and b_i are generated independently across users according to uniform distributions on the intervals $[0.5, 5]$, and $[0, 5]$ respectively. Sample outputs of the two mechanisms are reproduced on Fig. 2. In this specific output, we see that the approximation quality of the frequency response perturbation mechanism remains good at low frequencies, but much worse than the parameters perturbation scheme at high frequencies. This is mainly due to the fact that we use additive perturbations in Algorithm 2, which means that the noise tends to dominate the magnitude of the transfer function when the latter is small. Since in this case however the errors occur when the attenuation is already significant, the H_∞-norm of the model error

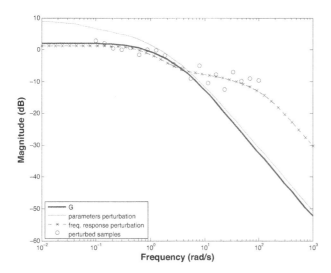

Figure 2: Examples of results produced by the mechanisms for a randomly generated model. We have $\|G - \hat{G}_1\|_\infty = 1.53$ and $\|G - \hat{G}_2\|_\infty = 0.28$, where G_1 is the model produced using parameter perturbation, and G_2 is the model produced via perturbed frequency response data.

for the frequency response perturbation mechanism still remains much smaller than for the parameter perturbation mechanism. The average H_∞ error obtained over 1000 randomly generated systems was found to be 0.97 for the parameter perturbation mechanism and 0.29 for the frequency response perturbation mechanism.

5. CONCLUSION

We have presented several privacy-preserving mechanisms that can be used to release a model describing the dynamics of a large group of users responding to a common input signal and producing an aggregate output signal. We expect the techniques described here to extend to more complex systems, with multiple inputs and outputs and potentially more coupled process dynamics. Future work will focus on analytically quantifying the approximation error achieved by the proposed mechanisms and will explore lower bounds on the model error achievable by differentially private release mechanisms.

Appendix: Proof of Proposition 1

As in (9), let us assume for concreteness that the data of the first participant is perturbed. From the Taylor-Lagrange formula, we have that for all $k \geq 0$,

$$|\hat{\beta}_1\hat{\alpha}_1^k - \beta_1\alpha_1^k| \leq k\tilde{\alpha}_1^{k-1}|\tilde{\beta}_1||\hat{\alpha}_1 - \alpha_1| + \tilde{\alpha}_1^k|\hat{\beta}_1 - \beta_1|,$$

where $\tilde{\alpha}_1 = \alpha_1 + \theta(\hat{\alpha}_1 - \alpha_1)$, $\tilde{\beta}_1 = \beta_1 + \theta(\hat{\beta}_1 - \beta_1)$, for some $\theta \in (0, 1)$. In particular,

$$\tilde{\alpha}_1 \leq e^{-\kappa_a h}, \quad |\tilde{\beta}_1| \leq \kappa_b h, \tag{13}$$

where the second inequality comes from the fact that

$$0 < \frac{1 - e^{-x}}{x} \leq 1, \forall x > 0.$$

We now bound the variations in the parameters α_1, β_1. Again, from the Taylor-Lagrange formula,

$$|\hat{\alpha}_1 - \alpha_1| = |e^{-\hat{a}_1 h} - e^{-a_1 h}| \leq \tilde{a}_1 h e^{-\tilde{a}_1 h} \frac{|\hat{a}_1 - a_1|}{\tilde{a}_1}$$

$$\leq 0.37\,\eta_m,$$

where $\tilde{a}_1 = a_1 + \theta(\hat{a}_1 - a_1)$ for some $\theta \in (0, 1)$, and we used the fact that $0 < xe^{-x} < 0.37$, for all $x > 0$. Finally,

$$|\hat{\beta}_1 - \beta_1| = \left| \frac{1 - e^{-\hat{a}_1 h}}{\hat{a}_1 h}\hat{b}_1 h - \frac{1 - e^{-a_1 h}}{a_1 h}b_1 h \right|$$

$$\leq \left| \frac{-1 + e^{-\tilde{a}_1 h} + \tilde{a}_1 h e^{-\tilde{a}_1 h}}{\tilde{a}_1^2 h^2} \right| |\tilde{b}_1|\, h\, |\hat{a}_1 h - a_1 h|$$

$$+ \frac{1 - e^{-\tilde{a}_1 h}}{\tilde{a}_1 h}h|\hat{b}_1 - b_1|$$

$$\leq 0.3\,\eta_m\,\kappa_b\,h + \rho_m h,$$

where $\tilde{\alpha}_1 = \alpha_1 + \theta(\hat{\alpha}_1 - \alpha_1)$, $\tilde{\beta}_1 = \beta_1 + \theta(\hat{\beta}_1 - \beta_1)$, for some $\theta \in (0, 1)$, and we used the fact that $|(-1 + e^{-x} + xe^{-x})/x| < 0.3$, for all $x > 0$.

Hence overall we get the bounds, for all $k \geq 0$,

$$|\hat{\beta}_1\hat{\alpha}_1^k - \beta_1\alpha_1^k| \leq h(0.37\,k\,\tilde{\alpha}_1^{k-1}\,\kappa_b\,\eta_m + \tilde{\alpha}_1^k(0.3\,\eta_m\,\kappa_b + \rho_m)),$$

and the result of the proposition follows from the formulas

$$\sum_{k=0}^{N-1} k\alpha^{k-1} = \frac{1 + (N-1)\alpha^N - N\alpha^{N-1}}{(1-\alpha)^2}, \quad \sum_{k=0}^{N-1}\alpha^k = \frac{1-\alpha^N}{1-\alpha}.$$

as well as (13).

6. REFERENCES

[1] K. J. Åström and B. Wittenmark. *Computer-Controlled Systems: Theory and Design.* Prentice Hall, 3rd edition, 1997.

[2] A. Blum, C. Dwork, F. McSherry, and K. Nissim. Practical privacy: the SuLQ framework. In *Proceedings of the twenty-fourth ACM SIGMOD-SIGACT-SIGART symposium on Principles of database systems (PODS)*, pages 128–138, New York, NY, USA, 2005.

[3] T.-H. H. Chan, E. Shi, and D. Song. Private and continual release of statistics. *ACM Transactions on Information and System Security*, 14(3):26:1–26:24, November 2011.

[4] T. M. Cover and J. A. Thomas. *Elements of Information Theory.* John Wiley and Sons, New York, NY, 1991.

[5] G. Duncan and D. Lambert. Disclosure-limited data dissemination. *Journal of the American Statistical Association*, 81(393):10–28, March 1986.

[6] C. Dwork. Differential privacy. In *Proceedings of the 33rd International Colloquium on Automata, Languages and Programming (ICALP)*, volume 4052 of *Lecture Notes in Computer Science.* Springer-Verlag, 2006.

[7] C. Dwork, K. Kenthapadi, F. McSherry, I. M. M. Naor, and Naor. Our data, ourselves: Privacy via distributed noise generation. *Advances in Cryptology-EUROCRYPT 2006*, pages 486–503, 2006.

[8] C. Dwork, F. McSherry, K. Nissim, and A. Smith. Calibrating noise to sensitivity in private data

analysis. In *Proceedings of the Third Theory of Cryptography Conference*, pages 265–284, 2006.

[9] C. Dwork, M. Naor, T. Pitassi, and G. N. Rothblum. Differential privacy under continual observations. In *STOC'10*, Cambridge, MA, June 2010.

[10] H. Garnier, M. Mensler, and A. Richard. Continuous-time model identification from sampled data: Implementation issues and performance evaluation. *International Journal of Control*, 76(13):1337–1357, 2003.

[11] B. Hoh, T. Iwuchukwu, Q. Jacobson, M. Gruteser, A. Bayen, J.-C. Herrera, R. Herring, D. Work, M. Annavaram, and J. Ban. Enhancing privacy and accuracy in probe vehicle based traffic monitoring via virtual trip lines. *IEEE Transactions on Mobile Computing*, 11(5), May 2012.

[12] S. Kung. A new identification and model reduction algorithm via singular value decompositions. In *Proceedings of the Twelfth Asilomar Conference on Circuits, Systems and Computers*, pages 705–714., November 1978.

[13] J. Le Ny and G. J. Pappas. Differentially private filtering. September 2012. Conditionally accepted for publication in the IEEE Transactions on Automatic Control, available at http://arxiv.org/abs/1207.4305.

[14] J. Le Ny and G. J. Pappas. Differentially private Kalman filtering. In *Proceedings of the 50th Annual Allerton Conference on Communication, Control, and Computing*, October 2012.

[15] A. Molina-Markham, P. Shenoy, K. Fu, E. Cecchet, and D. Irwin. Private memoirs of a smart meter. In *Proceedings of the 2nd ACM Workshop on Embedded Sensing Systems for Energy-Efficiency in Building*, pages 61–66, New York, NY, USA, 2010.

[16] B. Reis, C. Kirby, L. Hadden, K. Olson, A. McMurry, J. Daniel, and K. Mandl. Aegis: a robust and scalable real-time public health surveillance system. *Journal of the American Medical Informatics Association*, 14(5):581–588, 2007.

[17] M. Roozbehani, M. Dahleh, and S. Mitter. Dynamic pricing and stabilization of supply and demand in modern electric power grids. In *IEEE International Conference onf Smart Grid Communications*, October 2010.

[18] L. Sankar, S. R. Rajagopalan, and H. V. Poor. A theory of privacy and utility in databases. Technical report, Princeton University, February 2011.

[19] L. N. Trefethen and D. Bau, III. *Numerical Linear Algebra*. SIAM, 1997.

Algorithms for Determining Network Robustness

Heath J. LeBlanc
Department of Electrical & Computer
Engineering and Computer Science
Ohio Northern University
Ada, OH, USA
h-leblanc@onu.edu

Xenofon Koutsoukos
Department of Electrical Engineering and
Computer Science
Vanderbilt University
Nashville, TN, USA
xenofon.koutsoukos@vanderbilt.edu

ABSTRACT

In this paper, we study algorithms for determining the robustness of a network. Network robustness is a novel graph theoretic property that provides a measure of redundancy of directed edges between all pairs of nonempty, disjoint subsets of nodes in a graph. The robustness of a graph has been shown recently to be useful for characterizing the class of network topologies in which resilient distributed algorithms that use purely local strategies are able to succeed in the presence of adversary nodes. Therefore, network robustness is a critical property of resilient networked systems. While methods have been given to construct robust networks, algorithms for determining the robustness of a given network have not been explored. This paper introduces several algorithms for determining the robustness of a network, and includes centralized, decentralized, and distributed algorithms.

Categories and Subject Descriptors

C.2.4 [**Computer-Communication Networks**]: Distributed Systems; C.4 [**Performance of Systems**]: Fault tolerance

General Terms

Algorithms, Security, Theory

Keywords

Network Robustness; Resilience; Distributed Algorithm; Adversary

1. INTRODUCTION

Network connectivity has long been the key metric in the analysis of fault-tolerant and secure distributed algorithms [3]. This is because (strong) connectivity formalizes the notion of redundant information flow across a network through independent paths. Thus, for algorithms that seek to relay or encode information across multiple hops in the network, connectivity precisely captures the necessary property for analysis [3,5]. More generally, for tasks that require nonlocal information, such as detection of adversary nodes,

connectivity is the central property for characterizing the necessary topologies [11,15]. However, whenever purely local strategies are employed, connectivity is no longer the key metric.

For algorithms that use purely local information, the nodes make decisions and act based on their sensor measurements, calculations, dynamics, and direct interactions with neighbors in the network. No global information is shared or assumed to be known. Instead, information is disseminated within components of the network in an iterative or diffusive manner, rather than being relayed or routed across the network. For these reasons, purely local algorithms are well suited to large-scale dynamic networks. Indeed, purely local strategies are employed in biology and nature [13]; e.g., flocking of birds and schooling of fish are postulated to arise from local interaction rules [13]. From an engineering perspective, examples of algorithms that are explicitly designed to use purely local strategies include iterative function calculation and iterative consensus algorithms [14], as well as gossip-based algorithms [2,6].

Edge reachability and network robustness are important properties for analyzing algorithms that use purely local strategies [7, 9, 17]. It has been shown that any nontrivially robust network has a directed spanning tree [17]. In fact, 1-robustness[1] is equivalent to the existence of a directed spanning tree [17]. Moreover, for iterative consensus algorithms in a time-invariant network, existence of a directed spanning tree is a necessary and sufficient condition for achieving agreement among the nodes [12]. However, the full utility of edge reachability and network robustness is realized only when considering fault-tolerant and resilient dissemination of information in a network through purely local strategies. This is because edge reachability – which is defined for a nonempty set – captures the requirement that enough nodes inside the set are sufficiently influenced from outside the set. There are two forms of redundancy present in the definition of edge reachability: redundancy of incoming links from outside and redundancy of such nodes with redundant incoming links from outside. This dual redundancy enables resilience against faulty information produced by either a sufficiently small number of neighboring nodes from outside the set or from a sufficiently small number of nodes from within the set. Robustness is a network-wide property that stipulates a lower bound on the edge reachability properties of a sufficiently large number of subsets of nodes. Just as resilient distributed algorithms using nonlocal information utilize the redundancy of independent paths afforded by sufficient connectivity [11,15], resilient distributed algorithms using purely local information utilize the redundancy of local information present in robust networks [7,9,17].

In previous work, the utility of edge reachability and network robustness as metrics for analysis of resilient distributed algorithms that use only local information has been demonstrated [8,9,17]. In

---

[1] See Section 2 for the formal definition of robustness.

particular, it is shown in [9] that $(F + 1, F + 1)$-robustness is the necessary and sufficient condition for achieving resilient asymptotic consensus in a time-invariant network in the presence of up to F malicious adversary nodes that seek to disrupt consensus. Hence, determining the robustness of a network is important for determining whether resilient distributed algorithms can succeed. A growth model for constructing large robust networks from small ones has been given in [17] and extended in [9]. This growth model entails the preferential attachment model of scale-free networks [1], which implies that many scale-free networks are nontrivially robust. In [16], it has been shown that the threshold function of random graphs coincide for robustness and connectivity, which implies that random graphs with high connectivity are also highly robust. These results imply that many complex networks are in fact robust. However, as of yet, no algorithms have been given for determining the robustness of a network.

In this paper we propose algorithms to determine the robustness of a given network. In particular, two centralized algorithms are introduced. The first algorithm checks for a given amount of robustness and the second one determines the robustness of any network, regardless of its connectedness properties. These algorithms assume the topology of the network is given as input to the algorithm (encoded by the adjacency matrix). A decentralized algorithm is proposed that enables the individual nodes of an undirected, connected network to compute the robustness of the network in a decentralized manner by broadcasting information about their neighborhood in order to locally reconstruct the network topology. The centralized algorithm is then used at each node to determine the overall robustness. A modification to this decentralized algorithm is proposed in which each individual node only checks the edge reachability conditions for subsets in which it is *not* included, thus resulting in a truly distributed algorithm. For these algorithms, we analyze their complexity and examine the improvement gained by the distributed algorithm.

The rest of the paper is organized as follows. Section 2 reviews the definition of edge reachability and network robustness, and recalls several useful properties of robust networks. Section 3 describes the nature of the problem of determining network robustness and proposes centralized, decentralized, and distributed algorithms to do so. Section 4 summarizes the work and provides directions for future work.

2. NETWORK ROBUSTNESS

Network robustness is a property of a network that formalizes the notion of sufficient redundancy of directed information flow between subsets of nodes in the network. Therefore, this property is generally defined for a finite, simple directed graph $\mathcal{D} = (\mathcal{V}, \mathcal{E})$. Without loss of generality, $\mathcal{V} = \{1, 2, \ldots, n\}$ is the set of nodes in the network and each directed edge $(i, j) \in \mathcal{E}$ indicates that node i is capable of transmitting information to node j. In this case, node i is an *in-neighbor* of node j and node j is an *out-neighbor* of node i. The set of in-neighbors of node i is denoted $\mathcal{N}_i^{\text{in}} = \{j \in \mathcal{V} : (j, i) \in \mathcal{E}\}$ and the *in-degree* of node i is denoted $d_i^{\text{in}} = |\mathcal{N}_i^{\text{in}}|$. In order to define network robustness, we require the following definition [7,9].

DEFINITION 1 ((r, s)-EDGE REACHABLE SET). *Given a nontrivial digraph $\mathcal{D}$ and a nonempty subset of nodes $\mathcal{S}$, we say that $\mathcal{S}$ is an (r, s)-edge reachable set if there are at least s nodes in $\mathcal{S}$ with at least r in-neighbors outside of $\mathcal{S}$, where $r, s \in \mathbb{Z}_{\geq 0}$; i.e., given $\mathcal{X}_{\mathcal{S}}^r = \{i \in \mathcal{S} : |\mathcal{N}_i^{\text{in}} \setminus \mathcal{S}| \geq r\}$, then $|\mathcal{X}_{\mathcal{S}}^r| \geq s$.*

A general illustration of an (r, s)-edge reachable set of nodes is shown in Figure 1. The parameter s in the definition of (r, s)-edge

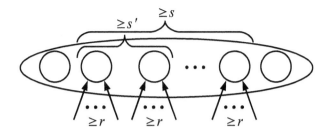

Figure 1: Illustration of an (r, s)-edge reachable set of nodes.

reachability quantifies a lower bound on the number of nodes in the set with at least r in-neighbors outside $\mathcal{S}$. Hence, the parameter r quantifies the redundancy of directed edges coming from outside and the parameter s quantifies the redundancy of nodes with sufficient outside influence.

Observe that, in general, a set is (r, s')-edge reachable, for $s' \leq s$, if it is (r, s)-edge reachable. At one extreme, whenever there are no nodes in $\mathcal{S}$ with at least r in-neighbors outside of $\mathcal{S}$, then $\mathcal{S}$ is only $(r, 0)$-edge reachable. At the other extreme, $\mathcal{S}$ can be at most $(r, |\mathcal{S}|)$-edge reachable. Edge reachability is used to define the global property of robustness [7,9].

DEFINITION 2 ((r, s)-ROBUSTNESS). *A nonempty, nontrivial digraph $\mathcal{D} = (\mathcal{V}, \mathcal{E})$ on n nodes ($n \geq 2$) is (r, s)-robust, for nonnegative integers $r \in \mathbb{Z}_{\geq 0}$, $1 \leq s \leq n$, if for every pair of nonempty, disjoint subsets $\mathcal{S}_1$ and $\mathcal{S}_2$ of $\mathcal{V}$ at least one of the following holds (recall $\mathcal{X}_{\mathcal{S}_k}^r = \{i \in \mathcal{S}_k : |\mathcal{N}_i^{\text{in}} \setminus \mathcal{S}_k| \geq r\}$ for $k \in \{1, 2\}$):*

(i) $|\mathcal{X}_{\mathcal{S}_1}^r| = |\mathcal{S}_1|$;

(ii) $|\mathcal{X}_{\mathcal{S}_2}^r| = |\mathcal{S}_2|$;

(iii) $|\mathcal{X}_{\mathcal{S}_1}^r| + |\mathcal{X}_{\mathcal{S}_2}^r| \geq s$.

By convention, if $\mathcal{D}$ is empty or trivial ($n \leq 1$), then $\mathcal{D}$ is $(0,1)$-robust. If $\mathcal{D}$ is trivial, $\mathcal{D}$ is also $(1,1)$-robust.[2]

Note that an $(r, 1)$-edge reachable set is abbreviated as r-edge reachable, and an $(r, 1)$-robust digraph is abbreviated as r-robust.

We adopt a total order for (r, s)-robustness that gives precedence to the r parameter in determining the relative robustness of a network. The maximal s in (r, s)-robustness is then used for ordering the robustness of two r-robust digraphs with the same value of r. The reason for adopting this convention is twofold. There are digraphs in which the parameter s may take on any value, and in such cases s loses its precise meaning. On the other hand, there are properties that show the utility of the parameter r in characterizing the robustness of a given digraph [8]. For example, the following properties provide the upper bound $r \leq \min\{\delta^{\text{in}}(\mathcal{D}), \lceil n/2 \rceil\}$ on the value of r for any digraph on n nodes, where $\delta^{\text{in}}(\mathcal{D})$ is the minimum in-degree of $\mathcal{D}$.

PROPERTY 1 (MAXIMUM ROBUSTNESS [8]). *No digraph $\mathcal{D}$ on n nodes is $(\lceil n/2 \rceil + 1)$-robust. Conversely, the complete digraph, denoted $K_n = (\mathcal{V}, \mathcal{E}_{K_n})$, with $\mathcal{E}_{K_n} = \{(i, j) \in \mathcal{V} \times \mathcal{V} : i \neq j\}$, is $(\lceil n/2 \rceil, s)$-robust, for $1 \leq s \leq n$. Furthermore, whenever $n > 1$ is odd, K_n is the only digraph on n nodes that is $(\lceil n/2 \rceil, s)$-robust with $s \geq \lfloor n/2 \rfloor$.*

---

[2] The trivial graph is defined to be both $(0,1)$-robust and $(1,1)$-robust for consistency with properties of robust networks for $n > 1$ [8].

PROPERTY 2 (MINIMUM IN-DEGREE [8]). *Given an (r, s)-robust digraph $\mathcal{D} = (\mathcal{V}, \mathcal{E})$, with $0 \leq r \leq \lceil n/2 \rceil$ and $1 \leq s \leq n$, the minimum in-degree of $\mathcal{D}$, $\delta^{in}(\mathcal{D})$, is at least*

$$\delta^{in}(\mathcal{D}) \geq \begin{cases} r + s - 1 & \text{if } s < r; \\ 2r - 2 & \text{if } s \geq r. \end{cases}$$

3. ALGORITHMS

3.1 Centralized Algorithms

In this section, we present centralized algorithms for checking and determining robustness. The direct manner to check a digraph to determine whether it is (r, s)-robust is a combinatorial problem. Because the sets in each pair considered are required to be nonempty and disjoint, the total number of pairs $R(n)$ that must be checked is

$$R(n) = \sum_{k=2}^{n} \binom{n}{k} \left(2^{k-1} - 1 \right), \tag{1}$$

where

- $n = |\mathcal{V}|$ is the number of nodes;

- each $k = 2, 3, \ldots, n$ in the sum is the size of the k-subsets of $\mathcal{V} = \{1, 2, \ldots, n\}$. Each k-subset of $\mathcal{V}$ is partitioned into exactly two nonempty parts, $\mathcal{S}_1$ and $\mathcal{S}_2$;

- $\binom{n}{k}$ is the number of k-subsets of $\{1, 2, \ldots, n\}$;

- $2^{k-1} - 1 = S(k, 2)$ is a Stirling number of the second kind, and is the number of ways to partition a k-set into exactly two nonempty unlabeled subsets (swapping the labels $\mathcal{S}_1$ and $\mathcal{S}_2$ results in the same pair)[3].

The form of (1) implies an algorithm for checking (r, s)-robustness of a digraph, *CheckRobustness*, which is shown in Algorithm 3.1. *CheckRobustness* takes as input values of r and s[4] and the adjacency matrix of the digraph, $A(\mathcal{D}) = [a_{ij}]$, which is defined by [4]

$$a_{ij} = \begin{cases} 1 & (i, j) \in E; \\ 0 & (i, j) \notin E. \end{cases}$$

CheckRobustness returns a Boolean variable indicating whether the digraph is (r, s)-robust along with a pair of sets with which the conditions fail. If the digraph is (r, s)-robust, the sets returned are empty sets. The algorithm iterates through all possible pairs of nonempty disjoint subsets, $\mathcal{S}_1, \mathcal{S}_2 \subset \mathcal{V}$, and checks conditions (i)-(iii) of Definition 2 using the adjacency matrix. To improve the performance on digraphs that fail the test, the algorithm returns the first pair that fails.

---

[3]The quantity may be argued directly by noticing that for each of the k elements, we have two choices: $\mathcal{S}_1$ or $\mathcal{S}_2$. But, we have to subtract the two sequences of choices resulting in $\mathcal{S}_1 = \emptyset$ or $\mathcal{S}_2 = \emptyset$. Finally, because the labels on the sets $\mathcal{S}_1$ and $\mathcal{S}_2$ are unimportant to the uniqueness of the nonempty partition, we divide by 2.

[4]Since all digraphs are 0-robust, and by Property 1 no digraph is r-robust with $r > \lceil n/2 \rceil$, it follows that one should only check $1 \leq r \leq \lceil n/2 \rceil, 1 \leq s \leq n$.

Algorithm 3.1: CHECKROBUSTNESS($A(\mathcal{D}), r, s$)

---

procedure ROBUSTHOLDS($A(\mathcal{D}), \mathcal{S}_1, \mathcal{S}_2, r, s$)
  $isRSRobust \leftarrow$ **false** , $s_{r,1} \leftarrow 0, s_{r,2} \leftarrow 0$
  for each $k \in \{1, 2\}$
  $\left\{ \begin{array}{l} \textbf{for each } i \in \mathcal{S}_k \\ \quad \left\{ \begin{array}{l} \textbf{if } \sum_{j \in \mathcal{N}_i^{in} \setminus \mathcal{S}_k} a_{ji} \geq r \\ \quad \textbf{then } s_{r,k} \leftarrow s_{r,k} + 1 \end{array} \right. \end{array} \right.$
  if $(s_{r,1} == |\mathcal{S}_1|)$ **or** $(s_{r,2} == |\mathcal{S}_2|)$ **or** $(s_{r,1} + s_{r,2} \geq s)$
    then $isRSRobust \leftarrow$ **true**
  return $(isRSRobust)$

main
  $isRSRobust \leftarrow$ **true**
  for $k \leftarrow 2$ **to** n
  $\left\{ \begin{array}{l} \textbf{for each } K_i \in \mathcal{K}_k \ (i = 1, 2, \ldots, \binom{n}{k}) \\ \textbf{comment: } \mathcal{K}_k \text{ is the set of } \binom{n}{k} \text{ unique } k\text{-subsets of } \mathcal{V} \\ \left\{ \begin{array}{l} \textbf{for each } P_j \in \mathcal{P}_{K_i} \ (j = 1, 2, \ldots, 2^{k-1} - 1) \\ \textbf{comment: } \mathcal{P}_{K_i} \text{ is the set of partitions of } K_i \\ \qquad \text{with exactly two nonempty parts} \\ \left\{ \begin{array}{l} \textbf{comment: } P_j = \{\mathcal{S}_1, \mathcal{S}_2\} \\ \textbf{if not } \text{ROBUSTHOLDS}(A(\mathcal{D}), \mathcal{S}_1, \mathcal{S}_2, r, s) \\ \quad \textbf{then } \left\{ \begin{array}{l} isRSRobust \leftarrow \textbf{false} \\ \textbf{return } (isRSRobust, \mathcal{S}_1, \mathcal{S}_2) \end{array} \right. \end{array} \right. \end{array} \right. \end{array} \right.$
  $\mathcal{S}_1 \leftarrow \emptyset, \mathcal{S}_2 \leftarrow \emptyset$
  return $(isRSRobust, \mathcal{S}_1, \mathcal{S}_2)$

The second algorithm, called *DetermineRobustness* (and given in Algorithm 3.2), determines (r, s)-robustness of *any* digraph, regardless of the number of components of the digraph. To do this, it requires the adjacency matrix $A(\mathcal{D})$ as input. *DetermineRobustness* first initializes r and s to the maximum values possible for any digraph on n nodes (see Properties 1 and 2). Then, as in *CheckRobustness*, *DetermineRobustness* iterates through all possible pairs of nonempty disjoint subsets, $\mathcal{S}_1, \mathcal{S}_2 \subset \mathcal{V}$, and checks conditions (i)-(iii) of Definition 2. In this case, instead of terminating upon a failing condition, the value of s is first decremented. Once all values of s are checked for the given value of r, the algorithm decrements r and restores s to its maximal value of n. If the digraph has no directed spanning tree (i.e., if it is not 1-robust), then *DetermineRobustness* returns $(r = 0, s = n)$. Using this approach, *DetermineRobustness* returns the maximal values r and s such that $\mathcal{D}$ is (r, s)-robust.[5]

It is clear from the form of $R(n)$ in (1) that these algorithms are not efficient. In fact, we show next that the algorithms are exponential in the square root of the size of the input (in this case, the adjacency matrix, which has size n^2). To analyze the complexity of the algorithms, we recall the following definition.

DEFINITION 3. *Given $f, g \colon \mathbb{R} \to \mathbb{R}$, then $f \in \mathcal{O}(g(x))$ if there exists $c \in \mathbb{R}_{>0}$ and $x_0 \in \mathbb{R}$ such that $|f(x)| \leq c|g(x)|$ for all $x \geq x_0$.*

We define the worst-case complexity of an algorithm as the maximal number of steps $T(m)$ required to complete the algorithm whenever the input is of size m. We say the worst-case complexity of an algorithm is $\mathcal{O}(g(m))$ if $T(m) \in \mathcal{O}(g(m))$.

---

[5]Recall from Section 2 that the total order on robustness compares the value of r first, and then compares the value of s for networks with the same r.

Algorithm 3.2: DETERMINEROBUSTNESS($A(\mathcal{D})$)

$r \leftarrow \min\{\delta^{\text{in}}(\mathcal{D}), \lceil n/2 \rceil\}$
comment: $\delta^{\text{in}}(\mathcal{D})$ is the minimum in-degree of $\mathcal{D}$

$s \leftarrow n$
for $k \leftarrow 2$ **to** n
  for each $K_i \in \mathcal{K}_k$ $(i = 1, 2, \ldots, \binom{n}{k})$
  comment: $\mathcal{K}_k$ is the set of $\binom{n}{k}$ unique k-subsets of $\mathcal{V}$

    for each $P_j \in \mathcal{P}_{K_i}$ $(j = 1, 2, \ldots, 2^{k-1} - 1)$
    comment: $\mathcal{P}_{K_i}$ is the set of partitions of K_i with exactly
          two nonempty parts
      comment: $P_j = \{\mathcal{S}_1, \mathcal{S}_2\}$

      $isRSRobust \leftarrow$ ROBUSTHOLDS($A(\mathcal{D}), \mathcal{S}_1, \mathcal{S}_2, r, s$)
      if ($isRSRobust ==$ **false**) **and** ($s > 0$)
        then $s \leftarrow s - 1$
      while ($isRSRobust ==$ **false**) **and** ($r > 0$)
        while ($isRSRobust ==$ **false**) **and** ($s > 0$)
          do $\begin{cases} isRSRobust \\ \quad \leftarrow \text{ROBUSTHOLDS}(A(\mathcal{D}), \mathcal{S}_1, \mathcal{S}_2, r, s) \\ \textbf{if not } isRSRobust \\ \quad \textbf{then } s \leftarrow s - 1 \end{cases}$
        do **if** ($isRSRobust ==$ **false**)
          then $\begin{cases} r \leftarrow r - 1 \\ s \leftarrow n \end{cases}$
      if $r == 0$
        then return (r, s)
return (r, s)

PROPOSITION 1. *Algorithms 3.1 and 3.2 have worst-case complexity $\mathcal{O}(m3^{\sqrt{m}})$ where $m = n^2$ is the size of the input (the adjacency matrix).*

PROOF. The procedure *RobustHolds* requires $\mathcal{O}(n^2)$ steps because $\mathcal{S}_k$ contains $\mathcal{O}(n)$ elements and the summation in the if-statement requires $\mathcal{O}(n)$ steps. In worst-case, there will be $R(n)$ calls to *RobustHolds* in Algorithm 3.1 and $R(n) + g(n)$ in Algorithm 3.2, where $g(n) \in \mathcal{O}(n^2)$ (since in Algorithm 3.2 there will be at most an additional $(\lceil n/2 \rceil - r)(n) + n - s$ calls to *RobustHolds* in an (r, s)-robust digraph caused by decrementing the values of r and s from their initial values). Therefore, in either case, there are $\mathcal{O}(R(n))$ calls to *RobustHolds*, and hence, $\mathcal{O}(n^2 R(n))$ steps in the worst case. Finally, to bound $R(n)$, we use the Binomial Theorem to obtain

$$
\begin{aligned}
R(n) &= \sum_{k=2}^{n} \binom{n}{k} (2^{k-1} - 1) \\
&\leq \sum_{k=2}^{n} \binom{n}{k} 2^k 1^{n-k} \\
&\leq \sum_{k=1}^{n} \binom{n}{k} 2^k 1^{n-k} \\
&\leq 3^n.
\end{aligned}
$$

Therefore, Algorithms 3.1 and 3.2 are $\mathcal{O}(m3^{\sqrt{m}})$, where $m = n^2$. $\square$

The complexity of Algorithms 3.1 and 3.2 are typical of any algorithm that determines the robustness of a network. This is because determining robustness is an NP-hard problem [16].

3.2 Network Model

The remaining algorithms operate in a decentralized manner in a time-invariant network. To model the network, we consider the undirected graph $\mathcal{G} = (\mathcal{V}, \mathcal{E})$, where $\mathcal{V} = \{1, \ldots, n\}$ is the *node set* and $\mathcal{E} \subset \binom{\mathcal{V}}{2}$ is the *edge set*. Each edge $\{i, j\} \in \mathcal{E}$ indicates that nodes i and j can exchange information. Each node $i \in \mathcal{V}$ is aware of its own identifier $i \in \mathcal{V}$ and its neighbor set $\mathcal{N}_i$. The diameter of the graph is denoted $diam$. Additionally, all nodes are normal; i.e., $\mathcal{V} = \mathcal{N}$. The network is assumed to be connected and fully synchronous with reliable communication. The execution of the distributed algorithm in the synchronous network progresses in rounds mapped to the nonnegative integers, $\mathbb{Z}_{\geq 0}$. We assume multiple messages may be sent in a given round and that messages may be of arbitrary size.

3.3 A Decentralized Algorithm

In this section, we present a decentralized algorithm for determining the robustness of a connected network. The main idea of the algorithm is for the nodes to share information about their neighborhood in such a way so that each node obtains the topological information about the network. Once this information is obtained, the centralized algorithm, *DetermineRobustness*, may be used to determine the robustness. The decentralized algorithm, *DecentralDetermineRobust* is shown in Algorithm 3.3. The algorithm uses several procedures: *LeaderElectBFSTree*, *InitiateConvergecast*, *ParticipateConvergecast*, *Broadcast*, *ParticipateBroadcast*, and *DetermineRobustness*.

The first procedure is *LeaderElectBFSTree*. *LeaderElectBFSTree* takes as input the node's ID and its neighbor set, and outputs a *leader* ID, a *parent* node, and a set of *children* nodes. *LeaderElectBFSTree* elects a leader in the network using parallel executions of Breadth-First Searches (BFSs) [10]. Each node initiates a modification of the *SynchBFS* algorithm of [10]. To do this, a calculation of the maximum ID is bootstrapped to the Breadth-First Search (BFS) tree construction. The node with the maximum ID is declared the leader, and the BFS tree with the leader as the root node is the BFS tree used in the subsequent convergecast and broadcast procedures.

Algorithm 3.3: DECENTRALDETERMINEROBUST($\text{ID}_i, \mathcal{N}_i$)

$(Leader, Par, Chldrn) \leftarrow$ LEADERELECTBFSTREE($\text{ID}_i, \mathcal{N}_i$)
if ($Leader == \text{ID}_i$)
  then $\begin{cases} A(\mathcal{G}) \leftarrow \text{INITIATECONVERGECAST}(\text{ID}_i, Chldrn) \\ \text{BROADCAST}(A(\mathcal{G}), Chldrn) \end{cases}$
  else $\begin{cases} \text{PARTICIPATECONVERGECAST}(\text{ID}_i, \mathcal{N}_i, Par, Chldrn) \\ A(\mathcal{G}) \leftarrow \text{PARTICIPATEBROADCAST}(Par, Chldrn) \end{cases}$
$(r, s) \leftarrow$ DETERMINEROBUSTNESS($A(\mathcal{G})$)
return (r, s)

In *LeaderElectBFSTree* all variables are associated to the initiating node's ID because n parallel executions run simultaneously. There are three types of messages involved in the BFS tree construction: *search*, *respond*, and *propagate* messages. The *search* message, with node i as the initiating node, contains the sending node's ID (initially i), the maximum ID seen so far (initially i), and the initiating node's ID (also i in the first round). Each node (other than i) is initially unmarked. Whenever an unmarked node receives a *search* message (or possibly multiple *search* messages from different neighbors), it becomes marked. The receiving node sets the maximum ID variable as the max of the received maximum

IDs and chooses one of the senders as its *parent*. It then sends a *respond* message to each neighbor from which it received a *search* message. The *respond* message contains its ID, a binary variable indicating whether the node was selected as *parent*, and the ID of the initiating node i. The next round, the marked node sends a *search* message to all of its neighbors to continue the construction of the BFS tree. Whenever a marked node receives a *respond* message, it checks to see if it is selected as the node's parent, and if so, it adds the node's ID to its *children* list. After each node sends its *search* message, it waits to receive all *respond* messages from neighbors. Once it receives all of its *respond* messages, it knows whether it is a leaf node in the BFS tree (i.e., if none of its neighbors selects it as *parent*). If a node is *not* a leaf node, it waits to receive *propagate* messages from all of its *children*. If it is a leaf node, it sends a *propagate* message to its *parent*, which contains the maximum ID it has seen. Once a non-leaf node receives *propagate* messages from all of its *children*, it takes the max of the maximum IDs and sends a *propagate* messages to its *parent*. Eventually, the initiating node i receives *propagate* messages from all of its *children* and then knows the maximum ID in the network. The node with the maximum ID asserts itself as the *leader*. The *parent* and *children* variables returned by *LeaderElectBFSTree* correspond to the node's *parent* and *children* in the BFS tree with the *leader* as the initiating node. If i is the leader, it selects itself as the parent (or the null symbol). *LeaderElectBFSTree* requires $\mathcal{O}(diam)$ rounds and $\mathcal{O}(diam|\mathcal{E}|)$ messages for each of the n parallel executions [10]. Hence, in total, *LeaderElectBFSTree* requires $\mathcal{O}(diam)$ rounds and $\mathcal{O}(n \times diam|\mathcal{E}|)$ messages.

Once *LeaderElectBFSTree* terminates, the leader node is determined and its BFS tree is constructed, which provides an efficient mechanism for convergecast and broadcast. In *DecentralDetermineRobust*, if node i is the leader, it initiates a convergecast using *InitiateConvergecast*. If node i is not the leader it participates in the convergecast using *ParticipateConvergecast*. *InitiateConvergecast* takes as input the leader's own node ID and the *children* list (which is just the neighbor set of the leader node). *ParticipateConvergecast* takes as input the node's own ID and its neighbor set, as well as the *parent* and *children* determined by *LeaderElectBFSTree*. In *InitiateConvergecast* and *ParticipateConvergecast*, there are two types of messages: *downstream* and *upstream* messages. *Downstream* messages are sent in the direction of leaf nodes, and *upstream* messages are sent in the direction of the *leader* (root) node. The leader node starts the convergecast by sending a *downstream* message containing its node ID and neighbor set to its children of the BFS tree constructed by *LeaderElectBFSTree*. Each node is initially unmarked and waits to receive a *downstream* message from its parent. Each *downstream* message contains a list of pairs, each containing a node ID and the neighbors of the node ID. Once a *downstream* message is received from its parent, the node becomes marked. The node adds it own node ID and neighbor set to the list of pairs, and sends this list in its *downstream* message to its children. Once the *downstream* message is sent, the node waits to receive *upstream* messages from all of its children. Whenever a leaf node receives its *downstream* message, it similarly adds its pair and sends the *upstream* message to its parents. The *upstream* messages are created by consolidating the neighbor lists in the *upstream* messages received from all of the node's children. Once the leader (root) node receives the *upstream* messages from its children, it can construct the adjacency matrix $A(\mathcal{G})$, which is the quantity returned in *InitiateConvergecast*. Once each non-leader node sends its *upstream* message, it begins its *ParticipateBroadcast* procedure. The convergecast procedure requires $\mathcal{O}(diam)$ rounds and $\mathcal{O}(|\mathcal{E}|)$ messages [10].

After the convergecast procedure terminates, the leader node has the adjacency matrix $A(\mathcal{G})$. It then initiates a broadcast using the BFS tree to provide the other nodes with the adjacency matrix. Each non-leader node waits for the adjacency matrix to arrive from its parent, and then relays the information to its children. Upon sending its message, the node then calls *DetermineRobustness* to obtain the values of r and s. The broadcast operation requires $\mathcal{O}(diam)$ rounds and $\mathcal{O}(|\mathcal{E}|)$ messages [10]. By combining the message and round complexity of the procedures in *DecentralDetermineRobust*, it follows that *DecentralDetermineRobust* requires $\mathcal{O}(diam)$ rounds and $\mathcal{O}(n \times diam|\mathcal{E}|)$ messages. Of course, *DecentralDetermineRobust* also inherits the worst-case complexity of *DetermineRobustness* given in Proposition 1.

3.4 A Distributed Algorithm

Here, we present a distributed algorithm for determining the robustness of a connected network. Instead of simply using the centralized algorithm, *DetermineRobustness*, after obtaining the adjacency matrix, as was done in Algorithm 3.3, in this case the computation required to determine robustness is reduced by only checking the edge reachability properties in subsets in which the node is *not* a member. The BFS tree construction is again used to elect a leader and provide an efficient means to broadcast information. In this algorithm, however, a second convergecast/broadcast sequence must be performed after the estimates of r and s are determined in order for the nodes to obtain the true values of r and s. *DistributedDetermineRobust* is given in Algorithm 3.4.

Algorithm 3.4: DISTRIBUTEDDETERMINEROBUST($\text{ID}_i, \mathcal{N}_i$)

$(Leader, Par, Chldrn) \leftarrow \text{LEADERELECTBFSTREE}(\text{ID}_i, \mathcal{N}_i)$
if $(Leader == \text{ID}_i)$
  then $\begin{cases} A(\mathcal{G}) \leftarrow \text{INITIATECONVERGECAST}(\text{ID}_i, Chldrn) \\ \text{BROADCAST}(A(\mathcal{G}), Chldrn) \end{cases}$
  else $\begin{cases} \text{PARTICIPATECONVERGECAST}(\text{ID}_i, \mathcal{N}_i, Par, Chldrn) \\ A(\mathcal{G}) \leftarrow \text{PARTICIPATEBROADCAST}(Par, Chldrn) \end{cases}$
$(\hat{r}, \hat{s}) \leftarrow \text{DETERMINEPARTIALROBUST}(A(\mathcal{G}), \text{ID}_i)$
if $(Leader == \text{ID}_i)$
  then $\begin{cases} (r, s) \leftarrow \text{INITIATECONVERGECAST2}(\hat{r}, \hat{s}, Chldrn) \\ \text{BROADCAST2}(r, s, Children) \end{cases}$
  else $\begin{cases} \text{PARTICIPATECONVERGECAST2}(\hat{r}, \hat{s}, Par, Chldrn) \\ (r, s) \leftarrow \text{PARTICIPATEBROADCAST2}(Par, Chldrn) \end{cases}$
return (r, s)

Before describing *DeterminePartialRobust*, we explain the difference in the second convergecast/broadcast sequence. In the second sequence, the nodes must determine the true values of r and s from their estimates. Therefore, the *downstream* and *upstream* messages of *InitiateConvergecast2* and *ParticipateConvergecast2* contain the minimum value of r seen along the downstream path, along with the minimum value of s seen for the given minimum value of r. For example, if a node's estimate is ($\hat{r} = 4, \hat{s} = 1$) and it receives a *downstream* message containing ($\hat{r} = 3, \hat{s} = 3$), then the pair sent in the next *downstream* message is ($\hat{r} = 3, \hat{s} = 3$). Similarly, once the downstream paths reach leaf nodes, the *upstream* messages are determined similarly. Once the leader node receives the *upstream* messages from its children, it can determine the true values of r and s. These values are used in the second broadcast.

DeterminePartialRobust is shown in Algorithm 3.5. Because the network is assumed to be connected, the network is at least 1-robust. Therefore, all subsets *not* including node i are always checked in *DeterminePartialRobust* when called from *Distributed-DetermineRobust* under the assumption of a connected network. Since decrementing r and s requires at most $\mathcal{O}(n^2)$ steps, this implies that all nodes will complete *DeterminePartialRobust* within $\mathcal{O}(n^2)$ steps of each other.

For the performance improvement of *DeterminePartialRobust*, observe that by eliminating the sets in which i is an element, *DeterminePartialRobust* effectively reduces the problem from size n to $n - 1$. That is, there are $R(n - 1)$ pairs of subsets to check in *DeterminePartialRobust*, instead of $R(n)$ pairs of subsets, as in *DetermineRobustness*. By using Pascal's Rule

$$\binom{n}{k} = \binom{n-1}{k} + \binom{n-1}{k-1},$$

we can show that the number of pairs of subsets that are avoided in *DeterminePartialRobust* is

$$R(n) - R(n-1) = \sum_{k=1}^{n-1} \binom{n-1}{k}(2^k - 1).$$

Notice that the number of pairs above is also the number of subsets in which i is a member. The difference between this number and $R(n - 1)$ is

$$n - 1 + \sum_{k=2}^{n-1} \binom{n-1}{k}(2^{k-1} + 1) > R(n-1)$$

Therefore, it is more than twice as efficient to check the subsets in which i is *not* a member rather than checking only subsets in which it *is* a member. However, the worst-case complexity of the algorithm is not improved. Also, the round and message complexity for rounds in which communication is needed coincide with the round and message complexity of the decentralized algorithm.

Algorithm 3.5: DETERMINEPARTIALROBUST$(A(\mathcal{D}), i)$

$r \leftarrow \min\{\delta^{\text{in}}(\mathcal{D}), \lceil n/2 \rceil\}$
comment: $\delta^{\text{in}}(\mathcal{D})$ is the minimum in-degree of $\mathcal{D}$

$s \leftarrow n$
for $k \leftarrow 2$ **to** $n - 1$
$\begin{cases} \textbf{for each } K_i' \in \mathcal{K}_k' \ (i = 1, 2, \ldots, \binom{n-1}{k}) \\ \textbf{comment: } \mathcal{K}_k' \text{ is the set of } \binom{n-1}{k} \text{ unique } k\text{-subsets of } \mathcal{V} \setminus \{i\} \\ \begin{cases} \textbf{for each } P_j' \in \mathcal{P}_{K_i}' \ (j = 1, 2, \ldots, 2^{k-1} - 1) \\ \textbf{comment: } \mathcal{P}_{K_i}' \text{ is the set of partitions of } K_i' \text{ with exactly} \\ \qquad\qquad \text{two nonempty parts} \\ \begin{cases} \textbf{comment: } P_j' = \{\mathcal{S}_1, \mathcal{S}_2\} \\ isRSRobust \leftarrow \text{ROBUSTHOLDS}(A(\mathcal{D}), \mathcal{S}_1, \mathcal{S}_2, r, s) \\ \textbf{if } (isRSRobust == \textbf{false}) \textbf{ and } (s > 0) \\ \quad \textbf{then } s \leftarrow s - 1 \\ \textbf{while } (isRSRobust == \textbf{false}) \textbf{ and } (r > 0) \\ \quad \textbf{do} \begin{cases} \textbf{while } (isRSRobust == \textbf{false}) \textbf{ and } (s > 0) \\ \quad \textbf{do} \begin{cases} isRSRobust \leftarrow \\ \quad \text{ROBUSTHOLDS}(A(\mathcal{D}), \mathcal{S}_1, \mathcal{S}_2, r, s) \\ \textbf{if not } isRSRobust \\ \quad \textbf{then } s \leftarrow s - 1 \end{cases} \\ \textbf{if } (isRSRobust == \textbf{false}) \\ \quad \textbf{then } \begin{cases} r \leftarrow r - 1 \\ s \leftarrow n \end{cases} \end{cases} \\ \textbf{if } r == 0 \\ \quad \textbf{then return } (r, s) \end{cases} \end{cases} \end{cases}$
return (r, s)

---

4. CONCLUSIONS

In this paper we have presented several algorithms for checking and determining the robustness of a network. We present two centralized algorithms, a decentralized algorithm, and a distributed one. All algorithms are inefficient; they are $\mathcal{O}(m3^{\sqrt{m}})$ in the size of the input. This is to be expected because the problem of determining the robustness of a network is NP-hard [16]. In order to improve on efficiency, one must consider approximate algorithms. We are currently investigating polynomial-time approximations that provide conservative estimates of the robustness of the network.

5. ACKNOWLEDGMENTS

This work has been supported in part by the National Science Foundation (CNS-1035655, CCF-0820088), the U.S. Army Research Office (ARO W911NF-10-1-0005), and Lockheed Martin. The views and conclusions contained herein are those of the authors and should not be interpreted as necessarily representing the official policies or endorsements, either expressed or implied, of the U.S. Government.

6. REFERENCES

[1] R. Albert and A. L. Barabási. Statistical mechanics of complex networks. *Rev. Mod. Phys.*, 74(1):47–97, Jan. 2002.

[2] S. Boyd, A. Ghosh, B. Prabhakar, and D. Shah. Randomized gossip algorithms. *IEEE Transactions on Information Theory*, 52(6):2508–2530, June 2006.

[3] D. Dolev. The Byzantine generals strike again. *Journal of Algorithms*, 3(1):14–30, 1982.

[4] C. Godsil and G. Royle. *Algebraic Graph Theory*. Springer-Verlag New York, Inc., 2001.

[5] S. Jaggi, M. Langberg, S. Katti, T. Ho, D. Katabi, and M. Medard. Resilient network coding in the presence of Byzantine adversaries. In *26th IEEE International Conference on Computer Communications, INFOCOM*, pages 616–624, Anchorage, AL, May 2007.

[6] D. Kempe, A. Dobra, and J. Gehrke. Gossip-based computation of aggregate information. In *44th Annual IEEE Symposium on Foundations of Computer Science*, pages 482–491, Cambridge, MA, Oct. 2003.

[7] H. J. LeBlanc. *Resilient Cooperative Control of Networked Multi-Agent Systems*. PhD thesis, Department of EECS, Vanderbilt University, 2012.

[8] H. J. LeBlanc, H. Zhang, X. D. Koutsoukos, and S. Sundaram. Resilient asymptotic consensus in robust networks. *To appear in IEEE Journal on Selected Areas in Communications, special issue on In-Network Computation: Exploring the Fundamental Limits*, 2013.

[9] H. J. LeBlanc, H. Zhang, S. Sundaram, and X. Koutsoukos. Consensus of multi-agent networks in the presence of adversaries using only local information. In *Proceedings of the 1st International Conference on High Confidence Networked Systems (HiCoNS)*, pages 1–10, Beijing, China, 2012.

[10] N. A. Lynch. *Distributed Algorithms*. Morgan Kaufmann Publishers Inc., San Francisco, California, 1997.

[11] F. Pasqualetti, A. Bicchi, and F. Bullo. Consensus computation in unreliable networks: A system theoretic approach. *IEEE Transactions on Automatic Control*, 57(1):90–104, Jan. 2012.

[12] W. Ren, R. W. Beard, and E. M. Atkins. Information consensus in multivehicle cooperative control. *IEEE Control Systems Magazine*, 27(2):71–82, April 2007.

[13] C. W. Reynolds. Flocks, herds and schools: A distributed behavioral model. *SIGGRAPH Comput. Graph.*, 21:25–34, August 1987.

[14] S. Sundaram and C. N. Hadjicostis. Distributed function calculation and consensus using linear iterative strategies. *IEEE Journal on Selected Areas in Communications*, 26(4):650–660, May 2008.

[15] S. Sundaram and C. N. Hadjicostis. Distributed function calculation via linear iterative strategies in the presence of malicious agents. *IEEE Transactions on Automatic Control*, 56(7):1495–1508, July 2011.

[16] H. Zhang and S. Sundaram. Robustness of complex networks with implications for consensus and contagion. *CoRR*, abs/1203.6119, 2012.

[17] H. Zhang and S. Sundaram. Robustness of information diffusion algorithms to locally bounded adversaries. In *Proceedings of the American Control Conference*, pages 5855–5861, Montréal, Canada, 2012.

S3A: Secure System Simplex Architecture for Enhanced Security and Robustness of Cyber-Physical Systems *

Sibin Mohan
Information Trust Institute
University of Illinois
Urbana IL 61802
sibin@illinois.edu

Stanley Bak
Dept. of Computer Science
University of Illinois
Urbana IL 61802
sbak2@illinois.edu

Emiliano Betti
System Programming
Research Group
University of Rome
"Tor Vergata", Rome
betti@sprg.uniroma2.it

Heechul Yun
Dept. of Computer Science
University of Illinois
Urbana IL 61802
heechul@illinois.edu

Lui Sha
Dept. of Computer Science
University of Illinois
Urbana IL 61802
lrs@illinois.edu

Marco Caccamo
Dept. of Computer Science
University of Illinois
Urbana IL 61802
mcaccamo@illinois.edu

ABSTRACT

The recently discovered 'W32.Stuxnet' worm has drastically changed the perception that systems managing critical infrastructure are invulnerable to software security attacks. Here we present an architecture that enhances the security of safety-critical cyber-physical systems despite the presence of such malware. Our architecture uses the property that control systems have deterministic (real-time) execution behavior to detect an intrusion within 0.6 μs while still guaranteeing the safety of the plant. We also show that even if an attacker is successful (or gains access to the operating system's administrative privileges), the overall state of the physical system still remains safe.

Categories and Subject Descriptors

D.4.7 [**Operating Systems**]: Organization and Design—*Real-Time Systems and Operating Systems; Cyber-Physical Systems; Safety-Critical Systems*; D.4.6 [**Operating Systems**]: Security and Protection—*Intrusion Detection*

Keywords

Real-Time Systems, Intrusion Detection, Cyber-Physical Systems, Stuxnet, Safety-Critical Systems, Secure Simplex, S3A.

1. INTRODUCTION

Many systems that have safety-critical requirements such as power plants, industry automation systems, automobiles, *etc.* can

---

*This work is supported in part by a grant from Rockwell Collins, by a grant from Lockheed Martin, by NSF CNS 06-49885 SGER, NSF CCR 03-25716 and by ONR N00014-05-0739. Opinions, findings, conclusions or recommendations expressed here are those of the authors and do not necessarily reflect the views of sponsors.

be classified as cyber-physical systems (CPS) – *i.e.* a tight combination of, and co-ordination between, computational and physical components. These systems (or parts of them) have stringent safety requirements and require deterministic operational guarantees (including real-time properties). Such systems have also traditionally been considered to be extremely secure since they *(a)* are typically not connected to the Internet; *(b)* use specialized protocols and proprietary interfaces ('security through obscurity') *(c)* are physically inaccessible to the outside world and *(d)* typically have their control code executing on custom hardware such as specialized processors or programmable logic controllers (PLCs). This misconception of ironclad security, however, has recently been exposed when the '*W32.Stuxnet*' worm [1] targeted and successfully infiltrated a Siemens WinCC/PCS7 control system [7]. Not only did it bypass all the security (digital/physical) techniques but it also reprogrammed the PLC that controlled the main system and *caused physical damage to the system.*

In this paper, we specifically address the problem of security for physical control systems with real-time requirements. Compared to general-purpose techniques, our work is different in that we focus on domain-specific characteristics of these systems and in particular, their *deterministic real-time nature*. We introduce a system architecture where an isolated and trusted hardware component is leveraged to enhance the security of the complete system. We present a novel intrusion detection mechanism that monitors context-specific side channels on the main CPU and in our initial prototype we use the *deterministic execution profile* of the system for this purpose [2].

Hence, we present the *Secure System Simplex Architecture* (S3A) to improve the security of cyber-physical systems that uses a combination of *(i)* knowledge of high-level control flow *(ii)* a *secure co-processor* implemented on an FPGA [3] *(iii)* deterministic execution time profiles and *(iv)* System Simplex [2, 21]. S3A detects intrusions that modify execution times by as low a value as $0.6\mu s$ on our test control system. With S3A, we expand the definition of 'correct system state' to include not just the physical state of the plant but also the *cyber state, i.e.* the state of the computer/PLC that executes the controller code. This type of security is hard for

---

[1] henceforth referred to as just 'Stuxnet'

[2] We elaborate on other potential side-channels in Sections 5.3 and 9.

[3] Can be a trusted processor/unwritable FPGA in the final implementation

an attacker to overcome by reverse engineering the code or the system especially since it involves *absolutely no changes to the source code/binary*. Even if an infection occurs and all of the security mechanisms are side-stepped (such as gaining access to the administrative privileges or the replication of our benevolent side channels), the trusted hardware component (secure co-processor) and the robust Simplex mechanism will still prevent the physical system from coming to harm, even from threats such as Stuxnet. Sections 4 and 5 present the details about our solution.

It is important to note that S3A is a *system-level solution that integrates multiple different solutions* to achieve security and safety in this domain. While we picked some mechanisms (execution time, Simplex, *etc.*), other concepts (Section 8) can be integrated to make the system that more secure and robust.

As the **main contribution** of this paper, we present the *Secure System Simplex Architecture* (S3A) where,

1. A **trusted hardware component** provides oversight over an untrusted real-time embedded control platform. The design provides a guarantee of plant safety in the event of successful infections. Even if an attacker gains administrative/root privileges she cannot inflict much harm since S3A ensures that the overall system (especially the physical plant) will not be damaged.

2. We investigate and use **context-dependent side channels for intrusion detection**, monitored by the trusted hardware component. They qualitatively increase the difficulty faced by potential attackers. Typically side-channel communication is used to break security techniques but we use them to our advantage in S3A. In this paper, we focus on side-channels in the context of CPU-controlled real-time embedded control systems as explained in Section 5.

3. We build and evaluate an **S3A prototype** for an inverted pendulum plant and discuss implementation efforts and the construction of side channel detection mechanism for *execution time-based side channels* using and FPGA in the role of the trusted hardware component. The side channel approach is shown to detect intrusions significantly faster than earlier plant-state-only detection approaches. This is explained in Section 5.4.

Further information on background, threat models, *etc.* is provided in Sections 2, 3 and Section 4

While intrusion detection is a broad area in computer security, our approach takes advantage of the real-time properties specific to embedded control systems. Also, most of the existing side-channel techniques/information (timing, memory, *etc.*) have traditionally been used to break the security of systems. This paper proposes a method so that these pieces of information are now used for *increasing* the security of the system. Also, such techniques have not been used before with the perspective of safety-critical control systems – hence we believe that this paper's contributions are novel.

We believe that our approach is generalizable to PLC and microcontroller-based CPS. Our justification is twofold; such systems *(i)* have stringent requirements for correct operation, *i.e.* the physical state of the plant must be kept safe under all conditions and *(ii)* often require the controller process to be deterministic.

Assumptions:

Important assumptions for the work presented in this paper are: *(a)* the system consists of a set of periodic, *real-time* tasks with stringent timing and deadline constraints managed by a real-time scheduler; such systems typically do not exhibit complex control flow, do not use dynamically allocated data structures, do not contain loops with unknown upper bounds, don't use function pointers, *etc.* – in

fact, they are often designed/developed with simplicity and determinism in mind *(b)* the hardware component must be trusted and can only be accessed by authorized personnel/engineers – this is not unlike the RSA encryption mechanism where the person holding the private key must be trusted *(c)* while we use an FPGA for a prototype implementation, the final hardware component could be implemented on an ASIC or custom processor or even an FPGA with its programmability turned off to prevent further tampering *(d)* the systems we describe are rarely updated and definitely not in a remote fashion (unlike, say, mobile embedded devices)[4].

Note: Our techniques are not specific to attacks mentioned in this paper (especially those in Section 2) and tackles the broader class of security breaches of controllers in safety-critical CPS.

2. MOTIVATION

Many control systems attached to critical infrastructure have traditionally been assumed to be extremely secure. The chief concern in such systems is *safety*, *i.e.* to ensure that the plant's operations remain within a predefined safety envelope. "Security" was attained by restricting access to such systems – no connection to the Internet and only a few people could access the computers that controlled these systems. Also, parts (or even all) of the control code executed on dedicated hardware (PLCs for instance).

2.1 Stuxnet

The *W32.Stuxnet* worm attack [7] overturned all of the above assumptions. It showed that industrial control systems could now be targeted by malicious code and that *not even hardware-based controllers were safe*. Stuxnet employed a really sophisticated attack mechanism that took control of the industrial automation system executing on a PLC. It took control of the system and operated it according to the attacker's design. It was also able to *hide these changes from the designers/engineers who operate the system*. To achieve these results, Stuxnet utilized a large number of complex methods the most notable of which was the *first known PLC rootkit*. In fact, Stuxnet was present on the infected systems for a long time before it was detected – perhaps even a few months. In this section we will focus on the real target of Stuxnet – the control code that manages the plants and the implications of such an attack.

Stuxnet had the ability to *(a)* monitor blocks that were exchanged between the PLC and computer, *(b)* infect the PLC by replacing legitimate blocks with infected ones and *(c)* hide the infection from designers. The PLCs are used to communicate with and control 'frequency converter drives' that manage the frequency of a variety of motors. The malicious code in the infected PLC affects the operational frequency of these motors so that they now operate outside their safety ranges. *E.g.*, in one instance, the frequency of a motor was set to 1410 Hz, then 2 Hz and then to 1604 Hz and the sequence is repeated – the normal operating frequency for this motor is between 807 Hz and 1210 Hz. Hence, in this instance, Stuxnet's actions can result in *real physical harm to the system*.

Note: Our focus is not on preventing the original intrusion or providing mechanisms to safeguard the Windows machines that are infected. We intend to detect the infection of the control code (on a PLC in this example, but could be any computer that runs it) and mainly safeguard the physical system from coming to harm.

2.2 Automotive Attack Surfaces and Other Examples

Researchers from the University of Washington demonstrated how a modern automobile's safety can be compromised by ma-

---

[4]See Section 4 for details.

licious attackers [4, 13]. They show how an attacker is able to circumvent the rudimentary security protections in modern automobiles and infiltrate virtually any electronic control unit (ECU) in the vehicle and compromise safety-critical systems (that have stringent real-time properties) such as disabling the brakes, stopping the engine, selectively braking individual wheels on demand, *etc.* – all of this, while ignoring the driver's inputs/actions. They were able to achieve this due to the vulnerabilities in the CAN bus protocols used in many modern vehicles. The attackers also show how malicious code can be embedded within the car's telematics unit that will completely erase itself after causing the crash.

There have been numerous other attacks that infiltrated critical systems *e.g.* wastewater treatment plants [1], NRG generation plants [17], medical devices [14], *etc.*

2.3   Discussion

As these examples show, safety-critical systems can no longer be considered to be safe from security breaches. While the development of cyber security techniques can help alleviate such problems, the real concern is for the control systems and physical plants that can be seriously damaged – often resulting in the crippling of critical infrastructure. Hence, we propose *non-traditional intrusion detection and recovery mechanisms* to tackle such problems. We use to our advantage the fact that the control codes running in a real-time system tend to be deterministic in behavior, simple to implement and exhibit strict timing properties. In fact, our techniques, if used on the above systems, could have gone a long way in mitigating (or at least quickly detecting) the attacks.

For the rest of this paper, we will show how such intrusions can be detected and the harmful effects mitigated by use of our *Secure System Simplex Architecture* (S3A). Hence, *our aim is to identify, as quickly as possible, that an infection has taken place and then ensure that the system (and its physical components) are always safe.* **Note:** as stated in the introduction, our work does not aim to prevent the original infections since that is a large problem that requires the development and implementation of multiple levels of cyber security techniques/research. We focus on the aftermath of the infection of control codes.

3.   THREAT MODEL

We deliberately will not delve too deeply into specific threat models, since we believe that our techniques will work well for a broad class of attacks that modify the execution behavior of embedded code in safety-critical systems. Attacks similar to those in Section 2 can be caught by the mechanisms presented in this paper. Hence, code could be injected by any of the mechanisms described in that section – as long as the malicious entity tries to execute *any new code* on the control side, we will be able to detect it. Hence, our threat model [12] is quite broad and can detect attacks such as: *(a) physical attacks*, i.e. code injected via infected/malicious hardware; *(b) memory attacks* where attackers try to inject malicious code into the system and/or take over existing code; *(c) in-*

sider attacks where the attackers try to gain control of the application/system by altering all or part of the program at runtime.

We will, instead, focus on what happens *after* attackers perform any of the above actions in order to execute their code. Hence, we intend to show how our architecture is able to quickly detect this and keep the system(s) safe particularly the physical systems. Since we don't care much about *what* executes and are more concerned with *how long* something executes, our "malicious entity" is a little more abstract as explained later in Sections 5.4.4 and 6.2.

4.   SYSTEM SIMPLEX OVERVIEW

The Simplex Architecture [21] utilizes the idea of *using simplicity to control complexity* in order to safely use an untrusted subsystem in a safety-critical control system. A Simplex system, shown in Figure 1, consists of three main components: *(a)* under normal operating conditions the `Complex Controller` actuates the plant; this controller has high performance characteristics and is typically unverifiable due to its complexity; *(b)* if, during this process, the system state becomes in danger of violating a safety condition, the `Safety Controller` takes over; *(c)* the exact switching behavior is implemented within a `Decision Module`. The Simplex architecture has been used to improve the safety of remote-controlled cars [5], pacemakers [2] and advanced avionics systems [19]. Early Simplex designs had all three subsystems located in software – at the application-level. This was updated in *System-Level* Simplex [2] by performing hardware/software partitioning on the system where the safety controller and the decision module are moved to a dedicated processing unit (an FPGA) that is different from the the microprocessor running the complex controller. We leverage this partitioning technique in S3A.

Untrusted Controllers: It is not that designers wish to use unverified (or untrusted) controllers in such systems. Most controllers that are intended to manage anything but the simplest of systems are typically complex and hard to verify. This is especially true if they must also achieve high levels of performance. Hence, there could be bugs and/or potential vulnerabilities in the system that attackers could exploit. Even if we assume that the controller is completely trusted, it can still be compromised (case in point – Stuxnet reprogrammed the controller in the PLC). Our technique can protect against any such intrusion, be it in trusted or untrusted controllers.

System Upgrades: Another issue is what happens if the system must be updated and that process either *(a)* breaks the safety and timing properties of the system or *(b)* introduces malicious code. This is particularly important if such updates were to happen in a remote fashion. While these would be serious issues in most general-purpose or even mobile embedded systems (*e.g.* cell phones), it is not a problem for safety-critical systems since the Simplex architecture has been shown to support upgrades to the complex controllers [20] in a safe manner. Also such systems are rarely updated, if at all. Any potential updates will have the following properties: *(1)* they are never performed remotely and carried

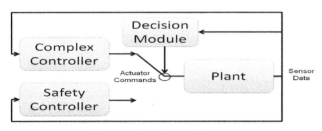

Figure 1: Simplex Architecture

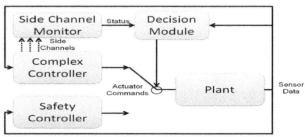

Figure 2: S3A Architecture

out by trusted engineers; *(2)* most updates are minor in that they only tune certain parameters and rarely, if at all, modify the control/timing structure of the code – hence they will not even modify the safety properties of the system and *(3)* major changes, if any, will require extensive redesign, testing, *etc.* – hence the real-time properties of the system must then be re-analyzed anyways.

Discussion: Our application of Simplex in S3A, in this paper, has several significant differences compared with earlier approaches. In the past, the primary motivation to use Simplex was to aid in the verification of complex systems. In this work, we instead apply Simplex to protect against malware that has infected the complex controller. Another key difference is that previously the decision module's behavior was determined completely by the physical state of the plant. In this work, we widen the scope of the "correct state" by using side channels from the computational part of the system, such as the timing properties of executing real-time tasks, in order to determine when to perform the switching. The Simplex decision module is now monitoring *both*, the physical system as well as the cyber state of the computational system.

5. INTEGRATED FRAMEWORK FOR SECURITY: SECURE SYSTEM SIMPLEX ARCHITECTURE (S3A)

We now present the *Secure System Simplex Architecture* (S3A) that prevents damage to safety-critical systems and also aids in rapid detection of malicious intrusions through side-channel monitoring. We first elaborate on the high-level logical framework of the architecture. We then discuss aspects of the execution time-based side channels that we have implemented in our S3A prototype and then follow it up with details on how to implement such a system – from the hardware aspects to the OS modifications; from the timing measurements to the control system that we use to show the effectiveness of our approach.

5.1 High Level Architecture

Figure 2 provides a high level overview of the system architecture. There is a `Complex Controller` that computes the control logic under normal operations. The computed actuation command is sent to the plant and sensor readings are produced and given to the controller to enable feedback control. There is also a `Decision Module` and `Safety Controller` in this architecture that are used not only to prevent damage to the plant in case of controller code bugs (as with the traditional Simplex applications) but also to prevent plant damage in the case of malicious actuation from attackers. We also have a `Side Channel Monitor` that examines the execution of the complex controller for changes in 'expected' behavior (in this paper it monitors the execution time of the complex controller to see if there is any deviation from what is expected). If the information obtained via the side channels differs from the expected model(s) of the system, the decision module is informed and control is switched to the safety controller (and an alarm can be raised). The types of side channels we can consider in a CPU-based embedded system include the execution time profiles of tasks, the number of instructions executed, the memory footprint and usage pattern or even the external communication pattern of the task. We will discuss timing side channels in more detail in the Section 5.2 and elaborate on the viability of the others in Sections 5.3 and 9.

This approach is qualitatively more difficult to attack than a typical control system. An attacker not only has to compromise the main system, but she also has to replicate all side channels that are currently being monitored. If the execution time is being monitored

then the attacker must replicate the timing profile of a correctly-functioning system. If the cycle count is being observed, her code must also execute for a believable number of instructions. Even if all the side channels match the expected models, the Decision Module will still monitor the plant state and, when malicious actuation occurs, prevent system damage.

The effectiveness of the side channel early-detection methodology depends on two factors. First, the constructed model of each side channel should restrict valid system behavior (not easily replicable). Second, the side channel itself must be secure (not easily forgeable). These factors are implementation specific and will be discussed later in Section 5.4.

5.2 Timing Side Channels

In this paper, we intend to secure a real-time embedded system. Therefore, we assume that the system has typical real-time characteristics, *i.e.* the system is divided into a set of periodic tasks managed by a real-time scheduler. Each task has a *known execution time* and each task periodically activates a job.

The monitoring module maintains a precise timing model of the system. Violations of this model occur when a job's, *(i)* execution time is too large; *(ii)* execution time is too small; *(iii)* activation period is too large or *(iv)* activation period is too small.

The monitoring module also needs to examine the execution of the *idle task*. This prevents a malicious attacker from allowing the real-time task to execute normally and perform malicious activity during idle time. Finally, the monitoring module should monitor the system activities that may result in timing perturbations.

In our prototype, we *monitor the control task* and the *idle task*. For rapid prototype development, we eliminate system noise (disable interrupts) while our control task is running to obtain a predictable timing environment[5] rather than patching system interrupts in order to receive their timing information. In an actual real-time system interrupts would be predictable and scheduled deterministically – hence we would be able to monitor them as well as the tasks. This addition could be made to our prototype in the future.

Execution times of the various real-time tasks in such systems are anyways obtained as part of system design by a variety of methods [22]. There is no extra effort that we have to perform to obtain this information. The worst-case, best-case and average-case behavior for most real-time systems is calculated ahead of time to ensure that all resource and schedulability requirements will be met during system operation. We use this knowledge of execution profiles to our advantage in S3A.

5.3 Other Potential Time-based Side Channels

In the assumed context of predictable real-time embedded control systems, several other side channels are available as part of the cyber state such as *task activation periodicity, memory footprint, bus access times and durations, scheduler events, etc..* Each of these is a candidate for *benevolent side-channels* that can be monitored to detect infections and would have to be individually replicated by an attacker to maintain control in an infected system, thus qualitatively increasing the difficulty for such actions.

Additionally, the specific side channels used may vary depending on the type of system. Here, we focus on CPU-based real-time control systems. Other systems, *e.g.* PLC-based ones, would likely need to either monitor the side channels using different methods or utilize a completely different (or additional) sets of side channels.

---

[5]Details in Section 5.4.5.

5.4 Implementation

We now describe a prototype implementation of S3A that we have created. The technical details of the prototype are listed in Table 1. We elaborate on key aspects of our implementation in detail: first, a hardware component overview is provided in Section 5.4.1. Then, the inverted pendulum hardware (our example 'safety-critical control system') setup is described in Section 5.4.2. The methodology for timing measurements of the control code is described in Section 5.4.3 and the methodology for timing-variability ('malicious code') tests is presented in Section 5.4.4. Section 5.4.5 gives essential details about the operating system setup during the measurements. Finally, Section 5.4.6 describes the specific design of the Decision Module and the timing Side Channel Monitor.

Component	Details
Inverted Pendulum	Quanser IP01
FPGA	Xilinx ML505
Computer with Controller	Intel Quad core 2.6 GHz
Operating System	Linux kernel ver. 2.6.36
Timing Profile	Intel Timestamp Counter (rdtsc)

Table 1: S3A Prototype Implementation Details

5.4.1 Hardware Components

A high-level hardware design of our prototype is shown in Figure 3. The prototype hardware instantiates the logical Secure System Simplex architecture previously described in Section 5 and shown in Figure 2. In our implementation, we run the complex controller on the main CPU. The Complex Controller communicates with a trusted hardware component, an FPGA in this case, to perform control of an inverted pendulum. Sensor readings are obtained by the FPGA over the PCIe bus using memory mapped I/O. The actuation command, in turn, is written to the memory-mapped region on the FPGA. Additionally, timing messages in the form of memory-mapped writes are periodically sent to the FPGA based on the state of execution (at the start/end of the control task and periodically during the Idle Task). This creates a timing side channel that can be observed by a timing channel monitor running on the FPGA. On the FPGA side, the timing channel monitor will measure the time elapsed between timing messages from the complex controller to ensure that the execution conforms to an expected timing model. The decision module will periodically examine the output of the Timing Channel Monitor, the actuation command from sent by the Complex Controller from shared memory on the FPGA, the actuation command from the locally-running safety controller and the state of the plant from a 'sensor and actuator interface' and decide which controller's actuation command should be used – the complex one on the CPU or the safe one on the FPGA. The actuation command is then output back to the Sensor and Actuator Interface.

The interface then, through a digital-to-analog converter, actuates the plant – in our case, an inverted pendulum. The Sensor and Actuator Interface also periodically acquires sensor readings through analog-to-digital converters and write their values to both shared memory accessible by the Complex Controller and to memory accessible by the trusted Decision Module and Safety Controller.

5.4.2 Inverted Pendulum

We used an inverted pendulum (IP) as the plant that was being controlled. An IP (e.g. Figure 4) is a classic real-time control challenge where a rod must be maintained in an upright position by moving a cart attached to the bottom of the IP along a one-dimensional track. It has two sensors (to measure the current pendulum angle and the cart position on the track) and one actuator (the motor near the base of the pendulum) used to move the cart. Two safety invariants must be met: (1) the pendulum must remain upright (can not fall over) and (2) the cart must remain near the center of the track. The specific inverted pendulum we used in our testbed was based on the Quanser IP01 linear control challenge [9].

Our setup varies slightly from an off-the-shelf Quanser IP01 as follows: we need to directly connect the sensors and actuators to the FPGA; the prebuilt setup requires a computer to do the data acquisition. We modified the system to redirect the sensor values and motor commands through an Arduino Uno microcontroller that communicates directly with the S3A FPGA through a serial cable. Although this may introduce latency into the system, we did not observe any issues with safely actuating the pendulum due to this small delay. The control code that manages the IP executes on a computer (Section 5.4.5 and Table 1) at a frequency of 50 Hz.

Note: The IP has been used quite extensively in literature as an appropriate example of a real-time control system [2,21]. Hence we believe it demonstrates an early prototype (and proof-of-concept) of our solutions. We are currently working on applying these techniques to other real control systems in conjunction with industry.

5.4.3 Timing

The implementation of the complex controller for the inverted pendulum is fairly simple with very few branches and most loops being statically decidable[6]. Hence it is fairly easy to calculate the execution time and number of instructions taken for such code. In our framework, we utilized simple dynamic timing analysis [22] methods to obtain an *execution profile* of the code. We used the Intel *time stamp counter* (rdtsc) [10] to obtain high resolution execution time measurements for the control code.

The control code was placed in a separate function and called in a loop. As part of our experiments, the loop was executed $1, 10, 100, 1,000, 10,000, 100,000$ and $1,000,000$ times on the actual computer where it would execute and measuring each set of executions. During each of these scenarios, the total time of the loop as well as the times taken up during each individual iteration

---

[6]This is typical of most control code in safety-critical and real-time control systems – hence our implementation of the controller for the inverted pendulum is also similar.

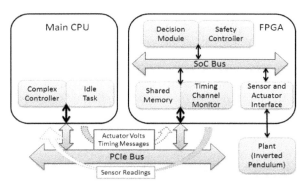

Figure 3: S3A Implementation Overview

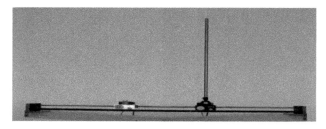

Figure 4: An inverted pendulum control system

was measured. From these traces we were able to determine the maximum (worst-case), minimum (best-case) and steady-case values for the execution time of the controller code. 'Steady-case' refers to the values obtained when the execution time has stabilized over multiple, repeated executions – *i.e.* when the initial cold cache related timing dilation at the start of the experiments no longer occur. To reduce the noise from instrumentation and overheads of the loops, function calls, *etc.* we used the 'dual-loop timing' method: *i.e.*, empty loops with only the measurement instrumentation were timed as a 'control' experiment. The execution times obtained for these instrumentation-only loops were subtracted from the execution times for the loops with the control code. While we used simple measurement-based schemes for obtaining the execution profile in this paper, it does not preclude the use of more sophisticated techniques [16, 22] to obtain better (and safer) timing estimates. This is especially true if the code is more complex than the one for the inverted pendulum. In fact, the better the estimation methods, the better S3A will be able to detect anomalies and intrusions.

Interrupts (all interrupts including inter-processor ones) were disabled during timing measurements. To reduce the effects of the operating system and other system issues we isolated our controller as best as we could as we will describe in Section 5.4.5.

5.4.4 Execution Time Variation

To mimic the effect of code modification on timing, we insert extra code into the execution of the control loop function described above. Specifically, the extra code is a loop with a varying upper bound (*i.e.* 1, 10, 100) that performs multiple arithmetic operations (floating point and integer). The idea is that the extra instructions that execute will make it look like an intrusion has taken place. Our S3A system will then detect the additional execution, raise an alarm and transfer control to the simple controller on the FPGA.

Note: As mentioned before, we are less interested in what kind of code executes "maliciously" because our detection does not depend on this detail. We only need to check whether whatever is executing has modified the timing profile of the system.

5.4.5 System and OS Setup

We used an off-the-shelf multi-core platform running Linux kernel 2.6.36 for our experiments (Table 1). Since we use a COTS system, there are many potential sources of timing noise such as cache interference, interrupts, kernel threads and other processes that must be removed for our measurements to be meaningful. In this section we describe the configuration we used to best emulate a typical uni-processor embedded real-time platform.

The CPU we used is an Intel Q6700 chip that has four cores and each pair of cores shares a common level two (last level) cache. We divided the four cores into two partitions: **1.** the *system partition* running on the first pair of cores (sharing one of the two L2 caches) handles all interrupts for non-critical devices (e.g., the keyboard) and runs all the operating system activities and non real-time processes (*e.g.*, the shell we use to run the experiments); **2.** the *real-time partition* runs on the second pair of cores (sharing the second L2 cache). One core in the real-time partition runs our real-time tasks together with the driver for the trusted FPGA component; the other core is turned off so that we avoid L2 cache interference among these two cores.

5.4.6 Detection

In our system, detection of malicious code can occur in one of two ways. The decision module observes both *(i)* the physical state of the plant (by traditional Simplex) as well as *(ii)* the computation state of the system (based on timing messages; S3A). A violation of the physical model or the computational model can trigger the decision module to transfer control to the safety controller on the FPGA. Based on a function of the track position and pendulum angle (the physical model), the decision module may choose to switch over to the safety controller [2, 21].

The computational system is monitored for violations of expected timing model of the system. Both, the control task as well as the idle task, are monitored in order to periodically send timing messages to the FPGA that contains an *expected timing model of the system as a finite state machine* (FSM) *running in hardware*. When timing messages arrive (or timers expire) the FSM advances. If malicious code were to execute, it would have a limited window of time to replicate the timing side channel before it was detected by the decision module.

Generally speaking, monitoring the timing progress of a real-time system can be performed by maintaining state about each task in the system. A task has two timers associated with it: **(I)** the first would enforce the execution time of the task and **(II)** the second will monitor periodic activation of the task. A stack is used to track task preemptions. Since typical real-time systems use priority-based execution, all task switches are directly observable by the FPGA through task start/task end messages.

For our specific prototype, we implemented the finite state machine (Figure 5), in hardware, on an FPGA. Our system contains two tasks: *(i)* the idle task and *(ii)* the controller task. Since only one task may be preempted (the idle task), we maintain a single variable as the call stack, $state_I$. Three timers are used: clk_C and clk_P maintain the execution time and period of the control task while clk_I maintains the execution of the idle task. In Figure 5, clk_C ticks while the control task is running (states C_1 and C_2) and clk_I ticks while the idle task is executing (states I_1 and I_2). Clk_P always ticks. The FSM is parameterized with six values: MustWait$_C$, CanWait$_C$, MustWait$_I$, CanWait$_I$, MustWait$_P$, and CanWait$_P$. These values are determined by the minimum and maximum time permitted between timing messages. The Must-Wait time indicates the minimum time that must elapse, whereas the CanTime indicates the jitter permitted between different iterations of the loop. Hence, MustWait is the minimum execution time of the task/idle loop/period whereas (MustWait + CanTime) is the maximum execution time.

In the FSM, initially the control task is running. State C_1 is entered and continued in until clk_C ticks from MustWait$_C$ to 0. Then state C_2 is entered. If clk_C ticks from CanWait$_C$ to 0 without the end task message then the control task has executed for too long and a timing violation occurs (indicated by dotted arrow in state C_2). Once the end control task message is received, the idle task begins to execute. Under normal operation, the state changes between I_1 and I_2 several times, until the control task is reactivated and state C_1 is again entered. Any messages that arrive without explicit tran-

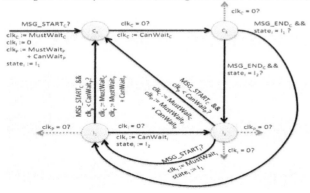

Figure 5: FSM for Detecting Timing Model Violations

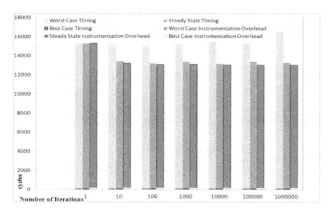

Figure 6: Summary of the Timing Results

sitions in the FSM are interpreted as errors in the prototype and trigger the decision module to switch to the safety controller. Additionally, dotted transitions in the FSM are timing violations that also trigger the decision module to take corrective action.

The FSM can also be used to tightly track the execution behavior of the code for more sophisticated controllers, *e.g.* if the code has many branches, function calls, *etc.* For instance, when the control code reaches a branch that affects the overall execution time, a message can be sent to the FSM about which side of the branch was taken. The FSM can now use this information to accurately track the execution of the program for all control constructs in the code.

6. EVALUATION

We now present an evaluation of S3A – Sections 6.1 and 6.2 present timing results obtained by analysis of the controller code – these values form the profile of the execution behavior used in the intrusion detection mechanism on the FPGA. Section 6.3 presents the details of the intrusion detection.

6.1 Timing Results and Execution Profile

Figure 6 presents a high level summary of the timing results used to obtain the execution profile of the complex controller code (Figure 2). We used dynamic/run-time timing analysis techniques to obtain the worst, best and steady state execution times for this code. The x-axis represents the number of times the controller code was repeatedly executed: from 1 to $1,000,000$ in steps of 10. The y-axis represents the execution time in *cycles*. Each grouping of vertical lines represents the 'worst-case', 'steady-state' and 'best-case' execution times for that experiment. 'Steady-state' refers to the execution time when successive executions of the controller code resulted in the same execution time – *i.e.* the situation when the execution reached a steady state. The 'worst-case' numbers in the graph are usually different from the first few iterations before the system effects (in particular the cache) have settled down. This is

the reason why there exists a slightly larger difference between the worst-case and best-case numbers.

Each vertical bar is split into two parts – the lower part shows the instrumentation overhead for that experiment[7], while the top part represents the timing for the control code only. We also see that the instrumentation overhead is almost the same across all experiments – oscillating between 260 and 270 cycles for all experiments.

As seen in the graph, the steady state and best-case values are very close, not just within the same experiment, but across experiments. The largest difference between the two is 360 cycles for the $n = 100,000$ experiment. This just shows that our assumption that controller codes in safety-critical systems are simple and have little variability is valid. This lack of variability is also evident from the fact that the worst-case execution cycles, across experiments, do not show much variance. The worst-case values for the last experiment $(1,000,000)$ has a slightly higher value of $16,560$ and this could be due to the initial cold cache and other system effects.

Figure 7 shows the execution profile for one timing experiment in particular – that of $100,000$ iterations. The x-axis is the iteration number while the y-axis is the number of cycles for each iteration. As this figure shows, the first few iterations take a little longer (around $17K$ cycles) and then most of the execution stabilizes to within a narrow band of:

$$1,590 \; cycles = 14,660 - 13,070$$
$$i.e. \sim 0.6 \, \mu s \; at \; 2.67 \, GHz$$

This band defines the '*accepted range*' of values that the FPGA uses to check for intrusions. Any execution that changes the steady state execution time by more than this narrow range will be caught by the FPGA. In fact, the FPGA will catch variance in either direction – *i.e.* increase/decrease in execution time.

The graph also shows that while the majority of execution times fall within a small band at the lower end of the above mentioned range, some values also fall into a narrow band at the top of the range (*i.e.* around the $14K$ value). This narrow band of increased execution times is due to latent system effects that we were not able to remove. The main culprit is the last level cache that, in this architecture, uses a random replacement policy. Hence, every once in a while a few of our controller's cache lines are evicted by periodic kernel threads that we could not disable (since we are running a COTS operating system) and these iterations take a few hundred cycles extra (anywhere from $500 - 900$) to execute. With a more predictable cache replacement policy, like the ones used in hard real-time systems, we would not see this behavior. To prove this theory we ran the same experiments on a PowerPC with pseudo-LRU (Last Recently Used) cache replacement policy in its last level and all the points are clustered into a single band. In fact,

---

[7]As explained in Section 5.4.3, we used dual-loop timing techniques to obtain the overheads due to the instrumentation.

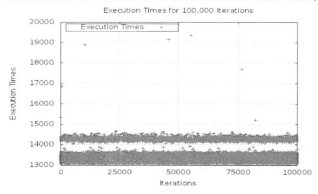

Figure 7: Execution Profile (100,000) with FPGA

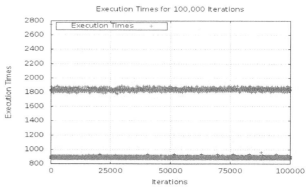

Figure 8: Execution Profile (100,0000) without FPGA

with LRU, tasks would not evict each other cache's lines unless the cache is not big enough to fit them at the same time[8]

Figure 7 also shows a few sporadic experiments exhibiting much higher execution times. Again, this is due to system effects and in particular, contention on the bus when communicating with the FPGA. The complex controller reads and writes messages to and from the FPGA to control the pendulum and to send the timing messages (Section 5.4.1). Many times, when the complex controller is waiting for data from the inverted pendulum that arrives on the common bus, the incoming messages experience unpredictable delays. These delays are due to bus contention among the FPGA and other peripherals sharing the same bus. To prove that the communication with the FPGA was the cause of these effects, we conducted timing experiments where the FPGA was switched off and all calls to communicate with it (read/write) resulted in null function calls. Figure 8 shows the results of these experiments for the $100,000$ iterations point. This experiment highlights two important points: *(1)* the random spikes at higher values no longer exist, thus showing that the bus contention due to communication with the FPGA was the main cause of the spikes; and *(2)* the same 'double-band' of execution results appears here; interestingly, the gap between the bands is almost identical to that of Figure 7, thus providing more evidence to the fact that the cache (and its replacement policy) is the culprit.

Such issues could be avoided when using actual hard real-time systems instead of the COTS-based experimental setup that we use here. In fact, a hard real-time system would use a more predictable bus, or other techniques [3], that allows designers to bound I/O contention and avoid random spikes.

6.2 Malicious code Execution Results

We introduce "malicious code" by inserting extra instructions (Section 5.4.4) – *i.e.* a loop of variable size within the complex controller code. The upper bounds for the malicious loop are one of $1, 10, 100$ – we stopped at the upper limit of 100 since anything over this value would put the execution of the "infected" control code over the real-time period of the task. Also, as we will see soon, even these small additional increases in execution times are caught by S3A.

Figure 9 shows the execution time (in cycles, on the y-axis) taken by the code for value of the malicious loop values (x-axis). The final bar in the graph represents the "base," *i.e.* the number of execution cycles taken up by the controller code without any malicious loop. As expected, the values for the malicious code increases significantly with each increase in the loop bound. Even the smallest sign of the presence of the malicious loop puts it outside of the narrow range ($0.6\mu s$) explained in Section 6.1. Hence, even this will be caught by S3A and control will be transferred over to the simple controller executing on the FPGA. **Note:** Since we don't re-

---

[8]If this is the case, we just have to account for it, when we compute the execution time for each task.

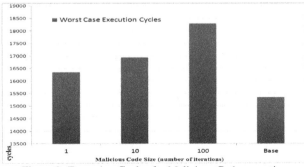

Figure 9: Execution Cycles for Malicious Code execution

ally care *what* executes as part of malicious code and *intend to only catch variations in execution time*, we only mimic the increased execution time effects by the methods discussed in this section.

6.3 Intrusion Detection

We now describe the evaluation of our timing side channel intrusion detection technique. First we describe timing measurements for obtaining key aspects of our architecture. Then, we demonstrate the *early detection of malicious code execution* using the timing side channel approach (S3A) and compare it with monitoring the plant state only (vanilla Simplex). The results for the inverted pendulum are summarized in Table 2.

Our first timing measurement was to obtain the *overheads for sending timing messages* to the FPGA. Although the message itself takes time to propagate through the PCIe bus to the FPGA, the CPU is not stalled during this time. By using the time stamp counter we measured the overhead on the CPU for sending a single timing message to be 130 cycles (50 nanoseconds). This time is extremely small and therefore each process could realistically send multiple messages during a single iteration of each control loop to reduce the time an attacker has to replicate the timing side channel. Another advantage of having multiple timing messages per iteration is that if the program contains branches, we could communicate to the FPGA timing monitor (at run-time) information about which branch was taken thus allowing for tighter monitoring of the timing requirements in the timing model FSM.

The second timing measurement was to quantify the *jitter of the timing messages* going to the FPGA(through the interconnect). We recorded the difference between the arrival of the start and end control iteration timing messages, in the FPGA, over several thousand iterations of the control loop. The reason for this jitter is twofold: *(a)* jitter of the execution time itself (the difference between the minimum and maximum execution time (Figure 5) and *(b)* varying time of message propagation through the PCIe bus.

Since our testbed is an off-the-shelf multicore system (with Linux), processes running concurrently on other cores as well as other independent bus masters (*e.g.* peripherals) may cause interference on the shared interconnect. In a deployed real-time control system, such noise would not be present or would at least be bounded. Nonetheless, we measured the typical timing variation caused by the interconnect to be about 0.6 microseconds, or less than $\frac{1}{8}^{th}$ of the iteration time of a single control iteration. The FPGA timing can now detect an intrusion using the timing-based side channel within $5.7\mu s$ and anything that changes the timing by $0.6\mu s$ would be caught (Table 2). We could add multiple timing messages in each control iteration (asthe CPU message overhead is so low) to further reduce the maximum intrusion detection delay.

The control task execution time (Table 2) was obtained from the execution time measurements in Section 6.1. The values are in absolute times that were converted from our cycle count measurements. Hence, the $4.6--5.7\mu s$ value for the 'Control Task Execution Time' is obtained from the (approx.) $13,000-14,000$ cycles that we discussed in Section 6.1 and Figure 7.

Due to the extra jitter caused by the interconnect, the enforced iteration time is expectedly larger than the measured control task ex-

Measured Quantity	Time (μs)
Control Task Exec. Time (single iter)	4.8 - 5.4
Interconnect Extra Jitter	~ 0.6
Enforced Iteration Time	4.6 - 5.7
Timing Anomaly Detection Time (for IP)	5.7
Vanilla Simplex Anomaly Detection Time	10,000
Timing Message CPU Overhead	0.05

Table 2: Measured Timings during Intrusion Detection

ecution time. The maximum enforced iteration time, $5.7\mu s$, is the maximum time the experimental framework can proceed without receiving a timing message before the safety controller takes over. Hence, in the FSM (Figure 5), the runtime value of $MustWait_C$ is $4.6\mu s$, and the runtime value of $CanWait_C$ is about $1.1\mu s$ ($mustWait_I$ and $canWait_I$ are much lower). Given these numbers, the side-channel monitor FSM will detect a missed timing message within $5.7\mu s$, *i.e.* the detection time reported.

We now compare the early detection of malicious code through timing side channels with the situation when only the plant state is being monitored (vanilla Simplex). In the timing side channel version, as discussed above, the maximum time that can proceed before without valid timing messages is $5.7\mu s$. For vanilla Simplex, we experimentally measured the amount of time needed to detect an intrusion. After taking control of the system, we tried to destabilize the pendulum by sending a maximum voltage value in the direction that would most quickly collapse the pendulum (in order to obtain a lower bound on the detection time when plant state is monitored alone). For vanilla Simplex, we were able to detect an intrusion after 5 control iterations, or 100 milliseconds. Hence, the use of timing side channels enables significantly faster detection of security vulnerabilities in real-time control systems: over four orders of magnitude faster than with traditional Simplex.

This test shows that if a smart attacker is able to override all of our checking mechanisms (say, by gaining root access) then *the physical system will still remain safe if she tries to destabilize it, since the base Simplex mechanism will kick in and take control.*

7. LIMITATIONS

S3A is not meant to be a silver bullet for intrusion detection in embedded control systems and does have some practical restrictions that may limit its applicability. First, to use S3A in a real system, the latter needs to be designed with the architecture in mind. While this is a limitation for some existing systems, we think that future architectures could provision for such techniques since it is never a bad idea to consider security while designing a new system.

One concern is making sure that an attacker cannot easily replicate our side channels. This could be overcome with minor modifications to the processor architecture or, in our prototype, allowing the FPGA to directly access the instruction count without explicit communication from the CPU.

Additionally, for each side channel, a model of the correct behavior must be created that restricts a malicious program. For the timing side channel, one problem could be that the execution times may have too much variability. While this is possible in general purpose systems, it is not very likely in real-time systems. Even so, this could be overcome at runtime by having each timing-behavior-modifying branch point send information to the FPGA indicating what path was taken, resulting in tight bounds on execution time. The construction and tuning of the timing parameters of the state machine is currently a manual process. We believe this could eventually become an automated step by performing a compile-time analysis of the control flow graph of the code combined with runtime analysis to perform precise timing measurements.

The implementation of the FPGA hardware in our framework must be correct for the system to be secure. This may seem like we have just moved the problem over to securing the FPGA system but this is not the case since: the FPGA and Safety Controller only need to maintain the safety of the plant. The Complex Controller, on the other hand, can perform useful work with the plant so any upgrades will be made to the Complex Controller and not to the FPGA's safety logic. Of course, we should not permit FPGA reconfiguration at runtime. One other issue related to the use of

FPGAs floating-point computation units are typically not present since they use up significant area. The FPGA in our architecture is used as a rapid prototype of the trusted simplex component. A deployment implementation could use a trusted microcontroller along with any capabilities (*e.g.* floating point units) that are needed for the various components. Also, the FPGA will only host the safety controller that maintains bare functionality. Hence, it is unlikely that it will need to perform fancy floating point calculations.

The original Simplex only protects systems from properties that are known to result in unsafe states. *E.g.* in Stuxnet, the malicious controller would actuate the plant motor for periods at very high frequencies and then for periods at very low frequencies in order to damage the motors. If the Decision Module was not monitoring this property, such unsafe actuation would still proceed to the plant.

8. RELATED WORK

Zimmer *et. al.* [24] use worst-case execution time (WCET) information to detect intrusions by instrumenting the tasks and schedulers with periodic checks on whether the execution has gone past expected WCET values. We focus on detecting intrusions in real-time control systems and ensuring that the plant remains safe even if the intruder is able to bypass all detection/security mechanisms. As compared to them, we ensure that the system remains safe even if an intruder gains root privileges to the system. Our monitoring is performed by a trusted hardware component, separate from the main system, thus increasing the robustness of the architecture.

The trusted computing engine (TCE) [11] and the reliability and security engine (RSE) [12] also use secure co-processors to execute security-critical code/monitor the access of critical data. We don't require the information about what data is critical or even touch the source code. We detect intrusions by observing the innate characteristics of the program at runtime.

The IBM 4758 secure co-processor could be used to perform intrusion detection [23]. This work contains a CPU, separate memory (volatile and non-volatile) along with cryptographic accelerators and comes wrapped in a tamper-responding secure boundary. While we could adapt this processor for use with our architecture, the main difference from S3A lies in the fact that we employ the inherent characteristics of the program to detect intrusions, especially in the CPS domain; also coupling with the System Simplex mechanism increases the robustness of the overall system. Flex-Core [6] uses a reconfigurable fabric to implement monitoring and book-keeping functions. Compared to FlexCore, we *(a)* don't need to know what types of attacks are taking place (as long as it modified the execution time behavior of our code) and *(b)* don't need to analyze the program structure/data.

Other related work includes Pioneer [18] (sophisticated checksum code and execution time information to establish safe remote execution on an untrusted computer), TVA [8] (provides guarantees that the software running on a general purpose computer is intrusion-free in conjunction with a hardware trusted component, TPM), and PRET [15] ('precision timed machines' to detect and protect against side-channel attacks). Our work is different from all of these in significant ways, since we don't touch actual code, try to protect local control systems with real-time properties and use side-channels to our benefit.

9. CONCLUSIONS

We presented a new framework, Secure System Simplex Architecture (S3A), that enhances the security and safety of a real-time control system. We use a combination of trusted hardware, benevolent side-channels, OS techniques and the intrinsic real-time nature (and domain-specific characteristics) of such systems to detect intrusions and prevent the physical plant from being damaged. We were able to detect intrusions in the system in less than 6 μs and changes of less than 0.6 μs – time scales that are extremely hard for intruders to defeat. We show that even if an attacker is able to bypass all security/intrusion detection techniques, the actual plant will remain safe. Another important characteristic of these techniques is that there are *no modifications required in the source code*. We believe that the novel techniques and architecture presented here will significantly increase the difficulty faced by would-be attackers thus improving the security and overall safety of such systems.

10. REFERENCES

[1] ABRAMS, M., AND WEISS, J. Malicious control system cyber security attack case study – maroochy water services. http://crc.nist.gov/groups/SMA/fisma/ics/documents/Maroochy-Water-Services-Case-Study_report.pdf, 2008.

[2] BAK, S., CHIVUKULA, D. K., ADEKUNLE, O., SUN, M., CACCAMO, M., AND SHA, L. The system-level simplex architecture for improved real-time embedded system safety. In *RTAS '09: Proceedings of the 2009 15th IEEE Real-Time and Embedded Technology and Applications Symposium* (Washington, DC, USA, 2009), IEEE Computer Society, pp. 99–107.

[3] BETTI, E., BAK, S., PELLIZZONI, R., CACCAMO, M., AND SHA, L. Real-time i/o management system with cots peripherals. *Computers, IEEE Transactions on PP*, 99 (2011), 1.

[4] CHECKOWAY, S., MCCOY, D., KANTOR, B., ANDERSON, D., SHACHAM, H., SAVAGE, S., KOSCHER, K., CZESKIS, A., ROESNER, F., AND KOHNO, T. Comprehensive experimental analyses of automotive attack surfaces. In *USENIX Security* (Aug 2011).

[5] CRENSHAW, T. L., GUNTER, E., ROBINSON, C. L., SHA, L., AND KUMAR, P. R. The simplex reference model: Limiting fault-propagation due to unreliable components in cyber-physical system architectures. In *RTSS '07: Proceedings of the 28th IEEE International Real-Time Systems Symposium* (Washington, DC, USA, 2007), IEEE Computer Society, pp. 400–412.

[6] DENG, D. Y., LO, D., MALYSA, G., SCHNEIDER, S., AND SUH, G. E. Flexible and efficient instruction-grained run-time monitoring using on-chip reconfigurable fabric. In *Proceedings of the 2010 43rd Annual IEEE/ACM International Symposium on Microarchitecture* (Washington, DC, USA, 2010), MICRO '43, IEEE Computer Society, pp. 137–148.

[7] FALLIERE, N., MURCHU, L., AND (SYMANTEC), E. C. W32.stuxnet dossier. http://www.symantec.com/content/en/us/enterprise/media/security_response/whitepapers/w32_stuxnet_dossier.pdf, 2011.

[8] GARFINKEL, T., PFAFF, B., CHOW, J., ROSENBLUM, M., AND BONEH, D. Terra: A virtual machine-based platform for trusted computing. *ACM SIGOPS Operating Systems Review 37*, 5 (2003), 193–206.

[9] INDUSTRIAL, Q. Inverted pendulum [ip] linear. Quanser IP01, 2011.

[10] INTEL. Using the RDTSC instruction for performance modeling. www.ccsl.carleton.ca/~jamuir/rdtscpm1.pdf.

[11] IYER, R. K., DABROWSKI, P., NAKKA, N., AND KALBARCZYK, Z. Reconfigurable tamper-resistant hardware support against insider threats: The trusted illiac approach. 133–152. 10.1007/978-0-387-77322-3_8.

[12] IYER, R. K., KALBARCZYK, Z., PATTABIRAMAN, K., HEALEY, W., HWU, W.-M. W., KLEMPERER, P., AND FARIVAR, R. Toward application-aware security and reliability. *IEEE Security and Privacy 5* (2007), 57–62.

[13] KOSCHER, K., CZESKIS, A., ROESNER, F., PATEL, S., KOHNO, T., CHECKOWAY, S., MCCOY, D., KANTOR, B., ANDERSON, D., SHACHAM, H., AND SAVAGE, S. Experimental security analysis of a modern automobile. In *Security and Privacy (SP), 2010 IEEE Symposium on* (may 2010), pp. 447 –462.

[14] LI, C., RAGHUNATHAN, A., AND JHA, N. Hijacking an insulin pump: Security attacks and defenses for a diabetes therapy system. In *e-Health Networking Applications and Services (Healthcom), 2011 13th IEEE International Conference on* (june 2011), pp. 150 –156.

[15] LIU, I., AND MCGROGAN, D. Elimination of side channel attacks on a precision timed architecture. Tech. Rep. UCB/EECS-2009-15, EECS Department, University of California, Berkeley, Jan 2009. This a class project report describing early work on eliminating side channel attacks using PRET.

[16] MOHAN, S., AND MUELLER, F. Hybrid timing analysis of modern processor pipelines via hardware/software interactions. In *IEEE Real-Time Embedded Technology and Applications Symposium* (2008), pp. 285–294.

[17] (NERC), N. A. E. R. C. Jan-june 2009 disturbance index. http://www.nerc.com/files/disturb09-January-June.pdf, 2009.

[18] SESHADRI, A., LUK, M., SHI, E., PERRIG, A., VAN DOORN, L., AND KHOSLA, P. Pioneer: verifying code integrity and enforcing untampered code execution on legacy systems. *ACM SIGOPS Operating Systems Review 39*, 5 (2005), 1–16.

[19] SETO, D., FERREIRA, E., AND MARZ, T. F. Case study: Development of a baseline controller for automatic landing of an f-16 aircraft using linear matrix inequalities (lmis). Technical Report Cmu/ sei-99-Tr-020.

[20] SETO, D., KROGH, B., SHA, L., AND CHUTINAN, A. Dynamic control system upgrade using the simplex architecture. *IEEE Control Systems 18*, 4 (Aug. 1998), 72–80.

[21] SHA, L. Using simplicity to control complexity. *IEEE Softw. 18*, 4 (2001), 20–28.

[22] WILHELM, R., AND ET AL. The worst-case execution time problem — overview of methods and survey of tools. *ACM Transactions on Embedded Computing Systems 7*, 3 (Apr. 2008), 1–53.

[23] ZHANG, X., VAN DOORN, L., JAEGER, T., PEREZ, R., AND SAILER, R. Secure coprocessor-based intrusion detection. *Proceedings of the 10th workshop on ACM SIGOPS European workshop beyond the PC EW10* (2002), 239.

[24] ZIMMER, C., BHATT, B., MUELLER, F., AND MOHAN, S. Time-based intrusion detection in cyber-physical systems. In *International Conference on Cyber-Physical Systems* (2010).

Towards Synthesis of Platform-aware
Attack-Resilient Control Systems [*]

Extended Abstract

Miroslav Pajic[1]   Nicola Bezzo[1]   James Weimer[1]   Rajeev Alur[1]
Rahul Mangharam[1]   Nathan Michael[2]   George J. Pappas[1]   Oleg Sokolsky[1]
Paulo Tabuada[3]   Stephanie Weirich[1]   Insup Lee[1]

[1]School of Engineering and Applied Science
University of Pennsylvania
Philadelphia, PA 19104
{pajic, nicbezzo, weimerj}@seas.upenn.edu
{rahulm, pappasg}@seas.upenn.edu
{sokolsky, alur, sweirich, lee}@cis.upenn.edu

[2] Robotics Institute
Carnegie Mellon University
Pittsburgh, PA 15213
nmichael@cmu.edu

[3]Department of Electrical Engineering
University of California, Los Angeles
Los Angeles, CA 90095
tabuada@ee.ucla.edu

Categories and Subject Descriptors

K.6.5 [**Management of Computing and Information Systems**]:
Security and Protection—*Unauthorized ccess (e.g., hacking, phreaking)*; C.3 [**Special-purpose and Application-based Systems**]: Process control systems, Real-time and embedded systems

Keywords

Attack-resilient control systems, cyber-physical system security

1. INTRODUCTION

Over the past decade, the design process in the automotive industry has gone through a period of significant changes. Modern vehicles present a complex interaction of a large number of embedded Electronic Control Units (ECUs), interacting with each other over different types of networks. Furthermore, there is a current shift in vehicle architectures, from isolated control systems to more open automotive architectures that would introduce new services such as remote diagnostics and code updates, and vehicle-to-vehicle communication. However, this increasing set of functionalities, network interoperability, and system design complexity may introduce security vulnerabilities that are easily exploitable.

Typically, modern vehicular control systems are not built with security in mind. As shown in [7], using simple methods an attacker can disrupt the operation of a car to either disable the vehicle or hijack it, giving the attacker the ability to control it instead. This problem is even more emphasized with the rise of vehicle au-

[*]This material is based on research sponsored by DARPA under agreement number FA8750-12-2-0247. The U.S. Government is authorized to reproduce and distribute reprints for Governmental purposes notwithstanding any copyright notation thereon. The views and conclusions contained herein are those of the authors and should not be interpreted as necessarily representing the official policies or endorsements, either expressed or implied, of DARPA or the U.S. Government.

tonomy; consequently, criticality analysis for various automotive components will have to be completely re-done.

To address these issues, we have introduced a design framework for development of high-confidence vehicular control systems that can be used in adversarial environments. The framework employs system design techniques that guarantee that the vehicle will maintain control, possibly at a reduced efficiency, under several classes of attacks. This comprehensive end-to-end approach to the development of vehicular control systems can be extended for the use in most networked control systems that may be subject to a variety of externally-originating attacks.

The overview of the development framework is shown in Fig. 1. To protect against the set of attacks that is as extensive and diverse as possible, we combine control-level techniques and code-level techniques:

- During the control design phase, it is necessary to address attacks on the environment of the controller, such as attacks on sensors, actuators, communication media (i.e., the network) and computational resources available to the controller. In this phase we build upon ways to introduce redundancy within the control loop, as well as methods for attack detection and identification. We utilize security-aware attack-resilient estimators that identify attacks and allow the controller to pursue a mitigation strategy. Therefore, we refer to these as *Control-level defenses*.

- In the system development phase, the framework employs *Code-level defenses* that prevent injection of malicious code into the operation of the controller itself. This is achieved by providing secure code synthesis for the derived controllers, with the goal to use a formal representation of the execution and code generation semantics to remove the uncertainty from the code generation process.

2. ATTACK-RESILIENT CONTROL SCHEMES

In this phase, we have built on the work from [3, 4] where methods for compressed sensing and error correction over the reals were used to derive a technique to develop secure state estimators when system sensors or actuators are under attack. We assume that control design for the nominal case, when no attacks are present, has

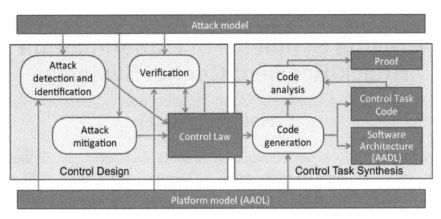

Figure 1: Overview of the approach.

already been performed. Hence, we focus on state estimation techniques that extend conventional state estimators to compensate for exogenous attacks or to provide indications to the controller that the system is under attack.

Most of the existing schemes for attack detection and identification (e.g., [8, 3, 4]) are based on the knowledge of the exact plant model. However, as the environmental conditions might affect some of the model parameters, we combine the resilient estimator with a controller scheme we have introduced in [9], which is resilient to both attacks and limited perturbations in model parameters. Thus, the overall controller design (shown in Fig. 2) guarantees that in the event the model becomes inaccurate, we can maintain a minimum performance level for the closed-loop system.

Our framework has been illustrated on a cruise control case study, in which a vehicle employs redundant sensor measurements (e.g., encoders, GPS, IMU) to maintain a predefined velocity even in the case of attacks. In this regard, we have created a simulator, based on the recently developed Robotic Operating System (ROS) [2], to emulate the dynamics of a real unmanned ground vehicle. Using this system, we have been able to demonstrate that our resilient control strategy can guarantee a safe performance when less than half of the sensors are under attack.

3. SAFE CODE GENERATION

Existing methods for designing secure control systems do not offer coordinated control-level and code-level defenses. Tools like Matlab allow us to model control laws and generate code, but security properties of the generated code are not well studied. Our aim is to prove that behavior of the control algorithm is preserved by code generation and that no vulnerabilities are introduced in the process.

The code of control tasks is executed on top of the underlying communication and computation platform. Therefore, proofs of control code execution need to take properties of the platform into account. We plan to precisely specify the services provided by the platform and use these specifications in proof construction. We use

architectural modeling to describe both the structure of the control software and the capabilities of the platform that runs it. To achieve this goal we utilize the Architecture Analysis and Design Language (AADL) [5], developed for modeling embedded control system architectures.

Code generation is performed by analyzing dependencies between expressions in the control law and generating code for the individual expressions in the topological order of dependencies. In this respect, code generation is similar to the one performed by the Simulink Real-Time Workshop tool [1]. Platform-dependent aspects — that is, access to specific sensors and actuators, handling of timers, etc. — should be "weaved in" afterwards. Currently, we perform this part manually. Our plan, however, is to enhance the code generator to perform this automatically based on the AADL model, using an approach similar to that of Ocarina [6].

4. REFERENCES

[1] Real-Time Windows Target - Run Simulink models on a PC in real time. http://www.mathworks.com/products/rtwt/.

[2] Robotic Operating System. http://www.ros.org.

[3] H. Fawzi, P. Tabuada, and S. Diggavi. Secure state-estimation for dynamical systems under active adversaries. In *49th Annual Allerton Conference on Communication, Control, and Computing (Allerton)*, pages 337–344, 2011.

[4] H. Fawzi, P. Tabuada, and S. Diggavi. Security for control systems under sensor and actuator attacks. In *Proceedings of the 51st IEEE Conference on Decision and Control*, 2012.

[5] P. Feiler, B. Lewis, and S. Vestal. The SAE AADL standard: A basis for model-based architecture-driven embedded systems engineering. In *Workshop on Model-Driven Embedded Systems*, 2003.

[6] J. Hugues, B. Zalila, L. Pautet, and F. Kordon. From the prototype to the final embedded system using the Ocarina AADL tool suite. *ACM Transactions on Embedded Computing Systems*, 7(4):42:1–42:25, 2008.

[7] K. Koscher, A. Czeskis, F. Roesner, S. Patel, T. Kohno, S. Checkoway, D. McCoy, B. Kantor, D. Anderson, H. Shacham, and S. Savage. Experimental security analysis of a modern automobile. In *2010 IEEE Symposium on Security and Privacy (SP)*, pages 447 –462, 2010.

[8] F. Pasqualetti, F. Dörfler, and F. Bullo. Attack detection and identification in cyber-physical systems. *IEEE Transactions on Automatic Control*, 2012. submitted.

[9] J. Weimer, N. Bezzo, M. Pajic, G. Pappas, O. Sokolsky, and I. Lee. Resilient adaptive control with application to vehicle cruise control. In *Workshop on Control of Cyber-Physical Systems*, 2012. submitted.

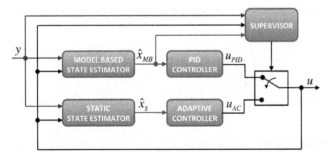

Figure 2: Diagram of the resilient controller.

Verifying Information Flow Properties of Hybrid Systems

Pavithra Prabhakar
IMDEA Software Institute
pavithra.prabhakar@imdea.org

Boris Köpf
IMDEA Software Institute
boris.koepf@imdea.org

ABSTRACT

In this paper, we study the problem of analyzing information flow properties of hybrid systems. We begin by formalizing non-interference – the baseline information flow property – for hybrid systems. We then present a type system for statically enforcing non-interference, together with a proof of soundness. We conclude with discussions on future work towards analyzing more permissive information flow properties.

Categories and Subject Descriptors

H.4 [**Information Systems Applications**]: Miscellaneous; C.1.3 [**Hybrid Systems**]: Security and Protection

Keywords

Information Flow Analysis

1. INTRODUCTION

With incidents such as Stuxnet attacking SCADA systems (see, e.g., [2]), the security of embedded control systems has come to the limelight. One of the most fundamental security properties is *confidentiality*, i.e., the requirement that secret information can only be learned by authorized parties. Security mechanisms such as access control, firewalls, and encryption [5] can ensure confidentiality while secrets are stored in databases or transferred over networks—but they cannot provide security guarantees while actual computation is being performed on the secrets. Information flow control [10, 8] protects secret information during computation, with the goal of achieving end-to-end confidentiality guarantees. The baseline information flow property is non-interference [4], which forbids any flow of information from classified (or *high*) to public (or *low*) domains.

A wide range of techniques have been proposed for reasoning about information flow properties in the context of discrete programs (see the survey [8]). Most of these techniques rely on static program analysis, which has the ad-

vantage of little or no run-time overhead when compared to techniques based on dynamic execution monitoring. Among the static analysis techniques for enforcing secure information flow, type systems for non-interference are probably the most popular approach. For example, in the type system by Volpano et al. [12], each program variable is annotated with a security type that specifies the domain of the data it stores, and each command is annotated with a security type that specifies the domain of the data it may affect. When type-checking a program, these annotations are combined using typing rules based on program syntax. A successful type check implies that the program will satisfy non-interference at run-time.

Unfortunately, the problem of enforcing information flow has received little attention in the context of *embedded control systems*, namely, systems in which embedded processors are employed for control. These include safety critical systems such as aerospace, automotive and medical devices among others. An inherent characteristic is the interaction of the embedded processors with a continuous environment. Due to the mixed discrete-continuous behavior exhibited by them, they are popularly referred to as hybrid systems.

In this paper, we investigate the use of type systems for enforcing non-interference for hybrid systems. To this end, we first present a syntax for hybrid systems that resembles that of discrete programs, along with a deterministic semantics. We formalize non-interference based on this model. Intuitively, non-interference for hybrid systems requires that for every two input signals that agree on the values of the variables of low security levels, the output signals also agree on the values of the variables of low security levels. Hence, the observable or low part of the output is invariant with respect to the high input.

We then present a static analysis method for inferring non-interference in hybrid systems. The analysis is based on the type system developed in [12] but includes additional typing judgments for the continuous specification of the system. The typing rule for the continuous dynamics needs to capture the interdependent nature of the evolution of the continuous variables. We prove the soundness of the type system, in the sense that a successful type check implies that the hybrid system satisfies non-interference. We conclude with directions for future work.

2. PRELIMINARIES

Let $\mathbb{N}$, $\mathbb{R}$ and $\mathbb{R}_{\geq 0}$ denote the set of natural, real and non-negative real numbers, respectively. Given a function f, we use $dom(f)$ to denote the domain of f.

HiCoNS'13, April 9–11, 2013, Philadelphia, Pennsylvania, USA.
Copyright 2013 ACM 978-1-4503-1961-4/13/04 ...$15.00.

A *sequence* is a function $\sigma : A \to B$, where A is $\{0, \cdots, n\}$ for some $n \in \mathbb{N}$. Length of a sequence $\sigma : \{0, \cdots, n\} \to B$ is the number of elements in its domain, namely, $n + 1$. Given two sequences σ_1 and σ_2, $\sigma_1 \sigma_2$ denotes the concatenations of σ_2 after σ_1. More precisely, if $\sigma_1 : \{0, \cdots, n_1\} \to A$ and $\sigma_2 : \{0, \cdots, n_2\} \to A$, $\sigma_1 \sigma_2 : \{0, \cdots, n_1 + n_2 + 1\} \to A$ such that $\sigma_1 \sigma_2(i) = \sigma_1(i)$ for $0 \le i \le n_1$ and $\sigma_1 \sigma_2(i) = \sigma_2(i - n_1 - 1)$ for $n_1 < i \le n_1 + n_2 + 1$. We denote by $\sigma[i, j]$, the subsequence of σ from the i-th element to the j-th element, that is, $\sigma[i, j] = \sigma(i) \cdots \sigma(j)$.

Given an element $\bar{x} \in \mathbb{R}^n$, we use $\bar{x}|_i$ to denote the projection of $\bar{x}$ to the i-th component, namely, $\bar{x}_i$, where $\bar{x} = (\bar{x}_1, \cdots, \bar{x}_n)$. Given a function $f : A \to \mathbb{R}^n$, the function $f|_i$ represent the projection of the image to the i-th component, that is, $f|_i : A \to \mathbb{R}$ such that for every $a \in A$, $f|_i(a) = f(a)|_i$.

3. DETERMINISTIC HYBRID SYSTEMS

Hybrid systems are systems exhibiting both discrete and continuous behaviors. The continuous behavior is typically modeled by a system of ordinary differential equations, and the discrete behavior corresponding to the control logic is modelled by a finite state automaton (see, for example, [6]). In general, the behavior of a hybrid system can be non-deterministic. In this paper, we focus on hybrid systems with deterministic behaviors, that is, systems which exhibit a unique behavior given an input signal and an initial state. To this end, we present a model which is analogous to a program.

3.1 Syntax

First, we present a simple syntax for expressing deterministic hybrid systems as a programming language.

Let us fix a set of input variables $Var^U = \{u_1, \cdots, u_k\}$ and a set of state variables $Var^X = \{x_1, \cdots, x_n\}$. A hybrid system $\mathcal{H}$ over (Var^U, Var^X) is defined inductively as follows:

$$\mathcal{H} := \quad \langle \dot{x}_1 = e, \cdots, \dot{x}_n = e, b \rangle \quad \text{(Flow)}$$

$$| \; [x_1 := e, \cdots, x_n := e] \quad \text{(Jump)}$$

$$| \; \mathcal{H}; \mathcal{H} \quad \text{(Sequential Composition)}$$

$$| \; \text{if } b \text{ then } \mathcal{H} \text{ else } \mathcal{H} \quad \text{(Branching)}$$

$$| \; \text{while } b \text{ do } \mathcal{H} \quad \text{(Looping)}$$

where e is an expression over $Var^U \cup Var^X$ formed from constants and variables using the arithmetic operators of addition and multiplication, and b is a boolean combination of predicates of the form $e > 0$. We will also treat b as an expression returning the boolean values 0 or 1 and as being formed using the binary operators $>$, $\neg$ (essentially $\neg b$ is interpreted as $1 - b$) and $\wedge$. We assume that the variables occurring in b are state variables.

The expression e represents a polynomial expression over the variables in Var, and the predicate b is a polynomial constraint over the state variables. The continuous dynamics of the system is specified using the system of n differential equations and an invariant, $\langle \dot{x}_1 = e_1, \cdots, \dot{x}_n = e_n, b \rangle$. The variables evolve according to the differential equations and satisfy the constraint specified by b at all times. The expression $[x_1 := e_1, \cdots, x_n := e_n]$ specifies the discrete jumps, namely, the value of a state variable x_i after the jump is

obtained by evaluating the expression e_i with the values of the variables before the jump. The operator $\mathcal{H}; \mathcal{H}$ specifies sequential composition, if b then $\mathcal{H}$ else $\mathcal{H}$ specifies branching and while b do $\mathcal{H}$ specifies looping.

3.2 Semantics

Next, we specify the semantics of the hybrid system. Before that, we define the notions of trajectories and transitions.

The continuous evolution of the system is given by a trajectory which is a solution of a system of differential equations given a continuously evolving input trajectory.

Definition. A *trajectory* is a continuous function $\tau : [0, t] \to \mathbb{R}^n$, for some $n \in \mathbb{N}$ and $t \in \mathbb{R}_{\ge 0}$. We denote the set of all trajectories with range $\mathbb{R}^d$ by $Traj(\mathbb{R}^d)$.

A trajectory $\tau' : [0, t'] \to \mathbb{R}^n$ is said to be a *prefix* of a trajectory $\tau : [0, t] \to \mathbb{R}^n$ if $t' \le t$ and $\tau'(t'') = \tau(t'')$ for every $0 \le t'' \le t'$.

The variables in $Var = Var^U \cup Var^X$ take values in $\mathbb{R}$. Hence, we define the input domain U to be $\mathbb{R}^k$, and the state domain X to be $\mathbb{R}^n$. An element $\bar{u} \in U$ is interpreted as a valuation which assigns $\bar{u}|_i$ to the input variable u_i, and similarly, an element $\bar{x} \in X$ is interpreted as a valuation which assigns $\bar{x}|_i$ to the state variable x_i. Hence, given an expression e, we denote by $[\![e]\!](\bar{u}, \bar{x})$, the result obtained by evaluating the expression after substituting each variable by the corresponding value from $\bar{u}$ or $\bar{x}$. Similarly, given a predicate b, we say that $\bar{x}$ satisfies b, denoted $\bar{x} \models b$, if substituting for the variables in b by the corresponding values in $\bar{x}$, the predicate evaluates to true; otherwise $\bar{x} \not\models b$.

We capture the state evolution in response to a continuous input by an input-state trajectory.

Definition. An *input-state trajectory* over (Var^U, Var^X) is an element $(\mathbf{u}, \mathbf{x})$ of $Traj(U) \times Traj(X)$ such that $dom(\mathbf{u}) = dom(\mathbf{x})$.

An input-state trajectory $(\mathbf{u}', \mathbf{x}')$ is a prefix of an input-state trajectory $(\mathbf{u}, \mathbf{x})$ if $\mathbf{u}'$ is a prefix of $\mathbf{u}$ and $\mathbf{x}'$ is a prefix of $\mathbf{x}$.

Assumption. We make the standard assumptions that the functions defined by the polynomial expressions in the right hand sides of the differential equations satisfy the conditions for existence and uniqueness of solutions of the differential equations (see, for example, [7], for details of such conditions).

An input-state trajectories $(\mathbf{u}, \mathbf{x})$ is *consistent* with a system of differential equations $\dot{x}_1 = e_1, \cdots, \dot{x}_n = e_n$, if $\mathbf{x}$ is a solution starting from $\mathbf{x}(0)$ on $\mathbf{u}$, that is, there exists a T with $dom(\mathbf{u}) = dom(\mathbf{x}) = [0, T]$, and for each $t \in [0, T]$ and $1 \le i \le n$,

$$d\mathbf{x}|_i / dt = [\![e_i]\!](\mathbf{u}(t), \mathbf{x}(t)).$$

The derivative of the projection of $\mathbf{x}$ to the i-th component at anytime t is equivalent to the value of the expression e_i evaluated at the values of $\mathbf{x}$ and $\mathbf{u}$ at time t.

The first state of $(\mathbf{u}, \mathbf{x})$, namely, $\mathbf{x}(0)$, is denoted as $first((\mathbf{u}, \mathbf{x}))$, and the last state, namely, $\mathbf{x}(T)$, where $dom(\mathbf{x}) = [0, T]$, as $last((\mathbf{u}, \mathbf{x}))$.

The transitions capture the discrete jumps in the systems due to impulse input.

Definition. A *transition* over (Var^U, Var^X) is an element of $X \times U \times X$.

The only prefix of a transition is the transition itself. As before, we define the first and last state of a transition, namely, $first((\bar{x}_1, \bar{u}, \bar{x}_2)) = \bar{x}_1$ and $last((\bar{x}_1, \bar{u}, \bar{x}_2)) = \bar{x}_2$.

An execution of the hybrid system is a sequence of input-state trajectories and transitions such that the last state of an element in the sequence matches with the starting state of the next element in the sequence.

Definition. An *execution* over (Var^U, Var^X) is a finite sequence σ of input-state trajectories and transitions over (Var^U, Var^X), such that, for every $i > 0$ in $dom(\sigma)$, $last(\sigma(i-1)) = first(\sigma(i))$. Let $Exec$ denote the set of executions over (Var^U, Var^X).

Note that an input-state trajectory or a transition is an execution with domain $\{0\}$. An execution σ' of length n' is a prefix of an execution σ of length n if $n' \leq n$ and $\sigma(i) = \sigma'(i)$ for every $0 \leq i < n'$ and $\sigma'(n')$ is a prefix of $\sigma(n')$.

Again, we use $first(\sigma)$ and $last(\sigma)$ for the first and last states of the execution σ, namely, $first(\sigma(0))$ and $last(\sigma(l))$, where $dom(\sigma) = \{0, \cdots, l\}$, respectively. An execution σ can be interpreted as a pair of sequences by separating the input and the state parts. We represent an execution σ also as a pair (σ_u, σ_x), where

- $dom(\sigma_u) = dom(\sigma_x) = dom(\sigma)$, and

- for each $i \in dom(\sigma)$,

  - if $\sigma(i) = (\mathbf{u}, \mathbf{x}) \in Traj(U) \times Traj(X)$, then $\sigma_u(i) = \mathbf{u}$ and $\sigma_x(i) = \mathbf{x}$; and

  - if $\sigma(i) = (\bar{x}_1, \bar{u}, \bar{x}_2)$, then $\sigma_u(i) = \bar{u}$ and $\sigma_x(i) = (\bar{x}_1, \bar{x}_2)$.

We call σ_u and σ_x, the input and state signal corresponding to σ, respectively.

The semantics of a hybrid system $\mathcal{H}$ over (Var^U, Var^X), denoted $[\![\mathcal{H}]\!]$, is given by a set of executions over (Var^U, Var^X). We define $[\![\mathcal{H}]\!]$ by induction on the structure of $\mathcal{H}$. We also need to define simultaneously the set of *complete* executions, those that execute $\mathcal{H}$ completely, denoted $[\![\mathcal{H}]\!]^c$.

- $[\![\langle \dot{x}_1 = e_1, \cdots, \dot{x}_n = e_n, b \rangle]\!]$ consists of executions which are input-state trajectories $(\mathbf{u}, \mathbf{x})$ consistent with the system of differential equations $\dot{x}_1 = e_1, \cdots, \dot{x}_n = e_n$ such that

  - for every $t \in [0, T]$, $\mathbf{x}(t) \models b$.

  where $dom(\mathbf{u}) = dom(\mathbf{x}) = [0, T]$.

  $[\![\langle \dot{x}_1 = e_1, \cdots, \dot{x}_n = e_n, b \rangle]\!]^c = [\![\langle \dot{x}_1 = e_1, \cdots, \dot{x}_n = e_n, b \rangle]\!]$.

- $[\![[x_1 := e_1, \cdots, x_n := e_n]]\!]$ is the set of transitions $(\bar{x}_1, \bar{u}, \bar{x}_2)$ such that $\bar{x}_2|_i = [\![e_i]\!](\bar{u}, \bar{x}_1)$.

  $[\![[x_1 := e_1, \cdots, x_n := e_n]]\!]^c = [\![[x_1 := e_1, \cdots, x_n := e_n]]\!]$.

- $[\![\mathcal{H}_1; \mathcal{H}_2]\!] = [\![\mathcal{H}_1]\!] \cup \{\sigma \in Exec \,|\, \exists \sigma_1 \in [\![\mathcal{H}_1]\!]^c, \exists \sigma_2 \in [\![\mathcal{H}_2]\!], \sigma = \sigma_1 \sigma_2\}$.

  $[\![\mathcal{H}_1; \mathcal{H}_2]\!]^c = \{\sigma \in Exec \,|\, \exists \sigma_1 \in [\![\mathcal{H}_1]\!]^c, \exists \sigma_2 \in [\![\mathcal{H}_2]\!]^c, \sigma = \sigma_1 \sigma_2\}$.

- $[\![\text{if } b \text{ then } \mathcal{H}_1 \text{ else } \mathcal{H}_2]\!] = \{\sigma \,|\, (first(\sigma) \models b \text{ and } \sigma \in [\![\mathcal{H}_1]\!])$ or $(first(\sigma) \not\models b \text{ and } \sigma \in [\![\mathcal{H}_2]\!])\}$.

  $[\![\text{if } b \text{ then } \mathcal{H}_1 \text{ else } \mathcal{H}_2]\!]^c = \{\sigma \,|\, (first(\sigma) \models b \text{ and } \sigma \in [\![\mathcal{H}_1]\!]^c)$ or $(first(\sigma) \not\models b \text{ and } \sigma \in [\![\mathcal{H}_2]\!]^c)\}$.

- $[\![\text{while } b \text{ do } \mathcal{H}]\!] = \{\sigma \in Exec \,|\, \exists \sigma_0, \sigma_1, \cdots, \sigma_l, \sigma = \sigma_0 \sigma_1 \cdots \sigma_l, \forall 0 \leq i \leq l, first(\sigma_i) \models b, \forall 0 \leq i < l, \sigma_i \in [\![\mathcal{H}]\!]^c, \sigma_l \in [\![\mathcal{H}]\!]\}$.

  $[\![\text{while } b \text{ do } \mathcal{H}]\!]^c = \{\sigma \in Exec \,|\, \exists \sigma_0, \sigma_1, \cdots, \sigma_l, \sigma = \sigma_0 \sigma_1 \cdots \sigma_l, \forall 0 \leq i \leq l, first(\sigma_i) \models b, \forall 0 \leq i \leq l, \sigma_i \in [\![\mathcal{H}]\!]^c, last(\sigma_l) \not\models b\}$.

Remark. Note that the set of complete executions associated with a hybrid system is a subset of the set of all executions associated with it, that is, $[\![\mathcal{H}]\!]^c \subseteq [\![\mathcal{H}]\!]$.

Remark. The set of executions $[\![\mathcal{H}]\!]$ is prefix-closed, that is, if $\sigma \in [\![\mathcal{H}]\!]$ and σ' is a prefix of σ, then $\sigma' \in [\![\mathcal{H}]\!]$.

3.3 Determinism

A set of executions is deterministic if corresponding to every input signal and initial state, there is at most one state signal.

Definition. A set of executions $E \subseteq Exec$ is said to be *deterministic* if for any pair of executions $\sigma = (\sigma_u, \sigma_x)$ and $\sigma' = (\sigma'_u, \sigma'_x)$ with $\sigma_u = \sigma'_u$ and $first(\sigma) = first(\sigma')$, $\sigma_x = \sigma'_x$.

The next proposition states that the semantics of a hybrid system is deterministic.

PROPOSITION 1. *Given a hybrid system $\mathcal{H}$ over (Var^X, Var^U), the set of executions $[\![\mathcal{H}]\!]$ is deterministic.*

Note that given an input trajectory and an initial state, the state trajectory if it exists corresponds to the unique solution guaranteed by the conditions of existence and uniqueness on the system of differential equations. The discrete jumps are correspond to a function from the initial state and input to a final state (as opposed to a relation), and hence is deterministic. The rest are standard constructs of a programming language which do not introduce any non-determinism. Details of the proof can be found in the Appendix.

Given an input signal and initial state, there might not always exist a corresponding state signal. For instance, for the flow construct, the solution of the differential equations corresponding to an input signal and an initial state may not satisfy the invariant. The other reason why a state signal might not exists is if the input is not of the expected type, that is, a discrete transition expects an impulse input and a continuous execution an input trajectory. Hence, we define the notion of a valid input for a given state.

Definition. An input signal σ_u is said to be *valid* for $\mathcal{H}$ and an initial state $\bar{x}_0$, if there exists an execution (σ_u, σ_x) in $\mathcal{H}$ with $first(\sigma_x) = \bar{x}_0$. In this case, we will denote the unique state signal corresponding to an input signal σ_u and an initial state $\bar{x}_0$ as $\Phi_{\mathcal{H}}(\sigma_u, \bar{x}_0)$.

When $\mathcal{H}$ is clear from the context, we drop the subscript $\mathcal{H}$ in $\Phi_{\mathcal{H}}$.

4. NON-INTERFERENCE

In this section, we present a notion of non-interference [4] for hybrid systems. There are various formalizations of non-interference on different system models; in the context of program semantics one typically requires that the values of high security variables do not affect those of low security variables [12, 8].

As is common, we consider a simple scenario with only two security levels H and L, for high and low security data, respectively. Non-interference requires that, for any two input signals that agree on their low security components, the corresponding state signals, if any, also agree on the low components. Hence, the effects of changes in the high security components is not observable.

More formally, let Var_L^U and Var_H^U be a partition of Var^U into low security and high security input variables, and similarly, Var_L^X and Var_H^X a partition of Var^X into low and high security state variables. The variable τ will be use to range over the security types, namely, H and L, and we assume the ordering $L < H$. We use $\bar{x}|_\tau$ and $\bar{u}|_\tau$ to represent the projection of the state $\bar{x}$ and the input $\bar{u}$ to the components corresponding to the variables with security type τ or lower, respectively; and similarly, we use $\sigma_u|_\tau$ and $\sigma_x|_\tau$ to denote the projection of the input signal and the state signal to the variables with security type τ or lower, respectively.

Definition. A hybrid system $\mathcal{H}$ over $(Var_L^U \cup Var_H^U, Var_L^X \cup Var_H^X)$ satisfies *non-interference* if for every pair of initial states $\bar{x}_0$ and $\bar{x}_0'$ and every pair of input signals σ_u and σ_u' such that $\bar{x}_0|_L = \bar{x}_0'|_L$ and $\sigma_u|_L = \sigma_u'|_L$, the following hold:

- σ_u is valid for $\bar{x}_0$ if and only if σ_u' is valid for $\bar{x}_0'$, and

- If σ_u is valid for $\bar{x}_0$ and σ_u' is valid for $\bar{x}_0'$, then
$$\Phi(\sigma_u, \bar{x}_0)|_L = \Phi(\sigma_u', \bar{x}_0')|_L.$$

We assume that the output variables are the same as the state variables, however, not all the state variables are observable, only the low security state variables are public.

Remark. A well-studied problem in control theory is observability, wherein, the question is to estimate the current state of the system by observing its output. Non-interference, on the other hand, refers to the problem of inferring the high input or the state by observing the low input or the state.

5. A SOLUTION BASED ON TYPE SYSTEMS

In this section, we present a security type system for statically reasoning about information flow in hybrid systems. The type system is sound, i.e., it guarantees that every well-typed hybrid system satisfies non-interference. Our presentation of the type system closely follows that of [12], but is extended with typing rules for the continuous specification of the system. The typing rules are given in Figures 1, 2, and 3 and are explained below.

(Int) $\lambda \vdash n : \tau \quad n = 0, 1$

(Var) $\lambda \vdash x : \tau\ var \quad \lambda(x) = \tau$

(R-Var) $\dfrac{\lambda \vdash x : \tau\ var}{\lambda \vdash x : \tau}$

(Op) $\dfrac{\begin{array}{l}\lambda \vdash e_1 : \tau \\ \lambda \vdash e_2 : \tau\end{array}}{\lambda \vdash e_1 \circ e_2 : \tau} \quad \circ\ \text{binary operator}$

Figure 1: Typing rules for expressions

A type system is used to derive judgments of the form $\lambda \vdash p : \rho$. Here, λ is an environment that assigns a security type H or L to each variable, p is either an expression, a variable, or a hybrid system, and ρ is either τ (corresponding to an expression), $\tau\ var$ (corresponding to a variable), or $\tau\ cmd$ (corresponding to a hybrid system).

(Jump) $\dfrac{\begin{array}{ll}\lambda \vdash x_i : \tau_i\ var & \text{for } 1 \le i \le n \\ \lambda \vdash e_i : \tau_i & \text{for } 1 \le i \le n \\ \tau \le \tau_i & \text{for } 1 \le i \le n\end{array}}{\lambda \vdash [x_1 := e_1, \cdots, x_n := e_n] : \tau\ cmd}$

(Flow) $\dfrac{\begin{array}{ll}\lambda \vdash x_i : \tau_i\ var & \text{for } 1 \le i \le n \\ \lambda \vdash e_i : \tau_i & \text{for } 1 \le i \le n \\ \lambda \vdash b : \tau & \\ \tau \le \tau_i & \text{for } 1 \le i \le n\end{array}}{\lambda \vdash \langle \dot{x}_1 := e_1, \cdots, \dot{x}_n := e_n, b \rangle : \tau\ cmd}$

(Comp) $\dfrac{\begin{array}{l}\lambda \vdash \mathcal{H}_1 : \tau\ cmd \\ \lambda \vdash \mathcal{H}_2 : \tau\ cmd\end{array}}{\lambda \vdash \mathcal{H}_1 ; \mathcal{H}_2 : \tau\ cmd}$

(If) $\dfrac{\begin{array}{l}\lambda \vdash b : \tau \\ \lambda \vdash \mathcal{H}_1 : \tau\ cmd \\ \lambda \vdash \mathcal{H}_2 : \tau\ cmd\end{array}}{\lambda \vdash \text{if } b \text{ then } \mathcal{H}_1 \text{ else } \mathcal{H}_2 : \tau\ cmd}$

(While) $\dfrac{\begin{array}{l}\lambda \vdash b : \tau \\ \lambda \vdash \mathcal{H} : \tau\ cmd\end{array}}{\lambda \vdash \text{while } b \text{ do } \mathcal{H} : \tau\ cmd}$

Figure 2: Typing rules for commands

(Subtype-1) $\dfrac{\begin{array}{l}\lambda \vdash p : \tau\ cmd \\ \tau' \le \tau\end{array}}{\lambda \vdash p : \tau'\ cmd}$

(Subtype-2) $\dfrac{\begin{array}{l}\lambda \vdash p : \tau \\ \tau \le \tau'\end{array}}{\lambda \vdash p : \tau'}$

Figure 3: Subtyping rules

The statements without a horizontal line are axioms. Statements with a horizontal line are inference rules, with the premise above and the conclusion below the line. A typing judgment is inferred from the type system, if it is the last statement in a sequence of statements such that each statement is either an axiom, or is inferred by an inference rule of the type system from previous statements in the sequence. We say that a hybrid system $\mathcal{H}$ is *well-typed* according to a variable typing λ if there exists a τ such that $\lambda \vdash \mathcal{H} : \tau\ cmd$ can be inferred.

A judgment with security type τ for an expression e implies that the information contained in e is of type τ or lower. A type $\tau\ cmd$ for a hybrid system $\mathcal{H}$ indicates that every variable which $\mathcal{H}$ assigns to has type τ or greater.

This information is used to prevent explicit and implicit flows of information. *Explicit* flows are prevented, e.g., by the typing rules for (Jump) in Figure 2: the rule requires equality between the security types of the variable on the left and the expression on the right, preventing the explicit flow of high data into a low variable. Note however that the rule (Subtype-2) in Figure 3 allows to change the security type of right-hand expression to a higher level, thereby allowing flow from low to high. *Implicit* flows are prevented, e.g., by the typing rule (If) in Figure 2: the rule again requires equality between the security types of the guard and that of the branches, which prevents typing of programs of the kind

$$\text{if } h = 1 \text{ then } [l := 1] \text{ else } [l := 0] \; ,$$

in which the control flow (rather than an assignment) leaks information from high to low. The rule (Subtype-1) in Figure 3 allows to use programs with assignments to high variables as branches under a low guard (but not vice versa). Note that we do not need the (Subtype-1) rule in our setting, since all the state variables are present in the (Jump) and (Flow) equations, which in turn sets the type of every command to be the lowest type of the state variables. However, in a more general setting, where the jump and flow equations do not contain all the state variables, one will need subtyping.

The remainder of the typing rules are standard, with the exception of the rule (Flow) in Figure 2 that deals with the continuous behavior of the hybrid system. Again, non-interference is enforced in a system of differential equations by local static syntax checks on each of the differential equations (as if they were assignments).

The following theorem shows that a successful syntactic type check implies the semantic notion of non-interference.

THEOREM 1. *Let $\mathcal{H}$ be a hybrid system over the variables $(Var_L^U \cup Var_H^U, Var_L^X \cup Var_H^X)$. Let λ be a mapping that assigns L to every variable in $Var_L^U \cup Var_L^X$, and H to the remaining variables. Then a successful type check $\lambda \vdash \mathcal{H} \colon \rho$ implies that $\mathcal{H}$ satisfies non-interference.*

PROOF. We will prove the following claims:

1. If $\lambda \vdash e \colon \tau$ can be inferred, then for any two states $\bar{x}_1, \bar{x}_2 \in X$ and any two inputs $\bar{u}_1, \bar{u}_2 \in U$ such that $\bar{x}_1|_\tau = \bar{x}_2|_\tau$ and $\bar{u}_1|_\tau = \bar{u}_2|_\tau$, then $[\![e]\!](\bar{u}_1, \bar{x}_1) = [\![e]\!](\bar{x}_2, \bar{u}_2)$.

2. If $\lambda \vdash \mathcal{H} \colon \rho$, then for every pair of initial states $\bar{x}_0$ and $\bar{x}_0'$ and every pair of input signals σ_u and σ_u' such that $\bar{x}_0|_L = \bar{x}_0'|_L$ and $\sigma_u|_L = \sigma_u'|_L$, the following hold:

   (a) σ_u is valid for $\bar{x}_0$ if and only if σ_u' is valid for $\bar{x}_0'$, and

   (b) if σ_u is valid for $\bar{x}_0$ and σ_u' is valid for $\bar{x}_0'$, then $\Phi(\sigma_u, \bar{x}_0)|_L = \Phi(\sigma_u', \bar{x}_0')|_L$.

   (c) if σ_u is valid for $\bar{x}_0$ and σ_u' is valid for $\bar{x}_0'$, then $(\sigma_u, \Phi(\sigma_u, \bar{x}_0))$ is a complete execution of $\mathcal{H}$ if and only if $(\sigma_u', \Phi(\sigma_u', \bar{x}_0'))$ is a complete execution of $\mathcal{H}$.

Proof by induction on the structure of the inference. More precisely, it suffices to show that each of the inference rules preserves the claims. First we show that the first claim holds for the inference rules corresponding to the expressions.

Case (Int): Here $e = n$, where $n = 0$ or 1. Since $[\![e]\!](\bar{u}, \bar{x}) = n$ for every $\bar{u}$ and $\bar{x}$, the claim is trivially satisfied.

Case (R-Var): Here $e = x$, where x is a variable. Note that $\lambda \vdash x \colon \tau$ *var* implies that $\lambda(x) = \tau$. Again, the claim is trivially satisfied.

Case (Op): Let $\bar{x}_1, \bar{x}_2 \in X$ be two states and $\bar{u}_1, \bar{u}_2 \in U$ be two inputs such that $\bar{x}_1|_\tau = \bar{x}_2|_\tau$ and $\bar{u}_1|_\tau = \bar{u}_2|_\tau$. Then $[\![e_1 \circ e_2]\!](\bar{u}_1, \bar{x}_1) = [\![e_1]\!](\bar{u}_1, \bar{x}_1) \circ [\![e_2]\!](\bar{u}_1, \bar{x}_1) = [\![e_1]\!](\bar{u}_2, \bar{x}_2) \circ [\![e_2]\!](\bar{u}_2, \bar{x}_2)$ (induction hypothesis) $= [\![e_1 \circ e_2]\!](\bar{u}_2, \bar{x}_2)$.

Case (Subtype-1): Let $\bar{x}_1, \bar{x}_2 \in X$ be two states and $\bar{u}_1, \bar{u}_2 \in U$ be two inputs such that $\bar{x}_1|_{\tau'} = \bar{x}_2|_{\tau'}$ and $\bar{u}_1|_{\tau'} =$

$\bar{u}_2|_{\tau'}$. Then, $\bar{x}_1|_\tau = \bar{x}_2|_\tau$ and $\bar{u}_1|_\tau = \bar{u}_2|_\tau$, since $\tau \leq \tau'$ implies that the variables with type τ is a subset of variables of type τ'. Therefore, $[\![e]\!](\bar{u}_1, \bar{x}_1) = [\![e]\!](\bar{x}_2, \bar{u}_2)$.

Next, we show that the second claim holds for the inference rules corresponding to the hybrid system. Let $\bar{x}_0$ and $\bar{x}_0'$ be states and σ_u and σ_u' be a pair of input signals that are valid for $\bar{x}_0$ and $\bar{x}_0'$, respectively, such that $\bar{x}_0|_L = \bar{x}_0'|_L$ and $\sigma_u|_L = \sigma_u'|_L$.

Case (Jump): The inputs signals corresponding to a jump are just elements of the input. The claim 2(a) is trivially true since every input for a discrete transition is valid for every state since $[\![e_i]\!]$ is a function. For claim 2(b), we need to show that for each variable x_i such that $\lambda(x_i) = L$, $[\![e_i]\!](\sigma_u, \bar{x}_0) = [\![e_i]\!](\sigma_u', \bar{x}_0')$. Since τ_i is L in this case, the hypothesis for the first part of the claim corresponding to e_i holds and hence $[\![e_i]\!](\sigma_u, \bar{x}_0) = [\![e_i]\!](\sigma_u', \bar{x}_0')$.

Case (Flow): First, we show that the solutions of the differential equations on $(\sigma_u, \bar{x}_0)$ and $(\sigma_u', \bar{x}_0')$ agree on the low variables. Let us denote by $\hat{\Phi}(\sigma_u, \bar{x}_0)$, the solution of the differential equations $\dot{x}_i = e_i$, $1 \leq i \leq n$. ($\hat{\Phi}$ differs from Φ in that it does not need to satisfy the invariant b).

For each $x_i \in Var_L^X$, $\tau_i = L$. Hence, e_i is independent of the variables in Var_H^X and Var_H^U. Hence, the set of differential equations corresponding to Var_L^X form a system of differential equations with Var_L^U as the input variables. Let us call the system S. Hence, $\hat{\Phi}(\sigma_u, \bar{x}_0)|_L$ (with initial state $\bar{x}_0|_L$) and $\sigma_u|_L$, and $\hat{\Phi}(\sigma_u', \bar{x}_0')|_L$ (with initial state $\bar{x}_0'|_L$) and $\sigma_u'|_L$, also satisfy system S. Since $\bar{x}_0|_L = \bar{x}_0'|_L$ and $\sigma_u|_L = \sigma_u'|_L$, and the solutions of the differential equations are unique (due to standard conditions of existence and uniqueness of differential equations), we obtain that $\hat{\Phi}(\sigma_u, \bar{x}_0)|_L = \hat{\Phi}(\sigma_u', \bar{x}_0')|_L$.

Suppose σ_u is valid for $\bar{x}_0$. Then $\hat{\Phi}(\sigma_u, \bar{x}_0)$ satisfies the invariant b. Since b has type $\tau \leq \tau_i$ for every i, b is of type low. Since $\hat{\Phi}(\sigma_u, \bar{x}_0)|_L = \hat{\Phi}(\sigma_u', \bar{x}_0')|_L$ and b is of type low, $\hat{\Phi}(\sigma_u', \bar{x}_0')$ also satisfies b and hence is valid. Therefore σ_u' is valid for $\bar{x}_0'$. The other direction is similar.

If σ_u is valid for $\bar{x}_0$ and σ_u' is valid for $\bar{x}_0'$, then $\hat{\Phi}(\sigma_u, \bar{x}_0)|_L = \hat{\Phi}(\sigma_u', \bar{x}_0')|_L$ implies that $\Phi(\sigma_u, \bar{x}_0)|_L = \Phi(\sigma_u', \bar{x}_0')|_L$.s

Case (Comp): Suppose σ_u is valid for $\bar{x}_0$ in $\mathcal{H}$. There exists an execution $\sigma = (\sigma_u, \sigma_x) \in Exec(\mathcal{H})$. Then there exist executions σ^f and σ^s such that $\sigma = \sigma^f \sigma^s$, where σ^f is a complete execution or σ^s is empty. We can apply the induction hypothesis on $\mathcal{H}_1$ to infer that the prefix σ_u' corresponding to σ_u^f, namely, $\sigma_u^{f'}$ is valid as well, that is, there exists an execution $\sigma_f' = (\sigma_u^{f'}, \sigma_x^{f'})$ of $\mathcal{H}_1$. Further, either σ^f and $\sigma^{f'}$ are both complete or are both not complete. Also, the lower part of last states of the executions coincide. Hence, we can apply the induction hypothesis again on the remaining input signal $\sigma^{s'}$ to obtain an execution for $\mathcal{H}_2$. Concatenating the two gives an execution for $\mathcal{H}$ which is valid for σ_u' and $\bar{x}_0'$. Further, the executions corresponding to both σ_u and σ_u' are either both complete or incomplete follows directly from the induction hypotheses corresponding to Claim 2(c) for $\mathcal{H}_1$ and $\mathcal{H}_2$. Finally, $\Phi(\sigma_u, \bar{x}_0)|_L = \Phi_{\mathcal{H}_2}(\sigma_u^s, (\Phi_{\mathcal{H}_1}(\sigma_u^f, \bar{x}_0)))|_L = \Phi_{\mathcal{H}_2}(\sigma_u^{s'}, (\Phi_{\mathcal{H}_1}(\sigma_u^{f'}, \bar{x}_0')))|_L = \Phi(\sigma_u', \bar{x}_0')|_L$.

Case (If): If σ_u is valid for $\bar{x}_0$, then either $b \models \bar{x}_0$ and σ_u is valid for $\mathcal{H}_1$ or $b \not\models \bar{x}_0$ and σ_u is valid for $\mathcal{H}_2$. First, we note that if there is at least one low variable in the system, then τcmd is always L (one can prove this by induction). Assuming $Var_L^X \neq \emptyset$ (otherwise there is nothing to prove), we infer that $\tau = L$. Since $\bar{x}_0|_L = \bar{x}_0'|_L$, and the type of b is

$L, b \models \bar{x}_0'$ if and only if $b \models \bar{x}_0$. We obtain from induction hypothesis of $\mathcal{H}_1$ and $\mathcal{H}_2$ that either $b \models \bar{x}_0'$ and σ_u' is valid for $\mathcal{H}_1$ or $b \not\models \bar{x}_0'$ and σ_u' is valid for $\mathcal{H}_2$. There fore σ_u' is valid for $\mathcal{H}$ with $\bar{x}_0'$ as the initial state. Also, note that state signals agree on the low variable values and on the completeness of the execution.

Case (While): The argument is similar to the case for (Comp). Here an execution is split into a finite number of sub-executions into two. If an input signal σ_u is valid for $\bar{x}_0$, then it can be split into sub-signals corresponding to the body of the while loop, namely, $\mathcal{H}$. Then induction hypothesis can be applied to each of these parts to obtain a valid execution for each of the sub-signals of σ_u'. These can then be concatenated to obtain an execution to the while loop, using the fact that the sub-executions agree on the low variable values and b only depends on the low variable values. □

Remark. The above theorem establishes the soundness of the type inference system. In fact, we can also show that every hybrid system, in which the expressions on the right hand sides have variables whose type is not higher than the type of the variable on the left, and the variables in the guards (of the if and while statements) is low, has a type inference using the type system.

Discussions.

Though the rules in the type system appear similar to that in [12], there are some fundamental differences between their interpretation in a hybrid system versus that in a discrete program. The variable assignments to all the variables happen concurrently in the hybrid system, and so does the evolution of the continuous variables. One can safely interpret a variable update as a sequence of updates to a fresh set of variables followed by a copy-back to the original variables.

However, such a sequential interpretation is not possible for the continuous evolution. In particular, one not only needs to ensure that in each of the individual differential equations $\dot{x}_i = e_i$, there is no unauthorized flow from the variables in e_i to x_i, but also needs to recursively ensure that there is no indirect path from a higher typed variable to x_i in the set of differential equations. However, it turns out that this is equivalent to ensuring that each individual differential equation is well-typed. More precisely, the typing rules impose a structure on the system of differential equations which decompose the system into two subsystems: (1) a subsystem whose statespace corresponds to only the low state variables, and inputs given by only low input variables; and (2) a subsystem whose statespace corresponds to the high state variables with inputs consisting of all the input variables and also the low state variables. It is clear that the solutions projected to the low state variables in such a system depend only the low variable values. For example, for a linear system $\dot{x} = Ax + Bu$, this implies that A and B have upper block triangular structure (for appropriate ordering of the state and input variables).

Example. Consider the simple hybrid system:

$$\mathcal{H} := \text{if } u > 0 \text{ then } \langle \dot{x} = 1, x > 3 \rangle \text{ else } \langle \dot{x} = 2, x < 0 \rangle,$$

where u is a high input variable and x is a low state variable. There is no direct flow of information from from u to x, but there is an implicit flow due to the condition $u > 0$. That is,

by observing x, one can deduce whether $u > 0$ or not. We will not be able to deduce $\gamma \vdash \mathcal{H} : \tau \, cmd$ for any τ.

Now suppose u is a low input variable and x is a high state variable. The following is a partial derivation of a judgment for $\mathcal{H}$.

1. $\lambda \vdash \langle \dot{x} = 1, x > 3 \rangle : H \, cmd$

2. $\lambda \vdash \langle \dot{x} = 2, x < 0 \rangle : H \, cmd$

3. $\lambda \vdash u > 0 : L$

4. $L \leq H$

5. (Subtype -2) $\lambda \vdash u > 0 : H$ (using 3 and 4)

6. (If) $\lambda \vdash \text{if } u > 0 \text{ then } \langle \dot{x} = 1, x > 3 \rangle \text{ else } \langle \dot{x} = 2, x < 0 \rangle : H \, cmd$ (using 1, 2 and 5)

Here, the derivations corresponding to 1, 2 and 3 are not given.

6. CONCLUSIONS AND FUTURE DIRECTIONS

We formalized a notion of non-interference for hybrid systems and proposed a type system-based static analysis for verifying non-interference. Non-interference is often considered to be too restrictive for practical scenarios. In the context of discrete programs, this restriction is typically circumvented by declassification [9] (which allows to specify which parts of the secret may be leaked) or by quantification [1] (which allows to specify bounds on the amount of leaked information). As ongoing work, we are investigating formalizations and analysis techniques for such relaxed notions in the context of hybrid systems.

Moreover, we will investigate hybrid systems counterpart to the interpretation of information-flow properties as a safety property over pairs of program runs [11]. Progress along those lines will allows us to use existing safety analysis tools for reasoning about information-flow properties in hybrid systems [3].

7. ACKNOWLEDGEMENTS

The authors would like to thank Richard Murray for useful inputs.

8. REFERENCES

[1] M. Backes, B. Köpf, and A. Rybalchenko. Automatic Discovery and Quantification of Information Leaks. In *Proc. 30th IEEE Symposium on Security and Privacy (SSP '09)*, pages 141–153. IEEE, 2009.

[2] A. A. Cárdenas, S. Amin, Z.-S. Lin, Y.-L. Huang, C.-Y. Huang, and S. Sastry. Attacks against process control systems: risk assessment, detection, and response. In B. S. N. Cheung, L. C. K. Hui, R. S. Sandhu, and D. S. Wong, editors, *ASIACCS*, pages 355–366. ACM, 2011.

[3] G. Frehse, C. L. Guernic, A. Donzé, S. Cotton, R. Ray, O. Lebeltel, R. Ripado, A. Girard, T. Dang, and O. Maler. Spaceex: Scalable verification of hybrid systems. In G. Gopalakrishnan and S. Qadeer, editors, *CAV*, volume 6806 of *Lecture Notes in Computer Science*, pages 379–395. Springer, 2011.

[4] J. A. Goguen and J. Meseguer. Security policies and security models. In *IEEE Symposium on Security and Privacy*, pages 11–20, 1982.

[5] G. S. Graham and P. J. Denning. Protection: principles and practice. In *Proceedings of the May 16-18, 1972, spring joint computer conference*, AFIPS '72 (Spring), pages 417–429, New York, NY, USA, 1972. ACM.

[6] T. A. Henzinger. The theory of hybrid automata. In *LICS*, pages 278–292, 1996.

[7] H. K. Khalil. *Nonlinear Systems*. Prentice-Hall, Upper Saddle River, NJ, 1996.

[8] A. Sabelfeld and A. C. Myers. Language-based information-flow security. *IEEE Journal on Selected Areas in Communications*, 21:2003, 2003.

[9] A. Sabelfeld and D. Sands. Dimensions and Principles of Declassification. In *Proc. IEEE Workshop on Computer Security Foundations (CSFW '05)*, pages 255–269. IEEE Computer Society, 2005.

[10] J. H. Saltzer, D. P. Reed, and D. D. Clark. End-to-end arguments in system design. *ACM Trans. Comput. Syst.*, 2(4):277–288, Nov. 1984.

[11] T. Terauchi and A. Aiken. Secure information flow as a safety problem. In *Proceedings of the 12th international conference on Static Analysis*, SAS'05, pages 352–367, Berlin, Heidelberg, 2005. Springer-Verlag.

[12] D. M. Volpano, C. E. Irvine, and G. Smith. A sound type system for secure flow analysis. *Journal of Computer Security*, 4(2/3):167–188, 1996.

APPENDIX

Proof of determinism of the hybrid system.

Proof of Proposition 1. We will prove the following statements by induction on $\mathcal{H}$.

- $[\![\mathcal{H}]\!]$ is deterministic.

- Given any execution $\sigma = \sigma_0 \sigma_1 \cdots \sigma_l$, there exists at most one i such that $\sigma[0, i] = \sigma_0 \sigma_1 \cdots \sigma_i$ is a complete execution of $\mathcal{H}$, that is, $\sigma[0, i] \in [\![\mathcal{H}]\!]^c$.

Proof by induction on the structure of $\mathcal{H}$.

- $\mathcal{H} = \langle \dot{x}_1 = e_1, \cdots, \dot{x}_n = e_n, b \rangle$: The continuous dynamics is deterministic by the assumptions of existence and uniqueness of the solutions of the differential equations. Further, given any execution $\sigma = \sigma_0 \sigma_1 \cdots \sigma_l$, if there exists an i such that $\sigma[0, i] \in [\![\mathcal{H}]\!]^c$, then $i = 0$. This is obvious from the definition of $[\![\mathcal{H}]\!]^c$.

- $\mathcal{H} = [x_1 := e_1, \cdots, x_n := e_n]$: Since $[\![e_i]\!]$ is a function mapping the input $\bar{u}$ and the initial state $\bar{x}_1$ to a unique state $\bar{x}_2$, $[\![\mathcal{H}]\!]$ is deterministic. Again, any complete execution of $\mathcal{H}$ has exactly one element.

- $\mathcal{H} = \mathcal{H}_1; \mathcal{H}_2$: By induction hypothesis, we have that both $\mathcal{H}_1$ and $\mathcal{H}_2$ are deterministic. Suppose $\mathcal{H}$ is not deterministic. Then there exist executions $\sigma = (\sigma_u, \sigma_x)$ and $\sigma' = (\sigma'_u, \sigma'_x)$ with $\sigma_u = \sigma'_u$ and $first(\sigma) = first(\sigma')$, and $\sigma_x \neq \sigma'_x$. Then there exist i and i' such that $\sigma[0, i] \in [\![\mathcal{H}_1]\!]^c$ and $\sigma'[0, i'] \in [\![\mathcal{H}_1]\!]^c$. Note that the length of σ and σ' are the same. Let us say that the length is l.

  We claim that $i = i'$. Otherwise, w.l.o.g, we can assume that $i < i'$. Since $[\![\mathcal{H}_1]\!]$ is prefix closed $\sigma'[0, i] \in [\![\mathcal{H}_1]\!]$. If $\sigma'[0, i] \neq \sigma[0, i]$, then it contradicts the determinism of $\mathcal{H}_1$. If $\sigma'[0, i] = \sigma[0, i]$, then $\sigma'[0, i]$ is complete, and it contradicts the second part of the induction hypothesis. Therefore $i = i'$. Further $\sigma[0, i] = \sigma'[0, i]$, otherwise, the determinism of $\mathcal{H}_1$ is contradicted. Note that since $\sigma[0, i] = \sigma'[0, i]$, the initial states of $\sigma[i, l]$ and $\sigma'[i, l]$ are the same. And the inputs are the same. Hence, determinism of $\mathcal{H}_2$ implies that $\sigma_x[i, l] = \sigma'_x[i, l]$. This contradicts our assumption that $\sigma_x \neq \sigma'_x$.

  The second part of the claim follows directly from the fact that if there exist two distinct prefixes of σ corresponding to $\mathcal{H}$, then there exists two distinct prefixes corresponding to either $\mathcal{H}_1$ or $\mathcal{H}_2$ contradicting the induction hypothesis.

- $\mathcal{H} = $ if b then $\mathcal{H}_1$ else $\mathcal{H}_2$: Given σ and σ' be executions of $\mathcal{H}$ with the same initial states and input signal, then both the execution belong to $\mathcal{H}_1$ or to $\mathcal{H}_2$ depending on whether the initial states satisfy b or not, respectively. Hence, the determinism of $\mathcal{H}_1$ and $\mathcal{H}_2$ imply that $\sigma_x = \sigma'_x$.

  Again, if the second part of the claim does not hold for $\mathcal{H}$, then it does not hold for either $\mathcal{H}_1$ or $\mathcal{H}_2$.

- $\mathcal{H} = $ while b do $\mathcal{H}^s$: Suppose there exist σ and σ' in $[\![\mathcal{H}]\!]$ with the same initial states and input signal. Suppose $\sigma = \sigma_0 \cdots \sigma_l$ and $\sigma' = \sigma'_0 \cdots \sigma'_{l'}$, where each $\sigma_i \in [\![\mathcal{H}^s]\!]$ and $\sigma'_j \in [\![\mathcal{H}^s]\!]$. We can show using the arguments similar to the case where $\mathcal{H} = \mathcal{H}_1; \mathcal{H}_2$ repeatedly, that $l = l'$ and the length of σ_i is the same as that of σ'_i for every i. Then, the determinism of $\mathcal{H}^s$ implies that $\sigma_i = \sigma'_i$ for each i.

  For the second part of the claim, assume that $\sigma[0, i]$ and $\sigma[0, i']$ are two prefixes of σ which belong to $[\![\mathcal{H}]\!]$. Then $last\sigma[0, i] \not\models b$. However, since $\sigma[0, i']$ contains a sequence of complete executions of $\mathcal{H}^s$ and this execution sequence coincides with that in the part $\sigma[0, i]$, hence $\sigma[i, i']$ also contains a sequence of complete executions of $\mathcal{H}^s$. Further, since all the executions in the sequence satisfy b at the initial states, $first\sigma[i, i'] \models b$. This is contradictions since $last\sigma[0, i] = first\sigma[i, i']$.

Achieving Resilience of Heterogeneous Networks Through Predictive, Formal Analysis

Zhijing Qin* Grit Denker† Carolyn Talcott† Nalini Venkatasubramanian*

*(zhijingq,nalini)@ics.uci.edu   †(grit.denker,clt)@sri.com

*Department of Computer Science
University of California, Irvine
Irvine, CA, USA

†Computer Science Laboratory
SRI International
Menlo Park, CA, USA

ABSTRACT

Rapid development and wide deployment of wireless technologies in recent years have brought an increasing number and variety of services that are accessible directly from mobile terminals via multiple network access technologies (e.g, Ethernet, WiFi, Bluetooth, LTE, etc). A particular traffic flow may go through different kinds of networks, which greatly increases the end-to-end connectivity opportunities. However, the disadvantage of multinetworks is that a failure or change in one network type may affect many traffic flows. Thus, the various networks in a multinetwork cannot be managed in isolation. Rather we need methodologies that analyze the effects of changes in these dynamic and heterogeneous network environments in unison. Traditional network analysis approaches only focus on static network attributes and do not fully consider the impact of failures on quality of services (QoS) across flows. In this paper, we design and implement a "what-if" analysis methodology using formal methods. Our methodology analyzes the impact of failures and changes in heterogeneous networks on QoS of flows. The results of the formal analysis can guide network administrators in their decisions to proactively adapt network configurations to achieve mission or application objectives. We illustrate our methodology with the help of use cases such as incorporating additional nodes in a network or reconfiguring the network due to failure. We compare our results with conventional network configuration approaches and show how our formal methodology provides more effective decision support than conventional network configuration approaches and that it scales better than simulation approaches.

Categories and Subject Descriptors

I.6.4 [Model Validation and Analysis]:

Keywords

Formal Analysis, Heterogeneous Networks

1. INFRASTRUCTURE DEPENDABILITY IN MULTINETWORKS

Instrumented Cyber Physical Spaces (ICPSs) are physical spaces that have been instrumented with "intelligence" through heterogeneous sensing, actuation and communication mechanisms. Sensing capabilities range from heat, pressure, movement, temperature, to images or videos to name a few. Devices can be actuated to achieve desired changes in the physical world. ICPSs are relevant for many application domains, including infrastructure security, health care, or smart homes. The power of ICPSs lies in achieving a common picture of the physical space–also called situational awareness (SA)–by observing sensors in unison and deciding how to best act upon that SA to achieve application, human or mission needs. We illustrate our vision of adaptive ICPSs with a campus emergency response scenario. Envision a university campus instrumented with cameras overlooking various areas and monitoring building hallways. Temperature sensors are installed throughout buildings to monitor for situations such as fires. Movement sensors observe pedestrian traffic and can determine whether areas are vacated or not. Mobile devices provide location information for individuals and can be a source of videos or images.

The ICPS can be viewed as a *multinetwork* consisting of devices that have a variety of communication capabilities and mobility profiles. Communication services range from Ethernet to sensor networks to wireless services such as Bluetooth, Zigbee, 802.11 or WAN. Achieving SA in such multinetworks to adapt them to mission needs is challenging. Take for example the case of a fire. Some of the cameras or the networks they are using to communicate data may no longer be operational. It is necessary to re-orient other cameras to ensure surveillance of the entire space. If the network has been partially rendered unusable through a fire, traffic may need to be rerouted or additional mobile routers might need to be deployed to support the network load. Increased traffic load may be due to first responders needing to coordinate their actions. All these changes will cause the network load to change and network administrators require information for decision making - networks may need to be reconfigured and additional network components may need to be deployed in order to best suit application needs under changed circumstances. This is but one example of an *ICPS multinetwork that can be dynamically adapted to new infrastructure situations or application quality-of-service (QoS) requirements.*

Our overall objective is to provide techniques for dependability and resilience in multinetwork ICPSs. While there are potential benefits in performance and QoS of Multinetworks, there are also potential new challenges. if one network goes down, it might affect various network traffic flows. Therefore, it is not longer sufficient to manage each network in isolation. Rather network administrators have to manage networks in the multinetwork in unison to achieve best performance across all network traffic and networks.

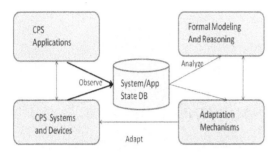

Figure 1: A Reflective CPS Architecture

We propose a reflective (observe-analyze-adapt (OAA)) architecture as shown in Figure 1 to achieve this objective. At the heart of the OAA paradigm is a database with system and application state information. This digital state information of the ICPS guides a range of "safe" adaptations to achieve end-to-end infrastructure and information dependability. There are many challenges that need to be solved to achieve this vision. In this paper we address one of those challenges: provide **resilience and dependability of ICPSs in the face of network or infrastructure failures**. We propose an approach to proactively deal with disruptions to the communication infrastructure of multinetworks. We use the OAA approach because the multinetwork has a model of itself, its objectives, and its effects on the environment. Our goal is to achieve network dependability and resilience through adaptation using runtime application of formal analysis methods.

Our work is set in the context of a multinetwork management platform called "Multinetwork INformation Architecture" (MINA). MINA (see Figure 2) is a middleware system developed on top of UC Irvine I-Sensorium [13]. MINA collects network state information from heterogeneous networks and provides management functions to address resource provisioning, configuration management and fault analysis.

MINA is organized into a three-tier architecture with mobile, but resource-constrained nodes in Tier 3, more stationary but also more powerful nodes in Tier 2, and a centralized server in Tier 1. Different kinds of networks are present in a multinetwork ranging from wired networks (solid lines in Figure2) to wireless networks (dashed lines in Figure 2). Accordingly nodes differ in their capabilities (mobility, computation, memory, power, etc) and edges in their link characteristics. Nodes may be equipped with more than one access technology.

The objective of our analysis is to ensure that quality-of-service (QoS) requirements of network flows are satisfied. A network flow is traffic flowing from a source node to one or more target nodes. For example, a flow may describe

imagery flowing from a camera installed on campus to the campus' security control center. Or a flow may describe the traffic that flows from the control center to all cameras in a building to disable power-safe modes on the cameras. The concept of network flow abstracts from the specific route the packets for this flow will take. To check satisfaction of flow QoS, we need network state information as collected in MINA. We employ formal analysis methods to check QoS satisfaction.

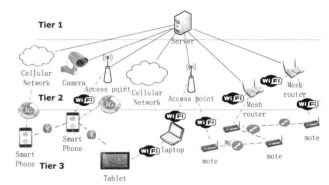

Figure 2: MINA: A Multinetwork Information Architecture

The proposed analysis methodology performs various "what if" analyses asking questions such as

- What happens if a node fails? The objective of this analysis is to determine how critical a node is, not just to one network flow, but to all flows.

- What should we do if we have additional network resource such as mobile routers? Where should we deploy them most effectively? The objective of the analysis is to determine where additional nodes would positively impact QoS of all flows.

- What happens if the load of selected flows changes and how can we best mitigate the effects?

- What happens if the link quality changes due to congestion or interference and how can we best mitigate the effects of degraded link quality?

Answers to these questions help to decide how to best utilize network resources or reconfigure the network to achieve better overall QoS requirements satisfaction. In turn, this will lead to better network resilience and dependability.

Related Work. Existing work on network analysis and prediction can be divided into static analysis and dynamic analysis. Static analysis only exams a snapshot of the the network. In [16], the authors determine the full network state including Internetwork Operating System bugs of devices, configuration errors, static/dynamic routing, and so on. They calculate all possible virtual paths according to the full network state and then compare the virtual paths with the available physical paths to check reachability. However, due to the large search state space, this approach is not very efficient. The same problem exists in [10]. The authors precompute routing tables for each state and employ formal methods to model every possible behavior of the network. [6] provides an effective way to reduce the state space. Both [10] and [16] only focus on the one time link failure and the network will converge to another stable state. In dynamic analysis a failure may cause other failures in future states. For example, a failing node does not only affect the flows going through that node, but also other flows due to flow rerouting. This is called cascading failures. In [8] the authors consider statistics of link failures and limited number of cascading failures. Different failures combinations can lead to loss of connectivity within a network or to severe congestion, as shown in [12]. They proposed a framework to analyze link availability in the context of link failures, changes of user behavior and routing. However, most of the cited approaches do not consider heterogeneous networks and do not study how the flows are affected by failures. In this paper, we provide an approach to handle (1) changing heterogeneous network topology (i.e. node failure, adding backup router, or network reconfiguration), while (2) taking into consideration how the flows' QoS performance are affected due to flow redistribution triggered by changes in the network topology. This approach is based on formal methods. Formal methods have been used to do network analysis [1], protocol proof [15] and network model checking [11]. To our best knowledge, there exist no tool that uses formal methods for the flow oriented predictive analysis of multinetworks.

The remainder of this paper is organized as follows: We introduce our formal model in Section 2. In Section 3 we present three use cases and compare the results our analysis method with conventional methods. Section 4 closes with concluding remarks.

2. FORMAL METHOD-BASED ANALYSIS METHODOLOGY

The objective of our analysis is to answer questions such as "what effect does a failing node have on all network flows" or "if one had more resources to deploy in the network, what would be the best location for an additional node." It turns out that underlying all of the questions listed in Section 1 is the concept of how critical a node is to the satisfaction of QoS requirements. We introduce the notion of "Node Criticality Index (NCI)." Nodes with the highest criticality index have the most negative effect on the overall QoS of flows when they fail. Thus, these nodes are the first targets when it comes to deploying backup nodes or relieving a node of high traffic loads. We distinguish our concept of NCI from conventional node importance measures used in existing work. The simplest node importance measure is node degree, which is defined as the number of neighbors a node has (see [2]). Closeness-based measure is another node importance measure that finds the distance center or the median of a graph. It has application in facility location [9], package delivery [3] and operations research problems. It is computed by summing up the distances from the current node to all remaining nodes. Betweenness is one of the most prominent node importance measures. It measures the influence of a node over the connection of other nodes by summing up the fraction of shortest paths between the other nodes that pass through it [4, 7]. However, none of these measures take into account how redistributed flows due to network changes influence overall QoS. The analysis methodology proposed here addresses that issue.

We use Maude [5] as our underlying formal method tool. Maude is a multiparadigm executable specification language encompassing both equational logic and rewriting logic. Maude allows modeling system states through user-defined data types and system dynamics through rewrite rules. The Maude interpreter is very efficient, allowing prototyping of quite complex test cases. Maude also provides efficient built-in search and model checking capabilities. Maude sources, executables for several platforms, the manual, a primer, cases studies, and papers are available from the Maude website http://maude.cs.uiuc.edu.

We formalize the analysis objectives as Maude models and rules. For example, if the analysis objective is to determine the most critical network node, then we provide a Maude specification and a set of rules that simulate in a network that a node fails, reroute affected flows and simulate QoS of the new network. Iterating this process over all nodes and comparing the resulting QoS of all flows allows us to determine the most critical node. If the analysis objective is to choose the best new access point for a wireless node when its access point fails, then we have a Maude specification and rules that simulates the overall performance for the different alternate access points. Thus, we generate a Maude specification according to the reasoning objective (step 3 in Figure 3). Information about the specific network topology and state and the flows is pulled from the MINA database (step 2 in Figure 3). We use the Maude engine to execute the specific analysis (step 4) and store any relevant analysis results (e.g., node criticality index or hints where new resources should be deployed) in the database (step 5). This information can be used by network administrators to devise new network reconfigurations and issue accordingly commands to the multinetwork (step 6).

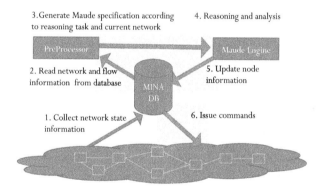

Figure 3: Workflow in the context of MINA

In the following we present some details about how we model networks and flows and what the rewriting rules to process network flows and determine QoS look like.

2.1 Network and Flow Specification

Information about networks and flows is stored in the MINA database as follows. A network node is represented by a 3-tuple containing *NodeId*, *neighbor list* and *weight list*. *neighbor list* contains all nodes directly linked to the node *NodeID*. The ith element in *weight list* represents the capacity of the link between *NodeId* and the ith element in the *neighbor list*. A flow is represented by an 8-tuple: *source*, *route*, *destination*, *flowID*, *type*, *throughput*, *packetlength* and *λ*. *route* is the sequence of nodes on the path of the flow from the source to the destination, *type* specifies the kind of traffic (e.g., ftp, audio, video, and so on), *packetlength* corresponds to the packet length when it is an ethernet packet or the length of the item sent on a different network, and *λ* is the mean packet arrival rate of this flow. Note the product of λ and *packetlength* is the throughput. In the following, we will show how we use the information about networks and flows that is stored in the MINA database to generate a Maude model.

We consider the nodes and links through which a flow goes as tandem queues (see Figure 4). The tandem queues refer to an arrangement of queues in which the queues are lined up one after the other: the outgoing traffic of the current queue is the incoming traffic of the next queue. A node consists of the queue and the network interface (NIC; there is possibly more than one NIC on a node). Currently we do not consider queue length limitations, or in other words, we assume there no packets are lost due to limited queues.

Since link propagation delay is extremely small, we only consider delay introduced by queueing and service time in the NIC. Thus, in our abstract model we assume the outgoing packet of one node to be the incoming packet of the subsequent node. This way, we divide an end-to-end flow into several sub flows, one for each hop along the path of the flow (see Fig 4). By doing so, we can iteratively propagate the QoS parameter computed in each node and accumulate the end-to-end QoS for a flow from its source to its destination. In this paper, we use delay as an example QoS parameter to illustrate our analysis methodology.

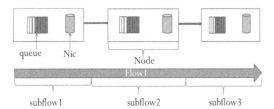

Figure 4: Network Flow Model

The flow model enables us to get the end-to-end delay by aggregating and propagating the delay incurred by each node. We use a simple M/M/1 model [14] to calculate the delay incurred by a single node. The M/M/1 represents the queue in a system having a single server, where arrivals are determined by a Poisson process and job service times have an exponential distribution. We denote the Poisson Arrival Distribution with (λ, n), where λ is the packet mean arrival rate and n is the packet length. The server's (network interface) mean service time is denoted by Ts. We use Poisson distribution to describe the flow pattern mainly because it is widely used to simulate network flow [14] and the Poisson distribution has perfect aggregation and partitioning attributes. For example, as shown in Fig 5(c), the Poisson pattern is not changed when a flow goes through a node with exponential service time. In Fig 5(b), flow A and B with mean arrival rate λ_1 and λ_2 are both the incoming Poisson flows at one node. After processing, the new aggregated flow is still a Poisson flow with a mean arrival rate $\lambda_1 + \lambda_2$. In Fig 5(a), a Poisson flow with mean arrival rate λ can be partitioned into two Poisson flows whose mean arrival rate's sum is still λ.

These important features enable us to apply the Possion-based delay calculation in each processor, regardless of how

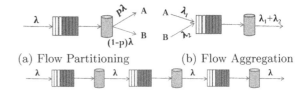

(a) Flow Partitioning   (b) Flow Aggregation

(c) Tandem Queue with Poisson Flow

Figure 5: Key Attributes of Flows with Poisson Arrival

the flows are distributed in the multinetwork:

$$Delay = n/(Ts - n)$$

2.2 Rewriting Rules for Analysis

We view the network as a set of nodes and flows. Each flow is a sequence of subflows, one subflow for each hop along the flow's path. Nodes and (sub)flows are basic concepts in our Maude model. We model the network as nodes N and sub flows SF. We also model the QoS parameters such as *delay*, throughput, jitter, packet loss and so on. So a network is modeled in Maude as a structure with the following elements: N(*node attributes*), SF(*subflow attributes*), *QoS attributes*.

Nodes N are modeled as a collection of attributes. Each attribute is represented as label(value)-pair. Variables (using capital letters) are used as a place holder for values in structures or rules. Attributes of nodes are the identity of the node (Nid(N1)), type of NIC (NIC(T))[1], transmission rate Tx(X)), Poison parameters (PoiPara(λ,n)), the number of flows expected to route through this node (Tot(S)), and the flows that have already arrived (Cur(C)). Thus a node is represented as N(Nid(N1),NIC(T),Tx(X),PoiPara(λ,n), Tot(S),Cur(C)).

Each subflow is modeled as a collection of attributes: identity of the parent flow Par(F1), the identity of the subflow Sub(S1), the identify of the source node of this subflow Src(N1) and its NIC type (SrcNIC(T)), and identity of the destination node of this subflow Dest(N2), the poison parameters PoiPara(λ_{in},n) for this subflow. and the incoming and outgoing QoS characteristics of this subflow. Since the examples in this paper only explore delay, we will only model incoming and outgoing delay (Delayin(DIN) and Delayout(DOUT)). Finally, we add a boolean flag to indicate whether the subflow was already processed by a rule (Proc(B)). Thus a subflow is represented as SF(Par(F1), Sub(SUB1),Src(N1), SrcNIC(T), Dest(N2), PoiPara(λ_{in},n_{in}), Proc(B), Delayin(DIN), DelayOut(DOUT)).

We have three main Maude rules that describe propagation of QoS characteristics of flows in the multinetwork: a) flow accumulation, b) flow processing, and c) flow propagation.

- *flow accumulation:* This rule is collecting all the sublows at one processor. The idea is that when multiple Poisson flows come into a processor, we aggregate the λ and n value for all flows to calculate the overall delay they have suffered given the service capacity of this processor (the capacity/transmission rate of the net-

---

[1] For simplicity and because of space limitation, we present our rules with one NIC per node.

work interface).

```
crl  N(Nid(N1), NIC(T), PoiPara(λ,n), Cur(C),...)
       SF(Src(N1), SrcNIC(T), PoiPara(λ_in,n_in),
           Proc(false), ...)

  => N(Nid(N1), NIC(T), PoiPara(λ',n'), Cur(C1),...)
       SF(Src(N1), SrcNIC(T), PoiPara(λ_in,n_in),
           Proc(true),...)
  if C1 := C + 1
     λ' := λ_in + λ
     n' := ( λ_in *n_in + λ * n)/(λ_in + λ).
```

Once the number of the accumulated flows reaches a predefined amount (indicated in processor by the value of attribute *total*), the *flow processing* rule will be triggered.

- *flow processing:* Once all incoming flows are accumulated, the node has a complete set of values of λ and n, and hence is able to calculate the new delay it incurred via the following rule. The new delay is added to the existing delay. Although we only focus on delay, we could similarly calculate other QoS attributes (e.g. jitter, packet loss, etc).

```
crl  N(Nid(N1), Tx(X), PoiPara(λ,n),...)
       SF(PoiPara(λ_in,n_in), Delayin(DIN)
           DelayOut(UNKNOWN),...)
  =>  N(Nid(N1), Tx(X), PoiPara(λ,n),...)
       SF(PoiPara(λ_in,n_in), Delayin(DIN)
           DelayOut(DOUT),...)
  if ( X - λ * n ) > 0
       DOUT := n_in / ( X - λ * n ) + DIN
```

- *flow propagation* Once the outgoing flow is generated by the node via the *flow processing* rule, it will be passed into the next node as an incoming flow. This way, the delay value can be propagated from the source to the destination.

```
rl  SF(Par(F1), Sub(S1), Src(N1), Dest(N2),
          Delayout(DOUT),...)
       SF(Par(F1), Sub(S2), Src(N2), Dest(N3),
          Delayin(UNKNOWN),...)
  =>  SF(Par(F1), Sub(S1), Src(N1), Dest(N2),
          Delayout(DOUT), ...)
       SF(Par(F1), Sub(S2), Src(N2), Dest(N3),
          Delayin(DOUT), ...)
```

2.3 Preliminary Validation

We performed a preliminary experiment to validate our Maude model. For this, we used the example network and flows shown in Fig 6(a) and Fig 6(b) as our test scenario. The example network has 30 nodes connected via links with different capacities (i.e. Ethernet 100Mbps, WiFi 10Mbps, BlueTooth 2Mbps), and 8 flows are specified with different arrival rate and packet lengths. Flow has two types: web/ftp (type 1) and audio/video (type 2). We compare end-to-end delays of flows calculated by Maude with those computed by Qualnet simulator where Qualnet models the same network and flows. In Qualnet, we use point-to-point links to simulate the links in Fig 6(a) and we use constant bit rate applications to simulate the flows in Fig 6(b). The results of simulating end-to-end delay (see Fig 8) show that the delays obtained

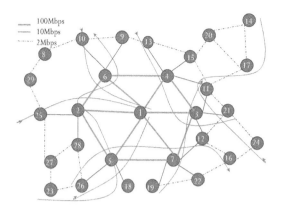
(a) network

route	flowid	type	TP	Item length (Mbits)	Arrival num (/s)
1,2,25	1	1	0.8	0.0016	500
1,5,26	2	1	0.8	0.002	400
19,7,3,11	3	1	0.8	0.0016	500
21,3,4,13	4	1	0.48	0.0016	300
1,6,10	5	2	0.48	0.0016	300
24,21,11,17,14	6	2	0.4	0.002	200
23,26,5,2,6,10	7	2	0.4	0.002	200
26,5,7,12,16	8	2	0.24	0.0008	300

(b) Flows

Figure 6: Preliminary Experimental Settings

for each flow (x-axis of Fig 8) by Maude are quite consistent with those determined by Qualnet, with an average error of less than 9%. Note that the objective of our formal model is **not** to have the exact same results as Qualnet, but rather achieve enough accuracy so that our prediction results will be viable, while at the same time our analysis method will be more efficient due to its abstraction level. We intend to determine with our formal methods analysis the trends of the delay performance in heterogeneous multinetworks and various kinds of flows. The preliminary experiment has validated our methodology. Next we further show that our methodology can provide solutions for three different case studies.

3. CASE STUDIES

We present three use cases. Each use case differs in its objective to adapt a multinetwork in the face of network failures. All use cases have application QoS requirements that must be satisfied. Different "what if" questions will provide guidance on how to best achieve QoS requirements. To compare the effectiveness of our formal method-based analysis approach with other approaches, we apply conventional strategies in each of the three use cases. We see that our analysis results suggest different adaptations than conventional analysis methods. We compare the suggested adaptation strategies from our analysis and conventional strategies by simulating the resulting networks to assess how well the adaptation strategy satisfies QoS requirements. We see that our analysis methodology provide superior guidance compared with conventional strategies.

3.1 Case 1: Node Criticality Index

Node Criticality Index (NCI) is an indicator of how important a node is. Generally the importance of a node can be measured by the impact of a node's failure on other nodes or network traffic. In this case study, we measure how end-to-end delays of flows are affected given a node failure. The node whose failure will cause the biggest end-to-end delay is the most important node. Traditional Node Critical Index approaches only focus on static attributes, e.g. node degree [2], centrality [9, 3], or workload/betweeness [4, 7]. These traditional measures are not taking into account the affect that a node failure will have on the flows that go through the failing node, and thus, the impact a failing node has on other flows due to contention caused by the redistribution of flows.

Our "what-if" analysis methodology and tool assumes that each node fails, one at a time, and generates a new network and new paths for the flows (using the Dijkstra algorithm to redistribute the flow, which is widely employed in routing protocols). We restrict failing of nodes to those nodes that are not source or destination of a flow. The reason is that if we would let those nodes fail, then we would not only change the paths of flows, we would also change the set of flows. And this would not allow us to compare the end-to-end delay results we generate for one node failing at a time. There are also nodes that are on the critical path of flow, meaning if these nodes fail, there is no longer a path between source and destination of at least one flow. Again, we assume these nodes do not fail so that we can consider the impact of a node failing under the same traffic load or set of flows. Thus, in summary, our analysis lets one node at a time fail—for those nodes that are not source, destination or critical path nodes—and compares the impact of a node's failure on all flows to compute which one has the most negative influence when failing. That node is deemed to be the most critical node.

In the following we refer to nodes that we do not let fail as *critical nodes* and those that we let fail as part of the analysis as *measurable nodes*. We are using the network and flows from Figure 6. The left table in Figure 7 below summarizes the average end-to-end delays on all eight flows in terms of the delay increase/decrease multiplication factor. The criticality rating is derived from the average multiplication factor, rating the most critical node to be the one with the biggest positive multiplication factor. We only show the top six most important nodes as determined by our Maude analysis (left table) or as determined using traditional approaches based on degree and workload (right table). For

Failed Node	Ave	Rank
Node 2	4.2	2
Node 3	4.4	1
Node 4	1.4	5
Node 5	1.1	6
Node 6	1.6	4
Node 7	1.9	3

Importance Ranking by Degree and load			
node	degree	load	Rank
5	6	1.44	1
3	6	1.28	2
7	6	1.04	3
4	6	0.48	4
2	5	1.2	5
6	5	0.88	6

Figure 7: Node Importance Ranking: Maude Based Results (left) vs. Degree/Workload Based Results (right)

example, when node 2 fails, the average end-to-end delay on all flows will be increased by 4.2 times, and when node 3

fails, then the multiplication factor is 4.4. In comparison, we get a different ranking with the traditional approach as shown in the right table of Figure 7.

To determine which analysis method delivers a better quality answer to the question "which node is the most important node?", we devised another experiment. The two most important nodes according to the "what-if" Maude analysis are node 3 and node 2 (labelled Maude Group in Fig 9), while traditional degree and workload-based analysis (labelled MaxDegree Group in Fig. 9) determine node 5 and node 3 to be the most critical ones. The next experiment assumes that the network administrator followed either the Maude analysis results of the MaxDegree analysis results and backed up those two most important nodes. Thus, it is very unlikely for those nodes to fail, but the remaining 16 nodes can still fail. For each group we model the networks in Qualnet and let the 16 nodes each fail for 300s. This means, there is a 4800s long experiment in Qualnet of each group (Maude Group and MaxDegree Group). The two 4800s experiments have the same original flow configuration. In addition, we run another experiment of 4800s without any node failures. We compare the end-to-end delay of the Maude Group and MaxDegree Group with the original network and flows (without any failure), to see how much increase in flow delay we get for either group. Fig 9 shows that if we protect the two modes selected by our "what-if" analysis tool, the average delay increase percentage is smaller (i.e., 25%) than if we protected the nodes chosen by a MaxDegree-based analysis (i.e., 34%)(Although some flows in MaxDegree group do not incur extra delay, i.e. 2, 6, 8). Thus, our "what-if" analysis is able to provide a more accurate NCI for this scenario.

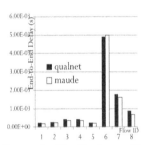

Figure 8: Preliminary Experimental Results

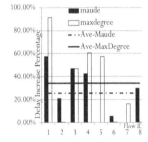

Figure 9: Delay increase (in %) for the two analysis approaches

3.2 Case 2: Adding an Additional Router

If one has limited resources available, it becomes a challenge to place them in the network in a way that ensures best use of the resource's capabilities. This is a common problem for network planning and administration. For example, if we have only one extra node which happens to be a router, where should we put it so that the overall end-to-end delay for all flows will be improved most? Traditional approaches usually put the extra router next to the node with the biggest workload. However, adding a new router will cause flow redistribution which will in turn impact the end-to-end delay of all flows. This aspect is usually not taken into consideration in traditional approaches. In our MINA architecture, wireless routers are in Tier 2 (Tier 1 is the centralized server and Tier 3 contains the mobile nodes), hence we determine that there are six tier two nodes (nodes 2-7) in Fig 6(a) that can be further supported by an additional router. Placing an additional router next to a node we assume that this router will have the exact same neighbors and links as that node. However, adding such extra router into the network means that the network changes and thus, flow routes will change too. Our "what-if" analysis tool examines end-to-end delay of each flow for possible position of the additional router and compares the results to determine the optimal placing of the additional router. We use again the network in Fig 6(a) and the flows in Fig 6(b) with exception of the differences indicated in Fig 12.

Flow ID	Ave Delay Inc.	Rank
2	98.71%	1
3	99.25%	2
5	99.61%	4
6	99.50%	3
7	99.99%	5

Figure 10: Best Position for additional router: Ranking by Maude analysis.

Node	Contention link	Flow ID	Load	Load sum	Rank
2	2-25	1	0.8	1.2	2
	2-28	9	0.4		
3	3-11	3	0.8	1.28	1
	3-21	21	0.48		
5	5-26	2	0.8	1.04	3
	5-26	8	0.24		
6	6-10	5	0.48	0.88	5
	6-10	7	0.4		
7	7-3	3	0.8	1.04	3
	7-5	8	0.24		

Figure 11: Best Position for additional router: Ranking by Workload-based analysis.

In Fig 10 we can see that when adding the extra router next to node 2, then the average end-to-end delay on all flows is 98.71% of the one without extra router. Thus this position has the best end-to-end delay improvement, according to our "what-if" analysis. In comparison, if traditional workload-based approach is used, the best position is node 3, as shown in Fig 11. Note: Node 4 is not in the Fig 11, because in order to do load balancing, nodes need to have at least two flows, and Node 4 only has one.

route	flowid	type	TP	Itemlength	Arrival num
13,4,3,21	4	1	0.48	0.0016	300
16,12,7,5,26	8	2	0.24	0.0008	300
1,2,28	9	2	0.4	0.0008	500

Figure 12: Flows in Case 2

Next we deploy the extra router next to nodes 2 and 3, respectively, and use Qualnet to test end-to-end delay improvement. The results show that the average delay decrease rate over all flows is 1.43% if we position the extra router next to node 2, while it is 0.01% if we position it next to node 3. Hence we can conclude that if we only have one extra router, node 2 is the better position to place, which is consistent with Maude "what-if" analysis.

3.3 Case 3: Network Reconfiguration

Mobile devices usually have more than one WiFi hotspot with which to associate. Properly selecting an access point is good for network resource utilization and application performance. We use again the network and flows as in Fig 6. If node 2 is down, node 25 and node 28 need to re-associate with either node 6 or node 5. Hence we have four network reconfiguration plans as determined by the possible combinations for node 25 and 28 re-associating with node 5 or 6. One of the four network reconfigurations and the new routes for flows are shown in Fig 13. We refer to NW1 where both

node 25 and node 28 re-associate with node 6 (25-6;28-6). NW2 is the network where node 25 re-associates with node 6 and node 28 re-associates with node 5 (25-6;28-5). NW3 is (25-5;28-5) and NW4 is (25-5;28-6).

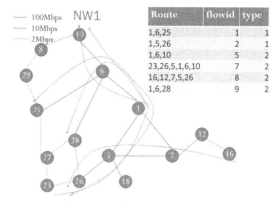

Route	flowid	type
1,6,25	1	1
1,5,26	2	1
1,6,10	5	2
23,26,5,1,6,10	7	2
16,12,7,5,26	8	2
1,6,28	9	2

Figure 13: One Possible Network Reconfiguration when Node 2 goes down

The "what-if" analysis tool calculated the end-to-end delay of flows for all four reconfigurations (see Fig 14). The results of the Maude analysis show that NW2 and NW4 will have less delay degradation compared with the one in original network (node 2 is on). However, if we use traditional load balance-based approach (called *LoadBalance*), NW3 and NW4 are the better choice, as shown in fig 15.

Network Config	Avg Delay Increase	Rank
NW1	54.0502%	3
NW2	27.6939%	1
NW3	65.6767%	4
NW4	28.5294%	2

Network config.	Node6 load:	Node5 load:	Delta	Rank
NW1	2.26	1.04	1.22	4
NW2	2.16	1.14	1.02	3
NW3	1.36	1.94	0.58	2
NW4	1.46	1.84	0.38	1

Figure 14: Best Reconfiguration Ranking using Maude

Figure 15: Best Reconfiguration Ranking by Workload

We then put these four resulting configurations into Qualnet to get the average end-to-end delay over all flows. As Fig 16 shows, Maude results are quite consistent with Qualnet results. I.e., Qualnet would prefer NW2 and NW4 over NW1 and NW 3, so does Maude. LoadBalance would prefer NW 4 and NW 3 over NW 1 and NW 2. Note the end-to-end delay generated by Qualnet is not exactly the same as the one generated by Maude "what-if" analysis tool. However, the trends and the relationship among different network configurations are quite similar.

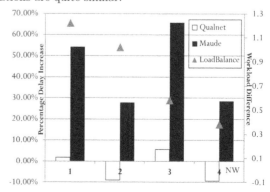

Figure 16: Verification by Qualnet

Note we use Qualnet as benchmark because it is a well known network simulator that can accurately describe the network behaviors across multiple layers. However, we cannot use Qualnet to replace "what-if" analysis tools. Maude is a high-level language providing conceptual abstractions. The three rules in our tools are the basic elements derived from the flow and queue models. Once these basic elements are in place, it is easy to set up and carry out analysis on various network without any further configuration. Network simulators usually need to simulate the packet/frame behaviors in all layers, which is more time-consuming. Moreover, having a human setting up these networks in Qualnet requires time and introduces the potential of misconfiguration by the human. In addition, increasing packet number means more calculation and time while our formal-method based tools scales up nicely due to abstraction. In Fig 17, we take the "No additional routers" scenario from case 2 and the "No failure happened" scenario from case 3 as examples to illustrate the efficiency and scalability of our Maude based "what-if" analysis tool. Maude only use 27ms and 11ms in two scenarios, respectively. Qualnet uses much more time in our experiments. Even if we only look at the time consumption in one second-this is the time used to simulate the same data amount with Maude, Qualnet still consumes more time. When we increased the number of packets by a factor of 10, then the time consumed by Maude is constant while it increases in Qualnet. Hence we argue that our formal language based "what-if" analysis tools have better scalability.

	Maude	Qualnet	Qualnet with 10 times packets
Case2: bp0	rewrites: 481 in (27ms real)	20.4160s/300s =68ms/1s	24.2847s/300s
Case3: nw0	rewrites: 295 in (11ms real)	12.9815s/300s =43ms/1s	14.8934s/300s

Figure 17: Time consumed by Maude and Qualnet

4. CONCLUSION AND FUTURE WORK

Traditional network analysis approaches mainly focus on faults and security problems in wired, homogeneous networks where nodes have enough capabilities and links are stable. In addition, those techniques do not take into consideration how changes to the network trigger flow redistribution that potentially impacts QoS of all flows.

In this paper, we proposed and evaluated a novel what-if analysis tool based on the formal language Maude. We modeled heterogeneous networks in Maude using a general flow and queue model and provided rules that compute how end-to-end delay in the network. Using these models, we can evaluate various kinds of network changes (i.e. failures, backup and reconfigurations) and determine improved network configurations. For example, we can determine what is the best position for additional resources or which nodes are most critical when it comes to failures. Experiments from three case studies have shown that our tool outperforms traditional approaches. The what-if analysis tool could be extended to adopt more QoS example parameters and heterogeneous applications in the future. Another area of future work is to investigate flow models for other types of traffic and formalize those in Maude. This would allow us to handle network traffic more comprehensively.

5. REFERENCES

[1] Model-based environment for validation of system reliability, availability, security, and performance https://www.mobius.illinois.edu/.

[2] P. Bonacich. Some unique properties of eigenvector centrality. *Social Networks*, 29(4):555 – 564, 2007.

[3] S. P. Borgatti. Centrality and network flow. *Social Networks*, 27(1):55 – 71, 2005.

[4] U. Brandes. On variants of shortest-path betweenness centrality and their generic computation. *SOCIAL NETWORKS*, 30(2), 2008.

[5] M. Clavel, F. Durán, S. Eker, P. Lincoln, N. Martí-Oliet, J. Meseguer, and C. L. Talcott, editors. *All About Maude - A High-Performance Logical Framework, How to Specify, Program and Verify Systems in Rewriting Logic*, volume 4350 of *Lecture Notes in Computer Science*. Springer, 2007.

[6] G. de Silva, P. Matousek, O. Rysavy, and M. Sveda. Formal analysis approach on networks with dynamic behaviours. In *Ultra Modern Telecommunications and Control Systems and Workshops (ICUMT), 2010 International Congress on*, pages 545 –551, oct. 2010.

[7] E. Estrada, D. J. Higham, and N. Hatano. Communicability betweenness in complex networks. *Physica A: Statistical Mechanics and its Applications*, 388(5):764 – 774, 2009.

[8] Q. Gan, Bjarne, , and E. Helvik. Dependability modelling and analysis of networks as taking routing and traffic into account. In *Next Generation Internet Design and Engineering, 2006. NGI '06. 2006 2nd Conference on*, 2006.

[9] P. Hage and F. Harary. Eccentricity and centrality in networks. *Social Networks*, 17(1):57 – 63, 1995.

[10] P. Matouek, J. R, O. Ryavy, and M. Svéda. A formal model for network-wide security analysis. In *Proceedings of the 15th Annual IEEE International Conference and Workshop on the Engineering of Computer Based Systems*, ECBS '08, pages 171–181, Washington, DC, USA, 2008. IEEE Computer Society.

[11] A. McIver and A. Fehnker. Formal techniques for the analysis of wireless networks. In *Leveraging Applications of Formal Methods, Verification and Validation, 2006. ISoLA 2006. Second International Symposium on*, pages 263–270. IEEE, 2006.

[12] M. Menth, M. Duelli, R. Martin, and J. Milbrandt. Resilience analysis of packet-switched communication networks. *Networking, IEEE/ACM Transactions on*, 17(6):1950 –1963, dec. 2009.

[13] Z. Qin and L. Iannario. Towards design of an overlay architecture in the multinetwork management system. Technical report, University of California, Irvine, http://www.ics.uci.edu/ dsm/cypress/publications.html, March 2012.

[14] W. Stallings. Queuing analysis, 2000.

[15] A. Ten Teije, Marcos, et al. Improving medical protocols by formal methods. *Artificial intelligence in medicine*, 36(3):193–209, 2006.

[16] G. G. Xie, J. Zhan, D. A. Maltz, H. Zhang, A. Greenberg, G. Hjalmtysson, and J. Rexford. On static reachability analysis of ip networks. In *in Proc. IEEE INFOCOM*, 2005.

Minimax Control For Cyber-Physical Systems under Network Packet Scheduling Attacks*

Yasser Shoukry
Electrical Engineering
UC Los Angeles
yshoukry@ee.ucla.edu

Jose Araujo
ACCESS Linnaeus Center
KTH Royal Institute of
Technology
araujo@kth.se

Paulo Tabuada
UC Los Angeles
tabuada@ee.ucla.edu

Mani Srivastava
UC Los Angeles
mbs@ee.ucla.edu

Karl H. Johansson
ACCESS Linnaeus Center
KTH Royal Institute of
Technology
kallej@kth.se

ABSTRACT

The control of physical systems is increasingly being done by re-sorting to networks to transmit information from sensors to con-trollers and from controllers to actuators. Unfortunately, this re-liance on networks also brings new security vulnerabilities for con-trol systems. We study the extent to which an adversary can attack a physical system by tampering with the temporal characteristics of the network, leading to time-varying delays and more impor-tantly by changing the order in which packets are delivered. We show that such attack can destabilize a system if the controller was not designed to be robust with respect to an adversarial scheduling of messages. Although one can always store delayed messages in a buffer so as to present them to the control algorithm in the or-der they were sent and with a constant delay, such design is overly conservative. Instead, we design a controller that makes the best possible use of the received packets in a minimax sense. The pro-posed design has the same worst case performance as a controller based on a buffer but has better performance whenever there is no attack or the attacker does not play the optimal attack strategy.

Categories and Subject Descriptors

J.2 [**Computer Applications**]: PHYSICAL SCIENCES AND EN-GINEERING Engineering, Electronics

Keywords

Out-of-order packets; Cyber-physical systems (CPS); networked control systems (NCS); Security; Resilient control; Minimax con-trol; Out-of-order messages; Long delays; Estimation

1. INTRODUCTION

The increased coupling between embedded computing technolo-gies and modern control systems has opened the door for develop-ing many engineering systems with growing complexity. In such systems, commonly termed *cyber-physical systems* (CPS), infor-mation from the physical world is quantized and processed using digital electronic components, and decisions taken by these "cyber components" are then applied to the physical world [20, 22]. Un-fortunately, this tight coupling between cyber components and the physical world oftentimes leads to systems where increased sophis-tication comes at the expense of increased vulnerability and secu-rity weaknesses. There exist several examples of attacks on CPSs such as the first-ever control system malware called Stuxnet [26, 23], and other staged attacks in power generators [16].

Therefore, the study of the effect and mitigation of attacks in CPSs has gained a great attention in recent years [21, 1, 6, 8, 25]. At the heart of CPSs is the network through which various components of the system exchange information. Hence, the analysis of attacks in the communication network, their detection, identification, and defense strategies are of major importance.

Recently, several researchers have studied the effect of attacks in the data communication of networked control systems [1, 10, 19, 32]. The work in [1, 10] focuses on the design of feedback con-trollers that minimize a control objective function. In this case, no delays are considered but only packet losses. The design of predic-tive controllers under delays and packet losses is proposed in [19], but out-of-sequence measurements are not explicitly considered in their solution. In [32], replay attacks are considered where the ma-licious node is able to replay old control messages that are sent to actuators.

In this paper, we devise a robust output-feedback controller which is resilient to an attack to the scheduling of packets in a networked

*This work is supported by the Knut and Alice Wallenberg Founda-tion, the Swedish Research Council, the HYCON2 EU project, the NSF grant CNS-1136174, and by DARPA under agreement number FA8750-12-2-0247. The U.S. Government is authorized to repro-duce and distribute reprints for Governmental purposes notwith-standing any copyright notation thereon. The views and conclu-sions contained herein are those of the authors and should not be interpreted as necessarily representing the official policies or en-dorsements, either expressed or implied, of DARPA or the U.S. Government

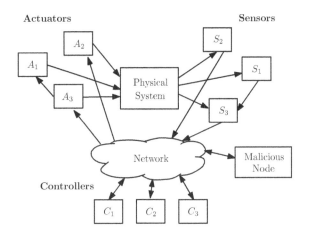

Figure 1: Typical networked cyber-physical system with an adversarial attack on the shared network.

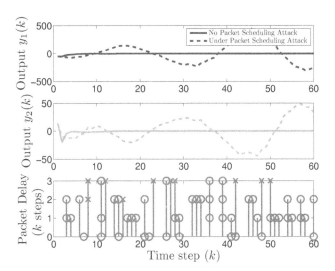

Figure 2: Example showing that packet scheduling attack can render the closed loop system unstable. The upper figure shows the response of the system under the attack (red, dashed line), versus the nominal behavior in the absence of the attack (black, solid line). The bottom figure shows the effect of the adversary on the packet delivery, the cross mark denotes a packet delivered out of its order, while the circle denotes packet received in the correct order. Height of the bars denotes the delay induced in the each received packet.

control system. An attack on the scheduling algorithm will lead to time-varying delays and more importantly can lead to a change in the order by which packets are received. The proposed controller uses the available information (received packets up to the current time) so as to be robust with respect to such attack. Notwithstanding this fact, such controller has no worse performance than a controller that stores the received messages, reorders them, and presents them to the controller with a constant delay. Moreover, the proposed controller has better performance whenever there is no attack or the attacker does not launch the worse possible attack.

The rest of this paper is organized as follows. Section 2 introduces how a packet scheduling attack can be mounted and the assumptions on the attacker. Formal presentation of the problem along with the proposed controller and simulation results are presented in Sections 3 and 6 respectively. Finally, Section 7 concludes this paper.

2. PACKET SCHEDULING ATTACKS

In typical networked cyber-physical systems, multiple sensors send information to controllers through a shared communication channel, and controllers transmit control packets to actuators that are connected to the physical system. An illustration of a networked cyber-physical system is shown in Figure 1.

Data packets are scheduled for transmission and they must arrive to their destination node before a certain allowed deadline. In our work, we consider one controller that is co-located with the actuators. Accordingly, we will focus on attacks mounted only in the path between the multiple sensors and controller. We also assume that all the network nodes use cryptographic algorithms to encrypt, decrypt and authenticate packets. This prevents an adversary from changing the content of the packets. Replay attacks are also excluded in our scenario since packets are timestamped before encryption and the timestamps can be used to detect the replay of old data.

We consider stealth or covert attacks in which an attacker does not want the attack to be detected. One possible such attack consists of influencing the temporal characteristics of the network. It will result in time-varying delays and data packets possibly received out-of-order. However, to remain stealth, the attacker will not be able to delay the packets beyond a maximum allowable delay consistent with the network protocol in place.

This attack, if not addressed by the controller, can lead to unstable behavior. Figure 2 shows an example of a system with a

classical Luenberger state observer and LQR controller (for formal definition of these terms please refer to [2]). In this example, the batch-reactor [27], a fourth order open-loop unstable system is simulated against both attacked and un-attacked packet schedules. The attack takes place in the path between from the sensor node to the controller node. Figure 3 shows how the packets are received where a cross sign indicates a message that is received out of its specified order and a circle indicates a packet received in the correct order. The height of the bars indicates the induced delay by the attacker. This example clearly shows that such attack on the packet scheduling can lead to instability.

Packet scheduling attacks can be easily mounted to both wired and wireless communication channels using several techniques. A direct way of performing this attack is by an adversary placing malicious software on one of the packet routers in the path between sender and receiver.

Another way of mounting this attack is by means of resource unfairness attacks [7]. Unfairness is a weak type of Denial-of-Service (DoS) attacks. Both wired and wireless communication channels are exposed to unfairness attack. In wireless communication channel, an adversary can exhaust the shared communication channel by repeatedly sending packets leading to packet collision and automatic re-transmission, leading packets to miss their deadlines. Even wired networks are subject to unfairness attack. For example the arbitration mechanism of CAN bus can be easily attacked by adding a node to the bus which is able to flip just one bit in the identification part of the CAN packet leading to a maliciously dropping of specific packets from the network and firing automatic transmission by the CAN controller [17].

From this discussion, the effect of packet scheduling attacks can be seen as an attacker who can adversarially: 1) add a time-varying delay to the network and 2) alter the order by which packets are received by the controller. This scenario is illustrated in Figure 3.

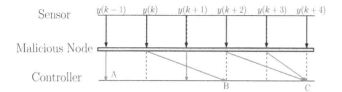

Figure 3: An adversarial attack affecting the packet scheduling sent by sensors to the controller node can introduce time-varying delays leading to, A) packets delivered within the allowed deadline B)Packets delivered out of its order C)multiple packets received at the same time instance.

The influence of the delay and missing data on the control system is a classic control analysis problem [9, 2]. Since the introduction of networked control systems, the analysis on the effect of fixed and time-varying delays as well as data loss on the control system has been the focus of much research [11, 12, 18, 31, 13, 29]. Even though the influence of short delays (lower than a sampling period) has been extensively studied, the effect of long delays and out-of-sequence messages has received less attention from the control community. The typical proposed solutions for a practical control system design under out-of-sequence messages is is to: 1) utilize a buffer with length equal to the maximum expected message delay, thus avoiding any out-of-sequence issues [11, 12, 18] or 2) discard any out-of-sequence messages, assuming that the penalty for not using such packets is low [24, 13]. Such approaches may not be suitable since in case 1) a fixed delay is introduced in the system and no improvement is made when messages actually arrive with no delay, and in case 2) such strategy may discard a large amount of messages for persistently out-of-sequence messages.

This could be allowed for specific robust control system designs, but it is obvious that it may in general exhibit low control performances, depending on the delay values.

Another approach was proposed in [15] where optimal control under long delays and out-of-sequence measurements for linear stochastic systems is discussed. Even though out-of-sequence measurements are utilized to improve the state estimate, a new control actuation is not performed whenever this occurs. This assumption is not motivated by the authors and it can suffer the same drawbacks as the buffer approach. Furthermore, it is unclear what is the right statistics to be used in the case of an adversarial attack. A similar approach is described in [14]. Several researchers have looked at the problem of optimal estimation under out-of-sequence measurements [3, 30, 28] but with no consideration of the control system.

A direct over-designed controller can be implemented in this case by inserting a buffer at the controller node where all packets are stored, correctly reordered and then used by the controller after a fixed delay. We argue that an opportunistic design that takes care of the varying-delay and/or the out-of-sequence behavior can lead to better performance measured by means of a cost function. We formalize these assumptions in the next section.

3. MINIMAX CONTROL UNDER PACKET SCHEDULING ATTACK

In this paper, we consider a discrete-time linear time-invariant control system subject to both state and output disturbances. The dynamics of the system are described by:

$$x_{k+1} = Ax_k + Bu_k + Dw_k,$$
$$y_k = Cx_k + Ew_k, \tag{3.1}$$

where $x_k \in \mathbb{R}^n, y_k \in \mathbf{Y} \subset \mathbb{R}^p, u_k \in \mathbf{U} \subset \mathbb{R}^m$, and $w_k \in \mathbf{W} \subset \mathbb{R}^d$ are the system state, output, control input, and disturbance input, all at time $k \in \mathbb{N}$ respectively. We have the following assumptions about the system and attacker capabilities:

(A1) There exists an upper bound T for the packet delay in the underlying network.

(A2) A cryptographic protocol is used to encrypt, decrypt and authenticate the packets.

(A3) Packets are timestamped before being encrypted.

(A4) The attacker is capable of introducing time-varying delays on the packets. However, in order for the attacker to be kept stealthy, he will not delay a packet by more than T time units.

The objective is to design a dynamic controller which is robust to the attack under consideration. It is beneficial to take the attacker's role to see how he should attack the system. The adversary by attacking the packet scheduling, i.e., by adding time-varying delays and/or altering the order of the packets, is actually preventing the controller from attenuating the effect of disturbances by preventing the controller from monitoring the exact state of the system. Hence, a natural defense strategy is to design a controller that is robust with respect to the worst disturbance input that is compatible with the received sequence of observations and the generated sequence of control actions. This leads to a minimax controller design using a dynamic game approach.

We follow the general framework of [4] to design a robust feedback controller using a zero-sum game-theoretic approach. The designed controller can be viewed as a dynamic game between two players. The controller is the minimizer player who tries to minimize the finite horizon quadratic cost (3.2) while the disturbance is the maximizer player.

$$J_\gamma(\mu, \nu) = |x_{K+1}|^2_{Q_f} +$$
$$\sum_{k=1}^{K} \left(|x_k|^2_Q + |u_k|^2 - \gamma^2 |w_k|^2 \right) - \gamma^2 |x_1|^2_{Q_0}. \tag{3.2}$$

Here, $\mu = \mu_1 \mu_2 \ldots \mu_k$ is the sequence of control inputs applied by the first player, $\nu = \nu_1 \nu_2 \ldots \nu_k$ is the sequence of disturbance inputs applied by the second player, K is the finite horizon length, x_1 is the unknown initial state of the system, and $\gamma \in \mathbb{R}$ is the disturbance attenuation level. We use the notation $|.|$ to denote the Euclidean norm with positive definite weighting matrices Q, Q_f and Q_0 of appropriate dimension.

The objective of the first player (controller) is to drive the state to zero while minimizing J. The objective of the second player (disturbance) and of the attacker is to increase the cost J as much as possible. Note that when the game admits a solution, the controller ensures the following bound for the effect of the disturbance:

$$||\zeta|| \leq \gamma ||\sigma||, \tag{3.3}$$

where

$$||\zeta|| = |x_{K+1}|^2_{Q_f} + \sum_{k=1}^{K} \left(|x_k|^2_Q + |u_k|^2 \right),$$

and

$$||\sigma|| = |x_1|^2_{Q_0} + \sum_{k=1}^{K} \left(|w_k|^2 \right).$$

We show in this paper that this game obeys the conditions required for certainty equivalence [5] even under the varying-delay and/or the out-of-order messages imposed by the attacker. Under certainty equivalence, one can split the design problem into two parts: the first is to design an observer which estimates the worst possible state that matches the sequence of available inputs and outputs; the second is to design a controller which makes use of the estimated state in order to generate the new control input.

Following these steps, the worst case state estimator works as follows. Whenever the observer receives an out-of-order packet, it starts by reordering the set of previous T messages, computes the worst case disturbance which is compatible with the available information, finds the corresponding worst case state estimate, and then plays the game as if the actual state was already located at this worst case estimate. The next two sections discuss the details of both the certainty equivalence property and how to construct the worst case observer and controller under the specified attack.

4. CERTAINTY EQUIVALENCE

Before we formulate the certainty equivalence property, we need to introduce some notation.

4.1 Notation

Recall that $u_k \in \mathbf{U}$ and $w_k \in \mathbf{W}$ denote the control input, and disturbance input at time k respectively. We reserve the symbols y, u, and w to denote the sequence of outputs, control inputs and disturbance inputs of finite length, i.e., $y \in \mathbf{Y}^*$, $u \in \mathbf{U}^*$, and $w \in \mathbf{W}^*$ respectively.

The overall disturbance ω is defined as the combination of the initial condition and the disturbance:

$$\omega := (x_1, w), \qquad \omega \in \Omega := \mathbb{R}^n \times \mathbf{W}^*. \tag{4.1}$$

We denote the solutions of (3.1) under the effect of sequences of inputs u and disturbances w as:

$$x_t = \phi_t(u, w, x_1), \tag{4.2}$$

$$y_t = \eta_t(u, w, x_1). \tag{4.3}$$

The conditions ensuring the certainty equivalence property are formulated in terms of the allowing information sets and its elements:

$$y^\tau \in \mathbf{Y}^\tau, \tag{4.4}$$

$$u^\tau \in \mathbf{U}^\tau, \tag{4.5}$$

$$w^\tau \in \mathbf{W}^\tau, \tag{4.6}$$

$$\omega^\tau \in \Omega^\tau = \mathbb{R}^n \times \mathbf{W}^\tau. \tag{4.7}$$

where X^ϵ denotes the ϵ-fold cartesian product of X with itself. Similarly we denote by η^τ to be the sequence of outputs $\eta_1 \eta_2 \ldots \eta_\tau$.

Let us consider the partial information problem. For any given integer $\tau \in \{1, 2, \ldots, k\}$ and sequence pair $(\bar{u}, \bar{y}) \in \mathbf{U}^\tau \times \mathbf{Y}^\tau$, we define the following subset $\Omega_\tau(\bar{u}, \bar{y})$ of Ω:

$$\Omega_\tau(\bar{u}, \bar{y}) = \{\omega \in \Omega | \eta_k(\bar{u}, \omega) = \bar{y}_k, k = 1, \ldots, \tau\}, \tag{4.8}$$

which denotes all the disturbance sequences which are compatible with the input and output strings up to time τ. We also introduce the following notation for the set of restrictions of Ω_τ:

$$\Omega_\tau^\tau(\bar{u}, \bar{y}) = \{\omega^\tau \in \Omega^\tau | \omega \in \Omega_\tau(\bar{u}, \bar{y})\}. \tag{4.9}$$

In the following discussion we drop the argument $(\bar{u}, \bar{y})$, however, one always needs to remember that Ω_τ and its restriction are only the disturbance strings that are compatible with the observed sequences of inputs and outputs.

4.2 Certainty Equivalence

In this subsection, we review the the conditions under which certainty equivalence is known to hold.

4.2.1 Information Process

The controller (first player) does not have complete knowledge about the disturbance string nor about the system state. The observation process θ_τ maps the observed inputs $u^\tau \in \mathbf{U}^\tau$ and outputs $y^\tau \in \mathbf{Y}^\tau$ to the set Ω_τ of all disturbances compatible with these observations. Hence θ_τ describes all the information about the disturbance that player 1 can extract from its observations. We note that θ_τ satisfies the following properties:

- Consistency:
$$\forall u \in \mathbf{U}^\tau, \forall \omega \in \Omega, \forall \tau \in [1, K], \omega \in \Omega_\tau(u, \eta^\tau(u, \omega)). \tag{4.10}$$

- Perfect Recall:
$$\forall u \in \mathbf{U}^\tau, \forall \omega \in \Omega, \tau' > \tau \Rightarrow \Omega_{\tau'} \subset \Omega_\tau. \tag{4.11}$$

- Strict non-anticipativeness:
$$\forall u \in \mathbf{U}^\tau, \forall \omega \in \Omega, \forall \tau \in [1, K], \omega \in \Omega_\tau \Leftrightarrow \omega^{\tau-1} \in \Omega_\tau^{\tau-1}. \tag{4.12}$$

4.2.2 Assumption I:

The perfect-state information two-person zero-sum game where the disturbance has access to u, admits a state feedback saddle-point solution leading to the upper value function of the Isaacs equation:

$$V_k(x) = \min_u \max_w V_{k+1}(Ax_k + Bu_k + Dw_k) + $$
$$+ \left(|x_k|_Q^2 + |u_k|^2 - \gamma^2 |\omega_k|^2 \right), \tag{4.13}$$
$$V_{K+1} = |x_{K+1}|_{Q_f}^2.$$

which represents the upper value of the game with performance index (3.2). Under this assumption, the minimum in u is unique for every (k, x).

4.2.3 Assumption II:

Introduce the following controller:

$$\hat{\mu}_\tau(\bar{u}^{\tau-1}, \bar{y}^{\tau-1}) := \mu_\tau^*(\hat{x}_\tau^\tau), \tag{4.14}$$

where, μ_τ^* denotes the optimal controller strategy for the perfect state measurement problem and $\hat{\mu}_\tau$ is the controller which is based on the worst case estimate of the state $\hat{x}_\tau^\tau$ up to time τ based on the available string of inputs and observations $\bar{u}^{\tau-1}, \bar{y}^{\tau-1}$.

The control sequence generated by this controller is such that the following saddle point property holds for all $\omega \in \Omega$ and $\tau \in [1, K]$

$$\min_u \max_{\omega \in \Omega_{\tau-1}} G_\tau(\bar{u}^{\tau-1}.u, \omega) = \max_{\omega \in \Omega_{\tau-1}} \min_u G_\tau(\bar{u}^{\tau-1}.u, \omega), \tag{4.15}$$

where G_τ is the auxiliary performance index:

$$G_\tau(u^\tau, \omega^\tau) = V_{\tau+1}(x_{\tau+1}) + \sum_{k=1}^K \left(|x_k|_Q^2 + |u_k|^2 - \gamma^2 |\omega_k|^2 \right). \tag{4.16}$$

4.2.4 Certainty Equivalence Principle:

For the partial information process and under assumptions I and II, the following problem has a solution for every τ:

$$\max_{\omega \in \Omega_{\tau-1}} G_\tau(\bar{u}^{\tau-1}, \omega^{\tau-1}), \tag{4.17}$$

Moreover, the solution of this problem yields a uniquely defined minimax controller $\hat{\mu}_\tau(\bar{u}^{\tau-1}, \bar{y}^{\tau-1})$. This result means there exists a worst case disturbance that matches the string of inputs and partial observations available up to time τ. Accordingly, the optimal minimax strategy for the first player is to construct a pair of controller and observer, where the controller is exactly the same as the optimal controller for the perfect state measurement, except it utilizes the state estimate instead of the measured state. The observer uses the information available up to time τ to estimate the worst case disturbance sequence and then use this information to estimate the worst case state trajectory which matches the string of inputs and outputs up to time τ.

5. MINIMAX ESTIMATOR AND CONTROLLER DESIGN

We now switch the focus into how to utilize the certainty equivalence principle to design a worst case controller and observer which satisfy assumption II from the previous section. We will start by stating the following results proved in [4] upon which we base our results.

Consider a linear time invariant system subject to disturbance modeled with (3.1), and, along with the cost function (3.2). Suppose that at time $k \geq T$ only information up to time $k - T$ is available to the controller and T is fixed. In other words, let's consider the information structure $\Omega_{\tau-T}$, this measurement process satisfies the three hypotheses (4.10)-(4.12). Accordingly, the auxiliary problem from Assumption II can be re-written as:

$$\max_{\omega^{\tau-1} \in \Omega_{\tau-T}^{\tau-1}} G_{\tau-1}(\bar{u}^{\tau-1}, \omega^{\tau-1}), \qquad (5.1)$$

where

$$G_{\tau-1}(\bar{u}^{\tau-1}, \omega^{\tau-1}) = V_\tau(x_\tau) + \sum_{k=1}^{\tau-T} \left(|x_k|_Q^2 + |u_k|^2 - \gamma^2 |\omega_k|^2 \right)$$
$$+ \sum_{\tau-T+1}^{\tau-1} \left(|x_k|_Q^2 + |u_k|^2 - \gamma^2 |\omega_k|^2 \right),$$

which will result in an observer which is able to estimate the worst case disturbance (and thus the system state) which matches the strings of inputs and outputs up to time $\tau - T$. Then, by using forward dynamic programming, another observer can be used to estimate the worst case disturbance for the remaining time $[\tau - T + 1, \dots \tau]$ where no observations are available to the controller.

Consider also the following dynamic controller which consists of the following controller/observer pair:

$$u_k = -B^T(M_{k+1}^{-1} + BB^T - \gamma^{-2}DD^T)^{-1}$$
$$\cdot A(I - \gamma^{-2}\Sigma_k M_k)^{-1}\widetilde{x}_k \qquad (5.2)$$

$$\widetilde{x}_{k+1} = A(I - \gamma^{-2}\widetilde{\Sigma}_k Q)^{-1}\widetilde{x}_k + Bu_k. \qquad (5.3)$$

$$\hat{x}_{k+1} = A\hat{x}_k + Bu_k + A(\Sigma_k^{-1} + C^T N^{-1}C - \gamma^{-2}Q)^{-1}$$
$$\cdot \left(\gamma^{-2}Q\hat{x}_k + C^T N^{-1}(y_k - C\hat{x}_k) \right). \qquad (5.4)$$

where $N = E^T E$ and with initial conditions

$$\begin{cases} \hat{x}_1 = 0, \ \widetilde{x}_1 = 0, & \text{if } \tau \leq T \\ \widetilde{x}_{\tau-T+1} = \hat{x}_{\tau-T+1}, & \text{if } \tau > T \end{cases} \qquad (5.5)$$

where $\hat{x}_k$ represents the closed-loop observer which incorporates the messages being received to update the current state estimate, while $\widetilde{x}_k$ represents the open-loop observer which runs over the

period with no messages being received while taking into account the worst case disturbance.

Additionally, M and Σ are the solutions of the following Game Algebraic Riccati Equation (GARE):

$$M_k = A^T(M_{k+1}^{-1} + BB^T - \gamma^{-2}DD^T)^{-1}A + Q^T Q,$$
$$M_f = Q_f \qquad (5.6)$$
$$\Sigma_{k+1} = A(\Sigma_k^{-1} + C^T N^{-1}C - \gamma^{-2}Q)^{-1}A^T + DD^T,$$
$$\Sigma_1 = Q^{-1} \qquad (5.7)$$
$$\widetilde{\Sigma}_{k+1} = A(\widetilde{\Sigma}_k^{-1} - \gamma^{-2}Q)^{-1}A^T + DD^T, \qquad (5.8)$$

where $\widetilde{\Sigma}_{k+1}$ has initial conditions

$$\begin{cases} \widetilde{\Sigma}_1 = Q^{-1} & \text{if } \tau \leq T \\ \widetilde{\Sigma}_{\tau-T+1} = \Sigma_{\tau-T+1} & \text{if } \tau > T \end{cases} \qquad (5.9)$$

PROPOSITION 5.1 (THEOREM 6.6 IN [4]). *The controller and observer pair described by (5.2)-(5.9), guarantees that minimax control for (3.1), with quadratic cost given by (3.2), achieves achieves the performance level of γ if the following conditions are satisfied:*

- *The Riccati equations (5.6) and (5.8) must admit a solution over $[1, K + 1]$, and the Riccati equation (5.7) has a solution over $[1, K - T + 1]$.*

- *The solution of the Observer Riccati equation (5.8) must satisfy:*

$$\rho(\widetilde{\Sigma}_k Q) < \gamma^2, \ \ k = 1, ..., K + 1. \qquad (5.10)$$

- *The solution of the two Riccati (5.6) and (5.8) equations must satisfy :*

$$\rho(\widetilde{\Sigma}_{k+1} M_{k+1}) < \gamma^2, \ \ k = 1, ..., K. \qquad (5.11)$$

This proposition show that this observer is able to always estimate the worst case state by using the information received up to time $k - T$ and then run a worst case open-loop observer for the period where no information is available.

Now we can generalize this result into the case of networked system under the specified attack.

5.1 Minimax Estimator and Controller under Packet Scheduling Attack

In order to design a minimax controller, we need first to check that all the assumptions required for certainty equivalence hold. First, lets examine the information structure presented in this situation. The packet scheduling attack affects mainly the information process and the amount of information presented at the controller at each time instance.

We can define the following set:

$$\mathbf{T} = \{k \in \{1, \dots, \tau\} | \text{packet is received and has timestamp} = k\} \qquad (5.12)$$

The information structure for the system under attack can be then defined as:

$$\widetilde{\Omega}_\tau(\bar{u}, \bar{y}) = \{\omega \in \Omega | \eta_k(\bar{u}, \omega) = \bar{y}_k, k \in \mathbf{T}\}, \qquad (5.13)$$

since packets are timestamped and can be reordered according to the time-stamps, it is not difficult to see that this information structure satisfies assumptions (4.10)-(4.12).

For the rest of the certainty equivalence assumptions, assumption I is not related to the packet reception behavior and thus it follows directly if the system without the attack does satisfy this assumption, thus the system under the attack satisfies them as well. Assumption II requires that the designed controller and observer satisfies the saddle point equation shown. This will be discussed in the remaining of this section.

Consider now the auxiliary problem defined in Assumption II. For the system under attack, the auxiliary problem can be written as:

$$\max_{\omega^{\tau-1} \in \bar{\Omega}_{\tau-1}^{\tau-1}} G_{\tau-1}(\bar{u}^{\tau-1}, \omega^{\tau-1}), \qquad (5.14)$$

where

$$G_{\tau-1}(\bar{u}^{\tau-1}, \omega^{\tau-1}) = V_\tau(x_\tau) + \sum_{k \in \mathbf{T}} \left(|x_k|_Q^2 + |u_k|^2 - \gamma^2 |\omega_k|^2 \right)$$
$$+ \sum_{k \notin \mathbf{T}} \left(|x_k|_Q^2 + |u_k|^2 - \gamma^2 |\omega_k|^2 \right).$$

With again the same intuition of having an observer which estimates the worst case disturbance over the time slots where the controller has information and then runs an open-loop (forward dynamic programming) to estimate the worst case for the remaining time where no information is available. Algorithm 1 utilizes this intuition.

As define above, Σ_k is used when there is a measurement reception, and $\widetilde{\Sigma}_k$ whenever the system is in open-loop and no measurement is received at the controller. We define $\bar{\Sigma}_k$ as taking the value of either Σ_k or $\widetilde{\Sigma}_k$ in the case of reception or no reception, respectively, of a message. An auxiliary state is also introduced as $\bar{x}_k$ which follows the same definition depending on the reception or no reception of a measurement. Additionally, we define the time step at which a packet is transmitted as t_k. The current time is denote as κ. The number of packets received at each time interval is denoted as N_{pkts}. Since multiple packets may arrive during the last time interval, we denote t_k^i as the time of each packet $i \in [1, N_{pkts}]$. We also define the buffers, $\Theta_x \in \mathbb{R}^{(n,T+1)}$, $\Theta_u \in \mathbb{R}^{(m,T+1)}$, $\Theta_y \in \mathbb{R}^{(p,T+1)}$ and $\Theta_\Sigma \in \mathbb{R}^{(n,n(T+1))}$, which store the values of $\widetilde{x}_k$, u_k, y_k and $\bar{\Sigma}_k$ in the interval $[\kappa - T - 1, \kappa]$. Values are stored in ascending order of transmission time and if a measurement does not arrive at the controller at a particular time k, then $\Theta_y(k) \in \emptyset$ (empty). We summarize this discussion in the following result:

THEOREM 5.2. *The implementation of the dynamic observer and controller pair shown in algorithm 1 guarantees that the minimax controller achieves the performance level of γ for the system under the packet scheduling attack, described by the assumptions (A1)-(A4), if the same conditions of proposition 5.1 are satisfied.*

PROOF. Algorithm 1 utilizes the same controller as proposition 5.1. Thus, with the conditions of Certainty Equivalence being satisfied, it is sufficient to show that the observer described in algorithm 1 constructs the worst case state estimate under the information pattern imposed by the packet scheduling attack. Define $y^\tau(\Delta)$ to be:

$$y^\tau(\Delta) = \begin{cases} y_i, & i = 1, \ldots \tau - \Delta \\ 0, & i > \tau - \Delta \end{cases} \qquad (5.15)$$

proposition 5.1 guarantees that the observer defined in (5.3) and (5.4) estimates the worst case state for the described output string $y^\tau(T)$. For the system under the attack, at each time k the observer reorders the packets in its correct order. The string of outputs can be shown as a concatenation of multiple $y^\tau(\Delta)$:

$$y_k = y^{\tau_1}(\Delta_1) y^{\tau_2}(\Delta_2) \ldots y^{\tau_n}(\Delta_n). \qquad (5.16)$$

Algorithm 1 Minimax control under packet scheduling attack

1: Define N_{pkts} and Θ_y based on the packets received between $[\kappa - 1, \kappa]$.
2: **if** $N_{pkts} = 0$ **then**　　　　　　　▷ No packet received
3: 　　$\bar{x}_{k+1} \leftarrow$ (5.3)
4: 　　$\bar{\Sigma}_{k+1} \leftarrow$ (5.8)
5: **else**　　　　　　　　　　　　▷ Packet(s) have received
6: 　　$t_k^{min} \leftarrow \min_{i=1,\ldots,N_{pkts}}(t_k^i)$
7: 　　$\bar{x}_{k+1} \leftarrow$ (5.5),　　　　　　　　▷ Initializations
8: 　　with initial $\bar{x}_{t_k^{min}-1} \leftarrow \Theta_x(\kappa - t_k^{min} - 1)$
9: 　　$\bar{\Sigma}_{k+1} \leftarrow$ (5.9)
10: 　　with initial $\bar{\Sigma}_{t_k^{min}-1} \leftarrow \Theta_\Sigma(\kappa - t_k^{min} - 1)$
11: 　　**for** $k = t_k^{min} - 1 : \kappa$ **do**　　　▷ Re-compute $\bar{x}$ and $\bar{\Sigma}$
12: 　　　　$u_k \leftarrow \Theta_u(\kappa - k)$
13: 　　　　$y_k \leftarrow \Theta_y(\kappa - k)$
14: 　　　　**if** $\Theta_y(k) \in \emptyset$ **then**　　　　▷ No packet arrival
15: 　　　　　　$\bar{x}_{k+1} \leftarrow$ (5.3)
16: 　　　　　　$\bar{\Sigma}_{k+1} \leftarrow$ (5.8)
17: 　　　　**else**　　　　　　　　　　▷ If packet arrived
18: 　　　　　　$\bar{x}_{k+1} \leftarrow$ (5.4)
19: 　　　　　　$\bar{\Sigma}_{k+1} \leftarrow$ (5.7)
20: 　　　　**end if**
21: 　　**end for**
22: **end if**
23: $M_k \leftarrow$ (5.8)
24: $u_k \leftarrow$ (5.2)

The observer constructed in algorithm 1 can be shown as multiple runs of the observer shown in proposition 5.1 over each $y^{\tau_j}(\Delta_j)$ separately, where Σ_k and $\widetilde{\Sigma}_k$ are now defined as $\bar{\Sigma}_k$. □

5.2 Memory and computation requirements

The proposed estimator and controller under packet scheduling attack requires the storage of the information Θ_x, Θ_u, Θ_y and Θ_Σ, at the controller/estimator unit as detailed in algorithm 1. In the case of the usage of a buffer approach, as discussed in Section 2, the implementation requires the storage of the same information as the proposed solution. This is the case as this approach computes equations (5.2)-(5.8) which require the same information set. Additionally, both implementations require the storage of the solution of the Riccati equation M_k.

With respect to the computational complexity, while the proposed controller/estimator requires de online computation of $\bar{\Sigma}$, in the buffer case this value can be pre-computed and stored in memory. However, this would increase the memory requirements when compared to the propose solution.

6. SIMULATION RESULTS

We now illustrate our results using a numerical example to validate the controller and estimator proposed in Section 5. The proposed solution is used for the control of the Batch Reactor process from [27] which is a fourth order unstable linear system with two inputs with system parameters defined as

$$A = \begin{pmatrix} 1.38 & -0.2077 & 6.715 & -5.676 \\ -0.5814 & -4.29 & 0 & 0.675 \\ 1.067 & 4.273 & -6.654 & 5.893 \\ 0.048 & 4.273 & 1.343 & -2.104 \end{pmatrix}$$

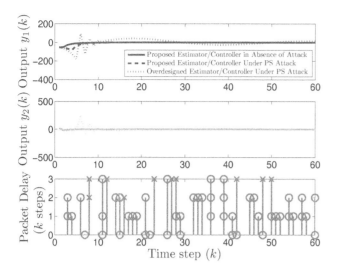

Figure 4: The upper figure shows the output value of the system under the three different cases. Lower figure depicts the packet delay induced by the attacker to each *received* packet.

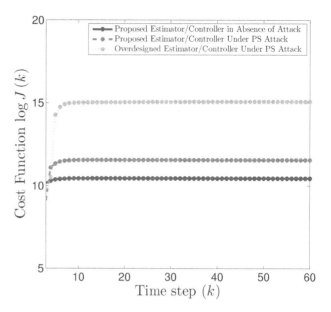

Figure 5: Evolution of the control cost $\log J(k)$ for each of the evaluated cases.

$$B = \begin{pmatrix} 0 & 0 \\ 5.679 & 0 \\ 1.136 & -3.146 \\ 1.136 & 0 \end{pmatrix}, \quad C \begin{pmatrix} 1 & 0 & 1 & -1 \\ 0 & 1 & 0 & 0 \end{pmatrix}, \quad D = \mathbf{0},$$

The worst-case process disturbance $w(k)$ for this system is defined in [4] and we use it also in our example. Additionally, the maximum allowed delay in the network is set to $T = 4$. The attacker will pick any delay between $[0, T]$ to affect the transmitted packet. Moreover, we select Q_f and Q as the identity matrix.

We evaluate the proposed solution in the absence of an attack and under a packet switching attack, and we compare it to the case where an over-designed estimator/controller would be used. The over-designed estimator/controller is the typical buffer case discussed in Section 2. The buffer length is defined to be the maximum delay $T = 4$.

Both the over-designed and our proposed estimator/controller are designed using a minimax approach where γ is picked to solve the algebraic Riccati equations (5.7)-(5.8) for the maximum delay. We set $\gamma = 36$ which is the minimum value which renders the system stable under the buffer implementation.

Figure 4 shows the time-response analysis for a 60 step simulation of the closed-loop control system, respectively. The upper figure shows the output value of the system under the three different cases, and lower figure depicts the packet delay induced by the attacker to each *received* packet. As the proposed controller and state-estimator makes use of all information up to time the current time step, an improved performance with respect to the over-designed implementation is obtained as shown in Figure 4.

The final cost in (3.2) obtained for the proposed minimax approach is 2.03% higher than the un-attacked scenario while the over-designed controller pays 103.3% more cost than the un-attacked scenario. This result reflects the opportunistic nature of our design. Figure 5 depicts the evolution of the logarithm of the control cost $\log J(k)$ under all cases.

7. CONCLUSIONS AND FUTURE WORK

In this paper, we have introduced a minimax defense for packet scheduling attacks. The main technical point is to show that the certainty equivalence property holds under the varying-delay and out-of-order information structure. It is then straight forward to design a worst case state-estimator and controller under this information structure. The final design is of opportunistic nature in the sense that it is designed for the worst case delay while immediately using the information in the received packets. The ability to immediately use the received information leads to better performance as measured by a quadratic cost. Simulation results show the feasibility of the proposed design.

As future work, we could generalize the results to the case where the attacker can mount attack on the path between the controller and the actuator. Another research direction is investigating the case where a system has more than one actuator, each actuator is controlled by a separate controller and the packet scheduling attack forces packets to arrive at different controllers in a different order. Such attack will lead to controllers with different knowledge about the system, yet they still need to be resilient.

8. ADDITIONAL AUTHORS

9. REFERENCES

[1] S. Amin, A. A. Cardenas, and S. Sastry. Safe and secure networked control systems under denial-of-service attacks. In R. Majumdar and P. Tabuada, editors, *Hybrid Systems: Computation and Control*, volume 5469 of *Lecture Notes in Computer Science*, pages 31–45. Springer Berlin Heidelberg, 2009.

[2] K. Åström and B. Wittenmark. *Computer controlled systems*. Prentice Hall Englewood Cliffs, NJ, 1990.

[3] Y. Bar-Shalom. Update with out-of-sequence measurements in tracking: exact solution. *Aerospace and Electronic Systems, IEEE Transactions on*, 38(3):769 – 777, jul 2002.

[4] T. Başar and P. Bernhard. *H-Infinity Optimal Control and Related Minimax Design Problems: A Dynamic Game Approach*. Modern Birkhäuser Classics. Birkhäuser Boston, 2008.

[5] P. Bernhard. A discrete-time min-max certainty equivalence principle. *Systems and Control Letters*, 24(4):229 – 234, 1995.

[6] A. A. Cárdenas, S. Amin, Z.-S. Lin, Y.-L. Huang, C.-Y. Huang, and S. Sastry. Attacks against process control systems: risk assessment, detection, and response. In *Proceedings of the 6th ACM Symposium on Information, Computer and Communications Security*, ASIACCS '11, pages 355–366, New York, NY, USA, 2011. ACM.

[7] X. Chen, K. Makki, K. Yen, and N. Pissinou. Sensor network security: a survey. *Communications Surveys Tutorials, IEEE*, 11(2):52 –73, quarter 2009.

[8] H. Fawzi, P. Tabuada, and S. Diggavi. Secure state-estimation for dynamical systems under active adversaries. In *Communication, Control, and Computing (Allerton), 2011 49th Annual Allerton Conference on*, pages 337 –344, sept. 2011.

[9] T. Glad and L. Ljung. *Control Theory: Multivariable and Nonlinear Methods*. Taylor & Francis, 2000.

[10] A. Gupta, C. Langbort, and T. Başar. Optimal control in the presence of an intelligent jammer with limited actions. In *Decision and Control (CDC), 2010 49th IEEE Conference on*, pages 1096 –1101, dec. 2010.

[11] Y. Halevi and A. Ray. Integrated communication and control systems. I - analysis. *ASME, Transactions, Journal of Dynamic Systems, Measurement and Control.*, 110:367 – 373, December 1988.

[12] Y. Halevi and A. Ray. Integrated communication and control systems. II - design considerations. *ASME, Transactions, Journal of Dynamic Systems, Measurement and Control.*, 110:367 – 373, December 1988.

[13] J. P. Hespanha, P. Naghshtabrizi, and Y. Xu. A survey of recent results in networked control systems. *Proceedings of the IEEE*, 95(1):138–162, 2007.

[14] H. Hirano, M. Mukai, T. Azuma, and M. Fujita. Optimal control of discrete-time linear systems with network-induced varying delay. In *American Control Conference, 2005. Proceedings of the 2005*, pages 1419 – 1424 vol. 2, june 2005.

[15] B. Lincoln and B. Bernhardsson. Optimal control over networks with long random delays. In *Proceedings of the International Symposium on Mathematical Theory of Networks and Systems*, Jan. 2000.

[16] J. Meserve. Staged cyber attack reveals vulnerability in power grid, Sept. 2007.

[17] M. Mostafa, M. Shalan, and S. Hammad. FPGA-based low-level can protocol testing. In *System-on-Chip for Real-Time Applications, The 6th International Workshop on*, pages 185–188. IEEE, 2006.

[18] J. Nilsson. *Real-Time control systems with delays*. PhD thesis, Lund Institute of Technology, Jan 1998. Ph.D. thesis.

[19] Z. H. Pang, G. P. Liu, and Z. Dong. Secure networked control systems under denial of service attacks. In *18th IFAC World Congress*, 2011.

[20] R. Poovendran, K. Sampigethaya, S. K. S. Gupta, I. Lee, K. V. Prasad, D. Corman, and J. Paunicka. Special issue on cyber - physical systems [scanning the issue]. *Proceedings of the IEEE*, 100(1):6 –12, jan. 2012.

[21] S. Radosavac, A. A. Cárdenas, J. S. Baras, and G. V. Moustakides. Detecting ieee 802.11 mac layer misbehavior in ad hoc networks: Robust strategies against individual and colluding attackers. *J. Comput. Secur.*, 15(1):103–128, Jan. 2007.

[22] M. Raya and J. Hubaux. Securing vehicular ad hoc networks. *Journal of Computer Security*, 15(1):39–68, 2007.

[23] T. Rid. Cyber war will not take place. *Journal of Strategic Studies*, 2011.

[24] P. L. Tang and C. de Silva. Compensation for transmission delays in an ethernet-based control network using variable-horizon predictive control. *Control Systems Technology, IEEE Transactions on*, 14(4):707 – 718, july 2006.

[25] A. Teixeira, D. Pérez, H. Sandberg, and K. H. Johansson. Attack models and scenarios for networked control systems. In *Proceedings of the 1st international conference on High Confidence Networked Systems*, HiCoNS '12, pages 55–64, New York, NY, USA, 2012. ACM.

[26] J. Vijayan. Stuxnet renews power grid security concerns, Jul. 26 2010.

[27] G. Walsh, H. Ye, and L. Bushnell. Stability analysis of networked control systems. *IEEE Transactions on Control Systems Technology*, pages 2876–2880, 1999.

[28] A. Westenberger, B. Duraisamy, M. Munz, M. Muntzinger, M. Fritzsche, and K. Dietmayer. Impact of out-of-sequence measurements on the joint integrated probabilistic data association filter for vehicle safety systems. In *Intelligent Vehicles Symposium (IV), 2012 IEEE*, pages 438 –443, june 2012.

[29] T. Yang. Networked control system: a brief survey. *Control Theory and Applications, IEE Proceedings -*, 153(4):403 – 412, july 2006.

[30] K. Zhang, X. Li, and Y. Zhu. Optimal update with out-of-sequence measurements. *Signal Processing, IEEE Transactions on*, 53(6):1992 – 2004, june 2005.

[31] W. Zhang, M. S. Branicky, and S. M. Phillips. Stability of networked control systems. *IEEE Control Systems Magazine*, 21(1):84 –99, Feb. 2001.

[32] M. Zhu and S. Martinez. On resilient consensus against replay attacks in operator-vehicle networks. In *American Control Conference (ACC), 2012*, pages 3553 –3558, june 2012.

Verifiably-Safe Software-Defined Networks for CPS

Richard Skowyra
rskowyra@bu.edu

Andrei Lapets
lapets@bu.edu

Azer Bestavros
best@bu.edu

Assaf Kfoury
kfoury@bu.edu

Computer Science Department
Boston University

ABSTRACT

Next generation cyber-physical systems (CPS) are expected to be deployed in domains which require scalability as well as performance under dynamic conditions. This scale and dynamicity will require that CPS communication networks be programmatic (i.e., not requiring manual intervention at any stage), but still maintain iron-clad safety guarantees. Software-defined networking standards like OpenFlow provide a means for scalably building tailor-made network architectures, but there is no guarantee that these systems are safe, correct, or secure.

In this work we propose a methodology and accompanying tools for specifying and modeling distributed systems such that existing formal verification techniques can be transparently used to analyze critical requirements and properties prior to system implementation. We demonstrate this methodology by iteratively modeling and verifying an Open-Flow learning switch network with respect to network correctness, network convergence, and mobility-related properties.

We posit that a design strategy based on the complementary pairing of software-defined networking and formal verification would enable the CPS community to build next-generation systems without sacrificing the safety and reliability that these systems must deliver.

Categories and Subject Descriptors

C.2.2 [**Network Protocols**]: Protocol Verification—*cyber-physical systems*; C.2.1 [**Network Architecture and Design**]: *software-de ned networking*

Keywords

Software-Defined Networking, OpenFlow, formal verification

1. INTRODUCTION

As the capabilities of modern computer technology continue to improve, an increasing number of safety-critical tasks are integrated with or replaced by automatic control and sensing systems (e.g., self-driving cars, unmanned aerial vehicles, mobile sensor platforms, smart-grid technologies, GPS navigation systems, and so on). These systems are frequently distributed and often must be either large-scale or require elasticity of scale as utilization or population fluctuates. Furthermore, many of these cyber-physical systems must interoperate over very large collections of interacting devices (possibly federated and running under multiple authorities), and they must be robust enough to handle churn, mobility, and other potentially unstable or unpredictable conditions. In order to operate under these conditions, CPSs will inevitably need to rely on increasingly more sophisticated data and control networks while maintaining strong safety and reliability guarantees. These requirements suggest that CPS communication networks be both programmatic (i.e., not requiring manual intervention at any stage) [25] and flexible to changing operating conditions.

Let us consider communication networks that must link multiple mobile end-hosts which communicate intermittently but reliably. On a small scale these networks can be easily built using multiplexed wireless communication like 802.11 or 802.15.4 Zigbee routers. As scale increases and it becomes possible that end-host mobility may span multiple routers or access points, however, significant overhead may be imposed by a naive attempt to maintain an updated, consistent network state that tracks end-host locations. This complexity may be compounded by the need to maintain QoS guarantees with respect to delay, loss rate, power consumption, etc. Ideally, any such communication network for next-generation cyber-physical systems would use existing physical infrastructure, but leverage domain-specific network designs and protocols to maximize these guarantees.

Recent advances in software-defined networking, specifically the OpenFlow initiative, allow precisely this flexibility in both physical infrastructure and software [23]. OpenFlow networks outsource routing logic to a domain-specific software controller written by the network designer, which runs on a remote machine (ranging from commodity hardware to custom FPGAs) connected to each switch via a secure channel. OpenFlow-enabled switches send unknown or unhandled packets to this controller, which responds by installing flow-rules (next-hop rules which trigger based on packet headers) in one or more of switches across the network. Compliant switches then route data-plane packets based on these flow rules.

OpenFlow routing hardware is supported by a number of major equipment vendors, often requiring only a firmware upgrade to existing, deployed routers [2]. OpenFlow has been used to implement a wide variety of network tools and protocols, including routing circuit-switch and packet-switched traffic over the same switch [10], wave-length path control in optical networks [21], in-network load balancers [26], wireless sensor networks [22], and wireless mesh networks [11].

While OpenFlow provides a powerful means for specifying control-plane logic and protocols, the resulting networks may not satisfy necessary safety conditions and QoS guarantees. In addition, controllers may contain not only implementation errors, but also critical design and logic flaws arising from insufficient or incorrect domain knowledge on the part of the designer, unexpected concurrency issues, misplaced assumptions about the operating environment, etc. These flaws could be extremely damaging if not detected before system deployment, especially in applications like vehicular control networks.

Fortunately, existing formal analysis and verification tools, applied to a model of the proposed system design, can be used to determine in a semi-automated manner that distributed systems built using OpenFlow do enforce their requirements in all cases. However, these tools are often limited to checking only properties in a small set of formal logics (LTL, relational calculus, process calculi, and so on). Real-world systems often have requirements spanning many such logics, all of which must be verified using different formalisms.

In this work, we present an infrastructure and associated tools for specifying and analyzing real-world, formally disparate properties of distributed systems, without requiring prior knowledge of any formal logics or languages. We provide an example using an OpenFlow-based network of learning switches to allow communication between mobile end-hosts. We investigate safety, stability, and probabilistic reliability properties, and use the result to iteratively design the system model until it verifiably satisfies all design requirements.

The rest of this paper is organized as follows. Section 2 describes the OpenFlow standard in more detail and discusses how communication systems controlled using OpenFlow programs may suffer from design or logical errors. Section 3 describes how these errors can be detected and fixed by analyzing formally specified properties of a model of the communication system prior to implementation. Section 4 describes an infrastructure for modeling distributed systems and automatically specifying and analyzing their properties. Section 5 describes related work, and Section 6 concludes.

2. OpenFlow

OpenFlow [23] is an emerging routing standard for software-defined networking that enforces a clean separation of the data and control planes. An OpenFlow switch routes data plane packets based on flow tables: ordered lists of rules guarded by a pattern to be matched over a packet header. These rules are installed by a controller, which is connected to each switch via a secure, dedicated link. Rules, at a minimum, can specify a port to route over, packet dropping, and forwarding of packets to the controller. If an incoming network packet's header does not match any flow rule, it is forwarded to the controller. Rules may also be set to expire after some time or duration, and be used to gather simple network statistics.

The OpenFlow controller is a software program running on a machine connected to each switch by a secure, dedicated control plane. The controller handles packets sent to it by OpenFlow switches and installs flow rules in the switches' flow tables. The functionality of the controller is determined completely by the application that it is being used to implement, but all controller programs must communicate with switches only by installing flow rules. Controllers can be written in a number of languages designed for the purpose. Popular choices include NOX/POX [16], Beacon [14], or Maestro [8], in addition to others [1].

An OpenFlow network provides a powerful, scalable infrastructure that can be used to tailor networks to specific tasks. Furthermore, all network design and planning beyond physical connectivity can be done in software, specifically in the design of the OpenFlow controller program. This allows for significantly richer network processing and routing functionality, but also introduces the possibility that (like any other software program) logical or design errors could lead to unsafe or incorrect behavior.

While network programming bugs may be tolerated in best-effort systems or those serving non-critical needs, many cyber-physical systems need iron-clad guarantees that a network routing mission-critical information will always (or with very high probability) meet its safety and correctness requirements. OpenFlow does not provide these guarantees, and so is not in its present form suitable for scalable network design in the cyber-physical realm. We propose that Verificare, a tool for formally verifiable distributed system design, can be used to bridge this gap.

3. DESIGN VERIFICATION

Significant prior work has been done on formal verification of software implementations [13]. Most of these techniques rely on the existence of a specification which is by assumption correct. The implemented software is then checked against this specification using formal techniques: the correct behavior of software is defined to be behavior which conforms to the software's specification, and bugs are defined as behaviors diverging from the specification.

However, as specifications (or languages for defining specifications) become more complex, another kind of correctness should be considered: how can a designer have confidence that the specification (or collection of specifications in multiple models) he defines is an accurate reflection of his intuitive and practical expectations regarding the correct behavior of the software? In particular, we are interested in some confirmation, from the perspective of a specification's designer, that the specification of a system correctly captures the behavior and requirements that the designer believes that it possesses. This is non-trivial, as there is no a priori correctness criterion against which a specification can be checked.

We address this issue by proposing that a specification should be constructed from a collection of formally modeled invariants, scenarios, and environments that are accompanied by familiar descriptions that a designer will recognize and understand within the context of the system's domain. On the back end, each invariant, scenario, or environment could potentially be represented in a distinct underlying

1. bind source address to source switch and port
2. if destination address is known:

   install fowarding rule to egress port for destination
3. if destination address is unknown:

   install forwarding rule to flood packets on all ports except source port

Figure 1: OpenFlow learning switch controller logic.

model or specification language that is appropriate for it. For example, the specification for a distributed file system which guarantees some level of availability could be constructed from a set of intuitive properties describing high-level notions of reliability; each intuitive property may map to multiple underlying specifications governing network behavior, data consistency, and data integrity.

We concentrate on the formal verification of distributed system design in the context of Verificare, a tool which allows specifications to be modeled and formally verified against properties chosen by the designer. This process is fast enough to allow rapid prototyping via formal verification, which can, for example, be used to iteratively model a specification as counter-examples to correctness claims are found.

Using the Verificare tool, it is possible to leverage OpenFlow's scalability without sacrificing confidence in the resulting system's safety and correctness. As an example application, we will model a network of OpenFlow learning switches, verify its key requirements, and demonstrate how this process can be used for rapid, iterative development of the specification. We chose to model a learning switch network because it is a well-known mobility solution that has a number of practical applications and deployment strategies, as well as a number of desirable properties which may be required to hold during its operation.

3.1 A Learning Switch Network

A learning switch is one that forms a routing table by binding the source address of network packets to the port on which those packets arrived. A network of these switches can be used to implement a communications network for mobile nodes such as autonomous mobile robots, warehouse floor staff, or mobile sensor platforms. As nodes move between locations, they connect to the network on different ports of different switches. These may, for example, be 802.11 wireless access points, 802.15.4 Zigbee routers, etc.

In order to ensure consistent network state, an OpenFlow controller maintains a network-wide routing table which it uses to install switch-specific packet forwarding rules. OpenFlow switches forward packets that don't match any forwarding rule to the switch, which records the packet's origin and installs a forwarding rule to describe its next hop (either to a specific switch port, or flooding to all switch ports but the origin). Specifically, the OpenFlow controller utilizes the logic in Figure 3.1 whenever it receives a packet sent to it by a switch.

In a traditional learning switch, every incoming network packet is sent to the controller, ensuring that the network state is as up-to-date as the last packet arrival. This minimizes the number of forwarding rules in the switch at any time, but can cause significant latency as all packets are forwarded to the controller for processing. In our exam-

ple application, more forwarding rules are used to minimize the number of packets which must be sent to the controller without impacting the consistency of the logical and physical network states. Other designs are certainly possible, and in fact Verificare could be used to explore their tradeoffs in detail.

Our example network has the topology shown in Figure 2. Every switch has a dedicated channel to the OpenFlow controller, a bidirectional link to another switch, and four ports available for nodes to connect on. Nodes are mobile end-hosts which connect to the network on a switch port for some time, send and receive messages with other nodes, then disconnect for some time before reconnecting elsewhere.

While the example network is small compared to most real-world implementations, significant empirical evidence suggests that most violations of specified properties can be detected using a small scale model [3]. This approach of checking a scoped version of a model is standard in model-checking and related verification paradigms. By necessity the approach is not complete, so un-detected counterexamples may exist. The approach is sound, however, guaranteeing that any counter-example to a property found by the system will indeed violate that property.

The requirements that we will verify for this model are as follows.

1. *no-forwarding-loops*: Any packet that enters the network will eventually exit the network.

2. *no-blackholes*: Any packet that is sent will eventually be received.

3. *stable-correct-receiver*: If all nodes cease being mobile, eventually all packets that are received will be received by the intended recipient.

4. *stable-no-floods*: If all nodes cease being mobile, eventually no more packets will be flooded.

5. *bounded-loss-rate*: The expected packet loss rate of mobile nodes is below a specified bound.

The first two properties represent invariant safety and correctness requirements for the network: packets cannot be routed in infinite cycles or lost within the network. The third and fourth properties represent network convergence properties: once nodes remain stationary, the actual and perceived (by the controller) locations of each node will correctly converge. The final property represents a probabilistic expectation about loss rate in the face of node mobility. Note that we could also reason about the probability of specific loss rates (i.e., that the loss rate is below a specified bound with some probability) using the same formalisms discussed below.

3.2 Formalizing Requirements

In order to verify the properties expressed above, it is necessary to represent them as formulas in a formal logic that makes it possible to automatically and provably solve them over the domain of possible models. Specifically, in order to specify correct behavior of systems (or any set of defined algorithms), it is first necessary to define a collection of mathematical objects $\mathcal{M}$ that corresponds to the set of possible systems $\mathcal{S}$, as well as a mapping $f : \mathcal{S} \rightarrow \mathcal{M}$ from individual systems $s \in \mathcal{S}$ to objects $m \in \mathcal{M}$. It is

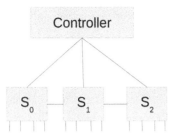

Figure 2: Learning switch network topology.

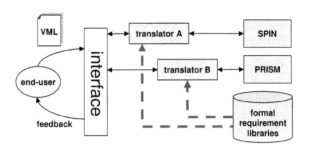

Figure 3: Verificare tool overview.

then necessary to establish some formal logical system $\mathcal{F}$, or *formalism*, that is sufficiently rich to express properties of objects in $\mathcal{S}$. Together $(f, \mathcal{M}, \mathcal{F})$ form one *model space* of the set of systems.

Given $(f, \mathcal{M}, \mathcal{F})$, it is possible to formally state what it means for a system to satisfy a property: a system $s \in \mathcal{S}$ satisfies some property φ iff it can be proven (either analytically or using a brute-force state space search) in the chosen formalism $\mathcal{F}$ that $f(s) \in \mathcal{M}$ satisfies a logical formula φ expressed in that formalism:

$$s \text{ satisfies requirement } \varphi \iff \varphi(f(s)) \in \mathcal{F}$$

However, adopting only one set of objects $\mathcal{M}$ and one formalism governing $\mathcal{M}$ that is sufficiently powerful to express all possible protocol properties is usually impractical. If some object $f(s) \in \mathcal{M}$ captured all possible aspects of a system $s \in \mathcal{S}$, determining whether that object satisfies some property may be intractable or undecidable.

A more tractable approach is to choose several different model spaces $(f_1, \mathcal{M}_1, \mathcal{F}_1), ..., (f_k, \mathcal{M}_k, \mathcal{F}_k)$ for systems, such that each model space can capture only some of the relevant properties of a system, and such that there exists a tractable or efficient algorithm for checking each property in its corresponding formalism.

In this work we consider two formalisms for describing properties of modeled systems: Linear Temporal Logic (LTL) and Probabilistic Computation Tree Logic (PCTL*) [5]. PCTL* formulas are logical statements governing probabilistic automata like discrete and continuous-time Markov chains; furthermore, these logical statements can contain probabilistic quantifiers. Assuming that there exists a mapping that can faithfully convert a protocol definition into a corresponding probabilistic automaton, it is then possible to construct a logical formula stating that the automaton (and thus, the protocol) satisfy, e.g., a certain expected packet loss rate.

LTL is a particular subset of PCTL*; LTL formulas are capable of expressing temporal properties about the existence of a state or set of states on the model which are of interest. For example, if there is a mapping that can faithfully convert a protocol definition into a Büchi automaton, then we can construct a logical formula stating that the automaton satisfies a property that will eventually (in some future state) always be true (over all states following it).

The first four properties defined above, *no-forwarding-loops*, *no-blackholes*, *stable-correct-receiver*, and *stable-no-floods*, are expressible as LTL formulas over a predicate which is true if and only if the corresponding model state is enabled. The final property, *bounded-loss-rate*, can be expressed in PCTL* using probabilistic quantifiers over the

stationary distribution of the model represented as a Continuous-Time Markov Chain (CTMC).

We should note that in practice, *checking* that a given model of a system satisfies one or more properties usually amounts to an exhaustive search of a pruned state space. Individual states represent snapshots of the model in operation, and transitions represent valid ways in which a state can progress. Such an approach to checking properties is employed in other application domains, such as hardware processor design [6].

4. VERIFICARE

In this section, we describe how the critical requirements (described in Section 3.1) for a network of learning switches can be formally verified under multiple calculi using the Verificare tool. A key design principle of Verificare is rapid prototyping of a distributed system specification prior to its implementation. The tool consists of three related components, diagrammed in Figure 3.

- **Verificare Modeling Language (VML):** VML is a lightweight modeling language designed to permit rapid, iterative development of specifications. It is discussed in detail in Section 4.1.

- **Formal Requirement Libraries:** Verificare includes libraries of formal requirements which can be automatically bound to user-created VML code. These libraries are used to separate model development from requirement specification, and are described further in Section 4.3.

- **VML Translator:** Verificare offloads model verification to off-the-shelf verification engines using implemented translators to and from VML and tool-specific languages. These translators enable properties in a variety of logics to be checked, even if no individual tool supports all of the logics being used. Translation is discussed further in Sections 4.3 and 4.4.

In order to analyze a system under development, a designer uses VML to model relevant aspects of that system. Properties and requirements to be checked are selected from the formal requirement libraries and optionally augmented with user-defined requirements. The combined model and requirement specification is translated automatically to one or more backend verification engines; the output is then presented to the user as statements about the VML model.

By way of example, we first model an initial, naive version of the learning switch network in VML. We then describe how the properties to be verified are added to the model, and

```
1 send(
2   int link=0,
3   set<host> dest=self.links[0],
4   msgtype(a,b,...)
5 )
6
7 recv(
8   link=all,
9   msgtype(var1, var2,...),
10  mfields='m'
11 )
```

Figure 4: VML send and receive primitives.

iteratively analyze and update the model until all necessary properties verifiably hold.

4.1 VML

Before modeling the network of learning switches, it is necessary to briefly introduce the Verificare Modeling Language, VML. VML is a specification modeling language inspired by Promela [17], Alloy [18], and Python. It is designed to capture sketches of specifications of distributed systems, and to abstract away implementation details in order to analyze architectural and design-specific properties.

VML supports typed sequences, sets, and dictionaries, in addition to integers and boolean values. In addition to basic indexing, insertion, and removal from these datastructures, VML allows simple containment checks, mapping of VML statements over sequences and sets, and comprehensions over sets. A non-deterministic pick primitive is also provided for sets, which allows a comprehension whose maximum size is bounded by the user. These features allow simple declarative reasoning about systems abstracted from implementation details, as is seen in the learning switch model.

In order to permit formal analysis of concurrency-related properties, control structures in VML are based on Dijkstra's Guarded Command Language [12]. VML supports if and do structures, each of which consists of a sequence of predicates guarding execution of a sequence of VML statements. If at any point multiple guards are true, the selection of which code block to execute is made non-deterministically.

4.1.1 The Network Abstraction

In addition to the features described above, VML provides a configurable network abstraction to simplify the modeling of distributed systems. Under this abstraction, a VML model consists of uniquely identified, independent, concurrent hosts communicating over a network. Each host has its own internal variable scope, state, and control logic.

Each host has a sequence, links, of sets of hosts, which denotes one or more links to the network over which some subset of other hosts are reachable. Messages sent over links are user-defined tuples prefixed with a message type.

Message sending is provided via the built-in send primitive in Figure 4.1.1, which sends a message to a (possibly empty) set of hosts over a specified link. If a host is not reachable over the specified link, it will not receive the message. The dest parameter may be any expression which evaluates to a set of hosts, such as a set comprehension. This allows simple reasoning about unicast (single hosts), multicast (set comprehensions) and broadcast (all hosts on the link) communication without needing separate implementations of each message-passing paradigm. If left empty,

```
1 host opf_Controller():
2   dict<hid><dict<hid><int>> routes
3   loop true:
4     recv(msg(saddr, daddr, sp)):
5       all {switch | switch in routes.keys()}:
6         if:
7           (switch == m.src): #Bind source addr to source port
8             routes[switch][saddr]=sp
9           (switch != m.src): #Bind source addr to source switch
10            routes[switch][saddr]=routes[switch][m.src]
11      ?(!(daddr in routes[m.src].keys())):
12        routes[m.src][daddr]=-1
13      send(dest=sw_id, forwarding_rule(sp, saddr, daddr,
14        routes[switch][daddr])
15      send(dest=sw_iditch, msg(saddr, daddr))
```

Figure 5: Learning switch controller (naive model).

send's link and dest parameters default to a host's first link and all hosts reachable via that link, respectively.

Messages are received using the recv primitive in Figure 4.1.1, which receives messages over one or more links. If messages are waiting on multiple links, the selection is made non-deterministically. By default, recv receives messages over all inks. The message type parameter imposes a criterion that only a message of type msgtype will be received; other messages waiting in the receiver will not trigger this statement.

The message must have as many tuple elements, with each of a matching type, as variables specified in the recv statement. After execution, each specified variable will contain the value of that message tuple field. Variables may be singletons, sets, or sequences. In the case of sequences, the length of the receiving sequence must be at least equal to the length of the sequence sent via the message. The optional mfields parameter provides a string to use as a prefix when accessing implicit message variables (such as the link a message arrived over).

4.2 A Learning Switch Network in VML

Recall that an Openflow network consists of three components: the controller, network switches which route packets based on flow tables, and end-hosts which send and receive packets. Our initial modeling attempt will specify a network of switches with flow tables, mobile end-hosts, and a controller with a standard learning switch functionality.

The learning switch network relies on bi-directional connections between ports, of which switches have several and end-hosts have one. This can easily be represented in the network abstraction by making each element of a host's links sequence correspond to a single port, restricting the size of the corresponding set of hosts per link to one, and ensuring mutual inclusion in two connected hosts' links sequences. Section 4.2.3, which models mobile end hosts, covers the process in detail. Similar syntax is used to set up the static topology shown in Figure 2 as the network's initial state.

4.2.1 The Openflow Controller

The naive VML model of an Openflow learning switch controller is presented in Figure 5. The routes datastructure provides a mapping of $(switch\_id, destination\_address) \mapsto port$, and allows the controller to look up the egress port from a switch to a destination address.

The remaining VML code is the controller's event handling loop. In lines 6-11, the controller updates its knowl-

```
1 host opf_Switch():
2  seq<pair<(int, int, int)><int>> flow_table
3  int match=-2
4  int saddr, daddr, p
5  loop true:
6   if:
7   (len(self.links[0]) == 0):
8    if:
9    recv(msg(saddr, daddr)):
10    for rule in flow_table:
11     if:
12     ((m.link, saddr, daddr)==rule.first):
13      match=rule.second
14      break
15    if:
16    (match>-2):
17     if:
18     (match > -1]):
19      send(link=match, msg(saddr, daddr))
20     (match ==-1):
21      all {port | port in self.links
22            && port != 0
23            && len(links[port])}:
24       send(link=port, msg(saddr, daddr))
25     else:
26      send(link=0, msg(saddr, daddr, m.link))
27    else: skip
28   else:
29   recv(link=0, msg(sp, saddr, daddr)):
30    for rule in flow_table:
31     if:
32     ((sp, saddr, daddr)==rule.first):
33      match=rule.second
34      break
35    send(link=match, msg(saddr, daddr))
36   recv( link=0,
37        forwarding_rule(sp, saddr, daddr, dp)
38        ):
39    flow_table.insert(
40      0, pair((sp, saddr, daddr), dp)
41    )
```

Figure 6: VML model of an Openflow switch.

```
1 host end_host():
2  hid switch
3  int port
4  loop true:
5   if:
6   (len(self.links[0])):
7    if:
8    recv(msg(saddr, daddr)): drop
9    true:
10    daddr = pick 1 {n | n in _hosts
11                   && n is end_host }
12    send(msg(self.id, daddr))
13   true:
14    open_ports[switch].add(port)
15    _hosts[switch].links[port].remove(self.id)
16    self.links[0].remove(switch)
17   else:
18    switch = pick 1 {s | s in open_ports.keys()
19                   && len(open_ports[s])}
20    port = pick 1 {p | p in open_ports[switch]}
21    open_ports[switch].remove[port]
22    _hosts[switch].links[port].add(self.id)
23    self.links[0].add(switch)
```

Figure 7: VML model of a mobile end-host.

a flood instruction. Figure 6 presents the VML model of an Openflow switch.

Lines 8-27 model normal packet routing. The Openflow standards do not, to the authors' knowledge, explicitly state that packets arriving from the controller should be dealt with prior to packets arriving over normal links. We modeled it as such since the alternative allows, for example, indefinite delays on the installation of forwarding rules. The flow table is modeled as a sequence of tuples mapping to switch egress ports. This is an ordered ranking, which uses the **for** operator to iterate over the sequence by index order. The first rule which matches the packet's header tuple is triggered.

Lines 28-41 handle messages received from the controller. These are either forwarding rules, or forwarded packets that are re-sent after the installation of a forwarding rule.

4.2.3 The End-Host

End hosts are modeled as hosts that send and receive messages while connected to the network. Mobility is formalized by the ability to non-deterministically disconnect and to later reconnect on any open port. The end host VML model is presented in Figure 7.

Lines 7-12 handle message reception and sending. Lines 13-23 handle disconnection and re-connection, which consists of out-of-band adjustments to the network abstraction and a global **open_ports** dictionary tracking available ports. The semantics of the **send** function ensure that adding or removing an identifier to an element of a host's **links** sequence enables or disables the ability to send to that host. During the connection procedure, an end-host adds itself to the switch's link in order to receive messages, and adds the switch to its own link in order to send messages.

4.3 Specifying and Verifying Properties

In Verificare, properties to be formally verified are usually selected from a domain-specific library and not developed by the system designer. As distributed systems often cover multiple domains of expertise, it is unreasonable to assume that all systems designers will be well-versed in both

edge of the origin's current switch and port. The route is set to the source port in the case of the originating switch, or to the originating switch in the case of other switches.

At line 11, the controller checks the message destination against its network state. If the destination has been seen before, it instructs the switch to install the appropriate forwarding rule, which maps a network address to a port. If the destination has not been seen before, it sets the destination port to -1, which is interpreted by the switch as a flood. It then re-sends the packet to the querying switch for re-transmission.

4.2.2 The Openflow Switch

Openflow switches have no intelligence beyond the ability to match packet header fields against a table of forwarding rules and to contact the controller if a packet does not match any rule. For the purposes of this application, we modeled these forwarding rules as tuples of the form (*source port, sender address, destination address*). This ensures that a packet will be sent to the controller when the destination is unknown, or when the sender's current location (i.e., the specific binding of switch, source address, and port) is not already known to the controller. Responses from the controller are a forwarding rule that either specifies an output port or

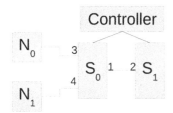

Figure 8: Modeled network topology.

Node	Controller	S_0	S_1
N_0	S_1	2	1	2
N_1	S_0	4	-	-

Figure 9: Forwarding loop network routing state.

the subtleties of relevant domains and the formal expression of those domains' traits. Furthermore, many critical properties (such as network connectivity, black-holes, etc.) are shared over many systems in the same domain. These can be formalized once and re-used many times.

```
1 host opf_Controller():
2   dict<hid><set<int>> end_host_ports
3   ...
4   loop true:
5     recv(msg(saddr, daddr, sp)):
6       if:
7         (sp in end_host_ports[m.src]):
8           ...
9         else: skip
```

Figure 10: Modified OpenFlow controller.

Properties are stored in libraries in two forms: as a high-level English-language statement, and as low-level formulas capturing that statement in one or more logics. While logical formulas are themselves general, the predicates and atoms used in a formula must be instantiated on a per-model basis. Network-related properties that consist entirely of statements about the state of the network abstraction and messages traversing it can be instantiated automatically. Others must be manually instantiated, with user-defined predicates to test relevant states and variables to bind as atoms.

The network safety properties *no-forwarding-loops* and *no-blackholes* can both be automatically instantiated, as they pertain only to the state of the network. The network convergence properties *stable-no-floods* and *stable-correct-receiver* primarily requires the user to label the relevant guarded code blocks and define a predicate to check the node identifier and destination address, respectively.

The network reliability property *bounded-loss-rate* requires the user to provide additional information, as explained in Section 4.4.2.

Once properties are selected and instantiated, the VML model is translated to one or more back-end verification engines using standard compiler implementation techniques [4]. These can range from single algorithms (e.g., non-interference checking) to off-the-shelf tools like Spin [17], Alloy [18], PRISM [20], and ProVerif [7]; the only requirement is that a

1. N_0 sends (N_0, N_1).
2. S_0 gets (N_0, N_1) on port 3, sends it to the controller.
3. The controller binds N_0 to port 3 on S_0.
4. The controller instructs S_0 to flood the message.
5. S_0 sends (N_0, N_1) to port 1.
6. S_1 gets $(N0,N1)$ on port 2, sends it to the controller.
7. The controller binds N_0 to port 2 on S_1.
8. N_1 sends (N_1, N_0).
9. S_0 gets $(N1, N0)$ on port 4, sends it to the controller.
10. The controller installs $(N_0 \to 1)$ on S_0.
11. The controller re-sends the packet.
12. S_0 gets (N_1,N_0) from the controller, forwards it to port 1.
13. S_1 gets (N_1, N_0) on port 2 sends it to the controller.
14. The controller installs $(N_0 \to 2)$ on S_1.
15. S_0 gets (N_1, N_0) from port 1,forwards it to port 1.
16. S_1 gets (N_1, N_0) on port 2, forwards it to port 2.

Figure 11: Execution trace for counter-example to *no-forwarding-loops*.

VML translator for the tool has been written.[1] Only properties that are checkable under that engine's formalism will be compiled along with the model. This may impose constraints on the order in which the user-selected properties can be checked. Packet loss ratios due to mobility, for example, should only be checked once it has been established that packets will not be lost when nodes are stationary.

4.4 Model Analysis

In this section, we analyze the naive model of a learning switch network with respect to the network safety and reliability properties defined above. The network safety properties are verified using the Spin model checker, which checks properties expressible in LTL (or more generally, any ω-regular property) via state-space search over a Büchi automaton. The network reliability properties are analyzed using PRISM, which performs probabilistic analysis of the system (modeled as a Continuous-Time Markov Chain) using user-specified transition rates. Note that these tools are property-specific, and are not a part of Verificare per se. Rather, the VML translator allows these tools to be treated as plugins to the system.

4.4.1 Network Safety and Convergence

The *no-blackholes*, *no-forwarding-loops*, *stable-no-floods* and *stable-correct receiver* properties were verified by translating the VML model to Promela, the modeling language used by the Spin model checker. Spin found a counter-example to the *no-forwarding-loop* property based on the naive controllers' mechanism for updating its routing table. In the following example, nodes are denoted using N_i and switches are denoted using S_i. Tuples denote a message sent from the first address to the second. The initial network state is as depicted in Figure 8. While the complete verification trace shown in Figure 11 is lengthy, relevant steps in the counter-example trace are as follows.

The final routing state is shown in Figure 9. The controller has bound N_0 to port 2 of S_1, which has resulted in flow rules that bind N_0 to port 1 on S_0 and port 2 on S_1. These rules will bounce a message for N_0 back and forth

---

[1]Translators for Spin and PRISM are currently under development. Others will be implemented in future work.

indefinitely. Note that this is also a violation of the *no-blackholes* property, as the message will never be received by the destination on port 3 of S_0. The root of the problem is in using a naive learning switch controller to manage multiple switches. Ports are expected to originate only traffic directly from nodes, not traffic forwarded from other switches. We introduced a new datastructure in the controller, `end_host_ports`, to track this distinction. The relevant portion of the modified controller is shown in Figure 10, in which a containment check within the sending switch's set of node ports is used as a guard over the route updating procedure.

After modifying the model to account for end-host ports, re-verification finds no counter-examples to network safety properties. A counter-example to *stable-no-floods* is found, however. Since rules never expire in the current model, a flood rule once installed will never be updated. Adding an expiration time (modeled as a non-deterministic option to expire) to flood rules and re-verifying the model now returns no counter-examples to the checked properties.

4.4.2 Network Reliability

Once network safety and convergence properties are verified, it is possible to analyze network reliability and performance with respect to average packet loss rates. Verificare currently uses PRISM to analyze such properties, as it can perform probabilistic analysis of Markovian processes. In this case, the system will be represented as a continuous-time Markov chain. Since transition rates are used to probabilistically change state and time, the VML translator requires guarded code blocks to be labeled with transition rates by the user. If a guard is not labeled, it is assumed to have a transition rate of 1. This allows the user to choose to only label guards that are relevant to the property under analysis.

For this example we chose to model packet loss rate only as a factor of mobility (the rate at which nodes join and leave) and send rate. Other potential factors could also be considered with minimal changes to the model, such as the rate at which forwarding rules expire, etc. The user would only have to assign rates the the respective guarded code blocks.

Given the structure of the VML model, mobility is modeled as two rates: a leave rate which models the frequency of disconnections, and a join rate which models the frequency of re-connections. This can be thought of as the rate at which nodes pass through service areas of access points and the amount of time to associate with the next access point, for example. The chart in Figure 12 uses a static join rate of 2, with leave and send rates as shown in the figure. In this analysis Verificare utilizes PRISM's capability to perform multiple verification runs using different parameter settings and to track the results.

5. RELATED WORK

We are unaware of any work wholly comparable to Verificare, but a number research communities intersect with specific aspects of the tool and its use. In this section, we compare relevant aspects of our work to work on provably safe and verifiable OpenFlow controllers, formal verification systems, and related work in the field of cyber-physical systems.

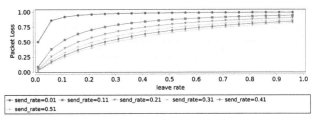

Figure 12: Packet Loss Rate

5.1 OpenFlow

In 2008, McKeown et al. proposed the OpenFlow standard [23]. A significant community in both industry and academia has since grown around this standard, including a number of researchers seeking to add provable or verifiable guarantees to OpenFlow controller programs.

Frenetic [15] is a declarative network programming language designed to allow safe programming of OpenFlow controllers. Frenetic provides a query abstraction that allows provably safe composition of controller functions, as well as modular controller design.

NICE [9] is a model checker specifically designed for OpenFlow controllers. It provides a library of common properties to be checked, and can analyze NOX [16] source code directly. NICE integrates symbolic execution with model checking to dramatically reduce the size of the state space to be searched by identifying equivalences among packet types.

Reitblatt et al. provide several formally verified consistent network update abstractions [24]. The authors define notions of per-packet and per-flow consistency, both at a high level and with respect to a mathematical network model presented in the paper. They define verifiable notions of trace invariants that allow model-checking of both notions of consistency.

Flog [19] is a logic-programming language that allows OpenFlow controller programs to be developed rapidly and in only a few lines of code. Flog breaks controllers into a flow-identification phase that specifies flows of interest, an information processing phase based on exhaustive triggering of inference rules, and a policy generation phase that generates forwarding rules to be installed on one or more switches.

5.2 Formal Verification

A key strength of Verificare is in the integration of off-the-shelf engines for formal verification of models. These verification tools each have a modeling language, property specification language, and formal system allowing automatic checking of properties over the model. Each tool excels at checking those properties which are capable of being expressed in its specification language.

The SPIN model checker [17] is designed to analyze concurrent processes communicating over channels. Models are written in Promela, which is a C-like language supporting non-determinism and providing a channel abstraction for modeling of inter-process communication. Properties are written in Linear Temporal Logic (LTL) or as never-claims, which are capable of expressing any ω-regular property. Spin translates the model and properties into Büchi automata, which are synchronously composed. The composed automaton's state space is then exhaustively searched for an instance that constitutes a reachable counter-example.

Alloy [18] is a declarative modeling and specification language based on first-order logic, relational algebra, and set theory. Models and properties to be checked are not distinct in Alloy; properties are constraints over the space of model instances. Verification is done by translation of a scoped model to a Boolean formula, which is then passed to a SAT solver for satisfiability testing.

PRISM [20] is a verification tool that analyzes models written in a guarded-command language based in part on earlier languages [12]. Models correspond to probabilistic automata. Properties to be checked are written in Probabilistic Computation Tree Logic (PCTL*), which includes probabilistic and temporal quantifiers. PRISM also supports reward-based property verification, in which states and transitions can be labeled with rewards that are incremented whenever that state or transition is reached. PRISM has both model-checking (for qualitative verification of models) and numeric computation (for quantitative verification of models) libraries.

ProVerif [7] is a tool for analyzing cryptographic security properties of protocols. ProVerif models are represented as Horn clauses and verified using logical resolution. Checkable properties include reachability of defined states, observational equivalence of models, and correspondence.

6. CONCLUSIONS

In this work, we presented Verificare, a design and modeling tool for distributed systems. Verificare allows for real-world system properties from multiple domains to be verified against a system model or countered with example execution traces highlighting a property violation.

We also argued that Verificare can be used to bridge the gap between software-defined networking and QoS, safety, or reliability guarantees. This indicates a viable design methodology for the construction of scalable, verifiable communication networks for cyber-physical systems. We provided an example of this methodology in the form of an OpenFlow learning switch network. The system was modeled in Verificare, and network safety, convergence, and reliability properties were analyzed. Counter-examples to these properties were used to iteratively refine the system's design until all requirements were satisfied.

7. REFERENCES

[1] Openflow components, 2011.

[2] Open networking foundation members, 2012.

[3] A. Andoni, D. Daniliuc, S. Khurshid, and D. Marinov. Evaluating the "small scope hypothesis". *Unpublished*, 2003.

[4] A. W. Appel. *Modern Compiler Implementation in C: Basic Techniques.* Cambridge University Press, New York, NY, USA, 1997.

[5] C. Baier. On algorithmic verification methods for probabilistic systems. Habilitation thesis, Fakultät für Mathematik & Informatik, Universität Mannheim, 1998.

[6] S. Berezin, E. Clarke, A. Biere, and Y. Zhu. Verification of out-of-order processor designs using model checking and a light-weight completion function. *Form. Methods Syst. Des.*, 20(2):159–186, Mar. 2002.

[7] B. Blanchet. Proverif automatic cryptographic protocol verifier user manual. *CNRS, Departement dInformatique, Ecole Normale Superieure, Paris*, 2005.

[8] Z. Cai, A. Cox, and T. Maestro. A system for scalable openflow control. Technical report, Technical Report TR10-08, Rice University, 2010.

[9] M. Canini, D. Venzano, P. Peresini, D. Kostic, and J. Rexford. A NICE way to test OpenFlow applications. In *NSDI*, 2012.

[10] S. Das, G. Parulkar, N. McKeown, P. Singh, D. Getachew, and L. Ong. Packet and circuit network convergence with openflow. In *Optical Fiber Communication (OFC), collocated National Fiber Optic Engineers Conference, 2010 Conference on (OFC/NFOEC)*, pages 1–3. IEEE, 2010.

[11] P. Dely, A. Kassler, and N. Bayer. Openflow for wireless mesh networks. In *Computer Communications and Networks (ICCCN), 2011 Proceedings of 20th International Conference on*, pages 1–6. IEEE, 2011.

[12] E. Dijkstra. Guarded commands, nondeterminacy and formal derivation of programs. *Communications of the ACM*, 18(8):453–457, 1975.

[13] V. D'Silva, D. Kroening, and G. Weissenbacher. A survey of automated techniques for formal software verification. *Computer-Aided Design of Integrated Circuits and Systems, IEEE Transactions on*, 27(7):1165–1178, 2008.

[14] D. Erickson. Beacon, 2012.

[15] N. Foster, R. Harrison, and M. Freedman. Frenetic: A network programming language. *ACM SIGPLAN Notices*, 46(9):279–291, 2011.

[16] N. Gude, T. Koponen, J. Pettit, B. Pfaff, M. Casado, N. McKeown, and S. Shenker. Nox: towards an operating system for networks. *ACM SIGCOMM Computer Communication Review*, 38(3):105–110, 2008.

[17] G. Holzmann. *The SPIN Model Checker: Primer and Reference Manual.* Addison-Wesley, Boston, 2005.

[18] D. Jackson. Alloy: a lightweight object modelling notation. *ACM Transactions on Software Engineering and Methodology*, 11(2):256–290, Apr. 2002.

[19] N. P. Katta, J. Rexford, and D. Walker. Logic Programming for Software-Defined Networks. In *XLDI*, number 1, 2012.

[20] M. Kwiatkowska, G. Norman, and D. Parker. PRISM 4.0: Verification of Probabilistic Real-time Systems. In *23rd International Conference on Computer Aided Verification*, pages 585–591. Springer, 2011.

[21] L. Liu, T. Tsuritani, I. Morita, H. Guo, and J. Wu. Openflow-based wavelength path control in transparent optical networks: a proof-of-concept demonstration. In *Optical Communication (ECOC), 2011 37th European Conference and Exhibition on*, pages 1–3. IEEE, 2011.

[22] A. Mahmud and R. Rahmani. Exploitation of openflow in wireless sensor networks. In *Computer Science and Network Technology (ICCSNT), 2011 International Conference on*, volume 1, pages 594–600. IEEE, 2011.

[23] N. McKeown, T. Anderson, H. Balakrishnan, G. Parulkar, L. Peterson, J. Rexford, S. Shenker, and J. Turner. Openflow: enabling innovation in campus networks. *ACM SIGCOMM Computer Communication Review*, 38(2):69–74, 2008.

[24] M. Reitblatt, N. Foster, J. Rexford, C. Schlesinger, and D. Walker. Abstractions for network update. *Proceedings of the ACM SIGCOMM 2012 conference on Applications, technologies, architectures, and protocols for computer communication - SIGCOMM '12*, page 323, 2012.

[25] V. K. Sood, D. Fischer, J. M. Eklund, and T. Brown. Developing a communication infrastructure for the smart grid. In *Electrical Power & Energy Conference (EPEC), 2009 IEEE*, October 2009.

[26] R. Wang, D. Butnariu, and J. Rexford. Openflow-based server load balancing gone wild. In *Proceedings of the 11th USENIX conference on Hot topics in management of internet, cloud, and enterprise networks and services*, pages 12–12. USENIX Association, 2011.

Bounding the Smallest Robustly Control Invariant Sets in Networks with Discrete Disturbances and Controls

Danielle C. Tarraf
Department of Electrical & Computer Engineering
The Johns Hopkins University
Baltimore, MD 21218
dtarraf@jhu.edu

ABSTRACT

This paper is concerned with the reliability of logistics networks, specifically the problem of guaranteeing their robustness to uncertainties in operating conditions while maintaining economical storage costs. Indeed, we investigate logistics networks in a setup where both the disturbances and control actions take their values in prescribed finite alphabet sets, we revisit recently derived bounds on the 'l_∞' norm of the smallest invariant hyperbox sets, we show that the existing bounds are conservative, and we propose a tighter new lower bound.

Categories and Subject Descriptors

J.2 [**Computer Applications**]: Engineering

Keywords

Logistics networks; Invariant sets; Robustness; Finite alphabets

1. INTRODUCTION

Society is critically dependent on the reliable operation of vast and diverse infrastructure networks, ranging from transportation networks (air, rail, etc...) to production and distribution networks, under uncertain operating conditions. On the one hand, robustness of these logistics networks to fluctuations in supply and demand is a desirable property that needs to be guaranteed. On the other hand, this guarantee should come at a reasonable cost, thereby ensuring that the infrastructure and its operation remains economically viable.

Logistics networks can be modeled as network flow problems, in which the nodes are associated with available raw materials, products, or resources, and in which the edges are associated with flows of the relevant raw materials, products or resources. The accumulated differences over time between the input and output flows at the n interconnected nodes is captured by the n-dimensional state of the system: Practically, this represents resources and/or products available (stored) at the n production stages or warehouses. The dynamics of the network are described by a discrete-time linear time-invariant (LTI) model, with the matrices defining the model describing which and in what quantity resources and products are involved in a unit flow. In this model, control inputs denote controlled flows such as production or distribution, and disturbance inputs denote uncontrolled flows such as consumer demand or the supply of raw material. In this context, robustly control invariant sets can be re-interpreted as storage or stockpiling needs, with associated construction and storage costs. As such, the existence of robustly control invariant sets [9, 15], and the sizes of the smallest such sets, are both questions of interest. These and other related questions have been previously considered in the literature [3, 5–8, 10–13]. The existing results typically assume *analog* control and disturbance actions, and examine polytopic or ellipsoidal invariant sets.

In contrast in this paper, we study logistics networks in which both the control actions and the disturbances take their values in prescribed finite alphabet sets. This finite alphabet model is justifiable from both practical and theoretical perspectives: Indeed, materials and goods are usually processed in batches in practice. On the other hand, the study of systems under discrete controls and disturbances has sparked much interest in recent years as evidenced by the literature on finite alphabet and boolean control [2, 14, 16, 20–22], mixed integer model predictive control [1], and discrete team theory [23], to cite a few. Building on our recent results in which we derived necessary and sufficient conditions for the existence of robustly control invariant hyperboxes [4, 18, 19], we revisit the question of *size* of the smallest such invariant sets, when they do exist. In particular, we assess the existing bounds [17, 19] on the size of the smallest robustly control invariant hyperbox set, when size is measured in an 'l_∞' sense. Finding the established bounds to be conservative in general, we derive tighter lower bounds.

The paper is organized as follows: We introduce the system model, state the question of interest, and explain its significance in Section 2. We briefly survey our relevant recent results in Section 3, reviewing questions of existence of robustly control invariant sets as well as summarizing recently derived upper and lower bounds on the 'sizes' of such sets. We then present our main results: We first show in Section 4 that the existing bounds are conservative in general.

We then propose in Section 5 a new, tighter lower bound. We conclude with directions for future work in Section 6.

A word on notation: $\mathbb{R}$, $\mathbb{Z}$, $\mathbb{R}_+$ and $\mathbb{Z}_+$ denote the reals, integers, non-negative reals and non-negative integers, respectively. $[x]_i$ denotes the ith component of $x \in \mathbb{R}^n$, while $\mathbf{1}$ denotes the vector in $\mathbb{R}^n$ whose entries are all equal to one. For $\mathcal{A} \subset \mathbb{Z}$, $M \in \mathbb{Z}^{n \times m}$, $M\mathcal{A}^m$ denotes the image of $\mathcal{A}^m$ by M, that is $M\mathcal{A}^m = \{a \in \mathbb{Z}^n | a = Mb \text{ for some } b \in \mathcal{A}^m\}$. Given a set $X = [0, x_1^+] \times \ldots \times [0, x_n^+] \subset \mathbb{R}^n$, V_X denotes its set of vertices, that is $V_X = \{x \in \mathbb{R}^n | [x]_i \in \{0, x_i^+\}\}$. $\mathbb{B}^n$ denotes the set of vertices of the unit hypercube, that is $\mathbb{B}^n = \{0, 1\}^n$. Finally, $\neg$ denotes boolean negation: Thus $\neg 0 = 1$ and vice versa.

2. SETUP

2.1 Problem Statement

Consider the system described by

$$x(t+1) = x(t) + Bu(t) - Dw(t), \qquad (1)$$

where time index $t \in \mathbb{Z}_+$, state $x(t) \in \mathbb{R}^n$, control input $u(t) \in \mathcal{U}^m$ and disturbance input $w(t) \in \mathcal{W}^p$. The control alphabet set $\mathcal{U} = \{a_1, \ldots, a_r\} \subset \mathbb{Z}$, the disturbance alphabet set $\mathcal{W} = \{b_1, \ldots, b_q\} \subset \mathbb{Z}$, and non-zero matrices $B \in \mathbb{Z}^{n \times m}$ and $D \in \mathbb{Z}^{n \times p}$ are given.

Definition 1. *A hyperbox*

$$X = [0, x_1^+] \times \ldots \times [0, x_n^+] \subset \mathbb{R}^n$$

is robustly control invariant if there exists a control law $\varphi : X \to \mathcal{U}^m$ such that for every $x(t) \in X$,

$$x(t+1) = x(t) + B\varphi(x(t)) - Dw(t) \in X$$

for any disturbance $w(t) \in \mathcal{W}^p$.

Definition 2. *The l_∞-norm of a hyperbox $X = [0, x_1^+] \times \ldots \times [0, x_n^+] \subset \mathbb{R}^n$, denoted by $\|X\|_\infty$, is de ned as*

$$\|X\|_\infty = \max_{i \in \{1, \ldots, n\}} x_i^+$$

In this work, we are interested in answering the following question:

Problem: When a robustly control invariant hyperbox exists, compute the size of the smallest such set, measured in the l_∞-norm.

Note that in practice, deriving an exact expression for the size is expected to be a difficult task, as it was found to be difficult even in the case of a degenerate network ($n = 1$) considered in our previous work [19]. As such, a more practical goal is to derive upper and lower bounds for this quantity, to assess the gap between these bounds, and to subsequently refine if possible. Indeed, this will be the direction we take in this work.

2.2 Relevance of the Problem Statement

The dynamics in (1) represent a unified general abstract model for various types of logistic networks, including production networks and distribution networks. In the case of production networks, the nodes of the model represent "products" (raw materials, intermediate products or finished products), the ith component of the state vector represents the amount of product i, and the edges represent production processes or activities, some of which may be fully or partially controlled by the operator of the network. The network may interact with its external environment through both controlled and uncontrolled flows representing generally uncertain supplies of raw material and demands of various products. The '$Bu - Dw$' term thus encodes the various production processes, supplies and demands, with matrices B and D representing the network topology and inputs u and w representing the controlled and uncontrolled flows, respectively. In the case of distribution networks, the nodes represent warehouses or hubs, the ith component of the state vector represents the quantity of commodities present in the ith warehouse or hub, and the '$Bu - Dw$' term encodes the various distribution protocols, supplies and demands, with matrices B and D again representing the network topology and inputs u and w again respectively representing the controlled flows and uncertainty in the system, respectively.

It is desirable to contain each component of the state vector within two bounds, a zero lower bound and a positive upper bound: The lower bound guards against shortages and interruptions in the production process, or against the underuse of distribution resources. The upper bound ensures that the storage capabilities of the system are not exceeded. The question of existence of robustly control invariant sets, specifically hyperboxes, thus naturally arises. By the same token, since storage is associated with costs, it is desirable to limit the storage capabilities of the system in the worst case setting, as encoded by the l_∞-norm. The question of characterizing the smallest robustly control invariant set in the l_∞ norm, considered in this paper, thus also arises and is practically meaningful.

3. OVERVIEW OF RELEVANT RESULTS

In this Section, we present a brief overview of relevant recent results: We begin in Section 3.1 by reviewing the question of existence of robustly control invariant hyperboxes. We then review in Section 3.2 recently established bounds on the size of the smallest such robustly control invariant sets.

3.1 Existence of Robustly Control Invariant Hyperboxes

We beginning by briefly reviewing some relevant notions and notation. Consider the following sets for $i \in \{1, \ldots, n\}$:

$$\begin{aligned} \mathcal{U}_+^i &= \{u \in \mathcal{U}^m | [Bu - Dw]_i \geq 0, \forall w \in \mathcal{W}^p\}, \\ \mathcal{U}_-^i &= \{u \in \mathcal{U}^m | [Bu - Dw]_i \leq 0, \forall w \in \mathcal{W}^p\}, \\ \mathcal{U}_c^i &= \{u \in \mathcal{U}^m | u \notin \mathcal{U}_-^i \cup \mathcal{U}_+^i\} \end{aligned}$$

Associate with every $x \in \mathbb{R}_+^n$ a *signature*, namely an n-tuple $s(x) = (s_1(x), \ldots, s_n(x))$ with $s_i(x) = +$ if $[x]_i = 0$ and

$s_i(x) = -$ if $[x]_i > 0$, and a subset of $\mathcal{U}^m$ defined by

$$\mathcal{U}_x = \mathcal{U}^1_{s_1(x)} \cap \ldots \cap \mathcal{U}^n_{s_n(x)}.$$

We can now state the relevant necessary and sufficient condition:

Theorem 1. *(Adapted from Theorem 1 in [18]). The following two statements are equivalent:*

(a) *There exists a set $X = [0, x_1^+] \times \ldots \times [0, x_n^+]$ that is robustly control invariant.*

(b) *The following condition holds*

$$\mathcal{U}_z \neq \emptyset, \ \forall z \in \mathbb{B}^n. \tag{2}$$

The proof of Theorem 1 hinges on two Lemmas that will be of use to us in the present work. We therefore complete this section by reviewing these two statements:

Lemma 1. *(Adapted from Lemma 1 in [18]). Let $X = [0, x_1^+] \times \ldots \times [0, x_n^+]$ be robustly control invariant, and consider a control law $\varphi : X \to \mathcal{U}^m$ as in Definition 1. Then at every vertex $x \in V_X$, we have*

$$\varphi(x) \in \mathcal{U}_z$$

where z is the unique element of $\mathbb{B}^n$ whose signature is identical to that of x.

Lemma 2. *(Adapted from Lemma 2 in [18]). If the following condition holds*

$$\mathcal{U}_z \neq \emptyset, \ \forall z \in \mathbb{B}^n \tag{2}$$

the set $X = [0, 2L_1] \times \ldots \times [0, 2L_n]$ is robustly control invariant for any choice $u_z \in \mathcal{U}_z$ whenever

$$L_i \geq L_i^o = \max_{w,z} \Big| [Bu_z - Dw]_i \Big|.$$

3.2 Previously Established Bounds

The following upper and lower bound were recently established for the general setting ($n \geq 1$):

Theorem 2. *(Adapted from Theorem 2 in [17]). Consider a network as in (1) and assume that condition (2) holds. Let l denote the l_∞ norm of the smallest robustly control invariant set. We have*

$$l \leq 2 \min_{\{u_z \mid u_z \in \mathcal{U}_z, z \in \mathbb{B}^n\}} \max_{i,w,z} \Big| [Bu_z - Dw]_i \Big|. \tag{3}$$

Theorem 3. *(Adapted from Theorem 3 in [17]). Consider a network as in (1) and assume that condition (2) holds. Let l denote the l_∞ norm of the smallest robustly control invariant set. For every $z \in \mathbb{B}^n$, define*

$$L_i(z) = \min_{u \in \mathcal{U}_z} \max_w \Big| [Bu - Dw]_i \Big|. \tag{4}$$

We have

$$l \geq \max_{i,z} L_i(z). \tag{5}$$

Additionally, a set of bounds were derived for the degenerate case of a network consisting of a single node ($n = 1$). The dynamics in this case reduce to

$$x(t+1) = x(t) + bu(t) - dw(t) \tag{6}$$

where b and d are given non-zero scalars. Define

$$\delta_+(u) = \max_{w \in \mathcal{W}} bu - dw, \delta_-(u) = \min_{w \in \mathcal{W}} bu - dw.$$

Note that $\delta_+(u) > 0$ when $u \in \mathcal{U}_c \cup \mathcal{U}_+$, and $\delta_+ \leq 0$ when $u \in \mathcal{U}_-$. Likewise, note that $\delta_-(u) < 0$ when $u \in \mathcal{U}_- \cup \mathcal{U}_c$ and $\delta_-(u) \geq 0$ when $u \in \mathcal{U}_+$. Now define

$$L_1^o = \min_{u \in \mathcal{U}_+} \delta_+(u),$$

$$L_2^o = \min_{u \in \mathcal{U}} |\delta_-(u)|,$$

$$L_3^o = \min_{u \in \mathcal{U}_c} \delta_+(u),$$

$$L_4^o = \min_{u \in \mathcal{U}_c} |\delta_-(u)|.$$

We are ready to state the established upper bound:

Theorem 4. *(Adapted from Theorem 6 in [19]). Let l be the size of the smallest robustly control invariant set. We have*

$$l \leq \min_{u \in \mathcal{U}_c} \Big(\max \Big\{ L_1^o + |\delta_-(u)|, L_2^o + \delta_+(u) \Big\} \Big). \tag{7}$$

Additionally, the upper bound established for this case is given by:

Theorem 5. *(Adapted from Theorem 5 in [19]). Let l be the size of the smallest robustly control invariant set. We have*

$$l \geq \max \Big\{ L_1^o + L_4^o, L_2^o + L_3^o \Big\} - \beta, \ \forall \beta > 0. \tag{8}$$

4. ASSESSING THE EXISTING BOUNDS

We begin by examining the lower bound given in Theorem 3 for the special case where $n = 1$, and we compare it to the bound given in Theorem 5, which was derived specifically for the degenerate case.

Proposition 1. *When $n = 1$, (5) reduces to*

$$l \geq \max\{L_1^o, L_2^o\}. \tag{9}$$

Proof: When $n = 1$, index i can be dropped, and $L_i(z)$ in (4) can be written as:

$$
\begin{aligned}
L(z) = L_i(z) &= \min_{u \in \mathcal{U}_z} \max_w \Big| [Bu - Dw]_i \Big| \\
&= \min_{u \in \mathcal{U}_z} \max_w |bu - dw| \\
&= \begin{cases} \min_{u \in \mathcal{U}_+} \max_w |bu - dw|, & z = 0 \\ \min_{u \in \mathcal{U}} \max_w |bu - dw|, & z = 1 \end{cases}
\end{aligned}
$$

Noting that where $u \in \mathcal{U}_+$, $bu - dw \geq 0$ for all w, hence $|bu - dw| = bu - dw$ and $\max_w |bu - dw| = \max_w bu - dw = \delta_+(u)$, we can write

$$
L(z) = \begin{cases} \min_{u \in \mathcal{U}_+} \delta_+(u), & z = 0 \\ \min_{u \in \mathcal{U}} \max_w |bu - dw|, & z = 1 \end{cases}
$$

Next, noting that where $u \in \mathcal{U}_-$, $bu - dw \leq 0$ for all w, $|bu - dw| = -(bu - dw)$ and $\max_w |bu - dw| = \max_w \{-(bu - dw)\} = |\min_w bu - dw| = \delta_-(u)$, we can write

$$L(z) = \begin{cases} \min\limits_{u \in \mathcal{U}_+} \delta_+(u), & z = 0 \\ \min\limits_{u \in \mathcal{U}} |\delta_-(u)|, & z = 1 \end{cases}$$

It thus follows that (5) can be written as

$$l \geq \max_{i,z} L_i(z) = \max_z L(z) = \max\{L_1^o, L_2^o\}.$$

$\square$

We conclude from this simple exercise that the lower bound derived in Theorem 3 is generally conservative, as

$$\max\{L_1^o, L_2^o\} < \max\{L_1^o + L_4^o, L_2^o + L_3^o\}$$

and we are thus unable to recover (8). We therefore wish to refine our lower bound.

5. A NEW LOWER BOUND

In parallel with what was done for the degenerate case, we begin by defining

$$\delta_+^i(u) = \max_{w \in \mathcal{W}}[Bu - Dw]_i, \delta_-^i(u) = \min_{w \in \mathcal{W}}[Bu - Dw]_i.$$

We can now propose the following improved lower bound:

Theorem 6. *Consider a network as in (1) and assume that condition (2) holds. Let l denote the l_∞ norm of the smallest robustly control invariant set. We have*

$$l \geq \max_{z,i}\left\{ \min_{u \in \mathcal{U}_{s_i(z)}^i \cup \mathcal{U}_c^i} |\delta_{s_i(z)}^i(u)| + \min_{u \in \cup \mathcal{U}_{\neg s_i(z)}^i} |\delta_{\neg s_i(z)}^i(u)| \right\} - \beta, \forall \beta > 0 \quad (10)$$

Proof: Assume that the hyper box $[0, l_1] \times \ldots \times [0, l_n]$ is robustly control invariant under control law $\varphi^* : X \to \mathcal{U}^m$. Note that at 0, by Lemma 1, we have

$$u \in \mathcal{U}_0 = \mathcal{U}_+^1 \cap \ldots \cap \mathcal{U}_+^n.$$

For each i, define

$$\bar{\epsilon}_i = \min_{u \in \mathcal{U}_c^i \cup \mathcal{U}_+^i} \delta_+^i(u) \leq \min_{u \in \mathcal{U}_+^i} \delta_+^i(u).$$

Note that $l_i \geq \bar{\epsilon}_i$, otherwise the hyper box cannot be invariant contradicting the assumption.

Now consider x_t where $[x_t]_i = l_i - \epsilon_i$ with $0 \leq \epsilon_i < \bar{\epsilon}_i$ for all i. x_t thus is in X, with associated input $u^* = \varphi^*(x_t)$. We require $x_{t+1} = x_t + Bu^* - Dw \in X$, for all $w \in \mathcal{W}^p$. Equivalently, we can rewrite this as

$$0 \leq l_i - \epsilon_i + [Bu^* - Dw]_i \leq l_i, \forall i, w$$

$$\Leftrightarrow \begin{cases} [Bu^* - Dw]_i \leq \epsilon_i, & \forall i, w \\ \text{and} \\ Bu^* - Dw]_i \geq \epsilon_i - l_i & \forall i, w \end{cases}$$

$$\Leftrightarrow \begin{cases} \max\limits_{w \in \mathcal{W}^p}[Bu^* - Dw]_i \leq \epsilon_i, & \forall i \\ \text{and} \\ \min\limits_{w \in \mathcal{W}^p}[Bu^* - Dw]_i \geq \epsilon_i - l_i & \forall i \end{cases}$$

$$\Leftrightarrow \begin{cases} \delta_+^i(u^*) \leq \epsilon_i, & \forall i \\ \text{and} \\ \delta_-^i(u^*) \geq \epsilon_i - l_i & \forall i \end{cases}$$

Now consider the first inequality. We have:

$$\delta_+^i(u^*) \leq \epsilon_i < \bar{\epsilon}_i = \min_{u \in \mathcal{U}_c^i \cup \mathcal{U}_+^i} \delta_+^i(u)$$

Since the last inequality is strict, we conclude that

$$u^* \in \mathcal{U}_-^i.$$

Since this holds for every i, we have

$$u^* \in \mathcal{U}_-^1 \cap \ldots \cap \mathcal{U}_-^n.$$

Under this condition, for every i we have $\delta_-^i(u^*) \leq 0$ and $|\delta_-^i(u^*)| = -\delta_-^i(u^*)$.

With this in mind, the second inequality can be written as:

$$\delta_-^i(u^*) \geq \epsilon_i - l_i, \forall i$$
$$\Leftrightarrow \epsilon_i - \delta_-^i(u^*) \leq l_i, \forall i$$
$$\Leftrightarrow \epsilon_i + |\delta_-^i(u^*)| \leq l_i, \forall i$$
$$\Rightarrow \epsilon_i + \min_{u \in \mathcal{U}} |\delta_-^i(u)| \leq l_i, \forall i$$

Finally, noting that $0 \leq \epsilon_i < \bar{\epsilon}_i = \min_{u \in \mathcal{U}_c^i \cup \mathcal{U}_+^i} \delta_+^i(u)$, we can write

$$\min_{u \in \mathcal{U}_c^i \cup \mathcal{U}_+^i} |\delta_+^i(u)| - \beta + \min_{u \in \mathcal{U}} |\delta_-^i(u)| \leq l_i, \forall i, \beta > 0$$

or equivalently

$$l_i \geq \min_{u \in \mathcal{U}_c^i \cup \mathcal{U}_+^i} |\delta_+^i(u)| + \min_{u \in \mathcal{U}} |\delta_-^i(u)| - \beta, \forall i, \beta > 0.$$

Finally, we have

$$l \geq \max_i \left\{ \min_{u \in \mathcal{U}_c^i \cup \mathcal{U}_+^i} |\delta_+^i(u)| + \min_{u \in \mathcal{U}} |\delta_-^i(u)| - \beta \right\}, \forall \beta > 0.$$

Repeating a similar argument at each of the vertices V_X and maximizing over the vertices, we get the desired expression for the lower bound. $\square$

Next, we show that this new lower bound reduces to the lower bound established in Theorem 5 in the case where the network is degenerate.

Proposition 2. *When $n = 1$, we have*

$$\max_{z,i} \left\{ \min_{u \in \mathcal{U}_{s_i(z)}^i \cup \mathcal{U}_c^i} |\delta_{s_i(z)}^i(u)| + \min_{u \in \mathcal{U}_{\neg s_i(z)}^i} |\delta_{\neg s_i(z)}^i(u)| \right\}$$
$$= \max\{L_1^o + L_4^o, L_2^o + L_3^o\}.$$

Proof: When $n = 1$, we can drop index i and write

$$\max_{z,i} \left\{ \min_{u \in \mathcal{U}_{s_i(z)}^i \cup \mathcal{U}_c^i} |\delta_{s_i(z)}^i(u)| + \min_{u \in \mathcal{U}_{\neg s_i(z)}^i} |\delta_{\neg s_i(z)}^i(u)| \right\}$$

$$= \max_{z \in \{0,1\}} \left\{ \min_{u \in \mathcal{U}_{s(z)} \cup \mathcal{U}_c} |\delta_{s(z)}(u)| + \min_{u \in \mathcal{U}_{\neg s(z)}} |\delta_{\neg s(z)}(u)| \right\}$$

Now

$$\min_{u \in \mathcal{U}_{s(z)} \cup \mathcal{U}_c} |\delta_{s(z)}(u)| + \min_{u \in \mathcal{U}_{\neg s(z)}} |\delta_{\neg s(z)}(u)|$$

$$= \begin{cases} \min\limits_{u \in \mathcal{U}_+ \cup \mathcal{U}_c} |\delta_+(u)| + \min\limits_{u \in \mathcal{U}} |\delta_-(u)|, & z = 0 \\ \min\limits_{u \in \mathcal{U}} |\delta_-(u)| + \min\limits_{u \in \mathcal{U}_+} |\delta_+(u)|, & z = 1 \end{cases}$$

$$= \begin{cases} L_3^o + L_2^o, & z = 0 \\ L_4^o + L_1^o, & z = 1 \end{cases}$$

since $\delta_-(u) < 0$ and $\delta_+(u) > 0$ when $u \in \mathcal{U}_c$. This concludes our proof. □

6. FUTURE WORK

Future work will focus on several directions: First, establishing a tighter upper bound on the l_∞ size of the smallest robustly control invariant hyperbox. Second, analyzing the size of the smallest robustly control invariant hyperbox in alternative meaningful norms, such as the l_1 norm. Third, studying the scenario where the uncertainty stems from *malicious* disruptions in supplies or raw materials, rather than natural fluctuations in supplies and demands.

7. ACKNOWLEDGMENTS

This research was supported by NSF CAREER award ECCS 0954601 and AFOSR YIP award FA9550-11-1-0118.

8. REFERENCES

[1] D. Axehill, L. Vandenberghe, and A. Hansson. Convex relaxations for mixed integer predictive control. *Automatica*, 46(5):1540–1545, June 2010.

[2] D. Bauso. Boolean-controlled systems via receding horizon and linear programming. *Journal of Mathematics of Control, Signals and Systems*, 21(1):69–91, 2009.

[3] D. Bauso, L. Giarrè, and R. Pesenti. Robust control of uncertain multi-inventory systems via linear matrix inequality. *International Journal of Control*, 83(8):1723–1740, 2010.

[4] D. Bauso and D. C. Tarraf. Control of production-distribution systems under discrete disturbances and control actions. In *Proceedings of the 50th IEEE Conference on Decision and Control and European Control Conference*, pages 680–6813, Orlando, FL, December 2011.

[5] A. Ben-Tal, B. Golany, and S. Shtern. Robust multi-echelon multi-period inventory control. *European Journal of Operational Research*, 199(3):922–935, 2009.

[6] D. P. Bertsekas. Infinite-time reachability of state-space regions by using feedback control. *IEEE Transactions on Automatic Control*, 17(5):604–613, 1972.

[7] D. P. Bertsekas and I. B. Rhodes. On the minmax reachability of target sets and target tubes. *Automatica*, 7:233–247, 1971.

[8] D. Bertsimas and A. Thiele. A robust optimization approach to inventory theory. *Operations Research*, 54(1):150–168, 2006.

[9] F. Blanchini. Set invariance in control. *Automatica*, 35(11):1747–1767, 1999.

[10] F. Blanchini, S. Miani, R. Pesenti, F. Rinaldi, and W. Ukovich. Robust control of production-distribution systems. In S. O. R. Moheimani, editor, *Perspectives in Robust Control*, volume 268 of *Lecture Notes in Control and Information Sciences*, pages 13–28. Springer, 2001.

[11] F. Blanchini, S. Miani, and W. Ukovich. Control of production-distribution systems with unknown inputs and system failures. *IEEE Transactions on Automatic Control*, 45(6):1072–1081, June 2000.

[12] F. Blanchini, F. Rinaldi, and W. Ukovich. Least inventory control of multi-storage systems with non-stochastic unknown input. *IEEE Transactions on Robotics and Automation*, 13(5):633–645, 1997.

[13] F. Blanchini, F. Rinaldi, and W. Ukovich. A network design problem for a distribution system with uncertain demands. *SIAM Journal on Optimization*, 7(2):560–578, May 1997.

[14] G. C. Goodwin and D. E. Quevedo. Finite alphabet control and estimation. *International Journal of Control, Automation and Systems*, 1(4):412–430, 2003.

[15] S. V. Rakovic, E. Kerrigan, D. Mayne, and K. I. Kouramas. Optimized robust control invariance for linear discrete-time systems: Theoretical foundations. *Automatica*, 43(5):831–841, 2007.

[16] D. C. Tarraf. A control-oriented notion of finite state approximation. *IEEE Transactions on Automatic Control*, 56(12):3197–3202, December 2012.

[17] D. C. Tarraf. On the smallest robustly control invariant sets in finite alphabet logistics networks. In *Proceedings of the Sixth International Conference on Network Games, Control and Optimization*, Avignon, France, November 2012.

[18] D. C. Tarraf and D. Bauso. Robust finite alphabet control of dynamic networks. Under review. Manuscript available at http://arxiv.org/abs/1111.0700.

[19] D. C. Tarraf and D. Bauso. Robust control of networks under discrete disturbances and controls. In *Proceedings of the Fifth International Conference on Network Games, Control and Optimization*, pages 1–6, Paris, France, November 2011.

[20] D. C. Tarraf, A. Megretski, and M. A. Dahleh. Finite state controllers for stabilizing switched systems with binary sensors. In A. Bemporad, A. Bicchi, and G. Buttazzo, editors, *Hybrid Systems: Computation and Control*, volume 4416 of *Lecture Notes in Computer Science*, pages 543–556. Springer, April 2007.

[21] D. C. Tarraf, A. Megretski, and M. A. Dahleh. A framework for robust stability of systems over finite alphabets. *IEEE Transactions on Automatic Control*, 53(5):1133–1146, June 2008.

[22] D. C. Tarraf, A. Megretski, and M. A. Dahleh. Finite approximations of switched homogeneous systems for controller synthesis. *IEEE Transactions on Automatic Control*, 56(5):1140–1145, May 2011.

[23] P. R. D. Waal and J. H. V. Schuppen. A class of team problems with discrete action spaces: Optimality conditions based on multimodularity. *SIAM Journal on Control and Optimization*, 38(3):875–892, 2000.

Contract-based Blame Assignment by Trace Analysis

Shaohui Wang
University of Pennsylvania
shaohui@seas.upenn.edu

Anaheed Ayoub
University of Pennsylvania
anaheed@seas.upenn.edu

Radoslav Ivanov
University of Pennsylvania
rivanov@seas.upenn.edu

Oleg Sokolsky
University of Pennsylvania
sokolsky@cis.upenn.edu

Insup Lee
University of Pennsylvania
lee@cis.upenn.edu

ABSTRACT

Fault diagnosis in networked systems has been an extensively studied field in systems engineering. Fault diagnosis generally includes the tasks of fault detection and isolation, and optionally recovery (FDIR). In this paper we further consider the blame assignment problem: given a system trace on which a system failure occurred and an identified set of faulty components, determine which subsets of faulty components are the *culprits* for the system failure.

We provide formal definitions of the notion *culprits* and the *blame assignment* problem, under the assumptions that only one system trace is given and the system cannot be rerun. We show that the problem is equivalent to deciding the unsatisfiability of a set of logical constraints on component behaviors, and present the transformation from a blame assignment instance into an instance of unsatisfiability checking. We also apply the approach to a case study in the medical device interoperability scenario that has motivated our work.

Categories and Subject Descriptors

C.2.3 [**Network Operations**]: Network monitoring; D.2.1 [**Requirements/Specifications**]: Methodologies—*blame assignment*; D.2.4 [**Software/Program Verification**]: Formal methods

Keywords

Blame Assignment; Component-based System; Trace Analysis; Fault Diagnosis

1. INTRODUCTION

A central idea in systems engineering is that complex systems are built by assembling components. Component-based systems are desirable because they allow independent development of system components by different suppliers, as well as their incremental construction and modification. The down side of component-based development is that no single entity – neither the integrator, nor component suppliers – have a complete understanding of component behaviors and possible interactions between them. This incomplete knowledge, in turn, requires us to resort to black-box analysis methods, when only the input-output behavior of a component is specified.

In this work, we are interested in the forensic analysis of a system following the discovered violation of system safety properties. While this problem is common to all safety-critical domains, our immediate motivation comes from the domain of medical devices. In the United States, the Food and Drug Administration (FDA) is responsible for assessing safety of medical devices and regulating their use in health care. When a system failure that harms a patient, known as an *adverse event* occurs, the hospital is required to report it to the FDA-maintained database [8]. Diagnosis of the root cause is crucial for the subsequent recovery and follow-up prevention measures. Such diagnosis requires recording of system executions leading to the failure, as well as methods for the efficient analysis of the recorded data.

There has been a great amount of research following the seminal work of [5] and [16] in the study of fault diagnosis. In this paper, we take a step further and consider the problem of blame assignment for component-based systems. The system model we use is described in Section 4.1. In this framework, the correct system behavior is captured by a *system contract*. The correct behavior for each component is captured in turn by a *component contract*.

We assume that no information is available about the internal behavior while only the values into and out of a component can be observed. This is especially true in most medical devices used currently, which has motivated collaborative efforts to bring open-source devices to hospitals [2]. We further assume that only one trace is observed. The technique of rerunning the system under varying conditions to observe more traces has been used in some of the existing diagnosis approaches (e.g., [16, 5, 20]). However, rerunning may not always be feasible in practice given the time, financial cost or the potential impact on patients [14, 3].

We make an initial attempt in defining the *blame assignment problem* with the aforementioned assumptions. Intuitively, blame assignment is one step further than fault diagnosis: assuming the faulty components in the system are identified, the blame assignment problem aims to determine the subsets of the faulty components that are responsible for the observed system failure.

We propose a formal solution to the blame assignment problem. Given only the observed trace, we provide formalized reasoning rules to determine how the system would behave if a suspected set of components are replaced with correct ones. This yields a reconstructed set of all potential system traces that could happen. On each reconstructed trace in the set, we check whether the system violation disappeared, and make a decision of whether to blame a subset of suspected components accordingly. In this paper, we focus on a conservative policy of casting blame, i.e., we require the system violation to disappear on *every* reconstructed trace so as to blame a subset of faulty nodes. In such a case, we call the subset a *culprit*. Based on our formulation, different blame assignment policies can be easily expressed and are discussed in Section 2.

Further investigation of the relations between the identified culprits yields a minimal culprit set. Soundly identifying minimal culprits can make system maintenance cost-effective, as it is enough to only replace components in the minimal culprits instead of all faulty components.

The proposed approach is illustrated with a running example described in Section 4. This example is adapted from a typical medical device interoperability scenario [1, 13].

The paper is organized as follows. We first define the blame assignment problem in Section 2 and discuss related work in Section 3. Then we show the system models used in our approach in Section 4. Our approach is then discussed in Section 5 and Section 6. Finally we conclude with our current work on tool implementation for blame assignment (Section 7) and a discussion in Section 8. A case study based on a medical device interoperability scenario is used throughout the paper to illustrate the approach.

2. THE BLAME ASSIGNMENT PROBLEM

Given an observed trace Tr for system S on which a system property φ_S is violated (denoted $Tr \not\models \varphi_S$), define

$$\mathcal{F} = \{A \mid A \text{ is a component in } S \text{ and } Tr \not\models \varphi_A\} \quad (1)$$

to be the set of faulty components for the violation of φ_S, where φ_A is the constraint on component A's behavior. Not all faulty components in $\mathcal{F}$ necessarily contribute to the system violation. For example, some components may be faulty but unrelated with a certain system property.

In this paper we focus on identifying the subsets of faulty components $\mathcal{F}$ which are the culprits of the violation of system property φ_S. To formally define the notion of a culprit set, we consider a suspected subset $\mathcal{A} \subseteq \mathcal{F}$ of faulty components. Replacing every component in $\mathcal{A}$ with a correct one would result an alternative system S'. Let

$$TR_{\mathcal{A}} = \{tr \mid tr \text{ is a trace for } S' \text{ and}$$

$$tr \text{ has the same system input as observed on } Tr\} \quad (2)$$

be the set of possible system traces for S' when rerunning the system S' with the same system input. A formal characterization of $TR_{\mathcal{A}}$ is given after Proposition 2 of Section 6. Intuitively, $\mathcal{A}$ is a contributory cause[17] for the system property violation if for *some* $tr \in TR_{\mathcal{A}}$, $tr \models \varphi_S$, i.e., the violation of system property φ_S disappears on *some* system traces after replacing the components in $\mathcal{A}$ with correct ones.

Let $Corr(\mathcal{A}) = \{tr \mid tr \in TR_{\mathcal{A}} \text{ and } tr \models \varphi_S\}$. We define a ratio $p : 2^{\mathcal{F}} \to [0, 1]$ as

$$p(\mathcal{A}) = \frac{|Corr(\mathcal{A})|}{|TR_{\mathcal{A}}|}. \quad (3)$$

Proposition 1. *A subset $\mathcal{A} \subseteq \mathcal{F}$ of faulty components is a contributory cause for the violation of a system property φ_S on an observed trace Tr if and only if $p(\mathcal{A}) > 0$.*

For the computation of the value of $p(\mathcal{A})$, explicit enumeration of the sets $TR_{\mathcal{A}}$ and $Corr(\mathcal{A})$ can be a choice for small-sized, discrete event systems[4, 19]. As the system complexity increases, the size of the set $TR_{\mathcal{A}}$ could grow intractable. Instead of computing the value for p, sampling in the potential trace space to obtain an estimate $\hat{p}$ of p could be used. Similar techniques have already been used in the work of fault diagnosis [5, 20].

The ratio p can be viewed as a measure of likelihood for a subset $\mathcal{A}$ of faulty components to be the contributory cause. The larger the value, the more likely the components in $\mathcal{A}$ contributed to the system property violation.

When assigning blame to components causing system property violation, the ratio p can also reflect different blame assignment policies. If a policy postulates that at least one subset $\mathcal{A}_1$ must be blamed, one may choose the subset which maximizes the ratio p:

$$\mathcal{A}_1 = \arg\max_{\mathcal{A} \in 2^{\mathcal{F}}} p(\mathcal{A}). \quad (4)$$

The calculated or estimated p ratio can also be compared to an empirical value $p_{blame} \in [0, 1]$, where the blame is assigned to a subset $\mathcal{A}$ only when $p(\mathcal{A}) > p_{blame}$. An aggressive policy would choose a small value of p_{blame} (e.g., 0 for the most aggressive policy) and blame a subset $\mathcal{A}$ whenever $p(\mathcal{A}) > p_{blame}$. A conservative policy may choose a much larger threshold p_{blame} in the range $[0, 1]$.

In the wide spectrum from aggressive policies to conservative ones, in this paper, we are interested in the special case where $p(\mathcal{A}) = 1$. It represents the most conservative blame assignment policy with the highest confidence level. Such a subset $\mathcal{A}$ of faulty components represent the main contributory cause[17] for the observed system property violation. By using the approach we introduce in this paper, we are able to cast blame on such a subset $\mathcal{A}$ with the highest confidence level.

In cases where for two subsets $\mathcal{A}$ and $\mathcal{A}'$ such that $p(\mathcal{A}') = p(\mathcal{A})$ and $\mathcal{A}'$ is a proper subset of $\mathcal{A}$, $\mathcal{A}'$ is blamed instead of $\mathcal{A}$. This also indicates a conservative policy where, blaming less is preferred to blaming more. The behaviors of the faulty, but non-blamed, components are not deemed as the main contributory cause for the observed system failure.

We say that a subset $\mathcal{A}$ is minimal at a value p_c if $p(\mathcal{A}) = p_c$ and there does not exist a subset $\mathcal{A}'$ such that $\mathcal{A}' \subseteq \mathcal{A}$, $\mathcal{A}' \neq \mathcal{A}$, and $p(\mathcal{A}') = p_c$. We define a subset $\mathcal{A}$ to be a *culprit* if $p(\mathcal{A}) = 1$. Given a system S and a trace Tr such that $Tr \not\models \varphi_S$, let $\mathcal{F}$ be as defined in (1), then the *blame assignment* problem is to identify the set

$$Culprit = \{\mathcal{A} \in 2^{\mathcal{F}} \mid \mathcal{A} \text{ is minimal at 1}\}. \quad (5)$$

3. RELATED WORK

Comparison with fault diagnosis. Fault diagnosis [5, 16, 7, 4, 19] in component-based, discrete event systems has been studied in various work in different settings. In these works, a *fault* is defined as "a physical condition that causes a device, a component or, an element to fail to perform in a required manner[4]." Faults may cause *errors* in individual components, which may then propagate through components and lead to system *failures*. Fault diagnosis generally includes the tasks of fault detection and isolation, and optionally recovery (FDIR). Fault detection aims at determining whether the components contain faults; fault isolation aims at determining the type and location of the faults; whereas fault recovery aims at providing steering feedbacks or remedy actions to the system.

Different from the task of fault isolation, the blame assignment problem is to assign blame to components responsible for the system property violation with the highest confidence level. By assuming that fault detection on an observed system trace has been performed and its result is an input to our approach, we focus on identifying the minimal culprits for system property violations.

Therefore, one difference of our work from fault isolation is that, the identified culprit sets can be proper subsets of $\mathcal{F}$. This indicates a scenario where not all faulty components should be blamed for the system property violation: some faulty components's behaviors may have been caused by others producing the wrong input, or some may be irrelevant to the system property, though being faulty. In the worst case, our approach gives the set $\mathcal{F}$ as the culprit, meaning that the faulty behaviors of all components in $\mathcal{F}$ are the main contributory cause for the system property violation.

Use of the ratio p. In this paper, we define the problem using the ratio p that we showed in Section 2. In addition to blame assignment, several existing techniques [4, 20] on fault diagnosis implicitly used such a ratio.

Comparison with the work in [10]. The work of Gössler et al. [10] has been a precursor to ours in attempting to establish the necessary and sufficient causal relationships between components' behaviors and system failure. Our work differs from [10] in the notion of causes and the rules by which traces are reconstructed. The culprits we define in this paper are in fact contributory causes [17], a characterization of an informal reasoning process. For trace construction, the approach in [10] requires to only change the faulty components' behaviors while keeping non-faulty components' behaviors (input and output) unchanged. This ignores the impact of changing one component's behavior on other components and imposes unnecessary constraints on trace reconstruction. The example in Subsection 8.5 illustrates the undesired limitation from this rule.

In addition, in this paper we provide a complete formalization of using state-of-the-art SAT/SMT solvers for efficient computation of culprits, which are not discussed in [10]. On the other hand, the work in [10] uses state machines as component models, which may lend their approach advantages in expressivity of component behaviors.

Comparison with work of higher order contracts. The work in [9] and [11] in the field of programming languages study should not be confused with ours, despite the same terms used such as contracts and blame. The contracts in their line of work refer to the correct type check of parameters in a function call, and blame is cast on either the caller or the callee. In contrast, the blame assignment problem we try to solve is for component-based systems.

4. SYSTEM MODEL AND TRACES

In this section, we present the language we use to define a component-based system. We first informally introduce a simple system that we will use as a running example throughout the paper. We then present the formal defini-

tions of a system in Section 4.1, and illustrate the definitions using our example system in Section 4.2.

The system S in Figure 1 consists of three *components* C, L, and V. Each component has named *input ports* and *output ports*, which are typed variables (a through h). The components are connected by two *channels*, one from port c to port d and the other from port e to port f. Unconnected component ports become the ports for the system S (a, b, g, and h).

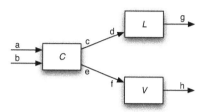

Figure 1: Example System

The behavior of each component is specified as a logical constraint on its input/output pairs of values, called its *contract*. For example, for L, if the the input port d and output port g are of type boolean, then the contract $\varphi_L := g = d$ requires that L produces the same output as the input.

A system contract is similarly defined on system input ports and output ports. We also refer to a system contract as a *system property*.

A *trace* for the system is a map from all ports to their respective observed values. For example, $\{a \rightarrow 92, b \rightarrow 95, c \rightarrow T, d \rightarrow T, e \rightarrow F, f \rightarrow F, g \rightarrow F, h \rightarrow F\}$ is a trace for the system S in Figure 1.

4.1 Formal Definitions

A port $x : \mathbb{T}_x$ is a typed variable with name x and type $\mathbb{T}_x$.

A component A is a tuple $\langle I_A, O_A, \varphi_A \rangle$ where
- $I_A = \{i_1, \ldots, i_m\}$ is a set of input ports,
- $O_A = \{o_1, \ldots, o_n\}$ is a set of output ports, and
- φ_A, called the *contract* for the component, is a logical constraint on ports in $I_A \cup O_A$.

A system $S = \langle A_1, \ldots, A_J, \theta, \varphi_S \rangle$ is a set of components $A_1, \ldots, A_J$ connected by a set θ of *channels*, with a system property φ_S.

A channel for S is a pair of ports (x, y) such that $\mathbb{T}_x = \mathbb{T}_y$, $x \in \bigcup_{j=1}^{J} O_{A_j}$, and $y \in \bigcup_{j=1}^{J} I_{A_j}$. x is called the source of the channel, and y is called the target of the channel. Intuitively, a channel (x, y) for S connects from the output port x of one component of S to the input port y of another component of S.

The system property φ_S for S is a logical constraint defined on unconnected ports of S. Formally, let $I_\theta = \{x \mid \exists y.(x, y) \in \theta\}$ and $O_\theta = \{y \mid \exists x.(x, y) \in \theta\}$, respectively; then, φ_S is a logical constraint defined on ports in $I \cup O$, where $I = \bigcup_{j=1}^{J} I_{A_j} \setminus O_\theta$, and $O = \bigcup_{j=1}^{J} O_{A_j} \setminus I_\theta$ are the input and output ports of S, respectively.

In this paper we make the following assumptions about system construction. (a) Fan-in connections are not allowed, i.e., it is required that $\forall (x_1, y_1), (x_2, y_2) \in \theta. y_1 \neq y_2$. (b) The connected system is acyclic. (c) Each component produces one output on each of its output ports in response to inputs on any subset of its input ports. (d) There is no name clash among port names. (e) Channels are reliable. A value passed into a channel will be successfully transmitted out to the connected component. In other words, we only consider traces Tr such that $Tr(x) = Tr(y)$ if (x, y) is a channel. Note that assumption (d) can be removed by qualifying port names with the associated component names, as is common in component-oriented languages.

We take a synchronous view of the system execution, where a set of external events arriving at the input ports of the system elicit outputs by the receiving components, which propagate along the connections within the system until outputs are produced on the output ports of the system, and then the system waits until the next set of external events arrive. Given the assumptions (a)–(c) above, each port will be used in any such reaction once. We can thus record the whole response in a single snapshot as values observed at each port. In this work, we consider contracts that describe component behavior in a single snapshot[1]; Section 8.2 discusses an extension to temporal contracts that involve multiple snapshots. Thus, to simplify the discussion, we consider a trace to contain a single snapshot, and formally define it as a map from a port name to the value observed at the port within the reaction.

The value at port x on trace Tr is denoted $Tr(x)$. The expression $Tr(x) = Tr(y)$ states a fact that the value at port x and port y are the same on trace Tr. Given a trace Tr, a component A is said to be *faulty* on Tr if $Tr \not\models \varphi_A$. A system S is said to have violated the property φ_S on the trace Tr if $Tr \not\models \varphi_S$.

Lastly we note that the language for component/system constraints description does not have to be limited to propositional logic. The approach can be generalized to logics whose satisfiability relation is decidable and the number of models for any formula is finite.

4.2 Medical Device Interoperability Case Study

The system S shown in Figure 1 is adapted from a medical device interoperability scenario described in [1, 13].

L is a controller which enables and disables a *laser scalpel* that a surgeon uses to perform chest operation on a patient. V is a controller for the patient ventilator to help keep the oxygen supply of the patient during whole body analgesia.

The system must ensure two properties: (a) the ventilator V is turned on whenever the patient's SpO2 (blood saturation with oxygen) level is below the threshold, and (b) the laser scalpel and the ventilator should not be both turned on.

For property (b), if L and V are both on, then the contact of laser with high concentration of oxygen could cause burn or fire, which is a hazardous situation that must be avoided.

To ensure that violations to properties (a) or (b) do not happen, a *coordinator* component C is used. The coordinator C reads (a) the patient's SpO2 level and (b) the threshold value for SpO2, from ports a and b respectively. If $a < b$, then it sends F to the laser scalpel in port c and T to the ventilator in port e, indicating that the laser scalpel should be disabled and the ventilator should be on; otherwise it sends T to c and F to e.

---

[1] A snapshot is similar to the notion of measurement in the literature on diagnosis [16], albeit constrained to one reaction.

The laser scalpel and ventilator controller components L and V forward the received instructions in ports d and f to the actual devices via ports g and h, respectively.

Formal definition of the example in Figure 1. The ports a and b are of type integers in between 0 and 100. Other ports are booleans. The formula for checking port value range is

$$\varphi_R(a, b) := (0 \leq a \leq 100) \wedge (0 \leq b \leq 100).$$

The system is defined as $S := \langle C, L, V, \theta, \varphi_S \rangle$, where $\theta = \{(c, d), (e, f)\}$, and

$$\varphi_S := \varphi_R(a, b) \wedge [(a < b) \wedge (\neg g \wedge h) \vee ((a \geq b) \wedge \neg(g \wedge h)]. \quad (6)$$

The component C is defined as $C := \langle I_C, O_C, \varphi_C \rangle$, where $I_C := \{a, b\}$, $O_C := \{c, e\}$, and

$$\varphi_C := \varphi_R(a, b) \wedge [((a < b) \wedge \neg c \wedge e) \vee ((a \geq b) \wedge c \wedge \neg e)]. \quad (7)$$

The component L is defined as $L := \langle I_L, O_L, \varphi_L \rangle$, where $I_L := \{d\}$, $O_L := \{g\}$, and

$$\varphi_L := d = g. \quad (8)$$

The component V is defined as $V := \langle I_V, O_V, \varphi_V \rangle$, where $I_V := \{f\}$, $O_V := \{h\}$, and

$$\varphi_V := f = h. \quad (9)$$

Finally, the constraint on the channels is defined as

$$\eta := (c = d) \wedge (e = f). \quad (10)$$

5. BLAME ASSIGNMENT

In this paper, we focus on blame assignment rather than fault isolation. In blame assignment, we start with the set $\mathcal{F}$ of faulty components for the system property violation on a given trace Tr, and analyze which subsets of $\mathcal{F}$ are the culprits for the system property violation. The set $\mathcal{F}$ is determined by the violations of component contracts observed within Tr.

The reasoning process for identifying culprits is called *trace reconstruction* in this paper. That is, if we suspect a subset $\mathcal{A} \subseteq \mathcal{F}$ to be the culprit, then we analyze how the system would behave should the faulty components in $\mathcal{A}$ be replaced with good ones as specified in their respective contracts. Due to the one-trace assumption that the system will not be rerun to obtain more traces for analysis, we perform this analysis based on information from the component contracts. Given an input to a specific component A, A's output will either be the correct values specified in A's contract, or the faulty value as observed on the trace Tr, depending on the trace reconstruction rules introduced in this section.

By following the approach, a set $TR_\mathcal{A}$ of potential system traces will be constructed. We use the definition of the culprit given in Section 2 to determine whether $\mathcal{A}$ is a culprit or not.

The result of blame assignment is usually a subset of $\mathcal{F}$ which caused the system property violation, whereas not all faulty components are blamed. To illustrate this, consider the trace $Tr = \{a \to 92, b \to 95, c \to T, d \to T, e \to F, f \to F, g \to F, h \to F\}$ for the system shown in Figure 1.

By the contracts of the components and the system, it is straightforward to decide that, on trace Tr, both C and L are faulty, and a violation to the system property φ_S occurs. In this case, it is intuitive to see that L should not be a culprit for the system violation, since the component C sends L the wrong instruction; even if L is a correct component, it cannot help prevent the violation of the system property.

In the rest of the section, we use the above example and trace Tr to illustrate a straightforward process of trace reconstruction and analysis for culprits. In the next section, we show how the blame assignment problem can be solved efficiently.

For the system shown in Figure 1 and trace $Tr = \{a \rightarrow 92, b \rightarrow 95, c \rightarrow T, d \rightarrow T, e \rightarrow F, f \rightarrow F, g \rightarrow F, h \rightarrow F\}$, components C and L are faulty and the system property φ_S is violated. We would like to determine which subsets of $\mathcal{F} = \{C, L\}$ are the culprits for the violation of φ_S, without additional reruns of the system to obtain new traces.

An informal analysis for the component L would proceed as: "even if L were behaving correctly, it could not prevent the system property from being violated since C is producing the wrong output." This analysis uses the implicit assumption that, even if L is replaced with a good one, the faulty component C would misbehave in the same manner as observed, given the same input for component C.

An informal analysis for the component C would proceed as: "the system property violation could have been prevented if component C were behaving correctly by giving $\{c \rightarrow F, e \rightarrow T\}$ as the output." Here, two implicit assumptions are used. First, when a component is replaced with a good one, its output would change to the correct values accordingly. Second, good components will keep correct behaviors in reconstructed traces.

Such implicit assumptions as in the above two examples are the best one can assume about components' behaviors, given the one-trace assumption in our problem definition.

As a first step in providing a formal approach to blame assignment, in this paper we explicitly state the informal assumptions as reasoning rules when one has to answer the question: "How would the system behave if a component is replaced with a good one, assuming that the same input is given to the new system?"

For a component A and a suspected subset $\mathcal{A} \subseteq \mathcal{F}$ of faulty components, the *traces reconstruction rules* are as follows.

(R1) If $A \notin \mathcal{F}$, then it is deemed as a good component. In the trace reconstruction, if its input is the same, then its output is kept the same as observed.

(R2) If $A \notin \mathcal{F}$ but its input has changed to other values than observed, then each of the correct output values corresponding to the changed input should be considered as a possible execution the component could perform.

(R3) If $A \in \mathcal{A} \subseteq \mathcal{F}$, then A is a faulty component that is replaced by a good one. Its behavior is the same as a good component in Rule (R2).

(R4) If $A \in \mathcal{F} \setminus \mathcal{A}$, i.e., A is faulty but not in the consideration of being suspected, then no matter whether its input has changed or not, its output remains the same as the value on the observed trace.

The rationale for Rule (R4) is that, for a faulty component which we do not replace due to the one trace assumption, we know no information on how it is supposed to behave other than as observed on the only available trace. Thus it is assumed that it will keep producing the same faulty value.

An example of using the rules is as follows. Consider the system in Figure 1, the trace $Tr = \{a \rightarrow 92, b \rightarrow 95, c \rightarrow T, d \rightarrow T, e \rightarrow F, f \rightarrow F, g \rightarrow F, h \rightarrow F\}$, and an analysis

session that only L is suspected (though C and L are both faulty on this trace).

We first take the same input $\{a \rightarrow 92, b \rightarrow 95\}$ as observed on the trace Tr. Then we consider the component behavior changes according to the topological order of their dataflow.

Since C is faulty but not suspected, the behavior of C is kept as observed on Tr, i.e. C keeps producing the values $\{c \rightarrow T, e \rightarrow F\}$ (Rule (R4)). Component V is not faulty, so it will behave correctly as specified in (9) to produce $\{h \rightarrow F\}$ (Rule (R1)). Component L is suspected, so it will be replaced and behave as a correct one, producing $\{g \rightarrow T\}$ as the output (Rule (R3)).

Therefore, the potential system trace after component L is replaced is the reconstructed trace $Tr' = \{a \rightarrow 92, b \rightarrow 95, c \rightarrow T, d \rightarrow T, e \rightarrow F, f \rightarrow F, g \rightarrow T, h \rightarrow F\}$. Thus we obtained a set of possible system behaviors after replacing L, i.e., $TR_{\{L\}} = \{Tr'\}$.[2] Since on Tr' the system property is still violated, we have $Corr(\{L\}) = \emptyset$, thus $p(\{L\}) = 0$. By definition in (5), $\{L\}$ is not a culprit.

By similar reasoning with trace reconstruction rules (R1)–(R4), we have $p(\{C\}) = 1$ and $p(\{C, L\}) = 1$, so they are culprits for the system violation. The subset $\{C\}$ is minimal at ratio 1, therefore $Culprit = \{\{C\}\}$.

In general, given a system $S = \langle A_1, \ldots, A_J, \theta, \varphi_S \rangle$ and a trace Tr such that $Tr \not\models \varphi_S$, the straightforward blame assignment process is as follows.

1. Compute the set $\mathcal{F}$ of faulty components.
2. Let $\mathcal{C}$ be an empty set.
3. For each non-empty subset $\mathcal{A} \subseteq \mathcal{F}$:
   3.1 Let $Corr(\mathcal{A})$ be an empty set.
   3.2 Use trace construction rules (R1)–(R4) to obtain the set $TR_{\mathcal{A}}$ of reconstructed system traces.
   3.3 Examine each trace Tr' in $TR_{\mathcal{A}}$, determine if $Tr' \models \varphi_S$. If yes, put Tr' into $Corr(\mathcal{A})$.
   3.4 Compute $p(\mathcal{A})$ according to the definition in Equation (3). If $p(\mathcal{A}) = 1$, put $\mathcal{A}$ into $\mathcal{C}$.
4. Compute $Culprit$ according to the definition in Equation (5), using the collected culprit sets in $\mathcal{C}$.
5. Output $Culprit$.

However, this straightforward computation is time consuming. Indeed, as shown in Theorem 1 in Section 6, an instance of the problem of determining whether $\mathcal{A}$ is a culprit is equivalent to an instance of an unsatisfiability checking problem in the logic used to express component contracts, whereas the latter is known to be a problem in the coNP-complete complexity class even for boolean logic[18].

On the other hand, also due to the equivalence shown in Theorem 1, we could transform the culprit determination problem into an equivalent unsatisfiability checking problem, for which standard best-effort solutions exist. State-of-the-art SAT/SMT solvers can be employed for efficient implementations to find culprits. This transformation is discussed in the next section.

---

[2]The example shown here is a special case, which only has one reconstructed trace. If a component allows non-deterministic outputs for an input, then a set of traces would be constructed when the component is non-faulty or suspected.

6. TRANSFORMATION INTO AN UNSATISFIABILITY CHECKING PROBLEM

The translation from deciding if $\mathcal{A}$ is a culprit to an unsatisfiability checking problem is made possible by the fact that both the conditions and the corresponding constraints on component behaviors in reconstruction rules (R1)–(R4) can be encoded in logical constraints analogous to Equations (6)–(9).

In this section, we present the transformation, assuming a given system $S = \langle A_1, \ldots, A_J, \theta, \varphi_S \rangle$, and a given trace Tr with $Tr \not\models \varphi_S$.

We first construct a series of subformulas used in later definitions (see Section 6.1 for details):

$$\iota, \eta, \tag{11}$$

$$\xi_{A_j,k}, \quad \text{for } (1 \le j \le J, \ k = 1, 2, 3, 4), \text{ and} \tag{12}$$

$$\kappa_{A_j}, \quad \text{for } (1 \le j \le J). \tag{13}$$

Here, ι is a formula constraining the input to the system be the same as observed on trace Tr. η is a formula constraining that the two values on the source and target ports of any channel are the same. $\xi_{A_j,k}$ represents the condition check of Rule (Rk) for component A_j. κ_{A_j} represents the constraint on component A_j's behavior if it is supposed to keep the output as on the observed trace in the trace reconstruction, i.e., if Rule (R1) or (R4) applies. The corresponding behavior of component A_j if it is non-faulty, or faulty and suspected (thus replaced with a correct one) is the same as its contract φ_{A_j}. Note that these definitions are parametric to the set $\mathcal{F}$ of faulty components and the set of suspected components $\mathcal{A} \subseteq \mathcal{F}$.

With the defined subformulas, it is then possible to define the behavior of a component in the trace reconstruction:

$$\psi_{A_j} := [(\xi_{A_j,1} \vee \xi_{A_j,4}) \wedge \kappa_{A_j}] \vee [(\xi_{A_j,2} \vee \xi_{A_j,3}) \wedge \varphi_{A_j}]. \tag{14}$$

Informally, this means, if Rule (R1) or (R4) applies, then the component A_j's behavior is constrained by κ_{A_j}; otherwise it is constrained by its contract φ_{A_j}.

Proposition 2. *The formula*

$$\psi := \iota \wedge \eta \wedge \psi_{A_1} \wedge \cdots \wedge \psi_{A_j} \tag{15}$$

defines the set $TR_\mathcal{A}$ of all the possible system behaviors with the same input as observed on Tr, after suspected components are replaced with correct ones.

Formally, $TR_\mathcal{A} = \{tr \mid tr \models \psi\}$ where ψ is defined in Equation (15) above.

According to the definition of $p(\mathcal{A})$ in Equation (3), for $p(\mathcal{A})$ to be 1, we are left to check that on every trace in $TR_\mathcal{A}$ the property φ_S is satisfied. This is equivalent to checking that

$$\psi \wedge \neg \varphi_S \tag{16}$$

is unsatisfiable.

Theorem 1. *Given a system $S = \langle A_1, \ldots, A_J, \theta, \varphi_S \rangle$ with components $A_1, \ldots, A_J$ and a system trace Tr such that $Tr \not\models \varphi_S$. Let $\mathcal{F}$ be defined as in (1) and let $\mathcal{A} \in 2^\mathcal{F}$. Then $\mathcal{A}$ is a culprit if and only if the formula $\psi \wedge \neg \varphi_S$ defined in Equation (16) is unsatisfiable.*

PROOF. First suppose (16) is unsatisfiable. Then for any trace tr, either (a) $tr \not\models \psi$ or (b) $tr \models \psi$ but $tr \not\models \neg \varphi_S$.

This means that if trace $tr \in TR_\mathcal{A}$, then it must be that $tr \not\models \neg \varphi_S$, i.e., $tr \models \varphi_S$, i.e., $tr \in Corr(\mathcal{A})$. Therefore $p(\mathcal{A}) = 1$, so $\mathcal{A}$ is a culprit.

Conversely, suppose $\mathcal{A}$ is a culprit, then $\forall tr \in TR_\mathcal{A}.tr \models \varphi_S$, so $tr \not\models \neg \varphi_S$, hence $tr \not\models \psi \wedge \neg \varphi_S$. On the other hand, for trace $tr \notin TR_\mathcal{A}$, by the definition of $TR_\mathcal{A}$, $tr \not\models \psi$, hence $tr \not\models \psi \wedge \neg \varphi_S$. Therefore, for any trace tr, Equation (16) is not satisfied, i.e., (16) is unsatisfiable. $\square$

6.1 Formula Construction

We now expand the definitions in Equations (11)–(13). The construction is systematic for any system S and trace Tr as defined in Section 4.1, and parametric to the set $\mathcal{F}$ of faulty components and a non-empty subset $\mathcal{A} \subseteq \mathcal{F}$ of suspected components.

A constraint that a port x should have the same as observed on trace Tr is written as a logical formula

$$same(x) := x = Tr_x, \tag{17}$$

where Tr_x is the value of x as observed on trace Tr.

The constraint ι on system input is defined as

$$\iota := \bigwedge_{x \in I} same(x), \tag{18}$$

where I is the set of open input ports of system S.

The constraint η on channels is

$$\eta := \bigwedge_{(x,y) \in \theta} x = y. \tag{19}$$

The test of whether a component A_j is in a set $\mathcal{A}$ is a logical disjunction:

$$in(A_j, \mathcal{A}) := \bigvee_{A \in \mathcal{A}} A = A_j. \tag{20}$$

For a component A_j, the conditions for Rules (R1)–(R4) can then be defined respectively as follows.

$$\xi_{A_j,1} := \neg in(A_j, \mathcal{F}) \wedge \bigwedge_{x \in I_{A_j}} same(x). \tag{21}$$

$$\xi_{A_j,2} := \neg in(A_j, \mathcal{F}) \wedge \neg \bigwedge_{x \in I_{A_j}} same(x). \tag{22}$$

$$\xi_{A_j,3} := in(A_j, \mathcal{A}). \tag{23}$$

$$\xi_{A_j,4} := in(A_j, \mathcal{F}) \wedge \neg in(A_j, \mathcal{A}). \tag{24}$$

The constraints κ_{A_j} on the components output if their output values should be the same as observed is defined as:

$$\kappa_{A_j} := \bigwedge_{x \in O_{A_j}} same(x). \tag{25}$$

For each subset $\mathcal{A}$, using the formulas defined in (17)–(25) to replace those used in (14)–(16), we obtain an instance of the unsatisfiability problem. By courtesy of Theorem 1, we can check for the unsatisfiability of the constructed formula instead of explicitly constructing the set $TR_\mathcal{A}$ and checking system property φ_S on every trace in $TR_\mathcal{A}$.

6.2 Case Study Continued

Currently we are working on employing the presented approach to perform analyses on the laser scalpel/ventilator interoperability case study, shown in Section 4.2. As an illustration, we show the case for the system trace $Tr = \{a \to$

$92, b \rightarrow 95, c \rightarrow T, d \rightarrow T, e \rightarrow F, f \rightarrow F, g \rightarrow F, h \rightarrow F\}$ and suspected set $\mathcal{A} = \{L\}$ which is a subset of $\mathcal{F} = \{C, L\}$ of faulty components.

The logical formulas for the case are constructed according to Equations (18) through (25). For instance,

$$\iota := (a = 92) \wedge (b = 95),$$
$$\eta := (c = d) \wedge (e = f).$$

For component C, $\xi_{C,1}$ and $\xi_{C,2}$ are defined to be

$$\xi_{C,1} := \neg in(C, \mathcal{F}) \wedge (a = 92) \wedge (b = 95),$$
$$\xi_{C,2} := \neg in(C, \mathcal{F}) \wedge \neg[(a = 92) \wedge (b = 95)],$$

while the definitions for $\xi_{C,3}$, $\xi_{C,4}$, and κ_C are the same as Equations (23), (24) and (25), respectively. Note that the formula

$$\kappa_C := (c = T) \wedge (e = F). \tag{26}$$

represents the case that the faulty component C keeps producing the same wrong values, according to Rule (R4).

The constructions for L are

$$\xi_{L,1} := \neg in(L, \mathcal{F}) \wedge (d = T) \wedge (g = F),$$
$$\xi_{L,2} := \neg in(L, \mathcal{F}) \wedge \neg[(d = T) \wedge (g = F)],$$

with $\xi_{L,3}$, $\xi_{L,4}$, and κ_L the same as in Equations (23), (24) and (25), respectively. This is similar for V.

Lastly, an instance of the formula $\psi \wedge \neg \varphi_S$ in Equation (16) is defined. This formula is *satisfiable*, which, by Theorem 1, means that the set $\{L\}$ is *not* a culprit. By similar processes, the sets $\{C\}$ and $\{C, L\}$ are culprits. By Definition 5, we have $Culprit = \{\{C\}\}$.

This example shows the difference of blame assignment and fault isolation. In fault isolation, after finding out that L and C are both faulty, the task is to find out what types of faults components L and C may have encountered and where the faults may be located inside the components L and C, respectively. In blame assignment, the task is to identify the minimal subsets of components which have contributed to the system property violation. In the above example, although the component L is faulty, the blame assignment analysis we have performed identifies C as the culprit for the violation, where L has been ruled out.

7. IMPLEMENTATION

The construction shown in Section 6.2 is a general process, given the system definition and a recorded trace. Existing state-of-the-art SAT/SMT solvers, such as Z3 from Microsoft Research[6] used in this paper, support the encoding of formula objects definitions. With the formulas encoded, a call to the theorem prover to check whether the formula in Equation (16) is satisfiable is issued, and the result is parsed for determining a culprit.

To automate this process, we have implemented a Python utility that employs the Z3 theorem prover to identify the *Culprit* set defined in (5). The system description and trace are written in two separate XML files and fed to the utility. Component contracts φ_{A_j} and system property φ_S are written as strings that will be parsed into Z3 formula objects.

After reading in and parsing the XML files, the utility (a) computes the set $\mathcal{F}$, (b) constructs the set $2^{\mathcal{F}}$, (c) for each (non-empty) $\mathcal{A} \in 2^{\mathcal{F}}$, constructs corresponding Z3 formula

objects used in (16), (d) calls the Z3 library for unsatisfiability check, (e) records the suspected set if it is a culprit, and finally (f) computes minimal culprits and outputs all the culprits it gathered.

8. DISCUSSION

8.1 Relationship Between Component and System Contracts

We assumed in the paper that component and system contracts are logically related to reflect the correct system design. Formally, for a system $S = \langle A_1, \ldots, A_J, \theta, \varphi_S \rangle$, we require that

$$\bigwedge_{j=1}^{J} \varphi_{A_j} \wedge \eta \rightarrow \varphi_S, \tag{27}$$

where η is the port constraint defined in Equation (19). That is, by composing components to design the system S, it should be made sure that the system property is not violated for any accepted input. If this requirement does not hold, the analysis in our approach would not proceed as the set $\mathcal{F}$ of faulty components can be spurious.

This can be illustrated using a slight variation of the case study shown in Subsection 4.2. Everything else being the same, suppose the contract for C had mistakenly included the assignment $\{a \rightarrow 92, b \rightarrow 95, c \rightarrow T, e \rightarrow F\}$ as a correct input/output pair. Then on the trace $Tr = \{a \rightarrow 92, b \rightarrow 95, c \rightarrow T, d \rightarrow T, e \rightarrow F, f \rightarrow F, g \rightarrow F, h \rightarrow F\}$ in the running case study, C would not even be identified as a faulty component in the first place. The set $\mathcal{F}$ of faulty components in this case is just $\{L\}$, whereas the blame assignment procedure introduced in our paper gives $Culprit = \emptyset$.

This spurious result is due to the violation of the condition in Equation (27). The given trace Tr in this case is an assignment for the port variables that falsifies (27).

8.2 Extending to Temporal Contracts

For the clarity of presentation, in this paper we have treated a trace as just one snapshot. In general, a system engages in repeated interactions with its environment, and contracts for both the system and individual components can describe relationships between values produced over multiple reactions.

The first complication in handling this general case is that interactions may overlap. For example, if a system is a chain of components, the last component in the chain may still be producing a system output for one reaction, while the first component may have already consumed the next system input, starting the next reaction. Isolating a set of values that belong in a snapshot is in itself a challenging problem and has been studied under the name of trace alignment [12].

Assuming such alignment is possible, we can represent the trace as a sequence of snapshots. We can then use a specification (for example, using a temporal logic) to describe relationships between values in different snapshots. For our case study, an example of a temporal property may be that whenever an SpO2 reading (port a) is less than the threshold (port b), then the output in port g of the laser scalpel component L must be F three snapshots later. We express this property using the "next snapshot" operator X of the linear temporal logic [15] as $a < b \Rightarrow XXX(g = F)$. In this case, a violation will be detected with a delay of three snapshots, once we observe the laser scalpel output. To perform the blame assignment analysis, we can start trace resonstruction three steps in the past from the moment a violation is observed.

In general, however, it is difficult to tell how far in the past the trace reconstruction should extend. In [10], trace reconstruction starts at the origin of the trace; however the complexity of trace reconstruction grows with the length of the trace. Incremental trace reconstruction may be one possibility to explore.

8.3 Dealing with Timed Systems

In this paper contracts of the system/components are specified as relations on input/output pairs. The analysis does not apply to cases where a system failure would consist of timing information of the values in component ports.

In general, modeling time in the proposed approach can be challenging. One has to provide abstractions to represent time in the system. In addition to considering different values a port could produce, one has to consider different times at which the value could be produced. This additional, orthogonal dimension of complication could dramatically increase the space of potential system traces after the replacement of components. The trace reconstruction idea presented in the paper has to be extended to cope with the time domain. This is currently one aspect of our ongoing work.

8.4 Scalability

Two aspects affect the scalability of our approach. First, in order to investigate each possible combination of faulty components, we explicitly constructed the power set $2^{\mathcal{F}}$ for the set $\mathcal{F}$ of faulty components for the observed system trace. The scalability of our approach is limited by the number of faulty components, rather than the total number of the components in the system.

Second, unsatisfiability problems for boolean logic are known to be coNP-complete[18], which imposes an algorithmic upper bound on analyzer capabilities. However, we envision that the scalability of our approach is only limited by the state-of-the-art SAT/SMT solvers being used. This is due to the fact that our transformation of blame assignment problem instances into unsatisfiability checking problem instances only imposes minimal overhead: as seen in Section 6, the number of variables for constructing logical formulas is the same as the total number of different ports of components, and the number of constructed clauses is linear to the number of components in the system.

We are now working with case studies of larger sizes to obtain empirical results on the above two aspects of limitations on the scalability of our approach.

8.5 Comparison of Reasoning Rules for Trace Reconstruction

In this subsection, we present a slightly revised version of the laser scalpel and ventilator interoperability case study which demonstrates the difference between our approach and the work presented in [10].

In summary, the approach used in [10] to trace reconstruction requires that all non-faulty components' behaviors be kept unchanged in the reconstruction. This effectively rules out traces where the input to non-faulty components has been changed. To accommodate the loss of reconstructed traces, the approach in [10] uses a different reasoning rule for assigning blame, that is, as we interpret, the suspected local component is blamed if and only if this test succeeds: in every possible reconstructed trace where non-faulty components' behaviors are kept unchanged, if the violation on the suspected local component disappears, then the system property violation must also disappear.

This trace reconstruction and reasoning rule is equivalent to ours with only one exception, which happens when there are good components lying downstream in the topological order according to data flow. The omission of certain traces in this approach could lead to spurious analysis results as we illustrate using the system S_1 in Figure 2. In addition to the system in Figure 1, two components L_1 and V_1 are added, whose behaviors are analogous to those of L and V, i.e., forwarding the received messages. However, the system property is now changed to

$$\varphi_{S_1} := \varphi_R(a,b) \wedge [((a < b) \wedge \neg k) \vee ((a \geq b) \wedge k)], \quad (28)$$

i.e., the output l of the lower branch of the system is not related to system property at all. (Note: This is a contrived system property, but it does illustrate the point.)

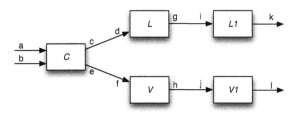

Figure 2: Modified Interoperability Case Study

In this case, on the trace $Tr = \{a \rightarrow 98, b \rightarrow 95, c \rightarrow T, d \rightarrow T, e \rightarrow F, f \rightarrow F, g \rightarrow F, h \rightarrow T, i \rightarrow F, j \rightarrow T, k \rightarrow F, l \rightarrow T\}$, the components L and V are faulty, and the global system property φ_{S_1} is violated.

When analyzing whether the subset $\{V\}$ is a culprit, the trace reconstruction using the approach in [10] is limited by the output of C and the input of V_1 on the observed trace, where $\{e \rightarrow F, j \rightarrow T\}$. This means on any possible reconstructed trace, it must be that $\{f \rightarrow F, h \rightarrow T\}$, where V's violation does not disappear. Thus, the precondition of the test rule in [10] for culprit is vacuously false, which makes the test for culprit vacuously succeed. Therefore V is blamed in this case.

This result is apparently spurious, since the system property φ_{S_1} has nothing to do with the component V (and V_1) by construction. In this case, an analysis engine should not ever cast blame on any subset of $\{V, V_1\}$.

As a comparison, our approach considers what the resulting traces would be should the faulty components be replaced with good ones. According to our analysis, the subsets $\{L\}$ and $\{L, V\}$ are culprits, while $Culprit = \{\{L\}\}$.

9. CONCLUSION AND FUTURE WORK

In this paper, we have proposed the blame assignment problem under the assumption that only one system trace is available. We showed that our presented approach casts blame on faulty components for the system property violation in a conservative yet high-confident manner.

The problem that we defined is equivalent to an unsatisfiability checking problem, for which state-of-the-art theorem provers exist. The theorem provers can be utilized for an efficient blame assignment engine implementation. Based on our Python utility which automates the processes of translating blame assignment instances and analyzing for culprits, larger-sized case studies will be studied for us to gain empirical results on the scaleability of our approach.

10. ACKNOWLEDGEMENTS

The research is supported in part by the National Science Foundation grants CNS-0834524, CNS-0930647, and CNS-1035715. We would like to thank FDA researchers Paul L. Jones and Yi Zhang for their motivating discussions on the problem of blame assignment. We would also like to thank Gregor Gössler for the in-depth discussion on their paper [10] and challenges in the blame assignment problem.

11. REFERENCES

[1] The MDPnP website. www.mdpnp.org.
[2] The OSMD website. http://osmdmadison.wordpress.com.
[3] Australian Transport Safety Bureau. In-flight upset–Airbus A330-303, VH-QPA, 154 km West of Learmonth, WA, 7 October 2008. Technical report, Australian Transport Safety Bureau, 2011.
[4] S. Bhattacharyya, Z. Huang, V. Chandra, and R. Kumar. A discrete event systems approach to network fault management: detection and diagnosis of faults. In *Proceedings of the American Control Conference*, volume 6, pages 5108–5113, 2004.
[5] J. de Kleer and B. C. Williams. Diagnosing multiple faults. *Artificial Intelligence*, 32(1):97–130, 1987.
[6] L. de Moura and N. Bjørner. Z3: An efficient SMT solver. In *TACAS'08*. Springer, 2008.
[7] A. Dubey, G. Karsai, R. Kereskenyi, and N. Mahadevan. Towards a real-time component framework for software health management. Technical Report ISIS-09-111, Vanderbilt University, 2009.
[8] FDA. FDA MAUDE Database.
[9] R. B. Findler and M. Felleisen. Contracts for higher-order functions. In *International Conference on Functional Programming*, ICFP '02, pages 48–59, New York, NY, USA, 2002. ACM.
[10] G. Gössler, D. L. Métayer, and J.-B. Raclet. Causality analysis in contract violation. In *Proceedings of the First international conference on Runtime verification*, RV'10, pages 270–284, 2010.
[11] M. Greenberg, B. C. Pierce, and S. Weirich. Contracts made manifest. *JFP*, 22(3):225–274, 2012.
[12] R. Jagadeesh Chandra Bose and W. van der Aalst. Trace alignment in process mining: opportunities for process diagnostics. *Business Process Management*, pages 227–242, 2010.
[13] C. Kim, M. Sun, S. Mohan, H. Yun, L. Sha, and T. F. Abdelzaher. A framework for the safe interoperability of medical devices in the presence of network failures. In *ICCPS'10*, pages 149–158, 2010.
[14] NERC Steering Group. Technical analysis of the August 14, 2003, blackout: What happened, why, and what did we learn? Technical report, North American Electric Reliability Council, 2004.
[15] A. Pnueli. The temporal logic of programs. In *Proceedings of FOCS '77*, pages 46–57, 1977.
[16] R. Reiter. A theory of diagnosis from first principles. *Artificial Intelligence*, 32(1):57–95, 1987.
[17] R. Riegelman et al. Contributory cause: unnecessary and insufficient. *Postgrad Med*, 66(2):177, 1979.
[18] S. Rudich and A. Wigderson. *Computational complexity theory*. American Mathematical Soc., 2004.
[19] M. Sampath, R. Sengupta, S. Lafortune, K. Sinnamohideen, and D. Teneketzis. Failure diagnosis using discrete-event models. *IEEE Transactions on Control Systems Technology*, 4(2):105–124, 1996.
[20] A. Zeller. Isolating cause-effect chains from computer programs. In *ACM International Symposium on Foundations of Software Engineering*, pages 1–10, 2002.

Distributed Model-Invariant Detection of Unknown Inputs in Networked Systems *

James Weimer
Department of Computer and
Information Science
School of Engineering and
Applied Science
University of Pennsylvania
Philadelphia, PA, USA
weimerj@seas.upenn.edu

Damiano Varagnolo
ACCESS Linnaeus Centre
School of Electrical
Engineering
KTH Royal Institute of
Technology
Stockholm, Sweden
damiano@kth.se

Karl Henrik Johansson
ACCESS Linnaeus Centre
School of Electrical
Engineering
KTH Royal Institute of
Technology
Stockholm, Sweden
kallej@kth.se

ABSTRACT

This work considers hypothesis testing in networked systems under severe lack of prior knowledge. In previous work we derived a centralized Uniformly Most Powerful Invariant (UMPI) approach to testing unknown inputs in unknown Linear Time Invariant (LTI) networked dynamics subject to unknown Gaussian noise. The detector was also shown to have Constant False Alarm Rate (CFAR) properties. Nonetheless, in large-scale systems, centralized testing may be infeasible or undesirable. Thus, we develop a distributed testing version of our previous work that utilizes a statistic that is maximally invariant to the unknown parameters and the non-local/neighboring measurements. Similar to the centralized approach, the distributed test is shown to have CFAR properties and to have performance that asymptotically approaches that of the centralized test. Simulation results illustrate that the performance of the distributed approach suffers marginal performance degradation in comparison to the centralized approach. Insight to this phenomena is provided through a discussion.

*The research leading to these results has received funding from the European Union Seventh Framework Programme [FP7/2007-2013] under grant agreement n°257462 HYCON2 Network of Excellence. The research was also supported by the Swedish Research Council and the Knut and Alice Wallenberg Foundation. Additionally, this material is based on research sponsored by DARPA under agreement number FA8750-12-2-0247. The U.S. Government is authorized to reproduce and distribute reprints for Governmental purposes notwithstanding any copyright notation thereon. The views and conclusions contained herein are those of the authors and should not be interpreted as necessarily representing the official policies or endorsements, either expressed or implied, of DARPA or the U.S. Government.

Categories and Subject Descriptors

H.1.1 [**Information Systems**]: Probability and StatisticsModels and Principles[Systems and Information Theory]

Keywords

Invariant Testing, Networked Systems

1. INTRODUCTION

Driven by the possibility of augmenting the flexibility and the reconfiguration capabilities of very complex systems, in many applications the current trend is to exploit multitudes of sensors and actuators, as in environmental monitoring [1], building energy management [2, 3], wireless communications [4] and power grids [5, 6]. The trend, however, comes with drawbacks: the high number of devices induces an increased possibility of faults with potentially disruptive ripple effects, like extended blackouts in power systems. There is thus a factual need for distributed fault detection algorithms.

We then consider that in every system, including dynamically networked ones such as the smart grid and building thermal dynamics, fault detection algorithms undoubtedly benefit from the knowledge of accurate models [6, 1, 3]. However, obtaining accurate models is often difficult or unrealistic due to the complexity of the system itself or the effects of environmental disturbances. For instance, in the smart grid security domain, it is common to assume the admittance of a transmission line is known [6]; however, the power line admittance is known to change with the temperature, humidity, and power flow, which leads to inaccurate models. Similarly, in building thermal dynamic modeling, even the simplest first-order heat equation model requires the knowledge of inter air-mass interactions, which change with the state of windows and doors (open or closed), the prevailing winds, the temperature, and the humidity. Thus, it is necessary to design fault detection schemes robust to these complex interactions.

If one were to consider large-scale networked systems, centralized approaches which apply model identification techniques in cascade with hypothesis testing may not be feasible. Similarly, when there are limited measurements, these identification and testing approaches tend to yield unexpected results, primarily due to the lack of information suitable for accurate parameter identification, see, e.g., [7, Example 1, page 46]. In this situation, distributed testing approaches that are designed to be invariant to the actual model parameters can result in better performance. In this paper we thus analyze if it is possible to derive distributed decision rules that do not depend on the model parameters and that are, in some sense to be defined, optimal with respect to the available information.

Literature review. Centralized classical hypothesis testing approaches usually use Generalized Likelihood Ratio (GLR) strategies, relying on obtaining Maximum Likelihood (ML) estimates of the unknown parameters under the various hypotheses and then testing their likelihood ratios. Maximally Invariant (MI) tests [8, Sec. 4.8] instead perform some additional preliminary operations so that the test is not influenced by the nuisance parameters. If MI tests are Uniformly Most Powerful Invariant (UMPI), then when the Signal to Noise Ratio (SNR) tends to infinity (e.g., when the number of measurements approaches infinity, see [9]), Generalized Likelihood Ratio (GLR) and UMPI strategies are asymptotically equivalent. When small datasets are available, nonetheless, MI tests can outperform GLR approaches [10].

Invariant strategies have been used in several applications, like detection of structural changes in linear regression models [11] or in spectral properties of disturbances [12]. The literature focuses mainly on finding invariant methods in linear models with unknown or partially known covariance matrices [13, 14, 15, 16, 17], with efforts specially in finding tests that exploit maximally invariant statistics and that have Constant False Alarm Rate (CFAR) properties.

Recently, there has been substantial research in distributed GLR tests for networked systems, e.g., in environmental monitoring, smart grid fault detection, and building HVAC failure detection and diagnostics applications. While all these approaches yield asymptotically accurate results as the number of measurements increases, their performance under limited measurements is sporadic and unpredictable. This motivates the need for distributed testing techniques which have predictable performance regardless of the number of measurements.

In our previous work [18], we considered the centralized detection of unknown inputs in unknown dynamically networked Linear Time Invariant (LTI) Gaussian systems and developed a UMPI test with CFAR properties. This work not only showed the existence on a UMPI test, but also established an upper bound on the performance of any distributed detection scheme.

Statement of contributions. here we again focus on LTI-Gaussian models, but reduce the prior information to be the smallest possible. More precisely, we assume the knowledge of *just* the fact that the system dynamics is networked, LTI with Gaussian driving noises and, furthermore, a weak knowledge on the structure of the input fault. We thus develop a distributed CFAR test that is invariant to the unknown parameters and the non-local/neighboring measurements describing the system. The distributed test is then numerically evaluated against the centralized test developed in [18] as well as the best case (assuming a known model) and the worst case (assuming no model) scenarios, where

it is shown empirically that the distributed test approaches the performance of the centralized UMPI test.

Structure of the paper. Section 2 reports the needed basic results and definitions on invariant hypothesis testing. Section 3 formulates precisely the problem considered. We propose our testing technique along with its statistical characterization in Section 4. Section 5 numerically compares the performance of the distributed detector against the performance of the centralized UMPI detector in [18] and strategies endowed with more prior information and no prior information for different operating points and systems. Finally, Section 6 reports some concluding remarks and proposes future extensions.

Notation. we use plain lower case italic fonts to indicate scalars or functions with scalar range, bold lower case italic fonts to indicate vectors or functions with vector range, and plain upper case italic fonts to indicate matrices. We also use $\otimes$ to denote Kronecker products, and $e_{i,j}$ to denote the elementary vector of dimension i consisting of all zeros with a single unit entry in the j-th position.

2. HYPOTHESIS TESTING PRELIMINARIES

Commiserate with [8], we recall definitions and methodology employed in designing UMPI tests. Let y be a r.v. with probability density $f(y \,;\, d, \delta)$ parametrized in d, δ. We define d to be the set of parameters of interest, and thus δ to be the set of nuisance parameters, which induce a *transformation group* G, i.e., a set of endomorphisms g on the space of the realizations y [8, Sec. 4.8]. This group of transformations partitions the measurement space into equivalence classes (or orbits) where points are considered equal if there exist $g, g' \in G$ mapping the first into the second and vice versa.

Definition 1 (Maximally Invariant Statistic [8]) A statistic $T[y]$ is said to be maximally invariant w.r.t. a transformation group G if it is:

invariant: $T[g(y)] = T[y], \quad \forall g \in G$

maximal: $T[y'] = T[y''] \Rightarrow \exists g \in G$ s.t. $y'' = g(y')$.

A statistical test, ϕ, based on an invariant statistic is said to be an invariant test:

Definition 2 (Invariant Test [8, Sec. 4.8]) Let G be a transformation group, $T[y]$ a statistic and $\phi(\cdot)$ a hypothesis test. ϕ is said to be invariant w.r.t. G if

$$\phi\big(T[g(y)]\big) = \phi\big(T[y]\big) \qquad (1)$$

for every $g \in G$.

The statistical performance of an invariant test ϕ is measured in terms of its *size* and *power*, where an invariant test is desired to be Uniformly Most Powerful Invariant (UMPI):

Definition 3 (Uniformly Most Powerful Invariant (UMPI) Test [8, Sec. 4.8]) Let G be a transformation group, $T[\boldsymbol{y}]$ a statistic and $\phi(\cdot)$ a test for deciding between H_0 and H_1 that is invariant w.r.t. G. Then $\phi(T[\boldsymbol{y}])$ is said to be an *uniformly most powerful invariant* (UMPI) test of size α if for every competing invariant test $\phi'(T[\boldsymbol{y}])$ it holds that

$$\text{(size)} \sup_{\boldsymbol{d},\boldsymbol{\delta} \text{ under } H_0} \Pr\Big[\phi(T[\boldsymbol{y}]) = H_1 \mid \boldsymbol{d},\boldsymbol{\delta}\Big] = \alpha;$$
$$\sup_{\boldsymbol{d},\boldsymbol{\delta} \text{ under } H_0} \Pr\Big[\phi'(T[\boldsymbol{y}]) = H_1 \mid \boldsymbol{d},\boldsymbol{\delta}\Big] \leq \alpha; \quad (2)$$

$$\text{(power)} \ \Pr\Big[\phi(T[\boldsymbol{y}]) = H_1 \mid \boldsymbol{d},\boldsymbol{\delta} \text{ under } H_1\Big] \geq$$
$$\Pr\Big[\phi'(T[\boldsymbol{y}]) = H_1 \mid \boldsymbol{d},\boldsymbol{\delta} \text{ under } H_1\Big]. \quad (3)$$

As a remark, thanks to the Karlin-Rubin theorem [8, Sec. 4.7, page 124], a scalar maximally invariant statistic whose likelihood ratio is monotone can be used to construct an UMPI test.

3. PROBLEM FORMULATION AND NOTATION

This section introduces a distributed hypothesis testing problem for deciding whether a signal, driven by unknown LTI networked Gaussian dynamics, lies also in a given subspace. Specifically, we consider a system of M interconnected nodes for which there exists an underlying interconnection graph, $\mathcal{G}(\mathcal{V},\mathcal{E})$, between the M nodes, where $\mathcal{V} := \{1,\dots,M\}$ is the vertex set, with $i \in \mathcal{V}$ corresponding to node i, and $\mathcal{E} \subseteq \mathcal{V} \times \mathcal{V}$ is the edge set of the graph. The undirected edge $\{i,j\}$ is incident on vertices i and j if nodes i and j share an interconnection, such that the neighborhood of node i, $\mathcal{N}_i$, is defined as

$$\mathcal{N}_i := \big\{ j \in \mathcal{V} \mid \{i,j\} \in \mathcal{E} \big\} \quad (4)$$

The inter-node dynamics are governed by discrete-time LTI-Gaussian dynamics

$$x_j(k+1) = x_j(k) + m_j \sum_{i \in \mathcal{N}_j} a_{ji}\Big(x_i(k) - x_j(k)\Big)$$
$$+ b_j d_j(k) + w_j(k) \quad (5)$$
$$y_j(k) = x_j(k) + v_j(k)$$

where:

- $k = 0,\dots,T$ is the time index (T even for notational simplicity[1]);

- $j = 1,\dots,M$ is the agent index;

- the states $x_j(k)$'s, measurements $y_j(k)$'s and inputs $d_j(k)$'s are scalar;

---

[1] For ease of notation and without loss of generality we assume that the available measurements are over a given period whose length is fixed *ex ante*.

- $m_j a_{ji} = m_j a_{ij} \in \mathbb{R}$ and $b_j \in \mathbb{R}$ denote respectively the gains between $x_i(k)$ and $x_j(k+1)$, and between $d_j(k)$ and $x_j(k+1)$;

- $w_j(k), v_j(k) \in \mathbb{R}$ are uncorrelated i.i.d. Gaussian process noise and measurement noise with moments

$$\mathbb{E}[w_j(k)] = \chi_{j,w} \quad \mathbb{E}[v_j(k)] = \chi_{j,v},$$

$$\mathbb{E}\Big[\big(w_j(k) - \overline{w}_j\big)^2\Big] = \sigma_{j,w}^2 \quad \mathbb{E}\Big[\big(v_j(k) - \overline{v}_j\big)^2\Big] = \sigma_{j,v}^2.$$

To compact the notation we let, for $j = 1,\dots,M$,

$$A := \big[\,\alpha_{ij}\,\big]$$
$$\alpha_{ij} := \begin{cases} 1 - m_j \sum_{n \in \mathcal{N}_j} a_{nj} & \text{if } i = j \\ m_j a_{ij} & \text{if } i \in \mathcal{N}_j, \ i \neq j \\ 0 & \text{otherwise} \end{cases}$$
$$B := \text{diag}[b_1,\dots,b_M]$$
$$\boldsymbol{y}_j := [y_j(0),\dots,y_j(T)]^\top$$
$$\boldsymbol{d}_j := [d_j(0),\dots,d_j(T)]^\top.$$

Additionally, we consider the following quantities: let $\mathcal{N}_j = \{i_1,\dots,i_J\}$ be the sorted list of neighbors of agent j. Then

$$\vec{\alpha}_j := [\alpha_{i_1 j},\dots,\alpha_{i_J j}]^\top$$
$$\vec{y}_j(k) := [y_{i_1}(k),\dots,y_{i_J}(k)]^\top$$
$$\vec{\boldsymbol{y}}_j := [\boldsymbol{y}_{i_1}^T,\dots,\boldsymbol{y}_{i_J}^T]^\top,$$

i.e., $\vec{y}_j(k)$ is the set of the measurements of agent j *and* its neighbors (sorted lexicographically) at time k, while $\vec{\boldsymbol{y}}_j$ is the set of *all* the measurements of agent j *and* its neighbors (again sorted lexicographically).

Consider then a *specific* agent $\ell \in \{1,\dots,M\}$. The structure of the input $\boldsymbol{d}_\ell$ is assumed to be as follows:

- $\boldsymbol{u}_\ell := \big[u_\ell(0),\dots,u_\ell(T)\big]^\top$ is a *desired* and *known* input signal;

- $\boldsymbol{s}_\ell^f := \big[s_\ell^f(0),\dots,s_\ell^f(T)\big]^\top$, $f = 1,\dots,N_\ell$ are some *known* signals defining the space of signals

$$\text{span}\big\langle \boldsymbol{s}_\ell^1,\dots,\boldsymbol{s}_\ell^{N_\ell}\big\rangle$$

(with $S_\ell := \big[\boldsymbol{s}_\ell^1,\dots,\boldsymbol{s}_\ell^{N_\ell}\big]$ being a shorthand for the $\boldsymbol{s}_\ell^f$'s);

- $\boldsymbol{\theta}_\ell \in \mathbb{R}^{N_\ell}$ is an unknown (but constant) signal selection parameter.

Then

$$\boldsymbol{d}_\ell = S_\ell \boldsymbol{\theta}_\ell + \mu_\ell \boldsymbol{u}_\ell \quad (6)$$

where the scalar μ_ℓ is an unknown parameter.

Summarizing, the information owned by agent ℓ is either *available* or *unavailable* as follows:

Assumption 4 Available information:

- the time-series measurements $\vec{\boldsymbol{y}}_\ell$

- the local desired input signal $\boldsymbol{u}_\ell$;

- the local nuisance subspace S_ℓ;

- the local weight m_ℓ;

- the fact that the state dynamics are LTI-Gaussian, constant in time, and with $b_\ell \neq 0$.

Assumption 5 Unavailable information:

- all the time-series measurements but $\vec{y}_j$;

- all the local desired input signals but u_ℓ;

- all the local nuisance subspaces but S_ℓ;

- all the local weights but m_ℓ;

- the weights A and B;

- the moments of the process and measurement noises $\chi_{j,w}, \chi_{j,v}, \sigma_{j,w}^2, \sigma_{j,v}^2, j = 1, \ldots, M$;

- the parameters $\boldsymbol{\theta}_j$ and μ_j;

- the initial conditions $x_1(0), \ldots, x_M(0)$;

- the input signals $\boldsymbol{d}_1, \ldots, \boldsymbol{d}_M$.

We then assume the unknown μ_ℓ to be either 0 or 1 and pose the following binary hypothesis testing problem:

Assumption 6 Structure of the fault μ_ℓ satisfies either one of the two following hypotheses:

H_0 **(null hypothesis):** $\qquad\qquad \mu_\ell = 0$

H_1 **(alternative hypothesis):** $\qquad \mu_\ell = 1$

In words, both hypotheses assume the actual $\boldsymbol{d}_\ell$ to be unknown, since $\boldsymbol{\theta}_\ell$ is unknown, but with a fixed and known functional structure. H_1 additionally assumes the presence of a known input u_ℓ.

*Our aim is thus: develop a distributed test that considers a **specific** agent $\ell \in \{1, \ldots, M\}$, and decides among the hypotheses H_0 vs. H_1 in Assumption 6 using only the information in Assumption 4 and, at the same time, being invariant to the unavailable information in Assumption 5.*

We note that the problem formulated in this section is fundamentally different from the problem formulated in [18]. Indeed, the novel test should be computable distributedly *and* should be invariant also to the non-local measurements (in addition to all the unavailable information in [18]).

We thus aim to find a test that detects whether node ℓ has a fault independently of whether a fault exists at any other node $j \neq \ell$ (fault isolation) *and* maximizes the probability of detection (power) for any probability of false alarm (size), i.e., we require the detector to be UMPI. Formally, thus, we aim to solve the following:

Problem 7

1. find a statistic $T[\vec{y_\ell}]$ that satisfies Definition 1 (maximal invariance) w.r.t. the transformation group induced by nuisance parameters in Assumption 5;

2. find a test $\phi\left(T[\vec{y_\ell}]\right)$ that satisfies Definition 3 (UMPI test) w.r.t. to the class of tests based on the previously introduced maximal invariant statistic $T[\vec{y_\ell}]$.

4. DISTRIBUTED INVARIANT TESTING

In this section we solve the previously posed problem and develop a distributed UMPI test that uses only local and neighboring measurements. The algorithm is based on the following novel result, solving the first part of Problem 7:

Theorem 8 A maximally invariant statistic that solves Problem 7-1 is

$$T[\boldsymbol{z}_\ell] = \frac{\boldsymbol{z}_\ell^\top P_\ell \boldsymbol{z}_\ell}{\dfrac{1}{N_\ell - 1} \boldsymbol{z}_\ell^\top (I_{N_\ell} - P_\ell) \boldsymbol{z}_\ell} \tag{7}$$

with

$$\begin{aligned}
\boldsymbol{z}_\ell &:= F_\ell Q \boldsymbol{y}_\ell \\
P_\ell &:= \frac{F_\ell Q \boldsymbol{u}_\ell \boldsymbol{u}_\ell^\top Q^\top F_\ell^\top}{\boldsymbol{u}_\ell^\top Q^\top F_\ell^\top F_\ell Q \boldsymbol{u}_\ell} \\
N_\ell &:= \frac{k}{2} - \|\mathcal{N}_\ell\|_0
\end{aligned} \tag{8}$$

and where the exploited quantities satisfy

$$\begin{aligned}
F_\ell^\top F_\ell &= I_{\frac{k}{2}} - \vec{Y}_\ell (\vec{Y}_\ell^\top \vec{Y}_\ell)^{-1} \vec{Y}_\ell^\top \\
Q &= I_{\frac{k}{2}} \otimes [\, 0 \quad 1 \,] \\
\vec{Y}_\ell &= \begin{bmatrix}
\vec{y}_\ell^\top(0) & (s_\ell^f(0))^\top & 1 \\
\vec{y}_\ell^\top(2) & (s_\ell^f(2))^\top & 1 \\
\vec{y}_\ell^\top(4) & (s_\ell^f(4))^\top & 1 \\
\vdots & \vdots & \vdots \\
\vec{y}_\ell^\top(T) & (s_\ell^f(T))^\top & 1
\end{bmatrix}
\end{aligned} \tag{9}$$

PROOF. The proof for Theorem 8 is provided in the appendix.

We observe that the maximally invariant statistic in (7) can be equivalently written as a ratio of independent chi-square random variables. This particular ratio is known to follow an F-distribution, which has a monotone likelihood ratio [8]. Thus we solve the second part of Problem 7 by applying the Karlin-Rubin theorem, obtaining directly the following:

Corollary 9 A distributed UMPI test of size α for Problem 7-2 is

$$\phi_\ell(\mathbf{z}_\ell) = \begin{cases} H_0 & \text{if } T_\ell[\mathbf{z}_\ell] < \mathcal{F}_{1,N_\ell-1}^{-1}(\alpha) \\ H_1 & \text{otherwise.} \end{cases} \qquad (10)$$

where $\mathcal{F}_{n,m}^{-1}(\alpha)$ is the inverse central cumulative F-distribution of dimensions n and m.

We remark that, w.r.t. the algorithm proposed in [18], test (10) can be performed in parallel and it is invariant to the non-local measurements. This comes with a price: the test exploits only about half of the available measurements (either local or from neighbors). The remaining local and neighbors' measurements are in fact lost in the attempt of obtaining invariance. Since the data set is smaller than the one exploited in [18], it is expected that the novel test will perform worse. In the following section we then numerically evaluate this loss.

5. NUMERICAL EXAMPLES

We perform three Monte-Carlo characterizations as follows:

1. we fix a desired probability of false alarms α (0.01, 0.1 and 0.25);

2. we randomly generate 500 stable networked systems of 10 agents like (5) as described in Table 1 (i.e., we discarded the unstable realizations);

3. for each of the 500 systems (5) we generated exactly one realization $y_j(1), \ldots, y_j(500)$, $j = 1, \ldots, 10$;

4. for each $T = 1, \ldots, 500$ and each of the 500 systems (5) we executed the following four tests, all with the same desired probability of false alarms α:

    (a) full information test: assume the perfect knowledge of the weights A and B; the moments of the process and measurement noises $\chi_{j,w}$, $\chi_{j,v}$, $\sigma_{j,w}^2$, $\sigma_{j,v}^2$; the parameters $\boldsymbol{\theta}_j$; the initial conditions $x_1(j)$ ($j = 1, \ldots, 10$). Then design the Uniformly Most Powerful (UMP) test for testing H_0 vs. H_1 given all this information;

    (b) centralized UMPI test: the UMPI test developed in [18], which is provided in the appendix using the notation introduced within this work;

    (c) distributed UMPI test (DUMPI): our test (10);

    (d) no information test: perform a weighted coin flip s.t. the desired probability of false alarms α is met.

The outcomes are then summarized in the following Figures 1, 2 and 3, that plot for each test and each T the average correct detection rate reached over the 500 considered realizations of system 5.

From the previous graphics we draw the following conclusions. Before the number of measurements (proportional to T) passes the threshold $\frac{T}{2} - N_\ell - M + 1$ (independent of the chosen α), both the centralized and distributed UMPI tests

$a_j, b_j \sim \mathcal{U}[-0.5, 0.5]$	$m_j \sim \mathcal{U}[1, 2]$
$\chi_{j,w}, \chi_{j,v} \sim \mathcal{N}(0, 1)$	$\sigma_{j,w}^2, \sigma_{j,v}^2 \sim \mathcal{U}[0.1, 1]$

Table 1: Random extraction mechanisms for the generation of the systems (5). $\mathcal{N}$ indicates Gaussian distributions, $\mathcal{U}$ uniform distributions. All the quantities are extracted independently.

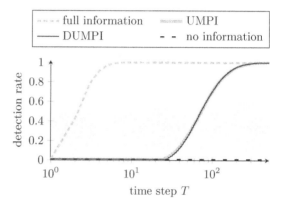

Figure 1: Monte-Carlo characterization of the detection tests given $\alpha = 0.01$.

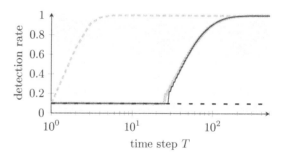

Figure 2: Monte-Carlo characterization of the detection tests given $\alpha = 0.1$. Legend as in Figure 1.

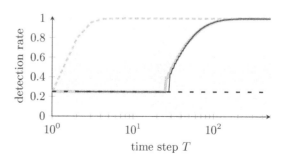

Figure 3: Monte-Carlo characterization of the detection tests given $\alpha = 0.25$. Legend as in Figure 1.

are equivalent to a coin flipping (since the amount of information is insufficient to take meaningful decisions). After that threshold, instead, the two test start increasing their correct detection rates (with different speeds, depending on the selected probability of false alarms), discerning better and better. Eventually they reach the same performance of the full information-based test, i.e., the best one might desire. We then notice that the difference in the correct detection rates between the centralized and distributed approaches starts small and vanishes quickly. This indicates that, from practical purposes, the distributed strategy performs well. The reason for such a similar performance between the centralized and distributed approaches lies in that the centralized approach from [18] (also provided in the appendix of this extended abstract), effectively disregards half of the measurements to achieve maximal invariance. In the distributed approach, the same measurements that are discarded by the centralized approach are employed to provide invariance to the local inter-node dynamics.

6. DISCUSSION AND FUTURE WORKS

We considered fault detection in networked Linear Time Invariant-Gaussian systems. More precisely, we defined a hypothesis testing problem over the structure of the inputs of the agents, and then derived a distributed Uniformly Most Powerful Invariant detector with Constant False Alarm Rate properties that is invariant to most of the parameters of the systems. We address the situation where there is little prior information available, and develop a distributed test starting from our previous centralized results described in [18]. 'Remarkably we obtain a distributed algorithm that has some capability of detecting faults even if knowledge of the overall system is really uncertain and the number of measurements is limited.

As in the centralized case, tests that exploit information of the system have better performance in terms of false positives / negatives rates. Nonetheless, the more measurements that are taken the more the distributed detector is shown to be perform better, achieving performance of its centralized counterpart quickly.

The value of the proposed strategy relies in its optimality properties, being in fact based on a maximally invariant statistic and being uniformly most powerful. This implies that in a certain sense it characterizes the performance that can be achieved when testing the posed hypotheses under the severe lack of knowledge assumed here.

The main future direction is thus to compare the developed strategy, both from practical and theoretical aspects, with the distributed fault detection algorithm that are based on dynamically identified systems. It is in fact necessary to understand if there are conditions s.t. the invariant test developed here is guaranteed to perform better than algorithms that start identifying the test and then perform tests on the identified model. Additionally, extensions of this work to feedback control applications where stabilizing control is desired in the presence of unknown parameters and disturbances is planned.

7. REFERENCES

[1] J. Weimer, B. Sinopoli, and B. Krogh, "An approach to leak detection using wireless sensor networks at carbon sequestration sites," *International Journal of Greenhouse Gas Control*, vol. 9, pp. 243–253, 2012.

[2] F. Oldewurtel, A. Parisio, C. N. Jones, D. Gyalistras, M. Gwerder, V. Stauch, B. Lehmann, and M. Morari, "Use of model predictive control and weather forecasts for energy efficient building climate control," *Energy and Buildings*, vol. 45, no. 0, pp. 15 – 27, 2012.

[3] J. Weimer, S.Ahmadi, J. Araujo, F. Mele, D. Papale, I. Shames, H. Sandberg, and K. Johansson, "Active actuator fault detection and diagnostics in hvac systems," in *ACM Workshop on Embedded Sensing Systems for Energy-Efficiency in Buildings (BuildSys)*, 2012.

[4] T. Arampatzis, J. Lygeros, and S. Manesis, "A survey of applications of wireless sensors and wireless sensor networks," in *IEEE International Symposium on Intelligent Control, MCCA*, 2005, pp. 719–724.

[5] S. Bolognani, A. Carron, A. Di Vittorio, D. Romeres, L. Schenato, and S. Zampieri, "Distributed multi-hop reactive power compensation in smart micro-grids subject to saturation constraints," in *51st IEEE Conference on Decision and Control*, 2012, pp. 785–790.

[6] I. Shames, A. Teixeira, H. Sandberg, and K. Johansson, "Distributed fault detection for interconnected systems," *Automatica*, vol. 47, no. 12, pp. 2757–2764, 2011.

[7] V. N. Vapnik, *Statistical learning theory*. New York: Wiley, 1998.

[8] L. L. Scharf, *Statistical Signal Processing, Detection, Estimation, and Time Series Analysis*. Addison-Welsley Publishing Company Inc., Reading, Massachusetts, 1991.

[9] J. Gabriel and S. Kay, "On the relationship between the glrt and umpi tests for the detection of signals with unknown parameters," *Signal Processing, IEEE Transactions on*, vol. 53, no. 11, pp. 4194–4203, 2005.

[10] H. Kim and A. Hero III, "Comparison of glr and invariant detectors under structured clutter covariance," *Image Processing, IEEE Transactions on*, vol. 10, no. 10, pp. 1509–1520, 2001.

[11] M. Hušková, "Some invariant test procedures for detection of structural changes," *Kybernetika*, vol. 36, no. 4, pp. 401–414, 2000.

[12] N. Begum and M. L. King, "Most mean powerful invariant test for testing two-dimensional parameter spaces," *Journal of Statistical Planning and Inference*, vol. 134, no. 2, pp. 536 – 548, 2005.

[13] S. Bose and A. Steinhardt, "A maximal invariant framework for adaptive detection with structured and unstructured covariance matrices," *Signal Processing, IEEE Transactions on*, vol. 43, no. 9, pp. 2164–2175, 1995.

[14] K. Noda and H. Ono, "On ump invariant f-test procedures in a general linear model," *Communications in Statistics-Theory and Methods*, vol. 30, no. 10, pp. 2099–2115, 2001.

[15] E. Conte, A. De Maio, and C. Galdi, "Cfar detection of multidimensional signals: an invariant approach," *Signal Processing, IEEE Transactions on*, vol. 51, no. 1, pp. 142–151, 2003.

[16] A. De Maio, "Rao test for adaptive detection in gaussian interference with unknown covariance

matrix," *Signal Processing, IEEE Transactions on,* vol. 55, no. 7, pp. 3577–3584, 2007.

[17] A. De Maio and E. Conte, "Adaptive detection in gaussian interference with unknown covariance after reduction by invariance," *Signal Processing, IEEE Transactions on,* vol. 58, no. 6, pp. 2925–2934, 2010.

[18] J. Weimer, D. Varagnolo, M. Stankovic, and K. Johansson, "Model-invariant detection of unknown inputs in networked systems," in *European Control Conference (under review),* 2013.

Appendix

This appendix provides a proof for Theorem 8. To identify a maximally invariant statistic requires identifying the the group of transformations induced by the unknown parameters. Identifying this group is achieved writing the measurement dynamics for node ℓ in 5 as

$$y_\ell(k+1) = y_\ell(k) + m_\ell \sum_{i \in \mathcal{N}_\ell} a_{\ell i}\Big(y_i(k) - y_\ell(k)\Big) + b_\ell d_\ell(k) + n_\ell(k) \qquad (11)$$

where

$$n_\ell(k) = w_\ell(k) + v_\ell(k+1) - \left(1 - m_\ell \sum_{i \in \mathcal{N}_\ell} a_{\ell i}\right) v_\ell(k) - m_\ell \sum_{i \in \mathcal{N}_\ell} a_{\ell i} v_i(k). \qquad (12)$$

We write the time-series concatenation of the measurements as

$$\boldsymbol{y}_\ell = \vec{H}_\ell \boldsymbol{\rho} + b_\ell \mu_\ell \boldsymbol{u}_\ell + \boldsymbol{n}_\ell \qquad (13)$$

where

$$\vec{H}_\ell = \begin{bmatrix} \vec{y}_\ell^\top(0) & (s_\ell^f(0))^\top & 1 \\ \vec{y}_\ell^\top(1) & (s_\ell^f(1))^\top & 1 \\ \vdots & \vdots & \vdots \\ \vec{y}_\ell^\top(T) & (s_\ell^f(T))^\top & 1 \end{bmatrix}$$

$$\boldsymbol{n}_\ell = [n_\ell(0), \quad n_\ell(1), \quad \ldots, \quad n_\ell(T)]^\top \qquad (14)$$

$$\mathrm{Cov}\,[\boldsymbol{n}_\ell] = \sigma_0^2 I + \sigma_1^2 \sum_{i=0}^{\frac{T}{2}} \left(\boldsymbol{e}_{2i}\boldsymbol{e}_{2i+1}^\top + \boldsymbol{e}_{2i+1}\boldsymbol{e}_{2i}^\top\right)$$

and $\boldsymbol{\rho}$ is a vector of unknown parameters such that each row of the time-series measurements is equivalent to the dynamics in (11). The unknown parameters induce a group of transformations on the measurements

$$G = \left\{ g \;\middle|\; g(\boldsymbol{y}_\ell) = \sigma_0 \left(I - \sum_{i=0}^{\frac{T}{2}} c_i \boldsymbol{e}_{2i}\boldsymbol{e}_{2i+1}^\top\right) \boldsymbol{y}_\ell + \vec{H}_\ell \boldsymbol{\rho} + \mu_\ell b_\ell \boldsymbol{u}_\ell \right\} \qquad (15)$$

where $c_i \in \mathbb{R}$ is an unknown gain induced by the unknown correlation and noise realization (which varies with time). It then follows that Theorem 8 is maximally invariant to the transformation group induced by the unknown parameters.

PROOF. Invariance: Observing the following:

$$Q\left[\sigma_0 \left(I - \sum_{i=0}^{\frac{T}{2}} c_i \boldsymbol{e}_{2i}\boldsymbol{e}_{2i+1}^\top\right) \boldsymbol{y}_\ell + \vec{H}_\ell \rho + \mu_\ell b_\ell \boldsymbol{u}_\ell\right] \qquad (16)$$

$$= \sigma_0 Q \boldsymbol{y}_\ell + \vec{Y}_\ell \rho + \mu_\ell b_\ell Q \boldsymbol{u}_\ell$$

and

$$F_\ell \left(\sigma_0 Q \boldsymbol{y}_\ell + \vec{Y}_\ell \rho + \mu_\ell b_\ell Q \boldsymbol{u}_\ell\right) = \sigma_0 \boldsymbol{z}_\ell + \mu_\ell b_\ell F_\ell Q \boldsymbol{u}_\ell \qquad (17)$$

then

$$T[g(\boldsymbol{y}_\ell)] = \frac{\sigma_0^2 \boldsymbol{z}_\ell P_\ell \boldsymbol{z}_\ell}{\sigma_0^2 \frac{1}{N_\ell - 1} \boldsymbol{z}_\ell (I_{N_\ell} - P_\ell) \boldsymbol{z}_\ell}$$

$$= \frac{\boldsymbol{z}_\ell P_\ell \boldsymbol{z}_\ell}{\frac{1}{N_\ell - 1} \boldsymbol{z}_\ell (I_{N_\ell} - P_\ell) \boldsymbol{z}_\ell} \qquad (18)$$

$$= T[\boldsymbol{y}_\ell]$$

Maximality: We observe that

$$T[\widehat{\boldsymbol{z}}_\ell] = T[\boldsymbol{z}_\ell]$$

$$\longrightarrow \frac{\boldsymbol{z}_\ell^\top P_\ell \boldsymbol{z}_\ell}{\boldsymbol{z}_\ell^\top (I - P_\ell)\boldsymbol{z}_\ell} = \frac{\widehat{\boldsymbol{z}}_\ell^\top P_\ell \widehat{\boldsymbol{z}}_\ell}{\widehat{\boldsymbol{z}}_\ell^\top (I - P_\ell)\widehat{\boldsymbol{z}}_\ell} \qquad (19)$$

$$\longrightarrow \widehat{\boldsymbol{z}}_\ell^\top \left(P_\ell - I \frac{\boldsymbol{z}_\ell^\top P \boldsymbol{z}_\ell}{\boldsymbol{z}_\ell^\top \boldsymbol{z}_\ell}\right) \widehat{\boldsymbol{z}}_\ell = 0$$

$$\longrightarrow \boldsymbol{u}_\ell^\top Q^\top F_\ell^\top \widehat{\boldsymbol{z}}_\ell = c \boldsymbol{u}_\ell^\top Q^\top F_\ell^\top \boldsymbol{z}_\ell, \quad \exists c \in \mathbb{R}.$$

and complete the proof for maximality as

$$\boldsymbol{u}_\ell^\top Q^\top F_\ell^\top \widehat{\boldsymbol{z}}_\ell = c \boldsymbol{u}_\ell^\top Q^\top F_\ell^\top \boldsymbol{z}_\ell$$

$$\longrightarrow \widehat{\boldsymbol{y}}_\ell = c \boldsymbol{y}_\ell + (I - P_\ell)(c \boldsymbol{y}_\ell - \widehat{\boldsymbol{y}}_\ell) \qquad (20)$$

$$\longrightarrow \widehat{\boldsymbol{y}}_\ell = g(\boldsymbol{y}_\ell), \quad \exists g \in G$$

Taxonomy for Description of Cross-Domain Attacks on CPS

Mark Yampolskiy, Peter Horvath, Xenofon D. Koutsoukos, Yuan Xue, Janos Sztipanovits
Vanderbilt University, Institute for Software Integrated Systems (ISIS)
myy@isis.vanderbilt.edu, phorvath@isis.vanderbilt.edu, Xenofon.Koutsoukos@Vanderbilt.Edu,
yuan.xue@Vanderbilt.Edu, janos.sztipanovits@vanderbilt.edu

ABSTRACT

The pervasiveness of Cyber-Physical Systems (CPS) in various aspects of the modern society grows rapidly and CPS become attractive targets for various kinds of attacks. We consider cyber-security as an integral part of CPS security. Additionally, the necessity exists to investigate the CPS-specific aspects which are out of scope of cyber-security. Most importantly, attacks capable to cross the cyber-physical domain boundary should be analyzed. The vulnerability of CPS to such cross-domain attacks has been practically proven by numerous examples, e.g., by the currently most famous Stuxnet attack.

In this paper, we propose a taxonomy for description of attacks on CPS. The proposed taxonomy is capable of representing both conventional cyber-attacks as well as cross-domain attacks. Furthermore, based on the proposed taxonomy, we define an attack categorization. Several possible application areas of the proposed taxonomy are extensively discussed. Among others, it can be used to establish a knowledge base about attacks on CPS that are known in the literature. Furthermore, the proposed description structure will foster the quantitative and qualitative analysis of these attacks, both of which are necessarily to improve CPS security.

Categories and Subject Descriptors

J.7 [**Computer in Other Systems**] Industrial control; Consumer products; Military; Real time; Process control

C.2.0 [**Computer-Communication Networks**] General – *Security and protection (e.g., firewalls).*

Keywords

Cyber-Physical Systems (CPS); CPS security; Cyber-Physical Attacks; cross-domain attacks; taxonomy.

1. INTRODUCTION

Currently, we are in the middle of an emergence of Cyber-Physical Systems (CPS) in almost all aspects of our life. Examples of CPS are manifold and include all kinds of unmanned or remote controlled vehicles, robotized manufacturing plants, critical infrastructure such as electrical power grid and nuclear power

plants, smart homes, smart cities, and many more. Based on our experience with computer and network security, CPS will become targets of adversary attacks.

Attacks on CPS are neither science fiction nor the matter of the distant future. Multiple attacks on various CPS have been already performed. Currently, the most famous attack is Stuxnet. Stuxnet is considered to be the first professionally crafted attack against CPS. This attack has reportedly damaged over 1000 centrifuges at an Iranian uranium enrichment plant [1]. Multiple further examples of attacks on various CPS have been reported or shown in the research literature. These include attacks on modern car electronics [2], attacks on remotely controlled UAVs via GPS spoofing [3], or even attacks which use CPS as a carrier to infect the maintenance computer [4].

There is a broad consensus among researchers that adversary goals of attacks on CPS might differ from the goals of attacks on cyber systems. For instance, many attacks on CPS would try to compromise the system's safety or physical integrity instead of data privacy usually considered in cyber-security.

However, technical aspects have even more severe implications on the CPS security. Figure 1 depicts various attacks which can be performed at targets located at different system layers. It is clear that attacks will affect the attacked targets. Additionally, due to the high degree of the dependencies and interdependencies between CPS elements at different layers, secondary effects can occur at CPS elements which have not been directly attacked. These induced effects can occur at elements located in different layers or even belonging to different (cyber or physical) domains. Such cross-layer and cross-domain attacks on CPS are very intricate and barely understood so far. Below, we will use qualifier "cross-domain" as a synonym for both cross-domain and cross-layer.

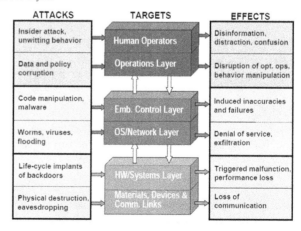

Figure 1. Layer Specific Attacks on CPS [12]

Surveying known attacks on CPS, one can notice that a significant portion exhibits cross-domain effects. This makes it extremely important to consider such attacks alongside with the conventional cyber-attacks. In order to do this, we first should be able to describe not only the single-domain but also cross-domain attacks.

Our contribution in this paper is as follows. We propose a taxonomy for description of attacks on CPS. The proposed taxonomy is capable of representing both conventional cyber-attacks as well as cross-domain attacks on CPS. Furthermore, based on the proposed taxonomy we define an attack categorization. Numerous examples illustrate the application of the proposed taxonomy for the attack description. Moreover, we provide an extensive discussion of possible taxonomy application areas. During this discussion we explain how the proposed taxonomy can be used for attack documentation, vulnerability assessment, and description of attack propagation.

The reminder of this paper is structured as follows. After discussing the state of the art regarding CPS security and cyber-security taxonomies in Section 2, we propose a novel taxonomy for description of attacks on CPS in Section 3. We discuss the taxonomy application areas in Section 4. We conclude this paper with the outline of our future plans and a short review in Sections 5 and 6 respectively.

2. RELATED WORK
We consider both known attacks on CPS and taxonomies elaborated in the cyber-security for classification and description of attacks on computer systems and networks.

2.1 Known Attacks on CPS
Compared to the vast amount of attacks on computer systems and networks we have faced in the last decades, the amount of attack on CPS is quite limited. Nevertheless, a fair amount of attacks on different kinds of CPS is known, including attacks on critical or industrial infrastructure, transportation systems, and remote controlled unmanned vehicles.

2.1.1 Critical or industrial infrastructure
Currently, the most famous attack on CPS is the Stuxnet [1], [5]. Stuxnet is considered to be the first professionally crafted attack on an industrial infrastructure. It contains very sophisticated techniques to infect targeted systems, to spread infection, and to evade its detection. However, from the cross-domain attack point of view, probably the most notable aspect of Stuxnet is the fact that it inflicts physical damage to the industrial infrastructure via manipulations in cyber-space.

However, it is wrong to assume that the Stuxnet was the only or even the first attack on CPS. According to [6], attacks on various industrial or critical infrastructures can be traced back as far as 1995. In [6], based on the analysis of 41 known security incidents in industrial control systems, authors present the attack trends. Whereas before 2001 most of the attacks were internal, i.e., carried out by company members, after 2001 the vast majority of the attacks are of external nature.

According to [7], the reasons for the growing vulnerability of CPS to various kinds of external cyber-attacks can be attributed to two main factors: urge to interconnect all devices and the usage of off the shelf solutions such as operating systems and network protocols.

A very good overview of various cyber-attacks on critical infrastructure can be found in [13]. From the cross-domain perspective, an attack on Maroochy Water Services on Queensland's Sunshine Coast in Australia is especially relevant for our discussion. In March 2000, a cyber-attack caused severe disruptions of this plant, including disruption of proper pump operation, suppression of alarms, and even releasing of untreated sewage into local waterways [14].

Additionally to the description real of security incidents, it became very common to discuss the implications of potentially possible attacks on critical infrastructure, such as electrical power grid, or national gas distribution system. Especially notable is the existence of various interdependences between various critical infrastructures. In [11], following four classes of interdependencies between critical infrastructures have been identified: physical, cyber, geographical, and logical. Because of these interdependencies, effects of an attack can propagate through different domains and inflict secondary damage to further infrastructure.

2.1.2 Transportation systems
Modern transportation systems, such as cars or airplanes, can be seen as CPS because they embody numerous embedded systems controlling various physical components. Among others, these systems are responsible for auto piloting, controlling of fuel injection and ABS, releasing airbags, etc. The controlling part of these functionalities is realized via millions of lines of code executed on tenths to hundreds internetworked Electronic Control Units (ECUs) [15]. Furthermore, the communication between ECUs is increasingly realized via wireless communication. The vulnerabilities of both running software and network communication to various attacks have had been extensively studies in cyber-security. Additionally, ECUs can be compromised by hardware Trojans. The detection of such Trojans is a very hard problem [21]. Regardless of how a control over a part of a CPS has been gained, it opens possibilities for numerous follow-up attacks.

There are numerous research papers describing experimental attacks on modern vehicles. For instance, in [2], the authors present a sequence of cyber-attacks executed on modern car's electronics. They experimentally show how attacks on ECUs can be prepared and performed, enabling execution of various cross-domain attacks endangering the safety of the car occupants. For instance, they have shown that it is possible to disable breaks, kill car engine during driving at a high speed, permanently lock the doors, manipulate speed indication, etc.

2.1.3 Remote controlled unmanned vehicles
Due to their proliferation, unmanned vehicles increasingly move into the focus of security concerns. In the recent years there were numerous reports that even military Unmanned Aerial Vehicles (UAVs) can become victims of cyber-attacks. From the cyber-security perspective, the example reported in [8] shows that a virus can spread even in a highly controlled environments, such as a military air base. In this example, the infection has been spread between vehicles through removable drives used for mission data updates. As it has been shown in [2], the infection of CPS can be used to perform cross-domain attacks and thus producing devastating consequences in physical domain.

It has been experimentally shown that a UAV can be hijacked by spoofing a GPS signal [3]. According to [13], such attacks can be classified as attack on the estimation algorithms. In the physical domain, such location estimation errors can lead to collisions, which, in turn, can cause physical damage of UAV and/or object it collides with.

Even though focusing on SCADA networks, the authors in [16] make very important observation that real-time operating systems (RTOS) "may be more susceptible to DoS attacks because even minor disruptions in device operation can lead to a significant loss of system availability in a real-time application." Applied to unmanned or remote controlled CPS, such susceptibility can also lead to consequences in the physical domain, e.g., because collision could not be avoided.

In [4], we have analyzed which attacks can be performed on a remotely controlled UAV via cyber means only. We have identified numerous effect propagation chains breaking out from the cyber into physical domain. It is remarkable that about a third of all identified attacks have shown domain crossing property. During the analysis, we have faced the problem that it was not possible to describe those cross-domain attacks with the means available in cyber-security. This experience has motivated our present work.

2.2 Attack Taxonomies in Cyber-Security

In network and computer security, taxonomies have been successfully used for single category classification, multi-dimensional characterization, attack description, and even for identification of new possible attacks. Several criteria for taxonomy have been elaborated, such as unambiguity, or mutually exclusiveness. However, as pointed out in [17], not all taxonomies should fulfill every listed criterion. For instance, not all taxonomies strive to be mutually exclusive.

2.2.1 Single category classification

There is a number of very good classification taxonomies proposed for various kinds of cyber-attacks. We have analyzed these taxonomies because most (if not all) attacks on computer systems and networks can be applied to CPS as well.

Classification taxonomies tend to focus on a particular aspect of cyber-security. For instance, in [18] the author focuses on the information security in wireless communication. The following attack classification groups are given: traffic analysis, active eavesdropping, unauthorized access, man-in-the-middle, session hijacking, and replay attacks.

Most of classification taxonomies we have analyzed do not take into account anything but cyber domain properties. However, there are also several classification taxonomies that consider physical domain properties. For instance, in [9] the authors present a taxonomy of attacks on embedded systems in Venn diagram form. This taxonomy distinguishes between the pure cyber-domain "logical" and cross-domain "physical and side channel" attacks. Even though the considered goals of such attacks are always within the cyber domain, techniques like power or electromagnetic analysis incorporate measurements in the physical domain.

2.2.2 Multi-dimensional characterization

Categorization of an attack in a single category is not always possible or reasonable. In some cases it is reasonable to characterize an attack based on a combination of multiple properties. Several taxonomies pursue this approach, organizing these properties as top-level tree elements. The elements in sub-trees are used to classify the attack within every dimension (similar to the single category classification described above).

The taxonomy for the characterization of computer worms proposed in [10] consists of the following dimensions: target discovery, distribution mechanism, activation, payload, and motivation. This taxonomy consists of two levels. For instance, for the distribution mechanism it lists following classification options: self-carried, second channel, and embedded.

The taxonomy presented in [19] is designated to characterize hardware Trojans. The top-level categories are physical characteristics, activation characteristics, and action characteristics. The overall tree has a slightly more complex structure as the sub-trees are of different depth. However, from our perspective, most interesting is the fact that the tree elements can characterize both cyber and physical properties.

Another example of taxonomy covering both cyber and physical aspects is presented in [11]. The authors focus on interactions and interdependencies between different critical infrastructures. The proposed taxonomy consists of six dimensions: Environment, Coupling and Response Behavior, Type of Failure, Infrastructure Characteristics, State of Operation, and Type of Interdependencies. Authors identify four types of interdependencies between critical infrastructures: Physical, Cyber, Logical, and Geographical.

2.2.3 Multi-dimensional description

Finally, there are taxonomies used for the description of attacks. Similar to the multi-dimensional characterization, they usually specify attack properties which have to be described. However, in contrast to the above outlined taxonomies, no fixed list of possible values is specified for these dimensions. Such taxonomies are required in bodies like CERT to describe newly discovered attacks, because often the categories within dimensions have to be extended.

A good example of such taxonomy is given in [17]. The authors discuss the characteristics of cyber-attacks and conclude that a tree-like taxonomy does not suit well to describe them. Instead they propose to describe attacks based on four dimensions: attack vector (i.e., method by which an attack reaches the target), attack target, exploited vulnerability, and additional payload or effect beyond the attack themselves. Although the authors propose several multi-level extensible categorizations within these dimensions, these are supposed to be extendible on demand.

3. TAXONOMY

Summarizing the related work presented in Section 2, there are several known attacks on CPS. However, their description mostly focuses on cyber means used to perform these attacks and tend to overlook the attack's cross-domain aspects. This provides us some knowledge but not really deep insights into cross-domain attacks. However, elaboration of a single category classification or multi-dimensional categorization taxonomy requires both broad amount of data about and deep insights into properties of attacks. As we currently have neither of them, a solution is to develop taxonomy for description of attacks on CPS.

In this section, we first propose a six-dimensional taxonomy for description of attacks on CPS. For every taxonomy dimension we describe its semantics. Based on the domain affiliation of two of these dimensions, we then introduce a categorization for various attacks on CPS.

3.1 Taxonomy Dimensions

In cyber-security, it is common to consider that an attack (action) on a target element (subject) causes effects on this element (state change). As this view considers only a single subject, which can belong either to cyber or to physical domain, no cross-domain attacks can be described.

In our proposal, we keep *Targets*, *Elements*, and *Attacks* as a top-level abstraction for three groups of taxonomy dimensions (see Figure 2). However, we propose an important redefinition of their semantics. An attack still can be viewed as an action, but we distinguish between *Attack Means* and *Preconditions* for these means to be successful. The Targets group contains both element(s) immediately influenced by an attack (subject) as well as the immediate influence (state change). We use the Effects group to describe effects induced by changes described in the group Targets. Similar to the Targets group, the Effects group contains *Victim Element* (subject) and *Impact on Victim* (state change) dimensions. Please note that this induction of Effects is caused by the high degree of dependencies and interdependencies between CPS components. In this paper, we focus on the description of the cause-effect relationships.

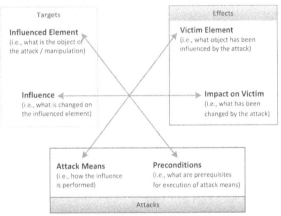

Figure 2. Taxonomy of Cyber-Physical Attacks

More formally, the semantics of every taxonomy dimension is defined as follows:

- **Influenced Element** describes the object that is manipulated by an attack. This element can reside in cyber or physical domain. It can be either an integral part of CPS or be part of cyber or physical environment CPS is interacting with.

- **Influence** describes the manipulation on the Influenced Element. In the case of an active attack on an element in the cyber domain, it can be the change of the element's state. If the influenced element belongs to the physical domain, influence describes the change of its physical property, e.g., temperature, or Signal to Noise Ratio (SNR). In the case of a passive attack, it can describe the fact of having knowledge about the element's state. Note that this dimension does not describe the means of the manipulation, but only the manipulation by itself. In other words, we distinguish between "what is done" (influence) and "how it is done" (means).

- **Victim Element** can be seen as a counterpart of the Influenced Element dimension. It can but should not necessarily be the same element. These elements can but should not necessarily belong to the same (cyber or physical) domain. Finally, these elements can but should not necessarily be at the same system layer or level of abstraction. The distinction between influenced and victim element is as follows: whereas the influenced element is directly manipulated by an attack, the victim element becomes manipulated via interactions existing in CPS.

- **Impact on Victim** is the counterpart of the Influence dimension. It describes the impact on the Victim Element. In the case of an active attack, it can be a change of the element's state or its physical property. In the case of a passive attack, it can describe the change of the knowledge about Victim Element. Please note that, in general, even a single Influence on a single Influenced Element can cause one or more Impact(s) on one or more Victim Element(s).

- **Attack Means** defines how the manipulation on the Influenced Element has been performed. Note that, in general, various means might exist to achieve the same influence on the same element.

- **Preconditions** dimension defines conditions under which Attack Means will lead to the consequences described in Effects dimensional group. Note that for the accomplishment of a particular Attack Means the fulfillment of several preconditions might be required. Therefore, this can take a form of a logical expression over state of one or more elements, existing vulnerabilities, and adversary knowledge.

We would like to illustrate the semantics of the proposed taxonomy dimensions describing the core of Stuxnet – a cross-domain attack, which is designated to inflict physical damage to centrifuges. However, the immediate effect of this attack is that the attacked centrifuge rotated with the speed exceeding its designated operational range (see Table 1). Note that this particular attack generates multiple impacts on the victim element.

Table 1. Cross-domain attack in Stuxnet

Influenced Element:	Victim Element:
- Centrifuge motor rotation controlling process	- Centrifuge
Influence:	**Impact on Victim:**
- Frequent changes of designated rotation speed between values below and above operational range	- Rotation with speed outside of the specified boundaries - Frequent changes of rotation speed - Excessive vibrations
Attack Means:	
- Send commands from the infected Programmable Logic Controller (PLC) to the centrifuge motor controller with the modifications of the designated rotation speed	
Preconditions:	
- PLC infected by Stuxnet	

3.2 Attack Categorization

The most significant feature of the proposed taxonomy is the clear distinction between Influenced Element and Victim Element. As both these dimensions are independent from each other, elements of these dimensions can belong to cyber or physical domain regardless of the domain affiliation of each other. Therefore, the description of cross-domain attacks becomes possible.

Furthermore, based on the domain of these elements, we can define following four attack categories: Cyber-to-Cyber (C2C), Cyber-to-Physical (C2P), Physical-to-Physical (P2P), and Physical-to-Cyber (P2C). These derivatives (see Figure 3) can be used to characterize attacks.

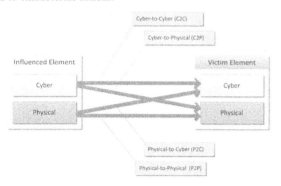

Figure 3. Characterization of attacks on CPS

In the Stuxnet's cross-domain attack presented in Table 1, the Influenced Element belongs to the cyber domain and the Victim Element belongs to the physical domain. Therefore, this attack can be characterized as a C2P attack. Currently, this category of attacks is the least understood one.

Table 2. Buffer overflow attack

Influenced Element:	Victim Element:
▪ Running process	▪ The same process
Influence:	**Impact on Victim:**
▪ Corruption of stack	▪ Process ether crashes or executes injected malicious code (depends on injected payload)
Attack Means:	
▪ Buffer overflow attack: send to the process more data than it expects under normal conditions	
Preconditions:	
▪ Unguarded buffer boundary	
▪ No W-xor-X Memory Protection[1]	

Cyber security focuses on C2C attacks, i.e., attacks with both Influenced and Victim Elements residing in cyber domain. Examples of such attacks are manifold and include buffer overflow, Denial of Service (DoS), man in the middle, and many other attacks. The C2C attacks have been intensively investigated for many years; they are comparatively well understood. In cyber-security, multiple methods have been elaborated for C2C attack prevention, detection, and mitigation. The description of the

---

[1] This protection mechanism is not effective against the Return Oriented Programming (ROP).

buffer overflow attack is presented in Table 2. Depending on the abstraction level of description, Influenced Element can be ether a running process or its stack. The Victim Element of this attack is the running process. As both elements belong to cyber domain, this attack can be categorized as C2C.

We have defined P2P attack as an attack with both Influenced and Victim Elements located in the physical domain. Despite the name similarity with the cyber security, physical security does not considers P2P attacks. Instead, it focuses on restricting physical access by unauthorized personnel to the equipment. Nevertheless, P2P attacks still can be seen as a well understood area, e.g., in material science which covers the wear of physical component under influence factors like speed, temperature, or vibration.

P2P attacks can either be executed by Attack Means manipulating Influenced Element, or as a consequence of Impact caused by some other attack. For instance, the immediate impacts of the Stuxnet's C2P attack described in Table 1 are excessive vibrations and rotation with speeds exceeding the normal operational range. These, in turn, can lead to accelerated wear (and thus to the reduction of life time) of centrifuge components and even to its irreparable physical damage (see Table 3). Please note that not all effects on the Victim Element of the original C2P attack cause effect propagation. Further, describing the effect propagation we don't have to specify Attack Means. However, it should not always be the case for Preconditions, as they can specify constraints under which the effect propagation is possible.

Table 3. P2P Effect Propagation

Influenced Element:	Victim Element:
▪ Centrifuge	▪ Centrifuge
Influence:	**Impact on Victim:**
▪ Rotation with speed outside out of the specified boundaries	▪ Reduced life time
▪ Excessive vibrations	▪ Physical damage
Attack Means:	
▪ N/A	
Preconditions:	
▪ N/A	

The security perspective of P2C effect propagation has been studied within the embedded system security. In this context, so called side-channel attacks use physical domain information in order to compromise the privacy of cyber domain. Applied to CPS, this principle can be used, e.g., for analysis of the used communication protocol. In Table 4 an attack is described which correlates the eavesdropped communication between a Remote Control (R/C) and the controlled UAV with the physical reaction of the UAV. This example presents a passive attack. Therefore, Influence describes the knowledge about Influenced Elements.

Concluding, with the exception of C2P all other categories of attacks have been more or less intensively studied. Unfortunately, all these categories have been studied independently of each other within different disciplines. However, in CPS we face the potential presence of all four attack categories. With the examples we have illustrated how the proposed taxonomy can be used to describe all four categories of attacks on CPS, i.e., C2C, C2P, P2P, and P2C.

Table 4. Protocol Analysis

Influenced Element: • R/C to UAV Communication • UAV Reaction	Victim Element: • Communication protocol
Influence: • Knowledge: R/C ⇔ UAV communication • Knowledge: UAV movement [changes]	Impact on Victim: • Inform. Disclosure: Command Meaning
Attack Means: • Correlation of eavesdropped communication and UAV's physical reactions	
Preconditions: • Statistically unique correlation possible	

4. APPLICATION AREAS

We see several application areas of the proposed taxonomy. In this section, we will outline three application areas which we consider as the most important: structured representation of attacks described in the literature, CPS vulnerability analysis, and representation of attack propagation.

4.1 Attack Documentation and Analysis

The most intuitive application of the proposed taxonomy is the structured representation of attacks on CPS described in the literature. Currently, without such structure, the comparison between attacks described in various case studies is very complicated and time consuming. Among others, it is very difficult to verify whether the described attack is a principally new one or just an already known attack applied to another CPS. Furthermore, for new attacks it is also important to understand what exactly is new. For instance, whether it is a new Attack Means which can be used to produce already known Influence on some Influenced Element, or whether it is a new to date not documented relationship between some Influence on an Influenced Element and the Impact on the Victim Element. For instance, in [2] and in [4] protocol analysis attacks are described (see also Table 4 and the corresponding description). These attacks differ solely in Influenced Elements, information about which is correlated.

Description of attacks from different case studies according to the same structure has several further advantages. This will enable the development of a catalogue listing known attacks on CPS in a similar structured manner. We consider such catalogue as a necessary prerequisite for further advances in the understanding of attacks on CPS. Most importantly, it will enable qualitative and quantitative analysis of known attacks.

Based on the qualitative analysis, it should be possible to identify elements in every dimension. Furthermore, we expect that the knowledge about and the analysis of these elements will enable construction of tree-like singe category classification taxonomies of elements belonging to particular dimensions. We expect that taxonomies elaborated in cyber-security can be integrated as parts of these "taxonomies within dimensions." This process can potentially transform our current proposal to multi-dimensional characterization taxonomy. Such knowledge is extremely important for the CPS vulnerability assessment, as it will provide the basis for the analysis whether CPS is susceptible to particular kind of manipulation or not.

The qualitative analysis is helpful to identify which elements within different dimensions are more common in different attacks. Such information is extremely important for assigning probabilities for different manipulations to occur. Such probabilities can be used, e.g., to compute comparable security grades of different CPS designs and/or configurations.

4.2 CPS Vulnerability Analysis

The common way to improve the system's security is to perform its vulnerability assessment and to make a cost-effective decision regarding which elements should be improved. The proposed taxonomy provides a good basis for both these tasks.

The taxonomy dimensions Influenced Element, Attack Means, and Preconditions are well known in cyber-security. For instance, it is common to analyze whether the network components or computers (i.e., Influenced Elements) are configured in the way (i.e., Preconditions) that it makes them susceptible to different attacks (i.e., Attack Means). This approach is also applicable to CPS. Especially in conjunction with the knowledge base containing information about possible attacks, the vulnerability assessment of a CPS model can become automated. Similar vulnerability assessment procedures for computer networks have been proposed in the literature, e.g., in [20].

Additionally, through distinction between dimensions within Targets and Effects groups, we foster the analysis of dependencies and interdependencies between Influenced Element and Victim Element(s) within a particular CPS. Please note that these dependencies can vary to a high extent between different CPS. Nevertheless, there are numerous modeling tools capable to compute with high accuracy which Effects can be caused, e.g., by increasing temperature or rotation speed of a particular Influenced Element of a CPS. The combination of the common cyber-security approach for the vulnerability assessment with the understanding of the cause-effect relationships existing in a CPS can result in an approach for the CPS vulnerability assessment.

Finally, it is common to weight the costs of measures for the security improvement against the costs which can be inflicted by an attack if these measures are not installed. Victim Element and Impact on Victim dimensions provide the basis for the analysis of costs of a successful attack. For instance, comparing two attacks described in [2], the attack capable of "killing" the engine can be seen as more severe (and more costly) than the one which permanently locks doors. Of course, these costs should be considered in conjunction with the probability of such Impact on the Victim Element to occur. The later can be computed based on the probabilities of all attacks leading to these Effects. As we have mentioned in the previous subsection, such probabilities can be derived based on the quantitative analysis of attacks described in the literature.

4.3 Attack Propagation and Encapsulation

As mentioned before, every CPS is a very complex heterogeneous system with multiple dependencies and interdependencies between its components. Therefore, an attack can take different paths how it influences the system, including cross-domain and cross-layer attacks. This makes the relationship between different sequences of attack steps and/or effect propagation stages much more complex and diverse than it is the case in the cyber systems. The proposed taxonomy is sufficient to capture various kinds of attack propagation and thus provides the basis for their analysis.

On the example of the Stuxnet attack we have already presented how the stages of the effect propagation can be described (see Table 1 and Table 3). It shows that elements of Victim Element and Impact on Victim can be "reused" as elements of Influenced Element and Influence in the induced attack. Please note that such cause-effect propagation chains are possible in all categories of attacks, and not only in P2P attacks.

Another kind of attack propagation is distinctive to complex attacks executed as a sequence of multiple stages. In the car case study [2], an infected Electronic Control Unit (ECU) spreads infection in two stages. In the first stage, it sends to a target ECU a request to enter the reprogramming mode. As no protection mechanisms is implemented, such as Authentication and Authorization (AA) of the command's issuer, the target ECU enters this mode (see Table 5).

Table 5. Entering Reprogramming Mode

Influenced Element:	Victim Element:
▪ Attacked ECU	▪ Attacked ECU
Influence:	**Impact on Victim:**
▪ Receive request to enter reprogramming mode	▪ Stops code execution ▪ Enters new state: reprogramming mode
Attack Means:	
▪ Send command to the attacked ECU via CAN bus	
Preconditions:	
▪ Target ECU is reprogrammable ▪ No physical access needed to enter this mode ▪ No AA protection for command verification	

From the attack propagation perspective, the first stage enables certain preconditions required for the second stage of this attack. In the particular case, the goal of the second stage is to reprogram the target ECU with a malicious code (see Table 6).

Table 6. Reprogramming ECU with a Malicious Code

Influenced Element:	Victim Element:
▪ Attacked ECU	▪ Attacked ECU
Influence:	**Impact on Victim:**
▪ Receive new code to update ECU	▪ Malicious code burned in ECU flash memory ▪ After burning and reboot, malicious code is running
Attack Means:	
▪ Send new program code to the attacked ECU via CAN bus	
Preconditions:	
▪ ECU current state: reprogramming mode ▪ No code verification mechanisms are implemented	

Additionally, we would like to discuss the reusability of the attack description. This is especially important because basic attacks can be used in numerous more complex attacks. The proposed taxonomy is capable to cope with the attack encapsulation too. Let us assume that the attack described in Table 5 has the unique ID #koscher10-enter-reprogram-mode. In this case one or more effects of this attack can be used to describe influenced element and influence of the more complex attack, the unique attack ID can be used as attack means causing these influences (see Table 7).

As shown in [2], this attack is even possible during car is driving at high speed. It is self-evident that if this attack is executed on a highway, it can cause a severe car accident. From the attack description perspective, we use this to show that this is possible to "fold" the exact effect propagation sequence in the attack description. Instead of description of the detailed effect propagation stages (i.e., if motor ECU enters reprogrammable state motors stops rotating, therefore car stops, therefore collisions become possible) it is possible to describe only relevant effects of the original attack.

Table 7. Reusability of attack

Influenced Element:	Victim Element:
▪ Motor ECU	▪ Motor ▪ Car ▪ Environment
Influence:	**Impact on Victim:**
▪ Enter reprogramming mode	▪ Motor: Stops rotating ▪ Car: stops ▪ Car & Environment: collisions, injuries
Attack Means:	
▪ #koscher10-enter-reprogram-mode	
Preconditions:	
▪ No command prevention during driving at high speed	

5. FUTURE WORK

We have analyzed the applicability and the limitations of the proposed taxonomy by describing attacks from three different case studies, the Stuxnet attack on industrial infrastructure [5], attacks on modern car [2], and attacks we have identified during the vulnerability assessment of a quad-rotor UAV [4].

In all these case studies, we have been able to represent both conventional cyber as well as CPS specific cross-domain attacks. Moreover, it was also possible to describe attacks which change the abstraction layer, e.g., between CPS element and the whole CPS. It is further possible to describe interactions with and impact on objects of CPS environment.

However, we have also faced several limitations of the proposed taxonomy. Most noticeable, although the proposed structure is suitable to capture all relevant information we could think of, the meta-information such as relationships between elements of different dimensions cannot be expressed intuitively. For example, in many cases an attack will generate multiple impacts on one or more influenced elements[2]. Furthermore, the cardinality relationship between different dimensions can vary to high extent between different attacks. Therefore, we are currently working on definition of *Cyber-Physical Attack Description Language* (CP-ADL). This is the natural extension of the proposed taxonomy. CP-ADL should be able to reflect meta-information such as relationship between dimensional elements. Additionally, this language should be useful for the storage of attack descriptions as

---

[2] We have presented one such example in Table 7. Another example with similar issues is jamming, which is nothing else but Influence on communication medium property (in physical domain) which leads to multiple Impacts at all network layers (in cyber domain). Even though the description of multiple pairs of Victim Element and Impact on Victim is possible, correlation between these elements described in a table form is not easy.

well as for the export of such information to other tools, e.g., for the automatic vulnerability assessment.

Another direction we consider for our future work is the automation of CPS vulnerability assessment. In [4] we have presented a systematic approach for the manual vulnerability assessment. As it has been successfully shown, e.g., in [20] for computer networks, an automatic vulnerability assessment is possible if the system model and the database of known attacks are available. However, we see the automatic vulnerability assessment rather as a plan for the distant future because first we have to understand which properties have to be reflected in the CPS model as well as to develop and to populate the knowledge base of known attacks on CPS.

6. CONCLUSION

Cyber-Physical Systems become increasingly embedded in our life. As we have seen through several examples, CPS are exposed to various kinds of attacks. Most noticeable, as CPS consist of highly interdependent components in both cyber and physical domains, attacks crossing this domain boundary become possible.

In this paper, we have proposed taxonomy for the structured description of cross-domain attacks on CPS. This taxonomy consists of six semantically clear distinct dimensions. We have illustrated the application of this taxonomy on numerous examples. We see our proposal as a first step on the way to the better understanding of cross-domain attacks and thus to the improvement of the CPS security. In this context, we have provided an extensive discussion of possible taxonomy application areas.

ACKNOWLEDGEMENT

This work is supported in part by the National Science Foundation (CNS-1035655), U.S. Army Research Office (AROW911NF-10-1-0005) and Lockheed Martin. The views and conclusions contained herein are those of the authors and should not be interpreted as necessarily representing the official policies or endorsements, either expressed or implied, of the U.S. Government.

REFERENCES

[1] Albright, D., Brannan, P., Walrond, C. 2010. Did Stuxnet Take Out 1,000 Centrifuges at the Natanz Enrichment Plant? In *Institute for Science and International Security* (ISIS) *report*.

[2] Koscher, K., Czeskis, A., Roesner, F., Patel, S., Kohno, T., Checkoway, S., Savage, S. 2010. Experimental security analysis of a modern automobile. In *Proceedings of Symposium on Security and Privacy* (SP), 447-462.

[3] Shepard, D. P., Bhatti, J. A., Humphreys, T. E., & Fansler, A. A. 2012. Evaluation of Smart Grid and Civilian UAV Vulnerability to GPS Spoofing Attacks.

[4] Yampolskiy, M., Horvath, P., Koutsoukos, X. D., Xue, Y., & Sztipanovits, J. 2012. Systematic analysis of cyber-attacks on CPS-evaluating applicability of DFD-based approach. In *Proceedings of the 5th International Symposium on Resilient*

Control Systems (Salt Lake City, Utah, August 14-16m 2012), 55-62.

[5] Falliere, N., Murchu, L. O., & Chien, E. 2011. W32. stuxnet dossier. *White paper*, Symantec Corp., Security Response.

[6] Byres, E., & Lowe, J. 2004. The myths and facts behind cyber security risks for industrial control systems. In *Proceedings of the VDE Kongress* (Vol. 116).

[7] Levy, E. 2003. Crossover: online pests plaguing the off line world. In *Security & Privacy*, 1(6), 71-73.

[8] Shachtman, N. 2011. Computer Virus Hits US Drone Fleet. In CNN.com.

[9] Ravi, S., Raghunathan, A., Kocher, P., & Hattangady, S. 2004. Security in embedded systems: Design challenges. In *ACM Transactions on Embedded Computing Systems*, 3(3), 461-491.

[10] Weaver, N., Paxson, V., Staniford, S., & Cunningham, R. 2003. A taxonomy of computer worms. In *Proceedings of the 2003 ACM workshop on Rapid malcode*, 11-18.

[11] Rinaldi, S. M., Peerenboom, J. P., & Kelly, T. K. 2001. Identifying, understanding, and analyzing critical infrastructure interdependencies. In *Control Systems*, 21(6), 11-25.

[12] Sztipanovits, J. 2012. Towards Science of System Integration for CPS. Keynotes at *The 1st ACM International Conference on High Confidence Networked Systems* (HiCoNS)

[13] Cárdenas, A. A., Amin, S., & Sastry, S. 2008. Research challenges for the security of control systems. In *Proceedings of the 3rd conference on Hot topics in security*, 1-6.

[14] Slay, J., & Miller, M. 2007. Lessons learned from the maroochy water breach. In *Critical Infrastructure Protection*, 73-82.

[15] Charette, R. N. 2009. This car runs on code. In *IEEE Spectrum*, 46(3), 3.

[16] Wang, J., & Yu, X. 2007. Security strategies for SCADA systems. In *Recent advances in security technology*, 378.

[17] Hansman, S., & Hunt, R. 2005. A taxonomy of network and computer attacks. In *Computers & Security*, 24(1), 31-43.

[18] Welch, D., & Lathrop, S. 2003. Wireless security threat taxonomy. In *Information Assurance Workshop*, 76-83.

[19] Rad, R. M., Wang, X., Tehranipoor, M., & Plusquellic, J. 2008. Power supply signal calibration techniques for improving detection resolution to hardware Trojans. In *Proceedings of the 2008 IEEE/ACM International Conference on Computer-Aided Design*, 632-639.

[20] Lippmann, R. P., Ingols, K. W., Scott, C., Piwowarski, K., Kratkiewicz, K. J., Artz, M., & Cunningham, R. K. 2005. *Evaluating and strengthening enterprise network security using attack graphs*. Project report.

[21] Agrawal, D., Baktir, S., Karakoyunlu, D., Rohatgi, P., & Sunar, B. 2007. Trojan detection using IC fingerprinting. In *Proceedings of Symposium on Security and Privacy*, 296-310.

Author Index